Pál Kelemen, Nicolas Pethes (eds.)
Philology in the Making

Digital Humanities | Volume 1

Pál Kelemen, Nicolas Pethes (eds.)

Philology in the Making

Analog/Digital Cultures of Scholarly Writing and Reading

[transcript]

Bibliographic information published by the Deutsche Nationalbibliothek
The Deutsche Nationalbibliothek lists this publication in the Deutsche Nationalbibliografie; detailed bibliographic data are available in the Internet at http://dnb.d-nb.de

Cover layout: Maria Arndt, Bielefeld
Typeset by Francisco Bragança, Bielefeld
Printed by Majuskel Medienproduktion GmbH, Wetzlar
Print-ISBN 978-3-8376-4770-9
PDF-ISBN 978-3-8394-4770-3
https://doi.org/10.14361/9783839447703

Table of contents

4. Technologies

Introduction

How do we know what we do? For a long time, this question has been a subordinate one in the history of the sciences in general and within the self-concept of philology in particular, because both seemed to be focused on the objects of this knowledge and not on the processes of its production. In the natural sciences, the discipline of Science Studies began to question this hierarchy between knowledge and practice and to ask about the tacit knowledge of the materially conditioned processes of research, social rituals of scientific communication, and media technologies used for the distribution of results.[1] Science Studies are based on the "practical turn"[2] because they consider knowledge to emerge from technically and institutionally embedded practices rather than from 'rational' and 'goal oriented' accounts that are given in retrospect once a project is completed. Contrary to such accounts, contemporary Science Studies consider contingencies, accidents, and involuntary findings as well as social hierarchies, technical equipment, and personal interaction equally relevant for the process of establishing valid facts, standards, and formats within a field.[3] Science, as Bruno Latour famously put it, is not "ready made" but "science in the making", and scientific facts are constructions by an isolated professional community rather than representations of the world out there or empirical manifestations of theoretical ideas.[4]

---

1 | Mario Biagioli (ed.), *The Science Studies Reader* (New York: Routledge, 1999).

2 | Cf. David G. Stern, "The Practical Turn", in *The Blackwell Guide to the Philosophy of Social Sciences*, eds. Stephen P. Turner and Paul A. Roth (Malden e.a.: Blackwell, 2003), 185-206; cf. Andrew Pickering, *Science as Practice and Culture* (Chicago: University of Chicago Press, 1992).

3 | Cf. Hans-Jörg Rheinberger, *Toward a History of Epistemic Things. Synthesizing Proteins in the Test Tube* (Stanford: Stanford University Press, 1997); Christoph Hoffmann: *Die Arbeit der Wissenschaften* (Zürich/Berlin: diaphanes, 2013).

4 | Bruno Latour, *Sciene in Action.* How to Follow Scientists and Engineers Through Society (Harvard: Harvard University Press 1987), 4; cf. Karin Knorr-Cetina, *The Manu-*

In the light of the success of Science Studies it is surprising that analyses of knowledge making practices within the humanities are still rare.[5] One of the reasons for this delay could be that philological research has been carried out methodically and technologically almost unchanged for over two centuries – so the knowledge of philological practices has actually remained tacit due to their assumed self-evidence. For this reason, it is no coincidence that the interest in "philology in the making" arises at a time when this methodological and technological continuity faces a challenge: the challenge of digitization.[6] As we witness the growing impact of e-books, full text-databases, hypertext editions, distant reading projects, and open access publications,[7] our awareness that these technological changes may have fundamental consequences for our understanding not only of literature and culture but also of scholarship in the humanities is raised. While new media often claim to simply enhance, accelerate, or expand the spatial and temporal range of previous communication devices and the cultural concepts that derive from them, the suspicion grows that they actually establish new modes of collecting, storing, editing, interpreting, and teaching literary history and philological theory. And if it

facture of Knowledge. An Essay on the Constructivist and Contextual Nature of Science (Oxford: Pergamon Press, 1981).

5 | Cf. Peter Becker/William Clark (eds.), *Little Tools of Knowledge. Historical Essays on Academic and Bureaucratic Practices* (Ann Arbor: University of Michigan Press, 2001); Steffen Martus/Carlos Spoerhase, "Praxeologie der Literaturwissenschaft", in *Geschichte der Germanistik* 35/36 (2009), 89-96, as well as the systematic account by Glenn Most (ed.), *Aporemata*, 5 vols. (Göttingen: Vandenhoek und Rupprecht, 1997-2001) and the suggestions by Hans Ulrich Gumbrecht, *The Powers of Philology. Dynamics of Textual Scholarship* (Urbana: University of Illinois Press, 2003).

6 | Cf. Pál Kelemen/Ernö Kulcsár Szabó/Ábel Tamás (eds.), *Kulturtechnik Philologie. Zur Theorie des Umgangs mit Texten* (Heidelberg: Winter, 2011); Marcus Krause/Nicolas Pethes, "Scholars in Action. Zur Autoreferenz philologischen Wissens im medialen Wandel", in *Deutsche Vierteljahresschrift für Literaturwissenschaft und Geistesgeschichte* 91 (2017), 73-108.

7 | Susan Schreibman/Ray Siemens/John Unsworth (eds.), *A New Companion to Digital Humanities* (Chichester: Wiley-Blackwell, 2016); Franco Moretti, *Graphs, Maps, Trees. Abstract Models for Literary History* (London: Verso, 2005); Adriaan Weel, *Changing our Textual Minds. Towards a Digital Order of Knowledge* (Manchester: Manchester University Press, 2011); Matthew L. Jockers, *Macroanalysis. Digital Methods and Literary History*, (Urbana: University of Illinois Press, 2011); Ann Burdick e.a., *Digital_Humanities* (Cambridge MA/London: The MIT Press, 2012); Alan Gross/Joseph Harmon (ed.), *The Internet Revolution in the Sciences and the Humanities* (Oxford: Oxford University Press, 2016).

is true that philology is "the fundamental science of human memory",[8] then the transfer of the praxeological approach from Science Studies to the study of philological practices is not only one possible extension of this methodological approach among many, but a crucial precondition for a fundamental understanding of the current consequences of the 'digital turn' for managing our cultural tradition as well as of the influence of our media technological competences on our self-understanding as a culture.

This awareness for the significance of media in philological scholarship also means to account for the actual materiality of objects and documents within the process of tradition. Contrary to an abstract notion of 'text' and the interpolation of its content or meaning, a praxeology of philological scholarship has to examine "the sociology of texts"[9] with respect to material specifities, medial differences, and everyday practices such as browsing, skimming, scrolling, and scanning. Thus, the concept of "material philology"[10] is extended far beyond the realm of book history and methodologies of editing.

The following articles will raise the question whether new media support or modify concepts of culture and tradition by examining philological practices such as collecting and comparing, archiving and editing, commenting and interpreting, quoting and referencing etc. with respect to the changes they underwent during the past two decades due to the introduction of digital media. They result from a two-year cooperation between the Departments of Literary Studies at the Universities of Budapest and Cologne, in the course of which the historical, methodological and theoretical prerequisites for such a philological praxeology were developed and discussed.[11] Two research questions were at the center of this cooperation:

8 | Jerome McGann, "Philology in a New Key", *Critical Inquiry* 39 (2013), 327-346: 345.

9 | D.F. McKenzie, *Bibliography and the Sociology of Texts* (Cambridge: Cambridge University Press, 1999); Jerome McGann, *A Critique of Modern Textual Criticism* (Charlottesville/London: University of Virginia Press, 1992).

10 | Stephen Nichols, "Why Material Philology? Some Thoughts", in *Philologie als Textwissenschaft. Alte und neue Horizonte* (*ZdPh* 116, 1997), eds. Helmut Tervooren and Horst Wenzel, 10-30; Almuth Gressilon, *Literarische Handschriften. Einführung in die "critique génétique"* (Frankfurt/M.: Peter Lang, 1999).

11 | The project "Die Praxis der Literaturwissenschaften" was funded by the *Deutscher Akademischer Austauschdienst*'s PPP-Program in 2016 and 2017 and brought together senior researchers, postdocs, and doctoral students from the Department of Comparative Literature and the Department of German Literature at Eötvös Lórand Tudományos Egyetem, Budapest, and the Departments of German Literature and the Department of English and American Studies at Universitaet zu Koeln for semiannual workshops. We would like to thank all participants of these meetings for their support and contributions and the DAAD for its generous funding.

1. What are the medial technologies and material appearances of what we will refer to as 'texts' in a digitized future? Does it change our notion of the literary artwork whether we read it on paper or on an electronic reader? Do new technologies of marking, referencing, quoting, and excerpting texts change the way we understand, interpret, use, and functionalize our textual heritage? Does it change our notion of a scholarly edition whether we have to look up numerous heavy volumes in a library or search for references online? And, through this simplified access: will digital media also transgress the border between academic and non-academic practices of reading and writing? It seems likely that computer technology will not replace 'paper culture' entirely but create an awareness of the historical role and ongoing function of using paper inside and outside the academia. But how do we avoid merely repeating the myths and fetishes of 'paper authenticity' and 'close reading'? Maybe the future for paper based media such as the book and paper based practices such as collecting will migrate into new contexts and forms of use that seem irritating only from a traditional point of view.

2. Which changes of practices connected to working with texts can be observed in the light of the digital turn in the Humanities? Since new media technologies never simply continue the *modus operandi* of old ones but rather implement fundamental changes in structures of communication as well as concepts of culture, knowledge, and art, new methods (e.g. quantitative analysis), formats (e.g. the digital catalogues), and institutions (e.g. divisions for Digital Humanities) have to be analyzed with respect to the transformation of practices, theories, and concepts within our routines of editing, analyzing, and teaching historical texts: What are the standards that scholars have to meet in order to successfully produce valid statements within a digitized scholarly community? How are authorities, categories, and methods implemented and canonized (or replaced) in the field? Will qualitative rereadings of selected texts still be a viable option for scholarship and teaching or will we have to contextualize these readings with the large data pools digital archives provide? Can we (and should we at all) maintain our understanding of humanities scholarship as a mode of aiming for the exemplary instead of for totality?

It may well be that computers will simply transfer the material sources, textual formats, and routines of reading from the paper realm into the digital one, so that eventually the formats of cultural tradition and philological communication are going to be similar *on* and *off* paper (as can already be observed on the e-book market). But it is also possible that entirely new arrangements of texts and reading may emerge (as some smart phone applications already suggest). Either way, this is the right time to take stock of both sides: Will cultural competences that evolved by using paper still be relevant in a computer age? Or will they become more and more obsolete once historical material will be available at all times to everybody? Is our notion of culture memory going to change once scholars realize it is not only based on great minds and ideas but rather on algorithms? How will the implementation of computer technologies (if not ubiquitous computing) recontextualize and maybe even change traditional paper-based practices of writing and reading, reconstructing and interpreting, or cross-referencing and applying knowledge?

Within the methodological framework of Science Studies, Actor-Network-Theory (ANT) seems especially useful for this approach because of its focus on semiotic structures: Latour is interested in the variety of scientific "inscriptions" and "paperwork" when he analyses the modes of "Drawing Things Together" *from* various sources of information *onto* the two-dimensional sphere of the written page.[12] That is to say, literary studies use paper and books not only as (historical) *objects*[13] but also as *tools* of scholarly writing[14] when they reconstruct and interpret written material of the past. Therefore, besides the *Laboratory Life* that Latour/Woolgar analyzed as a system of various types of "literature" in their study from 1979,[15] there is a *Library Life*[16] to be discovered as paper based institutions of knowledge undergo fundamental media changes, i.e.: fundamental changes within their network of materialities and agents.

To be sure: the debate about philology has been dominated by an ongoing diagnosis of changes, turns, and crises long before the advent of digitized text analysis (and probably ever since philology was introduced at Universities in the late eighteenth century). But the following articles will neither focus on the history of various philological disciplines nor on the constitution of what has been recently labeled "metaphilology", i.e. a philological analysis of historical positions within literary studies.[17] Neither is it going to contribute to the impressive number of manifestos on the "Return to Philology", on its redefinitions as "New", "Post", or "Future Philology", or to the debate on "Rephilologisierung" in Germany.[18] And they will not follow sociological approaches that reconstruct

12 | Bruno Latour, "Drawing Things Together", in *Representation in Scientific Practice*, eds. Michael Lynch and Steve Woolgar (Cambridge: MIT Press, 1990), 19-68.

13 | Christian Benne, *Die Erfindung des Manuskripts. Zur Theorie und Geschichte literarischer Gegenständlichkeit* (Frankfurt/M.: Suhrkamp, 2015).

14 | Michael Hagner, *Zur Sache des Buches* (Göttingen: Wallstein, 2015).

15 | Bruno Latour/Steven Woolgar, *Laboratory Lives. The Construction of Scientific Facts* (Princeton: Princeton University Press, 1979).

16 | Friedolin Krentel e.a., *Library Life. Werkstätten kulturwissenschaftlichen Forschens* (Lüneburg: meson press, 2015).

17 | Pascale Hummels (ed.), *Metaphilology. Histories and Languages of Philology* (Paris: Philologicum, 2009).

18 | Paul de Man, Paul, "The Return to Philology", in *The Resistance to Theory* (Minneapolis: University of Minnesota Press, 1986), 21-26; Jonathan Culler, "The Return to Philology", in *Journal of Aesthetic Education* 36 (2002), 12-16; Edward Said, "The

the process of scholarly knowledge making, but in doing so are focused on hierarchies and economic interests within institutionalized humanities[19] and only reluctantly extended to the analysis of practices.[20] Considering the practices of Digital Humanities as a challenge for philological knowledge is still an open field of research today: Computational Philology has been almost exclusively promoted programmatically[21] and hardly ever contextualized historically,[22] let alone praxeologically.[23]

On the basis of these considerations, the following essays deal with four overarching topics: With regard to the *theory* of philology, HANJO BERRESSEM proposes to reflect on the changing media environments of reading within the framework of an ecology of philology and to ask about the respective technical framings of producing meaning. MARCUS KRAUSE pursues the way in which the concept of 'philology' has become a label for the appropriate handling of texts, even though there is no stable theory of philology in the history of philology, but merely changing relations between theory and philology. Finally, BJÖRN SONNENBERG-SCHRANK asks how the establishment of Digital Humanities as a promising label was able to assert itself against this background by alluding to the old myths of totality and completeness, which can be evaluated

---

Return to Philology", *Humanism and Democratic Criticism* (New York: Columbia University Press, 2004), 57-84; Matthew Restall, "A History of the New Philology and the New Philology in History", *Latin American Research Review* 38 (2003), no. 1, 113-134; Michelle Warren, "Post-Philology", in *Postcolonial Moves. Medieval through Modern*, ed. Patricia C. Ingham and Michelle Warren (New York: Palgrave, 2003), 19-45; Sheldon Pollock, "Future Philology? The Fate of a Soft Science in a Hard World", in *Critical Inquiry* 35 (2009), 931-961; Walter Erhart (ed.), *Grenzen der Germanistik: Rephilologisierung oder Erweiterung?* (Stuttgart: Metzler, 2004).

19 | Pierre Bourdieu, *Homo Academicus* (Paris: de Minuit, 1984); Peter J. Brenner, *Geist, Geld und Wissenschaft. Arbeits- und Darstellungsformen von Literaturwissenschaft* (Frankfurt/M.: Suhrkamp, 1993).

20 | Peter Burke, "The Cultural History of Intellectual Practices", in *Political Concepts and Time. New Approaches to Conceptual History*, ed. Javier F. Sebastián (Santander: Cantabria University Press, 2011), 103-128.

21 | Starting with J.F. Burrows, "'Delta': A Measure of Stylistic Difference and Guide to Likely Authorship", in *Literary and Linguistic Computing* 17 (2002), 267-287; cf. Jerome McGann, *Radiant Textuality. Literature after the World Wide Web* (New York: Palgrave, 2014).

22 | David I. Holmes, "The Evolution of Stylometry in Humanities Scholarship", in: *Literary and Linguistic Computing* 13 (1998), 111-117.

23 | Vivian Lewis e.a., *Building Expertise to Support Digital Scholarship: A Global Perspective* (Council on Library and Information Resources, 2015).

negatively as a pathological hoarding as well as positively as a dissolution of boundaries in shape of 'cyborg philology'.

With regard to the concept of *materiality*, Ádam Rung reminds us that classical philology never disposed of original autographs anyway and instead followed the ideal of 'pure text' – a dematerialization that is currently drawn into question by Digital Humanities and their ability to visually depict the materiality of texts. Nicolas Pethes refers to the fundamental material basis of philological research before textual structures or digital storage media, paper, which in contemporary cultural studies becomes the focus of interest at the very moment when it threatens to transfer to a paperless culture. As Livia Kleinwächter shows, the next genetic stage corresponding to paper is manuscripts, which in the eighteenth and nineteenth centuries became both a reference point for the invention of authorship as for the historicist fetishization of authentic documents, and whose materiality still represents a boundary point for philological interpretation today. Charlotte Jaekel reconstructs how, in the 19th century, this knowledge of the materiality of culture was made more and more invisible, thus preparing the ground for methods in Science Studies that aim at revealing the inscription apparatuses of knowledge by way of 'reverse blackboxing'. In closing, Júlia Tóth-Czifra asks what significance traditional paper technologies still have in today's digitally supported editing practices and discusses practices archiving preliminary stages of the edited texts in digital databases.

With regard to the *practices* of philology, Matthias Bickenbach points to the practice of browsing as an approach to books that does not simply aim at decoding meaning and that cannot simply be reproduced digitally. It is therefore not the status of the text itself that changes through digitalization, but only the way in which it is used, i.e. the media differentiated body techniques of reading, which reconstitute the text anew in every reading event. Charlotte Coch reconstructs technically supported reading and memorizing techniques using the example of the slip box that Hegel still uses as an encyclopaedia of the mind but is reconceptualized by Niklas Luhmann as an active communication partner. Gábor Mezei deals with the complementary question of the operation of writing and analogizes it with the spatial design of maps, insofar as writing not only sketches a topography of signs, but is also structured by the gaps between them and can thus be revealed as a grid of interruptions. Julia Nantke concludes the section with a description of the mutual relationship between traditional philological practices and new digital technologies.

The last section is devoted to this interrelationship with a view to the new possibilities, but also to the implicit limitations of philological practice through digital *technologies*: In the sense of blackboxing, Gabor Palkó argues that the computer also generates a blind spot of research, especially since computer surfaces simulate old media practices. Daniel Kozák, on the other hand, shows how Digital Humanities in the field of editorial philology allows a broader commentary on ancient sources – without drawing the consequence that digital results necessarily have to be more objective than the analog ones, which they still supplement today. Amália Kerekes identifies the daily press since the 19th century as the most obvious modern corpus for DH, which even in predigital times could only be viewed as big data and raises the question of the relationship between macroanalysis (with respect to knowledge about journals) and microreading (with respect to understanding their contents). Conversely, Gábor Vaderna shows for historical research that computers must not only be understood as tools that change concepts of history by macroperspective analyses, but that microhistory can also be digitized. Melinda Vásári concludes the volume by showing that the relationship between philology and computer not only concerns digital text structures, but also the question of archiving and analyzing computers and hard disks of writers and scholars, so that philology approaches the practice of autopsy from forensics – an examination of dead bodies of data that once again underscores the vitality of philology in the digital age.

1. Theories

How We Read

Towards an Ecological Philology

Hanjo Berressem

"[t]here is no language in itself"[1]

"everything that is said is said by an observer"[2]

Introduction

In the wake of the ecological turn in the humanities, how to conceptualize an ecological philology? A scan of the academic landscape might suggest the implementation of philological research on topics such as 'philology in the anthropocene' or 'philology and global warning.' If neither of these topics feature in my paper, that is because I think the idea of an 'ecological philology' needs to be structural rather than topical. It should not be about the creation of a 'green philology,' but rather about addressing the field and practice of philology itself in its relation to not so much 'nature' even, but to 'the world in general.' In other words, an ecologization of philology should be robust enough to suffuse its main conceptual parameters and each of its research projects. Rather than serve as a starter kit for a superficial 'greening of philology,' it should aim at a truly philological ecology.

In this extended view of ecology, I will argue that much of philology already is ecological. At the same time, there are philological situations that might not only be revisited from an ecological point of view but that might actually profit from an ecological approach. It is this 'situationist' aspect of ecology that I take to be its most important characteristic. Every ecological intervention needs to

---

1 | Félix Guattari, *The Machinic Unconscious: Essays in Schizoanalysis* (Los Angeles: Semiotext[e], 2011), 27.

2 | Humberto R. Maturana, "Everything is said by an Observer", in *Gaia: A Way of Knowing: Political Implications of the New Biology,* edited by W.I. Thompson,65-82 (Hudson, NY: Lindisfarne Press, 1987).

be site- and time-specific. It needs to operate from within very specific and thus invariably singular situations.

For the specific situation of this essay, I will take Félix Guattari's notion of a "generalized ecology"[3] as my ecological reference. His 'ecosophy' does not only resonate with many concerns that define the philological field, it also goes beyond the more topical and by default 'environmental' aspects of ecology. Quite programmatically, in fact, it aims to combine "social ecology, mental ecology and environmental ecology".[4] Guattari develops the ontology and epistemology of that ecosophy in his book *Schizoanalytic Cartographies*. Although I will only be able to trace that project in its most general contours, I would hope that some of its 'spirit' can be felt to suffuse the following pages. It should function as one possible conceptual matrix for a more detailed investigation of an ecologization that I will develop from within the philological field itself: the ecologization of reading.

Default Positions

While a detailed ecologization of philology has not yet been developed, it is implicit in what we have come to call 'media ecology,' which concerns, by default, the interplay of various technological media and media platforms in any given situation. If environmental ecology concerns 'the household of nature,' media ecology concerns 'the household of media.' In German, the early name for such a media ecology was the more prosaic and more technical term *Medienverbund*.

The relation of media ecology to philology is that reading and writing, as media of communication, are everywhere part of that larger ecology. Consider how, in a guest lecture, everybody is part of a very specific media ecology. The speaker with papers, keynote presentation and smartphone, the audience with its various electronic devices and paper technologies. Each 'side' contributes to the overall media environment as both custodians and administrators. But then there are also anonymous custodians, such as the electric light that carries vision or the air-conditioned atmosphere, as the technologized 'natural' media through which vision and sound travel. Within this complex media milieu, speaking and reading are strapped into various electronic exoskeletons. While the speaker is reading, the visualization of textual quotes are generated through digital channels that represent letters as pixeled, electronic images. Even the process of reading is the result of a prior digitalization by way of the computer that during the talk projects the images of letters onto the screen by

3 | Félix Guattari, *The Three Ecologies* (London: Athlone Press, 2000), 52.

4 | Ibd., 41.

way of 'electronic light.' To free this channel, the reading might have to divert to the earlier medium of paper. One could, of course, use an iPad or a smartphone to read from, which are reading practices that are becoming more and more common.

For each moment of our existence, we could perform such an analysis of the media ecology we are immersed in and that we administer, even while it administers us as well. Neil Postman, who has defined media as "complex communication systems," considered media ecology as "the study of media as environments"[5] in the sense that we talk, more metaphorically, of media landscapes, media deserts, data mountains and the flow of data.

Early on, Marshall McLuhan has stressed the importance of the analysis of both technical and natural media ecologies and media practices, because we too often simply accept them and think too little about their functions and effects. We talk too soon about the contents that media transmit rather than about the modes of the presentation of these contents. His slogan that 'the medium is the message' refers to this awareness or alertness. In fact, for McLuhan, media are quite literally the unconscious of our culture. "Media effects are new environments as imperceptible as water is to a fish, subliminal for the most part".[6] TV, for instance, "is environmental and imperceptible, like all environments".[7] This is why we have to look at media from 'without.' "Fish don't know water exists till beached,"[8] McLuhan notes. At the same time, such an outside position might be deadly, because we are inside of and literally 'breathe media.' The awareness of this 'being within' is one of the most important ecological realizations of media studies and, in extension, a philological ecology. As scholars, users and humans we are, inevitably, part of the overall media ecology, especially if one does not restrict media studies to the study of technological media but also includes 'natural' media. Not only electric but also ambient light. Media

> are so pervasive in their personal, political, economic, aesthetic, psychological, moral, ethical, and social consequences that they leave no part of us untouched, unaffected,

---

5 | Neil Postman, "The Reformed English Curriculum", in *High School 1980: The Shape of the Future in American Secondary Education*, edited by Alvin C. Eurich, 160-168 (New York: Pitman, 1970), 161.

6 | Marshall McLuhan, *Counterblast* (Toronto: McClelland & Stewart Ltd, 1969), 22.

7 | Marshall McLuhan, *Understanding Media: The Extensions of Man* (New York: MIT Press, 1964), ix; "Literacy creates very much simpler kinds of people than those that develop in the complex web of ordinary tribal and oral societies" (Ibd., 59).

8 | Marshall McLuhan, *Culture Is Our Business* (Eugene: Wipf & Stock, 1970), 191.

> unaltered. The medium is the massage. Any understanding of social and cultural change is impossible without a knowledge of the way media work as environments.[9]

What the notion of media ecology implies is that media do not only follow each other but that, at any given moment, they traverse each other, comment on each other, critique each other and stage each other. It is a legacy of McLuhan that after a period of 'media history,' 'media archaeology' and 'media differentiation,' we are once again highlighting modes of what might be called media superposition. Already in *Understanding Me: Lectures and Interviews* (1977), McLuhan notes that to think ecologically about media means

> arranging various media to help each other so they won't cancel each other out, to buttress one medium with another. You might say, for example, that radio is a bigger help to literacy than television, but television might be a very wonderful aid to teaching languages. And so you can do some things on some media that you cannot do on others. And, therefore, if you watch the whole field, you can prevent this waste that comes by one canceling the other out.[10]

One must look, therefore, at media not so much as carriers of a specific content, but as procedures and practices, and at media as the content of other media. The 'content' of any medium is always another medium. "The content of writing is speech, just as the written word is the content of print, and print is the content of the telegraph".[11]

Today, most media ecologies are subsumed by the digital. Friedrich Kittler's *Gramophone, Film, Typewriter* from 1986 shows the fascination of these digital platforms, processes and practices. Kittler is quite literally enraptured:

> The general digitalization of information and channels erases the differences between individual media. Sound and image, voice and text have become mere effects on the surface [...]. And if the optical fiber network reduces all formerly separated data flows cables combine formerly separated dataflows to one standardized digital series of numbers, any medium can be translated into another.[12]

Jay David Bolter's term remediation addresses these transmedial movements, such as the relation of books to new media platforms, and as such it also

9 | Marshall McLuhan and Quentin Fiore, *The Medium is the Massage* (New York: Random House, 1967), 26.

10 | Marshall McLuhan, Stephanie and David Staines, *Understanding Me: Lectures and Interviews* (Toronto: McClelland & Stewart Ltd., 2004), 271.

11 | McLuhan, *Understanding Media*, 23 f.

12 | Friedrich Kittler, *Gramophon, Film, Typewriter* (Stanford: Stanford UP, 1999), 102.

addresses new sites and times of reading. As he describes remediation, "we call the representation of one medium in another *remediation*, and we will argue that remediation is a defining characteristic of the new digital media".[13] While Bolter is aware that this has always been the case, he argues that "at our historical moment, remediation is the predominant convention at work in establishing the identity of new digital media".[14] Henry Jenkins' *Convergence Culture: Where Old and New Media Collide* (2006), also addresses media milieus but is basically a how-to-do-it version for the greater media marketplace, delineating the various platforms on which media products can and will be placed in a media economy rather than a media ecology.[15]

Let me bring this down to a practical level and to a specific situation. In the work of American author Mark. Z. Danielewski, remediation implies a curious time reversal. Generally, novels remediate earlier forms of literature, such as illuminated manuscripts or epic poems, while cinematographic formats such as the 'new' format of quality TV, remediates earlier narrative forms such as serialized novels, or novels in general. In the case of Danielewski, however, somewhat in the way novels developed a 'filmic writing,' the novel remediates a very contemporary media format. *In The Familiar*, which is the first part of a planned 27 volume novel, philological serialization does not remediate earlier literary serializations, but rather contemporary TV serialization in a meeting of 'analog philology' and the digital logic of quality TV-series.[16] This remediation does not only open up novels to what is called horizontal storytelling and world building, it also comes to model processes of novelistic production, distribution and franchising on TV-series parameters, not only in that there is, similar to TV-series, a Wiki for the 'novel' as well as sites for 'reader feedback' but also, and perhaps more important, there are narratological implications, such as the fact that there is no longer a clear 'sense of an ending.' As Danielewski notes, "if it doesn't sell, then it dies".[17] In fact, as of 2018, with five volumes published, Pantheon has paused the publication of further 'seasons.'

While this example shows how 'the way we read' shifts within the digital media ecology, an ecologization of philology will also have effects on other levels

---

13 | Jay David Bolter and Richard Grusin, *Remediation: Understanding New Media.* (Cambridge: MIT Press, 2000), 45.

14 | Ibd., 54.

15 | Cf. Henry Jenkins, *Convergence Culture: Where Old and New Media Collide* (New York: New York UP, 2006).

16 | Cf. Mark Z. Danielewski, *The Familiar, Volume 1: One Rainy Day in May* (New York: Pantheon Books, 2015).

17 | Mark Danielewski and Dylan Foley, "The Rumpus Interview with Mark Danielewski", in *The Rumpus* (May 20th 2015), [http://therumpus.net/2015/05/the-rumpus-interview-with-mark-danielewski/].

of what I called analog philology. In fact, an analog philology does no longer exist in a pure state, because contemporary philological practice is in many of its facets an inherently computerized ecology that covers the full spectrum from the fractal space of a multitude of intersecting media platforms to 'big data mining,' computerized 'imaging' and 'distant reading' operations, as in Franco Moretti's big data logistics which applies the logic of computer linguistics to literary studies.[18]

An ecologization of philology must be able to address all levels, ranges and applications of philology, from the computer-aided work on editions and textual variants to its position vis-à-vis new theories of textuality and of reading; from the very 'heart' of philology, that is, to its most peripheral spaces. It is in this context that I will superpose the general ecosophy developed by Félix Guattari in his book *Schizoanalytic Cartographies* onto philology.

Schizoanalytic Philology

The conceptual center of *Schizoanalytic Cartographies* is formed by a rigorously abstract and yet at the same time everywhere concrete and time- and site-specific 'metamodel' that considers the world as an expressionist field that folds the actual and abstract on 'one side' onto the virtual and concrete on 'the other.'

Fig. 1: Diagram adapted from "figure 1.1. Discursivity and deterritorialization" in Félix Guattari, Schizoanalytic Cartographies (London: Bloomsbury 2013), 27.

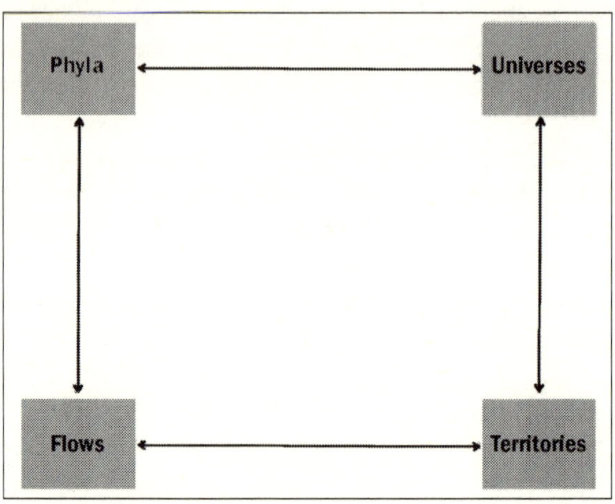

18 | Cf. Franco Moretti, *Distant Reading* (London: Verso, 2013).

The diagram's conceptual quadrophonics relate the 'domains' of Flows, Phyla, Territories and Universes. In telegrammatic reduction, Flows and Phyla are actual, as in material, while Territories and Universes are virtual, as in immaterial. On the actual side, which concerns an objective, quantitative, extensive and abstract, field: "1) Flows of matter and energy; 2) abstract machinic Phyla".[19] On the virtual side, which concerns a subjective, qualitative, intensive and 'concrete' field, "3) existential Territories, considered from the angle of their self-enjoyment (their 'for itself') and, finally, 4) incorporeal Universes, which escape from the energetic, legal, evolutionary and existential coordinates of the three preceding domains".[20] Not only actual and virtual, then, but also 'the world for-itself' on the one side, and 'its' entities, which Guattari calls 'consistencies,' on the other. "[T]here is the Given, thus there is the Giving",[21] Guattari notes, modulating Deleuze's differentiation, in *Difference and Repetition,* of 'the given' and 'the given as given.' The world 'as such' on the one side, and its 'spirit' as actualized, embodied and expressed in its beings on the other.

At the same time, there is a vertical differentiation: while Flows and Territories have a high degree of consistency and are tendentially continuous, Phyla and Universes, which have a low degree of consistency, are tendentially discontinuous. As Guattari notes, "the Phyla will constitute the 'integrals' of Flows, as it were, and the Universes, the 'integrals' of Territories".[22] Undifferentiated material flows and differentiated networks on the actual side, undifferentiated affects and differentiated thought on the other.

A fundamental proposition of the diagram is that the oppositions that define the diagram, such as extensive and intensive, actual and virtual, objective and subjective, and, from an ecological perspective, the world and its creatures, are 'in actual fact' not oppositions but complementarities. The same goes for the vertical vectors, which relate Flows or Phyla and Territories and Universes, both of which concern the complementarity of waves and particles. What counts for all of these is, as Niels Bohr noted, *contraria sunt complementa:* 'quantum ecology.' Given this structure, in order to chart a specific 'position' or 'situation' within the diagram one always needs at least two 'cursors' simultaneously, one scanning horizontally, the other vertically.

In terms of space, the 'expressive ecology' set up in the diagram rests on the notion of a fractal space that is defined by a quasi-infinite level of dimensions that allow for conceptual shifts between different levels of analysis. As Guattari states in "La transversalité," "[t]ransversality is a dimension that strives to

19 | Félix Guattari (1989), *Schizoanalytic Cartographies*, translated by Andrew Goffey (London: Bloomsbury, 2013), 52, emphasis added.

20 | Ibd.

21 | Ibd., 58.

22 | Ibd., 28.

overcome two impasses: that of pure verticality, and a simple horizontality. Transversality tends to be realized when maximum communication is brought about between different levels and above all in terms of different directions".[23]

How to relate this rigorously abstract diagram to philology? A first implication is that an ecological philology needs to deal equally with both actual and virtual assemblages, as in material 'books' and immaterial 'meanings.' In other words, both reading and writing practices are invariably embodied. A second implication is that every philological phenomenon is singular, as in time- and site-specific, as well as, like the world in general, radically constructed on all of its levels. There is nothing 'natural' in philology, as in 'simply given.' While both of these implications might be said to be already integrated into up-to-date versions of philology, a third implication might be less integrated. If entities 'express' rather than 'represent' the world, philology needs to become expressive rather than representative. It should be everywhere in touch with the life-world, that is, as well as with its specific form of functioning. If to be ecological means to create situations that are adequate to the operation of the world, which Guattari, following Michel Serres, defines as "a pure multiplicity of ordered multiplicities and pure multiplicities"[24] that generates newness, then any ecological administration of a given situation should, without in any way neglecting the level of the ordering of multiplicities, value multiplicity over simplicity.

Again, although these implications are abstract, they define very specific situations. In each situation, the four functors operate as 'attractors' that align specific affective and machinic aspects of 'the world' with specific affective and cognitive aspects of its creatures. The realm of Flows, for instance, can denote, depending on the situation, flows of metal, money, lava or data. If, as Guattari claims, any given situation can be defined in terms of these attractors and has a specific position in the model, let me test in how far it might help to address some of the 'situations' of philology. What would a schizoanalytic philology look like?

In terms of the inherent fractality of ecological space, for instance, the increasing importance of computing in philology inevitably impacts different 'dimensions of analysis,' from the purely technological level to the growing importance of quantification in the human sciences in terms of generating specific research agendas, and further to the ramification of distant reading practices within the larger field of reading practices. Any ecological philology, therefore, is not only site- and time-specific but also inherently multidimensional. In what spirit are such digital quantifications performed in a specific

23 | Félix Guattari, *Psychanalyse et Transversalité* (Paris: La Découverte 1974), 80.

24 | Michel Serres, *Genesis*, translated by Geneviève James and James Nielson (Ann Arbor: University of Michigan Press, 1982), 11.

situation? Are there ways to couple them to close reading practices and what are the conceptual architectures that define such practices? What kind of readings emerge from them? What effects do forms of distant reading have on practices of close reading, both institutionally and psychoanalytically? What are the affective scales and parameters that we use to measure reading ecologies? But also, what, in every moment of a research project, are the moments that allow for an intervention into the world that is productive of greater complexity and singularization?

In order to construct a site- and time-specific philology, therefore, every situation has to be understood as a complex, changing arrangement of interrelated levels and forces. Each situation, in other words, is already an ecology. In this context, the fact that all four functors are at play in any given situation brings to the fore the function of 'blackboxing' as a both pragmatic but also a conceptual research tool.[25] This concerns a number of questions. What, for instance, are the political, cultural and individual ramifications of blackboxing in specific philological research projects? Also, in a fully constructed, and thus what Guattari calls machinic world, blackboxing concerns the conscious or unconscious exclusion of certain levels or 'pockets' of machinic processes from one's research agenda. Despite such necessary exclusions, because no situation can be fully unfolded, the research agenda can either integrate the effects of these processes, in the sense that they are conceptually 'kept in mind,' or it can simply neglect them. In terms of philology, only the first approach allows for the ecologization of philology.

Philology in the New Media Ecology

To get an idea of the relevance of such questions about blackboxing, let me return for a moment to 'the situation of Danielewski' and the way his work addresses one of the most comprehensive framework of an ecological philology, which is encapsulated in the question of 'how do we read?' An ecologization of philology calls for an embodied view of reading that includes body practices, paper practices, digital practices and cultural practices, considered equally as 'practices of life.'

In this context, 'naturalization' concerns one of the more devious and insidious forms of blackboxing. Consider, in terms of philology, the naturalization of the reading process and the way Danielewski's book *Only Revolutions* (2006) literally dramatizes, by way of its actual form, that thoughts are invariably embodied, and what happens when a paper practice folds itself into a

25 | Cf. the article by Charlotte Jaekel in this volume.

body practice.[26] As such, it opens up areas that are usually blackboxed in terms of 'reading.' In *Only Revolutions* this happens by way of a truly revolutionary gesture in the sense of 'turning over;' a gesture that reorganizes body and mind in the process of reading. While reading is normally organized around a book's spine as the axis around which the pages – as well as the argument and narrative – are turned in a specific numerical and implicitly temporal order, it is now a rotation of this spine, as if one were to read the book forwards and backwards at the same time. *Only Revolutions.* Two stories, those of Sam and Hayley, are quite literally twisted into each other.

In this series of revolutions, the book brings about complex, new constellations and alignments between muscular and conceptual movements, as do, of course, 'mangas' and arabic books. For the 'western reader,' muscular operations, sensations and thoughts align into a new reading practice. The book addresses the performance of reading from the levels of its spatiality and posture to the performance of the eyes. Physiologically, 'we' tend to read the page from top to bottom. This is different on other media platforms. With eBooks, the eye still focusses the complete page. On the computer, however, one tends to scroll. With the eye held on one level, the text scrolls by, which is, physiologically, something completely different from the eye going down the page. Perhaps, one should consider, philologically, in how far this also changes and bears on the production of meaning: muscular philology, or perhaps physiological philology. Already at a time that saw the beginning of computer-aided design, Guattari developed, in his book *The Three Ecologies*, the notion of "computer-aided subjectivity".[27] Computer-aided reading would be one element of such a computer-aided subjectivation.

With *Only Revolutions* we are invited to turn the book every 7th page to follow the other person's story. As such, it dramatizes a new way of reading and of telling a story, denaturalizing – as in 'making perceptible' – the normalized practice of reading. Of course, this denaturalization is not completely new, because the format had already been used in 50s science fiction and thrillers, although on a different level. Danielewski's variation of the format implies to metricize and rhythmisize the literary and cognitive processes. And even this is not new. Paragraphs, chapters and subchapters do that as well. As do sentences with their syntactic modulations and melodies. Thus, any change helps us to understand better how we are 'normally' reading and thinking. Which is why these renewals are important. They show us new ways to read and to think. Where both of these things are the same.

These questions about reading bleed everywhere into questions about research and how to design research. If the default philology ties philology

26 | Cf. Mark Z. Danielewski, *Only Revolutions* (New York: Pantheon Books, 2006).

27 | Guattari, *The Three Ecologies*, 38.

and research to the laboratory of meaning and thus to what Deleuze calls in *Cinema 1* "the powers of the false,"[28] a philological ecology is aware that 'there is no philology in itself.' As such, it is interested in how to tie the powers of the false to the realm of 'true' intensity. In other words, how to tie philology to life? In today's philological research landscape we are often so far removed from this approach that we have largely forgotten that in the history of philology, this has always been a central question. Already Wilhelm Dilthey advocates that the registers of thought have to be steeped into the registers of life and Gilles Deleuze notes in *Cinema 2* that "[l]ife will no longer be made to appear before the categories of thought; thought will be thrown into the categories of life".[29] This is, in its deepest sense, what an ecologization of philology means. How to envision a philology that is steeped into the registers of life? In other words, can one imagine, from within a largely representative, mimetic philology, an inherently expressive philology?

The question of how philology relates to life once more implies blackboxing and as such the question 'where to draw the borders of philology?' Or those of film studies, or of architecture, for that matter? To ecologize philology has the same radical implications that Latour's network theory has, if we were to take it as seriously as it deserves to be taken in terms of what it implies for research. Where, then, are, in each situation, the exact fault lines of philological black-boxing?

One of these fault lines, which demarcates the 'function of philology,' is closely tied to what second-order cybernetics calls the observer, as the internal agency that is separated from the life of the entity in which it is embodied. It is the result of the separation of a metadomain within the entity that observes itself as a subsystem. '[D]iscriminatory indications,' processes of observation do not only need to have access to a semiotic and, more specifically, to a linguistic domain; rather, they are themselves the results of these domains.

Although the agency of the observer can never be separated from the entity in which it is embodied, the 'observer proper' recapitulates, within the entity, the distinction between that entity and its milieu. It sees and treats 'itself' as an object or environment. "Semantic relations, relations of meaning, symbols, etc., do not participate in the operation of the observer as a living system [...]. An observer operates in two non-intersecting phenomenic domains".[30] The other

28 | Gilles Deleuze, *Cinema 1. The Movement-Image*, translated by Hugh Tomlinson and Barbara Habberjam, (London: The Athlone Press, 1986), 149.

29 | Gilles Deleuze, *Cinema 2. The Time-Image*, translated by Hugh Tomlinson and Robert Galeta (London: The Althone Press, 1985), 189.

30 | (44-5) Humberto R. Maturana, "Cognition", in *Wahrnehmung und Kommunikation*, edited by Peter M. Hejl, Wolfram K. Köck and Gerhard Roth, 29-49. Frankfurt: Peter Lang, 1978.

domain is that of energetic, and as such meaningless 'structural couplings' that, in evolutionary terms, denote processes of automatic adaptation, as when a person enters a room and automatically adapts to its milieu both in terms of physical and psychic tensors, stressors and tensors.

The difference between 'energetic' and 'informational' registers is analogous to the one between a continuously changing set of irritations and its integrated version. Between a medium that touches and irritates systems on a quantitave level and the qualitative level of the integration of these irritations. This parallelism goes through all levels of the recursive assemblage of entities, down to their smallest elements. In the words of von Foerster, "[n]o [cell] codes the *quality* of the cause of an irritation, only the *quantity* of the irritation." From this position, objects are merely tokens of the consistency's eigenbehaviour: "our sense organs continuously 'report' only the more or less severe bumping against an obstacle, but they never convey features or characteristics of that which they bump against".[31] Dilthey calls this, quite beautifully, "the pressure of the world on the subject".[32] In fact, the system itself is nothing but a consolidated set of strategic resistances to these pressures: "The external world expresses itself in life as pressure through the relation of impulse to resistance".[33]

While the realm of energetic and of impulses – the "intensity of the stimulus"[34] – concerns the way structural couplings pilot structural changes. Observers, however, who have no conscious knowledge of most of these structural changes, perceive these 'immediately' as behavioral changes. If the observer is the agent of philology, structural changes are the philological unconscious.

The fundamental characteristic of a Guattarian ecology is to maintain that entities and the world are not opposed to each other but that entities express the world. They are, as James Lovelock maintained, "the equivalent of a central nervous system".[35] How are unconscious systemic histories, the energetic histories that define structural changes, related to the notations of these histories from within the cognitive platform that is responsible for behavioural changes? Again, in our concentration on the formal and conceptual complexities of life-writing, we have forgotten that this adequation of life and writing is, according to Dilthey, the basic question posed by of autobiography.

31 | Ernst von Glasersfeld (1992), "Eine Einführung", in *Schlüsselwerke des Konstruktivismus* (Wiesbaden: VS Verlag, 2001, 16-38), 21.

32 | Wilhelm Dilthey, *Selected Works. Volume III: The Formation of the Historical World in the Human Sciences.* (Princeton: Princeton UP, 2002), 264.

33 | Ibd., 352.

34 | von Foerster, *Wissen und Gewissen*, 274.

35 | James Lovelock, "The Quest for Gaia", in *New Scientist.* Vol. 65, Nr. 935 (February 6th, 1975), 304-306, here 306.

While one strategy of blackboxing is to consider structural couplings as a lower form of 'natural adaptation' that is, in the case of humans, replaced by higher, 'cultural' forms of adaptation, such as language, the crucial ecological as well as poetological point is that language and culture are also modes of structural coupling. In fact, meaning, which is extrapolated from the internal observation of structural change, is an 'attribute' of structural coupling. The level of language does not replace structural couplings, therefore, it is one form of structural coupling among a multitude of others.

One level of these, which Maturana calls third-order structural couplings, concerns the 'social domain' and considers communication itself as a form of structural coupling.[36] Maturana notes. This is one way of relating language to life and as such to the ecological. Language mediates between ontogenetically coupled organisms, language brings about "a consensual domain".[37]

While humans are linked to the world in terms of their energetics, from temperature to poetry, they are, as observers, formally apart from it. Even in being separated from the world, however, the entity is part of being in the world and of the world. Consider the 'philology' of Henry James, who is concerned with 'Impressions of Life' in the literal sense of pressures and the totality of the resonances between the writer or researcher and the milieu at each infinitely short moment of that writer's or researcher's existence.[38]

Situations of Reading

Let me address how an ecological approach to philology concerns the ways in which 'philological reading' differs from 'simply reading.' In fact, when I say 'reading,' that already implies a number of default positions, because in academia reading means, most of the time, the reading of fiction. 'Do you read?' means: Do you read fiction?, although 'reading fiction' is only a very small segment of the overall reading ecology and of the immensely complex cultural practice of reading and writing, all of which concern 'the philological.' Despite the various visual and the digital turns, we still live very much in a reading and a print culture, for instance, especially if one also includes technologically upgraded notions of print, such as WhatsApp – short-term, electronic print, that is. In our daily lives we are all relentlessly reading and readers. At the same time, many of today's more interesting concepts concerning philological reading are about machines reading rather than about readers reading,

36 | Maturana, *Erkennen*, 290: "The interactions within a consensual realm can be described as communicative interactions".

37 | Maturana, *Erkennen*, 150 f.

38 | Cf. Henry James, *The Art of Fiction* (London: Penguin, 1984).

such as the digital potentials of distant readings and their quantitative, big data logistics. What, then, about the practices of human reading 'in the 21st media ecology'?

Let me start with the following question: If a philological ecology of reading were to be understood in terms of 'the love of the word' and, more specifically, 'the love of literature,' what kind of love would that be? To address that question, let me turn to Roland Barthes, who sets, in *The Pleasure of the Text*, the pleasures against the *jouissance* of reading and who proposes, in opening sections of S/Z the deceptively easy, but often misunderstood distinction between the 'readerly' (lisible) and the 'writerly' (scriptible) text.

In 'the readerly,' Barthes notes, "everything holds together, everything must hold together as well as possible".[39] In other words, the readerly network of signs is tightly crocheted and "the discourse scrupulously keeps within a circle of solidarities".[40] One such solidarity is the solidarity of logic, which means, in terms of narrative, the solidarity of cause and effect: "The moral law, the law of value of the readerly, is to fill in the chains of causality".[41] Very simply: why did the characters do what they did? Does the narrative make sense? Are there logical inconsistencies?

One might say that the overall project of the readerly text is the artful assemblage of architectures of the signified: "we can say that any classic (readerly) text is implicitly an art of Replete Literature: literature that is replete: like a cupboard where meanings are shelved, stacked, safeguarded (in this text nothing is ever lost: meaning recuperates everything)".[42] For many, the text of philology is, by default, this readerly text, and perhaps the readerly text is in particular the text of digital philology and of the digital humanities, with their potentialities of new, very small but infinitely powerful electronic shelfs, stacks and modes of safeguarding the texts that they make available and insert into an electronic philology, as well as with its infinite archives of and clicks into more and more complex and "electronically organized [*zettelgekästelte*]" inter- and paratexts. A fully recuperable and unfoldable universe of references and of the tracings of meaning is one of the promises and utopias of a digitally enhanced philology, and it opens up vast field of future sites of research. However, and this should be a concern for the digital humanities, Barthes notes that this "readerly literature can no longer be written".[43]

Readerly texts, then, might be said to be in the first instance 'meaningful' texts. In the critical reception of Barthes' concept, however, readerly texts have

39 | Roland Barthes, *The Pleasure of the Text* (New York: Hill & Wang, 1998), 181.

40 | Ibd., 156.

41 | Ibd., 181.

42 | Ibd., 200 f.

43 | Ibd., 201.

often been identified, somewhat unfortunately and prematurely, as 'easy texts' because they provide closure and are written for a 'philologically informed public.' A public that is invested affectively and conceptually in the pleasurable construction of meaning. Readerly texts cater, the story goes, openly and gladly to our assumed reading practices and expectations; to what Barthes elsewhere calls the world of the 'studium.' In a psychoanalytic context, they address what Barthes calls 'the pleasures of the text,' which is a term to which I will return. Readerly texts, however, at least the best of them, are not at all easy. This is implied by the term 'studium.' What they are, rather, is 'serious' in the sense that their reading implies scholarly work and complicated operations of 'understanding.' Reading a readerly text consists of the consumption and reflection of the 'given meaning' provided by the text, regardless of whether that meaning is highly complex or extremely simple.

It is safe to say that much of philology concerns 'the studium of words,' and a lot of philological work concerns architectures of meaning and their administration. In what way is the writerly concerned with meaning? There are writerly texts that are very aware of the complexities and the paradoxes of meaning, and the way in which meaning is diffracted in the literary text. How it is multiplied and dispersed rather than how it constructs semantic architectures. If thought is considered from the position of assemblage, Guattari notes that the synapsis, which he situates within the ecological fold between Universes and Phyla, is a function of disruption 'before' it is a function of connection. Each construction of meaning, he notes, relies on the more powerful disruption of meaning.

The second question is how to address, philologically, the punctum. Is there a space for philological bliss? Again, this concerns a misreading of Barthes. If 'readerly' texts are often considered to be easy texts, which, as I just argued, they are not, 'writerly' texts are often taken to be difficult, such as the texts read in academia. Writerly texts are taken to be, both in terms of form and content, complex and difficult and thus not at all 'easy reads.' Not pleasurable, that is. They are texts in which the retrieval of meaning is difficult. This distinction, however, is not at all what Barthes is all about. In fact, if readerly texts are often not easy, writerly texts are often not difficult. But then what are they? Maybe the distinction needs to be drawn along different conceptual vectors.

On the background of the death of the author that famously causes the birth of the reader, Barthes' first parameter is that the writerly calls to the reader to participate actively in the production of the text. In this context and in terms of our contemporary media ecology and the various platforms on which 'quality TV' is assembled, John Fiske has, in his 1987 book *Television Culture*, introduced the term 'the producerly' into TV studies.[44] The producerly is a neologism that is positioned at the threshold of practices of reading and theories of

44 | Cf. John Fiske, *Television Culture* (London: Methuen, 1987).

seriality and that explicitly goes back to echoes Roland Barthes' distinction. It would be easy to relate the writerly text to what Espen Aarseth has called the 'ergodic' hypertext in that it is participatory. While this is, perhaps, and in a certain way, true, it misses Barthes' point in a very revelatory manner. What Barthes means by readerly participation is not that the writerly texts asks of the reader to play an active part of the creation of meaning, which is a given and indispensible participation in the world of the readerly, but that the reader should participate in the delight of creation and creativity [Schlegel]. The writerly text concerns precisely a philological *jouissance* – Lacan's term for delight or bliss – that unhinges the political economy of the 'literary institution' of writer, reader and philology as producer, consumer and market respectively. Symptomatically, Barthes reads this economy in terms of capitalism and the logic of consumption.

> Why is the writerly our value? Because the goal of literary work (of literature as work) is to make the reader no longer a consumer, but a producer of the text. Our literature is characterized by the pitiless divorce which the literary institution maintains between the producer of the text and its user, between its owner and its customer, between its author and its reader. This reader is thereby plunged into a kind of idleness - he is intransitive; he is, in short, serious.[45]

Apart from that economy, the interesting word is, of course, 'serious,' which is precisely the sentiment philology and the university asks for vis-à-vis the literary text. In terms of the literary market, it is the equivalent of 'work' and concerns the always serious, circumspect, often arduous reading practices of hermeneutics and exegesis. Of 'close reading,' if that is considered as operating on the level of meaning. Of the signified. As such, philology cuts itself off from the internal disruption of meaning as well as from the existential relation of the text to the reader, which is a relation that is singular, subjective, affective and not really communicable. It delineates the 'meaningless' aspect of the text. While meaning can be shared, the punctum is to a large degree incommunicable.

Also, and even worse one might say, philology cuts itself off from 'the non-serious.' But what exactly is the opposite of 'seriousness?' At this point, Barthes sets up a difficult and curious asymmetry. While readerly texts can be found in books, writerly texts are not only immaterial in that they emerge in-between a real book and an unserious reader. In other senses, they are not even texts. As Barthes notes,

45 | Roland Barthes, *S/Z: An Essay* (New York: Hill & Wang, 1991), 4.

the writerly text is not a thing, we would have a hard time finding it in a bookstore [...]. The writerly text is a perpetual present, upon which no consequent language (which would inevitably make it past) can be superimposed.[46]

As such, the writerly is impossible in a way that is very difficult for philology to think. It is a 'present text.' A text without history and without belatedness [*Nachträglichkeit*]. It is a constant, dynamic 'literary practice' without 'reification'. In both of these contexts, it is inherently paradoxical. In Barthes' beautifully elegant prose,

the writerly is the novelistic without the novel, poetry without the poem, the essay without the dissertation, writing without style, production without product, structuration without structure. But the readerly texts? They are products (and not productions), they make up the enormous mass of our literature.

Another surprising characteristic is that the writerly text has a direct relationship not to other words – what philology usually calls intertextuality – but rather to the world itself. It is here that philology becomes ecological.

[T]he writerly text is ourselves writing, before the infinite play of the world (the world as function) is traversed, intersected, stopped, plasticized by some singular system (Ideology, Genus, Criticism) which reduces the plurality of entrances, the opening of networks, the infinity of languages.

Add to that list 'capital letter' Philology. The writerly, then, denotes the pure potentiality of every text to embody the given multiplicity of the world. The world in and of pure play. And precisely that play, before it turns into work, is the opposite of philological seriousness. While the readerly highlights the signified, the writerly text is us 'reading' the world as a multiplicity of 'pure signifiers.' As Barthes notes, it is "a galaxy of signifiers, not a structure of signifieds [...]. [T]he systems of meaning can take over this absolutely plural text, but their number is never closed, based as it is on the infinity of language".[47] Barthes, then, affirms that the level of third-order coupling, language, reaches beyond its communicative function to include what Deleuze & Guattari would call its 'body-without-organs.' Still, while Barthes goes a long way to ecologize – as in somatize – language, he does not go quite as far as Guattari, who would add any form of signaletic material that has not yet congealed into linguistic material, the various codes that suffuse the abstract machine that is the world and to which its entities are linked.

46 | Ibd., 5.
47 | Ibd., 5 f.

The writerly, then, is not the text of pleasure, but of 'mindless pleasure' or *jouissance*. In semiotic rather than psychoanalytic terms, it is the text of the signifier before it is tied to regimes of meaning. It is, as Kristeva would note, the text of sound, or of the splendor of what Lacan called the 'stupidity [*betise*] of the signifier,' as set against the serious cleverness of the readerly.

The readerly text – the text of the signified, that is – can no longer be written, Barthes maintains, but of course he says that knowing full well that it is written. In fact, we are flooded by readerly, 'clever' and serious texts, and we have been at all times. The question about seriousness is not a historical one, but a question about the specific 'flows of seriousness across specific media platforms' and the specific forms and formats that carry seriousness at a specific moment.

Not only are we flooded by readerly texts today (consider the hopeless seriousness of sex in 50 *Shades of Grey*, the devastating seriousness of *The Lord of the Rings*, the general absence of humor). Also, mainly by way of Hollywood, we are flooded by readerly, or perhaps 'watchable' images and movies. In these readerly and watchable worlds, one might argue, everything is strangely über-clever. In this cleverness, however, everything proceeds as expected and already texts and films that deviate a fraction from the norm, the expectations and the genre, that is – the famous genre hybrids – are considered to be 'writerly.' If TV is 'readerly or watchable,' quality TV is 'writerly or filmable,' the simple story goes.

It is precisely in this context that Fiske proposes the term 'the producerly.' Taking the readerly to be the simple, popular text and the writerly to be the avant-garde, difficult text, Fiske finds in 'good' TV series an amalgamation of the best of both worlds. A way to have one's 'philological' cake and eat it too. TV texts are popular while being complex. Despite their complexity and thus difficulty, they turn the viewer into an active participant in the production. Thus: the 'producerly.' If the writerly is difficult and activating, Fiske argues, the producerly is popular, difficult and activating. Translated into today's terminology: quality TV is writerly, activating, and we still like to watch it.

In actual fact, however, Fiske's producerly texts are, in terms of quality TV, cover-ups for the relentless commodification of a misunderstood notion of the writerly. For instance, if quality TV producers incorporate gaps and mysteries into their products – which they like to call, with horrible because innocent frankness 'franchises' – this creates a field and demand for narrative extensions that provide the missing pieces in further texts that float across the various media platforms.

By way of the producerly, texts are inserted into the both additive and addictive logic of 'seriality' for purposes of commodification. If what Iser had called narrative gaps [Leerstellen] are simply 'gaps and deferred mysteries' that lead the spectators to actively or 'productively' become themselves investigators and consumers of more and more transmedial extensions of the original text or character, this is a fully commodified gap. Or take a second form of productivity, which lies in the fact that discussions on specific media platforms such as blogs may well lead the producers of the show to change the narrative development of the text. This is indeed activity and consumers becoming producers. Unfortunately, however, both of these productivities belong – of course and tragically – deeply to Barthes' readerly universe. They are something quite hellish, in fact. They are 'productions of consumption.'

As I have tried to show, the writerly is not at all to do with a classical hermeneutics and the extensions of meaning. Rather than creating a meaningful text, the writerly text expresses the endless complexity of language and of life. Its sheer and ultimately meaningless multiplicity. The writerly, as a mode of reading, is reading joyously. It is reading in the mode of polymorphous perversity. It does not imply supercharging texts with meaning. Quite the contrary, it celebrates the subtractions of meaning in a text. Its dissemination. It celebrates writing becoming multiplicity, which is precisely what Guattari's diagram asked for. It asks, in other words, for a specific sensibility of reading. In another Barthian terminology, it asks for the attention to the stupid, inexplicable but existential punctums rather than for the full embrace of the logic of the studium. It celebrates the surprising newness of every sentence, which makes the overall problematics, by the way, not at all a question of genre, or of high vs. low culture, because there are complex thrillers and simple sonnets, surprising melodramas and predictable tragedies. And, more importantly, there are freaky, joyous sentences and normal, dull ones.

All of this should not lead to the conclusion that only writerly reading is 'good reading.' The challenge is to describe reading not as an ideal, but rather as a particular cultural practice within different media ecologies and thus as radically site- and time-specific. When we're tired, we all read relatively easy, readerly texts. The political lesson of readerly texts is that they are useful to practice cultural patterns. At night, we read our children and ourselves not only into sleep but also into our culture. This is why TV is tendentially ideological. But then there is a reading for the moments that we are awake. In a different context, Homi Bhabha has called these aspects the 'didactic,' ideological side of reading and the 'performative,' experimental side of reading, which is when reading does not have so much to do with practicing the old but with thinking the new. When reading asks us to forget that which the readerly texts have taught us. In *The Pleasure of the Text*, Barthes emphasizes specifically that "we do not read everything with the same intensity of reading".[48]

What can the notions of the readerly and the writerly – in that they set bliss against pleasure – bring to philology? What, if there is one, is the 'bliss of phi-

48 | Barthes, *The Pleasure of the Text*, 108.

logy?' Are there deeply unserious moments at which philology – the love of words – embraces the body, the world and the present. Although Barthes envisions this bliss as the bliss of the signifier as the body of language, this signifier is ultimately the signifier of a multiplicitous world. Perhaps meaning and hermeneutics encapsulate moments of the stupid bliss of multiplicity. At the heart of philology, perhaps, lies the pure potentiality and plurality of creation, the potentiality of a meaningless, stupid splendor rather than a kernel of meaning. Its deeply unserious, joyful play. Not recuperation of meaning but the setting free of intensities.

However that will play itself out, in order to play well, one needs to be 'alert.' Awake. Not sluggish. The task is not, as in the demands of the notion of the 'producerly' and its entanglements, to look for more meaning in an attempt to buy oneself deeper into the franchises.

> To interpret a text is not to give it a (more or less justified, more or less free) meaning, but on the contrary to appreciate what plural constitutes it. Let us first posit the image of a triumphant plural, unimpoverished by any constraint of representation (of imitation). In this ideal text, the networks are many and interact, without anyone of them being able to surpass the rest.[49]

The ecological question would be whether new media technologies can be embraced not only in the pursuit of meaning, but also in the pursuit and in the cause of multiplicity. In other words, how to escape the generalizing force of 'the producerly', but then also, where in the producerly can one find lines of escape? As with the capitalist agenda, the ecological question is not to replace capitalism with any idealistic notion of total revolution, but how "to make an anti-capitalism within capitalism".[50] In philological terms, how "to make an anti-philology within philology." To do that would be a long way towards its ecologization.

49 | Barthes, *S/Z*, 5.

50 | Félix Guattari, *Soft Subversions: Texts and Interviews* (Los Angeles: Semiotext[e], 2009), 116.

"The Return to Philology"

About the Eternal Recurrence of a Theoretical Figure

Marcus Krause

The call for a 'return to philology' has become pervasive for many years now. Even more, this observation itself is so commonplace by now that it almost seems to be no longer possible to get oneself into a position of distance and deliberation towards the figure of a 'return to philology.' As it is usual for common places, for such places that are frequented by various persons over a longer period, the *locus communis* on which the demand for a return to philology is formulated has become crowded and confusing. This place has been visited so often that it has collected countless and contradictory theoretical opinions, methodical claims, and institutional necessities. Accordingly, it is very difficult to achieve a survey over this heterogeneous field. First and foremost, it is not clear what the 'philology,' to which one is to return, is or should be. Corresponding to this uncertainty, the question arises what the different concepts of the philological are that build the basis for the different demands for a 'return to philology.' A second issue is connected to this: From where – and why in the first place – is one to return? How does the place or the places look like which are to be left? What is so horrendous about these places that they must be abandoned at all costs? One can hope that especially the answers to this second set of questions are able to illuminate why the figure of a 'return to philology' is so attractive that it has been summoned time and again in various discussions of the last thirty years.

But at first, it is necessary to describe what the phrase 'return to philology' actually is supposed to denominate. It seems natural to begin this description with the theoretical or discursive primal scene (the 'Urszene') of the phrase. And – as is well-known – this primal scene is available in Paul de Man's short essay "The Return to Philology," which was first published in the year 1982 in the *Times Literary Supplement*.[1] Unfortunately, de Man's usage of the term 'philology' is not philological at all. To the contrary, it is quite imprecise. De Man

1 | *The Times Literary Supplement* 4158, 10 December 1982, 1355-1356.

introduces the term contiguous to the term 'rhetoric' as a "descriptive science"[2] in service of the academic teaching of literature. This characterization seems to allude to the classical trivium of dialectic, rhetoric, and grammar, thus putting philology – so unspectacular as historical inaccurate – into the position of grammar. After this first circumscription of philology the term vanishes from de Man's considerations and makes room for a debate that follows a well-known pattern. On one side, there is the evocation of a deep crisis of the humanities that are reproached for losing their moral compass and for forgetting their distinctive competencies. Typically, this evocation is accompanied by a demand for a return to a treatment of literature which is conform to classical humanistic ideals. On the other side stand those post-structural theories which are held responsible for this crisis, this alienation of philology from itself.

Who is Afraid of Walter Jackson Bate?

In Walter Jackson Bate, who taught English literature in Harvard and won two Pulitzer Prizes as well as a National Book Award, de Man chooses a worthy key witness for this confrontation.[3] It is Bate's essay "The Crisis in English Studies" which de Man quotes in order to delineate the front lines that characterize the battle for the conceptual direction of the humanities around 1982. Because of the central strategic position Bate's essay has for the course of de Man's argumentation, I will briefly summarize its basic hypotheses. The first hypothesis is a historical one: According to Bate, the philologies have been suffering from repeated specializations since the end of the 19th century (of which the New Criticism since the 1940s and the structuralism/post-structuralism since the 1960s build the last two phases). And because of these specializations, the philologies have neglected their original task dramatically. This task is determined anthropologically and consists of – if one is to believe Bate's second hypothesis – the interpretation of the great works of literature and their didactic imparting, thus teaching students "the whole experience of life – historical movements

2 | Paul de Man, "The Return to Philology", in: de Man: *The Resistance to Theory* (Minneapolis: University of Minnesota Press, 1986), 21-26, 26. De Man's main argumentation in the first paragraphs of his essay is – despite of its title – about the teaching of literature and not about philology which is presented incidentally as a subdiscipline of the academic teaching of literature.

3 | As an introduction to the life and opinions of Walter Jackson Bate cf. Robert D. Richardson, *Splendor of Heart: Walter Jackson Bate and the Teaching of Literature* (Boston: Godine, 2014).

and individual dilemmas in choice of values".[4] This definition may be quite traditional and not really impressive, but the recommendations deduced from it and made at the end of Bate's essay are quite striking. To counter the trivialization which follows the mentioned specialization in the study of literature and culminates in the post-structural and particularly deconstructive theorization of literary texts, Bate suggests a peculiar strategy. He demands a return to a philology that is not – as one might expect – based on its hermeneutic conception and the textual criticism of the 19th century but on an ideal which dates back to the Renaissance. It is the "legacy of *litterae humaniores*"[5] he wants to reestablish, a legacy based on the humanistic principles of a holistic study of the human being and the education of humankind, principles which are allegedly "almost forgotten" in the year 1982. Even more 'spectacular' than this enunciation of a golden age of literary anthropology or of an anthropological exegesis of literature are Bate's suggestions how this return to the humanistic roots of the university is to be accomplished. His essay concludes with a pretty simple "appeal [...] to administrations of universities and colleges"[6] which posts "terms that are fairly specific when the cards are down and a tenure appointment is to be made"[7]: According to these 'terms' only scholars whose modes of researching and teaching correspond to Bate's humanistic dicta should be hired or given tenure. In other words, those people who specialize in such fields as "women's studies" or "'gay' studies",[8] who engage in such topics like "Deconstruction as Politics" or "The Trickster Figure in Chicano and Black Literature"[9] should be denied positions in the university.

It is hardly surprising that de Man takes up this demand to denounce Walter Jackson Bate as a person who prefers for the resolution of a philological debate rather the application of "law enforcement [...] than a critical debate".[10] However, what de Man withholds during his recapitulation of Bate's essay is that his own recommendation for a 'return to philology' refers back to Bate's recommendation for a 'return to philology'. It is the diametrical opposition to Bate's supposition of an anti-theoretical return to the humanistic ideal of a philology that morally educates the human being. This reference and along with it the redetermination of the term 'philology' stays implicit during de Man's entire essay.

4 | Walter Jackson Bate, "The Crisis of English Studies", in: *Harvard Magazine* September/October 1982, 46-53, 53.

5 | Ibid., 51.

6 | Ibid., 52.

7 | Ibid., 53.

8 | Ibid., 51.

9 | Ibid., 52.

10 | De Man, "Return to Philology", 23.

The Distance of Close Reading

This latency corresponds to de Man's next step in his argumentation which aims at the contouring of a concept of reading that is theoretically unsuspicious and obviously tries to stay in the area of common sense. It is at least peculiar how restrained – in contrast to Bate's essay – de Man argues when he establishes a definition of a reading that is philological.[11] It is no coincidence that his characterization of reading refers to Reuben Brower, a Harvard colleague of Bate whose name does definitely not suggest ideas of a theoretical reevaluation and expansion of the philological but is connected to the New Criticism and its concept of *close reading*.[12] De Man summarizes Brower's teaching method in the following way:

> Students, as they began to write on the writings of others, were not to say anything that was not derived from the text they were considering. They were not to make any statements that they could not support by a specific use of language that actually occurred in the text. They were asked, in other words, to begin by reading texts closely as texts and not to move at once into the general context of human experience or history.[13]

---

11 | For a definition and problematization of the term 'philology' and its institutional position in the US, see the *Special focus issue "What is Philology?"* of the journal *Comparative Literature Studies* 27/1 (1990) and especially Jan Ziolkowski, "What is Philology? Introduction", ibid., 1-12.

12 | The concept of 'close reading' is probably one of the most ambiguous and mistakable concepts in the field of literary studies. Leaving aside the reinterpretations and appropriations of 'close reading' in theoretical domains outside of the new criticism (which would complicate the matter even further), it seems almost impossible to come up with a concise definition by looking into the classical studies of the new criticists (such as Empsons's *Seven Types of Ambiguity* (1930), Cleanth Brook and Robert Penn Warren's *Understanding Poetry* (1937), John Crows Ransom's *The New Criticism* (1941), or Brook's *The Well Wrought Urn* (1947)). The only consistent feature all close readings of the new criticists have in common can probably be seen in the concentration on the formal properties of literary texts, but what these formal properties are and how their interplay is organized, differs from study to study. The avoidance of all references to factors external to the text (be they biographical, historical, sociological, etc.) generally attributed to the New Criticism is not a consistent feature. For an overview of new criticism and its background see René Wellek, *A History of Modern Criticism, 1750–1950. Volume 6: American Criticism, 1900–1950* (New Haven: Yale University Press, 1988).

13 | De Man, Return to Philology, 23.

Based on this representation of Brower's understanding of the teaching of literature,[14] de Man moves on to the crucial turning point of his argumentation, a turning point which is also – without saying it out loud – supposed to be a mortal blow to Walter Jackson Bate's critique:

> Mere reading [...], prior to any theory, is able to transform critical discourse in a manner that would appear deeply subversive to those who think of the teaching of literature as a substitute for the teaching of theology, ethics, psychology, or intellectual history. Close reading accomplishes this often in spite of itself because it cannot fail to respond to structures of language which it is the more or less secret aim of literary teaching to keep hidden.[15]

These two sentences contain several implicit presumptions which de Man's essay never elucidates, but which are crucial for an understanding of his approach to a 'return to philology'. First: There is something like 'mere reading' and this 'purity' correlates to a perusal of texts which is totally unaffected by any theoretical presuppositions. Second: This 'mere reading' is contrary to a reading of literary texts which refers to any contexts in order to describe, explain, or interpret them. Third: *Close reading* is to be distinguished from this 'mere reading', although it is not clear what the differences are supposed to be, but both have in common that they have a subversive relationship to all context-based interpretations of literary texts. In contrast to 'mere readings,' a 'close reading' arrives at a critical stance which is based on a deep alertness towards the linguistic structures of texts 'in spite of itself,' as de Man puts it. This leads to the assumption that the procedures of 'close reading,' as they have been developed and differentiated in several textbooks since I. A. Richards's *Practical Criticism*, are based on certain hypotheses that put them in distance to the merits of 'mere readings'.[16] Four: Literary studies pursue a – more or less –

14 | That this representation is not accurate or - at least - incomplete, is already suggested by its reductive simplicity. A look into Reuben Arthur Brower's recapitulation of his teaching, his book *The Fields of Light. An Experiment in Critical Reading* (Philadelphia 2013, originally published 1951), confirms this. There, he suggests - for example - the concept of 'design' as an analytical category and suggests no less than seven of such designs that can be found in a literary text (grammatical, logical, chronological, imaginal, dramatic, metaphorical, ironic, and rhythmic). This is not really what I would characterize as a non-theoretical approach to reading or as 'mere reading'.

15 | De Man, Return to Philology, 24.

16 | One superficial look into Richards' *Practical Criticism* (1929) is enough to make evident that de Man's presentation of 'close reading' and its relation to 'mere reading' or the 'structures of languages' is very dubious, to say the least. If anything, Richard's study is about the insight that there is not anything like 'mere reading'. The first part of

secret objective in academic teaching because they try to hide the linguistic structures of literary texts by concealing such structures behind the already mentioned interests in theology, ethics, psychology, history of ideas, etc.

As this little overview suggests, most of de Man's listed basic premises are rather problematic, at least in the roughly implied manner they are presented in his essay. Accordingly, it is questionable where one is to find such angelic beings which are able to perform a 'mere reading' that perceives texts as abstract linguistics entities without taking any contexts into consideration and without being influenced by any theoretical premises. It is also questionable what exactly the difficulties are with which – according to de Man – *close readings* obstruct themselves and to which version of the New Criticism his reference to the concept of *close reading* alludes.[17] Finally and particularly, the questions arise who is behind the academic conspiracy to hide the linguistic structures of literary texts, who is be fooled and deceived by this conspiracy, and most of all: to what end? Even if the last question can be at least partially answered by indicating that de Man's postulation of a conspiracy in literary studies is intended to be a polemics against the universal anthropological claims Bate formulated in his attack against any theoretical turn in the humanities, the question remains whether Bate's opinions were indeed so widespread and prevalent that they can form the basis for a ubiquitous connivery.

In view of the general claim de Man's essays raise in regard to the precision and the attention to details of analytical readings, it is astonishing that such questions remain open and that de Man's phrasing in "The Return to Philology" moves on such shaky ground. The reason for that may be conjectured from a view at the next paragraph of the essay. There, de Man establishes a distinction between the consumers "and the *professors* of literature"[18] which constitutes a dichotomic difference between friend and foe, thus terminating all the differentiations that would be needed to answer the open questions. Within the scope of this distinction, even the term 'philological' finally reappears after

---

the book consists of a presentation of myriads of interpretations of poems Richards collected during his courses, a presentation that makes abundantly clear that every reading is based on a variety of presuppositions. The analyses of these presuppositions lead Richards to the formulation of no less than ten basic difficulties of criticism which illustrate that to 'merely read' without reflecting the process of reading and its premises can only lead to misunderstandings and exactly not to the observation of the structures of language proclaimed by de Man.

17 | See Mark Jancovich: *The Cultural Politics of the New Criticism* (Cambridge: Cambridge University Press, 1993) for a description of the various concepts of close readings and for a reevaluation of the role contextual knowledge plays for the classical protagonists of the New Criticism.

18 | De Man, "Return to Philology", 24.

a longer absence from the text because the 'professors of literature' are distinguished from the mere consumers of literature whose opinions are only based on "aesthetic appreciation" by the professors' "attention to the philological or rhetorical devices of language." What follows is the knack of de Man's essay. It consists of the identification of the quoted 'attention to the rhetorical devices of language' not only with philology but also with theory. In the words of de Man: "the turn to theory occurred as a return to philology, to an examination of the structure of language prior to the meaning it produces."[19]

The wording of this sentence reminds one of a very similar sounding formulation in another essay of de Man, in "The Resistance to Theory", an essay that also reveals what specific theories are addressed with the collective singular 'theory' used in "The Return to Philology."[20] This formulation reads as follows: "The advent of theory [...] occurs with the introduction of linguistic terminology in the metalanguage about literature."[21] According to this, the term 'theory' designates such theories that can be correlated to the *linguistic turn* or to structuralism in general. It is in this sense that de Man presents the two examples for such recent theories he mentions in *The Return to Philology*. According to this interpretation of theory, Foucault's *The Order of Things* is a description of "the referential relationship between language and reality [...] in the methodological innovations of social scientists and philologists" and Derrida's deconstruction "stresses the empirical powers of language over those of intuition and knowledge".[22] These summarizing characterizations adjust Foucault's and Derrida's analyses to the line of argument according to which the theoretical boost of the late 1960s and 1970s has to be interpreted as a consequence of a turn of language towards itself and its own mediality. But they are not really convincing, because they miss the real thrust of both discourse analysis and deconstruction which can rather not be described in structuralist terms. Even more: The notion that de Man's own readings of literary and philosophical texts are properly characterized by his own definition as an 'examination of the structure of language prior to the meaning it produces' should be challenged as well. The questions these readings raise about the aporetic relations between the constative and the performative dimension of these texts and the productivity of rhetorical figures for the bypassing of such aporias do not seem to fit too well to this definition. Thus, it definitively looks like the identifi-

19 | Ibid.

20 | For the relation of theory, philosophy, and reading in de Man's essays cf. Tom Cohen/Barbara Cohen/J. Hillis Miller/Andrzej Warminski (eds.), *Material Events: Paul de Man and the Afterlife of Theory* (Minneapolis: University of Minnesota Press, 2000).

21 | Paul de Man, "The Resistance to Theory", in: de Man, *The Resistance to Theory*, 3-20, 8.

22 | De Man, "Return to Philology", 24.

cation of the 'turn to theory' with a 'return to philology' is itself an example for a productivity of rhetorics which normally builds the central focus of de Man's readings. And it is rather not an example for a concise definition of the terms 'theory' and 'philology' or for an analytically strict argumentation concerning the relation between these two terms.

"Philology" as a Fighting Word

More significant than this connection of the 'return to philology' to rhetorics (because the term is linked to the 'turn to theory' mainly by the similarity between 'return' and 'turn') is the phrase as a strategic figure of a reappropriation, of a recapture of philology.[23] Despite the huge differences between de Man's and Bate's essays that de Man so harshly criticizes, they have one thing in common, namely the positive understanding of the word 'philology'. Both – Bate and de Man – press for a return to philology. Both avoid defining the term 'philology' so that its indeterminacy and vagueness allow it to connote exactly the qualities which correspond to their ideas of a good academic practice. The position into which both put philology (or the phantasm of philology) is precisely the one for which Lacanian psychoanalysis has developed the concept of the *sujet supposé savoir,*[24] of a subject that is supposed to know and that because of this general assumption can be used to serve as an object for various transferences. Accordingly, the philology to which one is to return signifies for Bate a holistic aesthetic education which stands in strict opposition to any theoretical specializations. For de Man and in contrast to this, philology and theory are in unison, even more: they are almost identical because they both can be characterized by the same autoreflexive treatment of language. The only thing de Man and Bate have in common is that they both think that it is philology that knows how to treat literature. But what this philology is or is supposed to be, could not be determined any more differently. Regarding this determination, the only common denominator between de Man and Bate is that both set down their own treatment of literature as philology or philological whereas everyone else's critical practice is unphilological.

23 | For a recapitulation of the current debate about such a recapture and further literature see Marcus Krause/Nicolas Pethes, "Scholars in Action. Zur Autoreferentialität philologischen Wissens im Wandel medialer Praktiken", in: *Deutsche Vierteljahrsschrift für Literaturwissenschaft und Geistesgeschichte* 91/1 (2017), 73-108.

24 | See Jacques Lacan, "Of the Subject Who is Supposed to Know, of the First Dyad, and of the Good'", in: ibd., *The Four Fundamental Concepts of Psychoanalysis* (London: Norton, 1979), 230-243.

The closing paragraphs of de Man's *Return to Philology* are dedicated to such unphilological practices for which Bate with his critique of theory and his belief in aesthetic education provides the figurehead. De Man characterizes the unphilological mainly as a reflective stagnation that relies on traditional aesthetic concepts and shares the connections between literature, ethics and epistemology established by such concepts without problematizing them. Reciprocally, this means that de Man understands the philological as a critique of all those conceptualizations and ideas he characterizes elsewhere as 'aesthetic ideology' and therefore also as a challenge to everything which his adversary Bate invokes against the theoretical turns in the humanities. In other words: philology as theory is criticism of ideology. Correspondingly, one can read near the end of the essay – in a renewed identification of philology with theory that is stated again without further comment: "Literary theory raises the unavoidable question whether aesthetic values can be compatible with the linguistic structures that make up the entities from which these values are derived."[25]

According to de Man, such a questioning of the compatibility between the epistemology of language and the ethics of its semantics should be proclaimed as a didactic project in and for colleges and universities. All literary studies, all humanities should dismiss all quasi-religious "standards of cultural excellence" and convey in their stead "a principle of disbelief [...] that is not so much scientific as it is critical".[26]

At the end of his essay, de Man suddenly turns against his own postulations when he argues morally and prophesies to all those who "refuse the crime of theoretical ruthlessness" that they "can no longer hope to gain a good conscience".[27] This remark may only be a preparation for the last sentence and punchline of the essay ("Neither, of course, can the theorists – but, then, they never laid claim to it in the first place"), but it is also fitting for an essay which suffers from terminological and argumentative inconsistencies otherwise untypical for de Man's analyses and readings. Be that as it may, it is time to conclude the recapitulation of de Man's essay and to correlate it to the questions raised at the beginning of this article.

Unfortunately, the conclusion can only be that especially the first question, the question about what constitutes the philology that is to be returned to, cannot be answered satisfactorily. The main reason for that lies in the weak definition of the concept of 'reading'.[28] Of course, one could refer de Man's

25 | De Man, "Return to Philology", 25.

26 | Ibid, 26.

27 | Ibid.

28 | In other essays and especially in reference to his own writing, de Man offers stronger definitions of the concept of 'reading', but a discussion of these definitions would take up too much room here. Besides, one could argue that there cannot be a

incantation of a 'mere reading' to Nietzsche's famous definition in *Morgenröthe*: There, the philologist is described as a 'teacher of slow reading' ("Lehrer des langsamen Lesens")[29] and Nietzsche characterizes himself in accordance to that as a 'slow writer.' Correspondingly, philology would be entrusted with three basic operations: the reading 'with tender fingers and eyes' ("mit zarten Fingern und Augen", as Nietzsche puts it),[30] the teaching of such readings, and the writing about such readings. There are worse definitions of philology, but it is also a definition that does not gain much in view of the conflict fought in *The Return to Philology* because de Man's antipode Walter Jackson Bate is unlikely to contradict such a minimal form of a definition of the philological. And similar referrals to the philological competence of reading can, for example, be found until today in the various programmatic manifests of the movement of a 'Rephilologisierung' in Germany,[31] a context which is not under strong suspicion of following de Man's theory and practice of reading.

But it is exactly because the philological in the figure of the 'return to philology' is such an open, such an underdetermined concept that so many philological practices can refer to it. And it seems to be this vagueness of the figure which makes it so attractive. Apparently, everybody, who intends to return to philology, determines for him- or herself what exactly the philology designates she or he wants to return to. And obviously, the figure of the 'return to philology' does not lose its rhetorical impact in spite of such different denotations and its lacking distinction. At this point, the reference to slow reading does not produce more discrimination. The intensity of slow reading and the extent of its perception of details is certainly (and should be) a matter of debate, but the more basic problems and differences commence with the conclusions drawn from such a reading. And these problems and differences point to the second set of questions asked at the beginning of this essay, to the questions from where one is to return and how the place looks like that is to be left. Concerning the answers to these questions, the difference between Bate and de Man could not be any more pronounced. Whereas the first declares the institutional sites of philology as uninhabitable because they alienated themselves from their proper purposes by too much theorization and dissolution of their traditional

---

theoretical definition of reading but only a practice of reading as shown in de Man's essays. For a discussion of de Man's reading (practices) in its relation to his theory of reading see Rodolphe Gasché, *The Wild Card of Reading. On Paul de Man* (Cambridge: Harvard University Press, 1998).

29 | Friedrich Nietzsche, *Mörgenröthe. Gedanken über die moralischen Vorurtheile*, in: Nietzsche: *Kritische Studienausgabe 3* (Berlin/New York: de Gruyter, 1988), 9-331, 17

30 | Ibid.

31 | See about this discussion Walter Erhart (ed.), *Grenzen der Germanistik. Rephilologisierung oder Erweiterung?* (Stuttgart: Metzler, 2004).

boundaries, the second identifies philology with theory and declares that every non-theoretical procedure is necessarily unphilological. This is where the total rejection of theory is opposed to its absolute affirmation. What exactly the demand for a return to philology is supposed to involve, seems in each case to be determined by the relation of philology to theory in a twofold manner: by the connection of theory and philology that is presumed and by the connection that is targeted.

The Eternal Recurrences of the "Return to Philology"

In my assessment, this insight leads to three options to follow up on the assumptions de Man's polemic essay made about the figure of the return to philology: the first option is a historical one which pursues how the figure is used and defined in bygone academic debates; the second option is contemporary and studies how the figure is updated in recent discussions and tries to reconstruct in which places and for which reasons the figure of a return to philology returns up to the current moment (and even up to the now of this present essay) again and again in multitudinous texts; the third option is systematic, interprets philology as a knowledge of reflexivity, and tries to understand the relation of philology to theory and to itself as theory.

First: Even a superficial glimpse into the history of philology conveys that the demand for a return to philology can be traced back to its own roots, to the origins of philology. The corresponding debate is basically as old as philology itself. At least, the debate accompanies every innovation or reform philology is subjected to, be they about its methods, its objects, or its institutional surroundings. The history of such changes and their discussions could be traced back from de Man and Bate via Friedrich Nietzsche and Ulrich von Wilamowitz-Moellendorf, Friedrich August Wolf and Johann Gottfried Herder,[32] via the self-understanding of the humanistic philologist Justus Lipsius that he was the first, who, put literary scholarship into the service of true wisdom to classical antiquity and Seneca's complaint about the decline of academic teaching he articulates in the phrase 'what was philosophy is now made into philology'. And it was Seneca who demanded in his *Epistulae morales ad Lucilium*: "[A]ll [...] reading should be applied to the idea of living the happy life, [...] we should not hunt out archaic or far-fetched words and eccentric metaphors and figures of speech, but [...] we should seek precepts which will help us, utterances of courage and spirit which may at once be turned into facts".[33] Even today, can

32 | Marcel Lepper, *Philologie zur Einführung* (Hamburg: Junius, 2012) offers a nice survey of the various conjunctures of philology.

33 | Lucius Annaeus Seneca, *Epistulae morales ad Lucilium*, CVIII, 35.

there be a more pronounced statement to take up position for Walter Jackson Bate and side against Paul de Man?

Second: For the different direction of the timeline and for the never waning interest in a return to the return to philology, I also want to give a few selected examples but only such that refer explicitly to de Man's essay. I confine the list to ten examples which lay no claim at all to any kind of completeness:

- 1990 – Lutz Ellrich/Nikolaus Wegmann: Theorie als Verteidigung der Literatur? Eine Fallgeschichte: Paul de Man[34]
- 1990 – Barbara Johnson: Philology: What is at Stake?[35]
- 1994 – Lee Patterson: The Return to Philology[36]
- 2002 – Jonathan Culler: The Return to Philology[37]
- 2005 – Jan M. Ziolkowski: Metaphilology[38]
- 2005 – Geoffrey Galt Harpham: Returning to Philology: The Past and Future of Literary Study[39]
- 2009 – Geoffrey Galt Harpham: Roots, Races and the Return to Philology[40]
- 2011 – Martin G. Eisner: The Return to Philology and the Future of Literary Criticisim: Reading the Temporality of Literature in Auerbach, Benjamin, and Dante[41]
- 2013 – Frances Ferguson: Philology, Literature, Style[42]
- 2017 – Andrew Hui: The Many Returns of Philology: A State of the Field Report[43]

One example which is very instructive in view of the discussion of the figure of a return to philology is not mentioned in the list because it does not explicitly treat de Man's essay. It is the third chapter of Edward Said's last book *Humanism and Democratic Criticism*. This chapter is called: "The Return to Philology".

34 | In: *Deutsche Vierteljahrsschrift für Literaturwissenschaft und Geistesgeschichte*, 64 (1990), 467-513.

35 | In: Comparative Literature Studies 27/1 (1990), 26-30.

36 | In: J. van Engen (ed.), *The Past and the Future of Medieval Studies* (Notre Dame: University of Notre Dame Press, 1994), 231-244.

37 | In: *The Journal of Aesthetic Education*, 36/3 (2002), 12-16.

38 | In: *The Journal of English and Germanic Philology* 104/2 (2005), 239-272.

39 | In: Ansgar Nünning/Koen Hilberdink (eds.), *New Prospects in Literary Research* (Amsterdam: Rodopi, 2005), 9-26.

40 | In: *Representaions* 106 (2009), 34-62.

41 | *California Italian Studies* 2 (2011), https://escholarship.org/uc/item/4gq644zp.

42 | In: *English Literary History* 80/2 (2013), 323-341.

43 | In: *Journal of the History of Ideas* 78/1 (2017), 137-156. A lot of further texts about various 'returns to philology' can be found here...

As present as de Man's essay has been in the academic discussion in the US in the 30 years since its publication, so absent is the essay in the chapter of Said's book bearing the same name as the essay. One can only surmise that this absence is meant to be a strong theoretical gesture. And considering what the text is about, this absence is not surprising at all because Said's demand for a 'return to philology' exhibits astonishing similarities to Walter Jackson Bate's demands. These similarities are founded in large measure on the conjuration of humanistic ideals, even if Said interprets humanism as a project which is considerably more political than Bate's understanding of it. Said's final goal is the enlightenment of the general public which is based on the representations of the human being in literary texts and the philological interpretation of them, whereas the objective of Bate's humanism is the education of individual subjects. For Said as well, philology consists of a sort of slow reading informed by attention to detail, a definition which is augmented over the course of the text by more and more characterizations: According to Said, "a true philological reading is active; it involves getting inside the process of language already going on in words and making it disclose what may be hidden or incomplete or masked or distorted in any text we may have before us."[44] To identify philology as a midwife of the hidden truths of a text, he puts philology into the vicinity of philosophy and even more: this argumentation seems to aim at the resuscitation of the dominion of the mind over the letter, an idea against which more than a few philological manifestos have been fighting in the past decades – for good reasons. Likewise, Said's next characterization of philological reading in the text is not really designated to bring joy to most philologists. It reads as following: "the act of reading is the act [...] of first putting oneself in the position of the author."[45]

In the light of such insistence on the unity of a sense which is to be unconcealed and the identification of the understanding of a text with the understanding of the position of its writer, it is not deeply surprising that de Man (as the originator of the catchphrase 'return to philology') is banned from Said's considerations. On the contrary, it is only consequent that he is not mentioned at all. Analogous to this elliptic gesture is Said's denunciation of Derrida and Foucault, the exact same theoreticians de Man's essay mentions for the defense of theory. Said accuses both of opposing the insight that "the actuality of reading is, fundamentally, an act of perhaps modest human emancipation and enlightenment that changes and enhances one's knowledge for purposes other than reductiveness, cynicism, or fruitless standing aside."[46]

44 | Edward Said, *Humanism and Democratic Criticism* (New York: Columbia University Press, 2004), 59.

45 | Ibid., 62.

46 | Ibid., 66.

Adding to these allegations Said's remarks about the argot of the humanities and the incomprehensibility of many of its representatives, it can be summarized that Said's text about the 'return to philology' gives vent to an animosity towards theory which can be described as an update of Bate's animosity towards theory for the 21st century. Aside from the fact that the vacancy that de Man's essay is exposed to in Said's manifesto marks it as anti-philological in the first place because the objective of philological practices can hardly be the crossing out or deletion of references but their reenactment, it is the kind of animosity towards theory hinted at above that prevents Said's actualization of the 'return to philology' from being suitable to determine the relation between theory and philology in a productive manner.

Third: In conclusion, I want to at least hint at a sketch of a possible systematization of this relation. According to such a systematization, philology and theory can be interrelated in four different ways: Firstly, as a theory of philology, secondly, as a theoretical philology, thirdly, as a philological theory, and fourthly, as a philology of theory.

Four Possible Relations between Philology and Theory

1. Theory of Philology

Theories of philology can be described as such deliberations which identify philological practices in a systematic manner and which describe the correlations between these practices and their interconnectedness. Therefore, these are observations that characterize philological practices especially with recourse to the unity of philology as an academic discipline as well as its difference to other disciplines and that do so drawing on the vocabulary of the philosophy (or theory) of science. Whereas there can be listed numerous such deliberations of the first half of the 19th century (ranging from Wolf, Schlegel, Ast and Schleiermacher to Boeckh's *Enzyklopädie und Methodenlehre der philologischen Wissenschaften*), it is hard to register an interest in such systematic descriptions of philology after that period until the end of the 20th century.[47] This may have changed in last two decades. But it is still striking that an interest in the theoretical examination of philology – in opposition to theoretical observations

47 | Glenn W. Most edited a series of books at the end of the 20th century with a similar encyclopedic scope: *Collecting Fragments/Fragmente sammeln* (Göttingen: Vandenhoek und Rupprecht, 1997); *Editing Texts/Texte edieren* (ibd., 1998); *Commentaries/Kommentare* (ibd., 1999); *Historicization/Historisierung* (ibd., 2001); *Disciplining Classics/Altertumswissenschaft als Beruf* (ibd., 2002).

about the natural and social sciences – seems to be limited to the philologies themselves.

2. Theoretical Philology

In contrast to theories of philology that can be postulated outside or inside of the discipline, theoretical philology is to be described as a subdiscipline of philology in correspondence to the specializations in other disciplines as in 'theoretical physics' or 'theoretical chemistry' and can be practiced only inside of philology.[48] The following types of studies can be subsumed under the term of a theoretical philology: on the one hand, studies that make observations on a higher level of abstraction (than philological analyses of single elements) about the concepts and terms used in analyses of a set or bodies of texts, of authors, of epochs, of genres, etc., on the other hand, studies that deal with the formalization of philological objects, the principles of philological modelling, and the description of methods used in philological studies. In terms of quantity, the field of theoretical philology seems to be disproportionally well staffed in comparison to other scientific disciplines. But systematic references of the heterogenous studies in this field to each other are as scarce as the willingness to a harmonization of the available observations and analyses. Moreover, there seems to be a lack of understanding about the insight that it cannot be the most important task of a theoretical philology to decide which methods and definitions are to be used and which ones are to be eliminated, but that a theoretical philology should primarily describe and classify the basics of the academic discipline without any evaluations. Not least because of the demands and challenges that the 'digital humanities' are presenting and are confronting the philologies with, it would be preferable to correct these defects.

Whereas the first two relations between theory and philology can at least draw on some traditional studies and the productivity of the distinction between a theory of philology and a theoretical philology has already been pointed out prominently elsewhere,[49] the distinction between a philological theory and a philology of theory is rather new territory.

48 | The distinction between Theory of Philology and Theoretical Philology follows the convincing deliberations in the introduction to Jörg Paulus: *Philologie der Intimität. Liebeskorrespondenz im Jean-Paul-Kreis* (Berlin/Boston: de Gruyter, 2013).

49 | Jörg Paulus, "Theoretische Philologie. Annäherung an eine disziplinäre und methodische Leerstelle", in: Cord-Friedrich Berghahn/Renate Stauf (eds.), *Philologie als Kultur* (Heidelberg: Winter, 2009), 33–50.

3. Philological Theory

Nevertheless or hence, I suggest to classify as philological theories such theoretical constructions as de Man's readings, in other words: such theories that start with philological observations, with the analyses of literary texts and that draw generalizing conclusions from the results of these analyses which transcend the range normally covered by philological readings. In this way, de Man reaches general assumptions about aesthetics, language, representation, or theory by way of the rhetorical reading of literary and philosophical texts, thus formulating analytical results which exceed the matrix of texts formerly analyzed and therefore leaving significantly the range of philological objects. Philological interpretations based on media theory, discourse analysis, theory of systems, and poetics of knowledge proceed in a similar way because they also make generalizing statements (about the functional principles of societies, media, or systems of knowledge) based on the reading(s) of literary texts.

4. Philology of Theory

In contrast to such philological theories, the term 'philology of theory' designates a philological treatment of theoretical texts. This treatment consists mainly of the two basic practices of textual criticism: the edition of theoretical texts on the one hand and on the other hand their annotation, that is a reading of theoretical texts which makes their contexts, rhetorical structures, intertextual affiliations, etc. accessible. With the establishment of an understanding of what a philology of theory can be and can achieve and what not, two different things could be accomplished. For one thing, one could confront the annoying custom that declares every (simple) reading of a theoretical text to be a theoretical statement or a theory itself, a custom which can be observed more and more frequently in the humanities and especially in cultural studies. And more importantly: the declaration of such a reading as a philology of theory (and not as theory itself) would make it possible to call for philological standards of precision and accuracy which such readings otherwise often lack. For another thing, the distinction between philology, theory, and philology of theory can be made productive for a deeper understanding of the figure of a 'return of philology' in the sense of de Man because this distinction makes it possible to avoid the mode of apodictic aporia into which almost all of de Man's essays get. Only by insisting on the non-identity of, on the differences between philology, rhetoric, and theory, it becomes evident that de Man produces the kind of amalgamations of aesthetics and epistemology that he constantly deconstructs in other texts. Only by keeping in mind that a philological attention to linguistic structures is not the same as a theoretical or a rhetorical one, de Man's demand for a 'return to philology' reveals itself as neither theoretically nor philologically convincing, but only as rhetorically persuading. In so doing, the famous phrase in "The Resistance to Theory", the institutionally and rhetorically less successful parallel text to the "Return to Philology", also dissipates into paradoxical complacence. The phrase is the following: "Nothing can overcome the resistance to theory since theory *is* itself this resistance".[50] The only reply to that can be that especially in de Man's essays it is precisely not theory that resists itself, but rather the "technically correct rhetorical readings", that is the philology of such theories, which accomplishes such resistance. And these readings may be – in de Man's own words – "boring, monotonous, predictable and unpleasant", but they do not need any revaluations or upgradings to theories.

Instead of a Punchline

After all this, one would be inclined to quote: 'Much ado about nothing'. But this quote again only bears witness to the indispensability of 'technically correct rhetorical readings' because only the philological commentary makes accessible the various levels the title of Shakespeare's comedy alludes to. The play is precisely not only about 'nothing'. Even more important seems to be the homophone 'noting' (pronounced the same as nothing during the Renaissance in England),[51] that is the character's perceiving and observing each other on the one hand and on the other hand the rumor, the hearsay, the eavesdropping (central elements of the plot of the play). And last but not least, the title also points to questions of gender as a main topic of the play by alluding to 'n O thing': a historical synonym for the female sex[52]...

50 | De Man: "Resistance to Theory", 19.

51 | Stephen Greenblatt, "Introduction to Much Ado about Nothing", in: *The Norton Shakespeare* (New York/London: Norton, 1997), 1381-1388, 1383.

52 | See Gordon Williams, *Shakespeare's Sexual Language: A Glossary* (London/New York: Continuum, 1997), 219.

Pathological Philology

Desire, Lack & the Digital Humanities

Björn Sonnenberg-Schrank

> "The real is full of holes and one can even make a vacuum in it."[1]

The *lack* (*manque*) Jacques Lacan has made famous as a defining factor for the subject is for him what produces desire: the *split subject* chases a lost unity, desires to restore the imaginary ideal state of completeness. Certainly, the pronounced interdependency of lack and desire, "the central lack in which the subject experiences himself as desire,"[2] is not an unproblematic concept, nor is it a sufficient explanation for *any*thing – but it can be brought in as an experimental working hypothesis when wondering about the motivation behind certain human endeavors, say, in the world of academia. Do scholars and scientists pursue a certain project because of the sheer fun it might bring them? For the sake of progress itself? Do they undertake it as an altruistic effort that might benefit humankind (even if only to a small segment of humankind, say: to the few people suffering from a rare disease or to the few people who work on an obscure author)? Is it, very unglamorously, a project that arises from the most basic of market principles, supply and demand: this is what is needed, or rather, in demand, right now (for whatever reason), therefore we should meet that demand before someone else does or before – perish the thought! – the demand wanes? Or could it after all sometimes be a case of lack, and the filling of knowledge gaps is less a question of progress and advancement and rather a striving for more insight which equals getting closer to an imaginary complete-

---

1 | Jacques Lacan, *The Seminar of Jacques Lacan. Book X: Anxiety. 1962-1963* (*Jacques Lacan in Ireland*, last modified June 2010, translated by Cormac Gallagher [http://www.lacaninireland.com/web/wp-content/uploads/2010/06/Seminar-X-Revised-by-Mary-Cherou-Lagreze.pdf], 171).

2 | Jacques Lacan, *The Seminar of Jacques Lacan. Book XI: The Four Fundamental Concepts of Psychoanalysis* (New York: W.W. Norton, 1998), 265.

ness, and the hunger for knowledge is really just that, a *hunger* that needs to be satisfied, a desire stemming from lack?

Compulsive Data Hoarding

The Digital Humanities (DH) as an exciting and open field with a growing number of well-stocked, well-staffed, well-funded "e-Humanities" and DH centers are currently finding their position as the 'machine in the garden' of the traditional humanities. One of the most exciting things about the field is that it is somewhat uncharted territory. From an outside, or even a semi-outside perspective it sometimes looks as if "digital" has become a prefix that enables unfundable projects to become fundable again, where the dear old humanities with their close readings, their semiotics, and idle enjoyment of the aesthetic value of theory and works of art can, under the guise of future-oriented digitality, benefit from the present discursive and monetary euphoria for specific new technologies and methods. The more interesting aspect of DH is what kind of work 'real' DH people do. Speaking in grossly oversimplified pictures, their work environments are not set up like the clichéd musty professor's office in which she broods in seclusion (except for the time when during office hours students interrupt the humanist peace), surrounded by books, papers, pens, and notes, reading and writing books and papers as a midwife in a process of paper cascades giving birth to more paper cascades.[3] DH centers in contrast are rather set up like proper 'IT laboratories,' in which a multitude of people, maybe not *in* white lab coats but almost as if, surrounded by expensive technology work on a paperless world of big data, archiving, collecting, computing. But what are the paperless cascades DH workers administer, manage, and produce? And what are some of the possible, the real, and the imagined benefits of letting computer-assisted methods and the humanities intersect, what kind of promise lies in big data, digital editions, and other DH pet projects?

For people who work with texts and among them especially the adherents of less hermeneutical approaches such as Genetic Criticism (GC) particularly digital editions must seem desirable: the utopia of GC to get as close as possible to a text and, if you will, its life-of-its-own – to avoid speaking of its meaning or even 'essence' – by assembling all traceable versions and incarnations, from an author's notebook or hard drive to existing publications and translations. On the other hand, it is hard to overlook that this detail-bent accumulation of bits and pieces has a dimension that – particularly when amplified in quantity and speed through the possibilities of modern high-performance computers – is

3 | Cf. the article by Nicolas Pethes in this volume.

quite obsessive-compulsive and more related to pathological hoarding[4] than to a philological quest for more clarity or a better, deeper understanding of any given object of concern.

I am not positioning GC (focus on the *process* from which the text emerged) against hermeneutics, traditionally in the form of a close reading (focus on one particular state of *text*), since both approaches, even when they deal with the same text, are fundamentally different.[5] Both can do without the other just as well as they can profit from each other. But is the philological gain, which undoubtedly exists, big enough to justify the time, funds, and disk space that goes into compiling such digital editions or is it mainly doubling and tripling of documents or of images of documents and are we slowly leaving the realm of the philological and entering the pathological?[6]

4 | "Compulsive hoarding" or "hoarding disorder" was defined as a mental disorder in the American Psychiatric Association's DSM (*Diagnostic and Statistical Manual of Mental Disorder: DSM*-5, 2013) for the first time as recently as 2013. In Germany, the common name is the Anglicism "Messie syndrome," which already contains the negative evaluation that a patient is not just hoarding, but being, and creating a *mess*. The behavior pattern is characterized by the inability to discard objects. It is closely related to the so-called "Diogenes syndrome" (or "senile squalor syndrome"), where again, the German name "Vermüllungssyndrom" (garbage cluttering syndrome) already contains a very negative judgement. It has its counterpart in the somewhat rarer "compulsive decluttering" (or "obsessive compulsive spartanism"), the excessive desire to discard objects a hoarder (or "messie") would hold on to - for the latter I don't see a (digital) humanities equivalent yet. Maybe browsing through a *Reader's Digest* version of a novel as the basis for a close reading?

5 | Especially regarding the idealism (in the Platonic sense of pertaining to the immaterial, mind-dependent realm of ideas) of GC: a close reading is subjective by nature and, obviously emerges from an individual's interaction with a text, a fact it does not hide as shortcoming, since this is its actual strength; however, the 'genetic edition' *can* never be complete as it is virtually impossible to include *all* the stages, elements, and traces of a text. Its nature is doomed, no matter *how* complete it is, to retain a certain lack.

6 | The almost compulsive longing for completeness and unearthing of versions, variations, and editions is by no means limited to literature and critical, complete, and/or digital editions, however there it is much easier to cloak as "philology" and thus as science, less as the desire of mere fans which fulfills no greater good than personal satisfaction. The same editorial and archival ambitions (not to say: collector's frenzy) can for instance be found in the field of popular music, on websites such as "Discogs", but also physically, especially when releases of artists with so-called cult followings (and called so for good - theological - reasons) are expanded by a surprising number of editions (not to mention bootlegs), often in the form of intricately curated box sets as beautiful aesthetic objects.

The underlying dream seems to be: I enlist a machine to help me read, process, comprehend the things I am not able to cover by myself and thereby I get closer to an imagined and imaginary idea of completeness (every findable line ever written by author X, including notes, manuscripts, sketches). Not only does the desire for completeness evoke Lacanian *manque* – in the form of philological desire stemming from philological lack – but also, obviously, repression: being a human – and humanities person – constantly reminds me of the limitations my being-human entails. Such limits could be body limits, knowledge limits, time limits, money limits, which all boil down to the most basic of human limits: the fact that I will never be able to find and read every text, watch every movie, visit every architecture, try every dish, simply because I will die before I can accomplish the *complete* task. However, DH methods allow me to – maybe not deny, but to temporarily forget, to repress the bleak reality that my *conditio humana* makes it simply impossible to reach the desired God state of completeness by replacing it with the dream that a digital all-seeing eye exists (to which I am, ideally, connected), and with it, a possibility of eternity – not in the sense of 'lasting forever,' but in the sense of 'being freed from the limitations of time.'

Literature as Big Data

> [...] the digital humanities have presented themselves as a radical break with the past, and must therefore produce evidence of such a break. And the evidence, let's be frank, is not strong."[7]

There is a danger when engaging critically with new media and/or technologies to be misread as (or actually, to *be*) caught up in the naïve binary of either embracing technological/medial advancements for the sake of progress, or as falling victim to the well-known reactionary anxiety about literally every new medium as potentially dangerous, corrupting, and corrosive.[8] Clearly, *not* to

7 | Franco Moretti, "Literature, Measured", in *Literary Lab Pamphlet* 12, last modified April 2016 [https://litlab.stanford.edu/LiteraryLabPamphlet12.pdf], 4 f.

8 | Some examples of noted new media fear narratives: comics corrupt the minds of children, television creates illiterate square-eyed zombies, video games breed cold-blooded killers, the internet isolates us and disables us to engage socially in the flesh, plus it destroys music, film and publishing industries and so on. There probably were concerned/incensed parents protesting the advent of the papyrus scroll as potentially destructive to the oral tradition and the social structure generated by orality.

keep the world of information technology and the humanities separated is only consequent and necessary in order to bridge and eventually erase such binaries.

One key moment in which DH took shape for many philologists is Franco Moretti's work at the Stanford Literary Lab, which culminated in his proposition of "distant reading" as one of the best-known DH projects.[9] Devising a method with which to approach texts by 'quantifying' them and turning them into *networks*, is an original thought because it not only uses computers to make traditional methods quicker and more expansive, but that is partly born from the genuine machinic features and operating modes of computers. After all, the mere utilization of a computer does not per se make a process modern, or even future-oriented; the way in which it is utilized, and in which its complex workings are integrated into the process however does. At least equally significant as his proposal itself is the fact that it did not work out as intended:

> The idea behind this study, clearly stated in its opening page, was, very simply, that network theory could offer a way to quantify plot, thus providing an essential piece that was still missing from computational analyses of literature. Once I started working in earnest, though, I soon realized that the machine-gathering of the data, essential to large-scale quantification, was not yet a realistic possibility. (Others, elsewhere, were already at work on this problem; but I wasn't aware of it). So, from its very first section, the essay drifted from quantification to the qualitative analysis of plot.[10]

Moretti deserves credit for his openness about the 'failure' of the initial aim and the admission that he "drifted from quantification to the qualitative analysis," because here, the operation becomes truly productive: if quantification is an additional tool *for*, but not one that is used *instead of* a qualitative analysis, it is

9 | In her article for the *New York Times Sunday Book Review* about Moretti's Distant Reading Kathryn Schulz states: "There will always be some people for whom new technologies seem to promise completeness and certainty, and Moretti, enthusing over the prospect of 'a unified theory of plot and style,' is one of them. Literature, he argues, is 'a collective system that should be grasped as such'. But this, too, is a theology of sorts – if not the claim that literature is a system, at least the conviction that we can find meaning only in its totality". (Kathryn Schulz, "The Mechanic Muse – What Is Distant Reading?". in *The New York Times Sunday Book Review*, last modified June 26th, 2011 [http://www.nytimes.com/2011/06/26/books/review/the-mechanic-muse-what-is-distant-reading.html], par. 11). Even though she has a different argument, she, too points out the theological underpinnings and the longing for completeness in which I locate the Lacanian lack of DH.

10 | Franco Moretti, "Network Theory, Plot Analysis", in *Literary Lab Pamphlet* 2. Stanford, last modified May 1st, 2011 [https://litlab.stanford.edu/LiteraryLabPamphlet2.pdf], 11.

a most helpful asset. It allows, if not a different, then certainly a deeper insight into the architecture of a text or even into a given totality of texts (like his research on 'the novel' in "Graphs, Maps, Trees") and thus provides a position from which to ask a new set of questions:

> [...] the asymmetry of a quantitative *explanandum* and a qualitative *explanans* leaves you often with a perfectly clear problem – and no idea of a solution [...] and problems without a solution are exactly what we need in a field like ours, where we are used to asking only those questions for which we already have an answer [...] I began this article by saying that quantitative data are useful because they are independent of interpretation; then, that they are interesting because they demand an interpretation; and now, most radically, we see them challenge existing interpretations, and ask for a theory [...] a theory – of diversity.[11]

A very simple example from the everyday practice of every philologist: If you turn a novel into a PDF-file[12], you can within seconds determine how often a word is used and how it is spread over the text-map, if there are identifiable segments in which a concentration is visible and so on. Talking about spread or visibility, one already enters the realm of abstract models and topology, of translating text into maps or graphs. This in turn can become useful for the qualitative analysis of plot, characters, settings, or style. Instead of slowly reading Frank Norris' *McTeague* (1899) and handpicking every instance something golden or the color of Trina's face in varying shades of red is mentioned, I can use the search function of my software and do it much quicker. But the computer's contribution remains quantitative: it can identify patterns, but it will not be able to make sense of them.[13] Furthermore, such pattern analyses are limited to immediate mentions and not mediated ones, which a human reader had no problems identifying, as the machine/software can only navigate the signifiers,

---

11 | Franco Moretti, "Graphs, Maps, Trees. Abstract Models for Literary History", in *New Left Review* 24, (Nov./Dec. 2003), 67-93, here 91.

12 | I would have liked to come up with a witticism that benefits from the typographical similarity of OCR and OCD and where a link might be established between Optical Character Recognition software's computerized conversion of text into characters and the desire for the repetition of patterns characteristic of Obsessive-compulsive Disorder. But then again, sometimes a cigar is just a cigar and not every computational achievement stems from *lack* or some pathology...

13 | "Forget the hype about computation making everything faster. Yes, data are gathered and analyzed with amazing speed; but the explanation of those results – unless you're happy with the first commonplace that crosses your mind – is a different story; here, only patience will do. For rapidity, nothing beats traditional interpretation" (Moretti, "Literature, Measured", 5).

not the signified. Even if we assume that algorithms can 'learn'[14] and granted that Artificial Intelligence's progress is impressive (albeit, it is never as good in reality as science fiction's lovable and/or terrifying sentient machines like HAL to the Terminator), there is still a dividing line between *recognizing* and *understanding*, between visible surfaces and less visible sublayers, between precise pattern analyses and those parts of the unconscious that simply do not follow patterns (because the unconscious simply *is not* structured like and produced by language, as Lacan proposes) but which factor in so significantly in cognitive processes.

But then, it is not a flaw that such distinctions remain. Regardless of one's stance towards the notion of totality, wholeness, or completeness in Moretti's project,[15] one very important aspect he (re)introduces is the emphasis on the collaborative (in *any* sense) nature of doing philology. He arrives at a position that we need to read as negating the existence of a division line that separates 'old' and 'modern,' singularities and laws, analog and digital reading, and in a way suggests what Donna Haraway might call Cyborg philology[16]: an improved

14 | The newest insight about the role of Big Data in recent political campaigning that surfaced in the context of the Cambridge Analytica scandal, like the ever-increasing presence of algorithms in, and their intrusion into the ever-increasing digital parts of our lives in general is something that we notice especially when it becomes visible through faultiness. In *Weapons of Math Destruction* (2016), Cathy O'Neil shows how algorithms use pattern analysis to make our behavior less opaque, on the one hand to cater to our preferences and thereby create a filter bubble in which our worldviews get constantly reaffirmed by drowning out offers that could contradict them (and thus potentially dangerous for democracy, which is based on plurality), on the other hand, to make us predictable (computable!): whether we are worthy of a bank loan or for which political candidate we are likely to vote. The gross mismatch between the size of the big data that formed the basis for the predictions on recent political votes (e.g. the UK's so-called Brexit in June 2016, and of course Donald Trump's surprising win of the 2016 US Presidential Election) and the inaccuracy of the predicted outcome was partly shocking, partly a healthy reminder that algorithms are far less able to foresee the future or individuals' behavior than often assumed and certainly no all-knowing God machines. This is not an argument against computational analysis, whether in voting patterns, nor in texts, but one for being a wary observer.

15 | "[...] a field this large cannot be understood by stitching together separate bits of knowledge about individual cases, because it isn't a sum of individual cases: it's a collective system that should be grasped as such, as a whole" (Moretti, "Graphs, Maps, Trees", 67).

16 | Also see Deleuze & Guattari's notion of an "assemblage," Gilles Deleuze and Félix Guattari, *Anti-Oedipus: Capitalism and Schizophrenia* (London: Bloomsbury Academic, 2013); Latour's "collective of humans and non-humans," (Bruno Latour, *Pandora's*

philology that expands itself by devices and methods, that does not discharge the solitary, subjective close reading of the human reader, but is no longer so exclusively centered around it.

WHOSE ARCHIVE? DIGITAL CULTURAL HERITAGE

One branch of Digital Culture that has less to do with the negotiation of traditional hermeneutics and more abstract models of computational methods, with different modes of reading (recognizing the signifiers vs. understanding the signified), and further paradigms, but is none the less an important part thereof is Digital Heritage (or DCH / Digital Cultural Heritage). Who would not find the idea attractive that for instance a digital museum makes it possible to study a hi-res image of every artifact in every museum or collection, especially since even most museums have more objects stowed away in storage than on display. No standing in line for the Mona Lisa, no travels to New York or Los Angeles to visit MoMA, Guggenheim, and Getty. Sure, I will miss out on the "aura," the hair of the brush dried into the oil paint, the ghostlike presence of the artist who had her hands on this very three-dimensional object, the immediacy of being in the same room with a statue and the physical act of walking around it – but losing some of the fetishistic aspects of the aesthetic experience is a fair price to pay for the chance to see pieces of art and artists' entire bodies of work that would be otherwise hard or impossible to ever lay an eye on.[17]

The premise of projects such as "Europeana.eu" sounds good and indeed democratic, a both pragmatic and idealistic application of digitality's and the internet's potential: turning Europe's cultural history into digital objects accessible for everybody. But there are built-in drawbacks: such an archive can never be complete and thus has to remain biased. And if it *were* complete, it would be as difficult to navigate as an uncurated museum – which is less a museum and more the den of a compulsive hoarder – and defeat its purpose of transparency. Then, there is the question of selection: what will be included in the archive in the first place? The world *in toto* still cannot be recorded and archived in the fashion of Adolfo Bioy Casares' fictional *Invention of Morel* (1940) (luckily,

---

Hope. Essays on the Reality of Science Studies (Cambridge: Harvard UP, 1999); or Barad's expanded notion of an "apparatus" and what it entails, Barad, Karen, *Meeting the Universe Halfway. Quantum Physics and the Entanglement of Matter and Meaning* (Durham: Duke UP, 2007).

17 | For a critique of the focus in digital media on representation (which, to some extent, I evoked here when I contrasted *seeing* with *experiencing*), see Kirschenbaum's notion of "screen essentialism," Matthew Kirschenbaum, *Mechanisms: New Media and the Forensic Imagination Cambridge* (London: MIT University Press, 2008).

since the lifelike copies Morel's invention produces also cause the originals to painfully fade from existence) and it does not 'objectively' record itself, not even in the form of less lifelike images and documents. It is necessary and inevitable to install curators who at the same time become gatekeepers: persons, apparatuses[18], or institutions determine what will constitute the digital cultural heritage. So, whose archive is it and who decides what will become a part and be left out of the narrative of "European culture?"[19]

Even though we like to think of the worldwide web and the digital culture it contains as much less territorialized than the world itself, digital culture has more borders and territories than meets the virtual eye, most evidently language. The amount of articles on Wikipedia in different languages not only indicates the size of the community of speakers, but furthermore (or *instead*, in fact) their access to the internet, and their willingness or inclination to post Wikipedia articles: there are almost six million English articles, by far more than in any other language, which makes perfect sense given the language's position in the world. In Sängö, the primary language spoken in the Central African Republic, there are slightly over one hundred articles and in Letzeburgesch, Luxemburg's language, there are over ten thousand articles. These numbers, however, do not represent the respective language's position in the world: Sängö is actively spoken by ca. five million people, Letzeburgesch by ca. 390.000. Depending on the area and influence of a language, the key technologies that are needed to build digital archives, are less or more advanced. Software developers are more inclined to devise and improve OCR or language pattern analysis software for languages with a higher dissemination, mainly because their market is automatically bigger: there are more potential buyers and users for a software that deals with English text than with text in Sängö. This means, that the size, velocity, and quality of the archives English speakers work on is automatically higher than those of their colleagues who work on archives of Hungarian, Sindhi, Gaelic, or Asturian texts and artifacts – not to mention cultures past and present with a distinct oral tradition or other modes of writing.

The archives in that sense do not only constitute a digital cultural heritage, they digitally reproduce and reinforce hegemonies and hierarchies – regardless of whether we are talking about Google Books, Wikipedia, Europeana or any other well-known and large-sized digital library or archive. While a democratic,

---

18 | Both in the sense of machinic devices as well as in the sense of power apparatuses, like the Althusserian state apparatus or the Foucauldian dispositif.

19 | For a media theoretical account of the interrelation of digital machines and the law, see Cornelia Vismann's in-depth study of archives (Cornelia Vismann, *Files: Law and Media Technology*, translated by Geoffrey Winthrop-Young (Stanford, CA: Stanford UP, 2008).

transparent archive is filled with more digital objects and the best intentions, simultaneously Eurocentrism and geopolitical as well as technological divides between North and South are digitally multiplied.[20]

THE DISEMBODIED ARCHIVE IN THE ETHER AND THE DESIRING DEMON THAT SEES EVERYTHING AND NEVER FORGETS

Our affection for seemingly immaterial archives sometimes blanks out that they *do* have a material side. Beginning with the metaphor, the "cloud" – presents itself as an ethereal archive: invisible, not corporeal, unlimited, omnipresent, suggesting that we can finally throw out the piled-up external hard drives we bought over the years and the USB sticks cluttering our desks and purses and hand the data over to the data angels, who will from then on keep all our documents safely guarded somewhere and everywhere. The image is so alluring that we almost become enmeshed in a reproduction of Plato's allegorical cave in which for the unknowing chained people staring at the wall, shadows seem like the real thing and not as a mediated copy thereof, as they can neither see the real objects nor the light source that causes the shadow images. But for the shadowlike, disembodied cloud, *somewhere* there *is* a very material and very big hard drive from which it 'emanates.' And it can be harmed by similar factors that are potentially harmful for our own private hard drives, magnetic tapes, CDRs, flashdrives or even proper libraries, museums, and other 'real' (as opposed to 'data') archives: insufficient storage space, fire, humidity, mold, decay, loss, bad caretaking, theft. Instead of factors that are less threatening to a cloud, others enter the picture that are less threatening to a real-material archive such as hacking or computer viruses. Certainly: matter in any form has a finite life whereas 'the virtual,' at least theoretically, isn't time-critical. But the virtual is always bound to matter: no data without data storage, so naturally the digital is time-critical, too. It may not look and feel like an organism, but just like an organism, it has a bodily dimension and can die (it even has drives!).

A related truism is the ominous "once it's out there, it's out there," the notion that the internet never forgets anything; there it is again: the all-seeing,

20 | Even more obvious than the territorialization of the web through language is the case of for instance China or Russia, where the internet does not constitute a connection to the world, but on the contrary a genuine parallel world, which indeed is not dictated or produced by language and its borders, but digitally reproduces political power structures. The idealistic utopia of a rhizomatic, borderless web gets debunked as romantically naive by the clarity of the fact that 'the digital' is not fundamentally different than the 'real' hierarchies and hegemonies of (state) apparatuses, power relations and their flows.

all-knowing, all-remembering data God looming over the image of the completely interconnected web. While not wrong per se, as indeed data can stay present and/or circulating practically unrestrictedly[21] and almost as if leading an indelible life of its own, as a matter of fact more data on the internet is deleted than stored.[22] It is by no means a bottomless container programmed to amass a complete archive of all the traces ever left. To conceive of the internet as all-encompassing data hoarding entity is reminiscent of Laplace's Demon, a 19th century premonition of present-day big data aspirations (and often used as a personification of a deterministic universe), which can be thought of as a superintelligence that knows everything that ever happened anywhere and can calculate a possible future from this knowledge.[23]

---

21 | This, of course, can also be very productive: when objects – in this case digital objects – keep circulating, their value might change eventually due to historic contexts changing and data garbage may become 'data gold,' following the logic of Thompson's "Rubbish Theory," Michael Thompson, *Rubbish Theory: The Creation and Destruction of Value* (Oxford: Oxford UP, 1979).

22 | Commonly, data is for instance deleted due to unpaid server bills, but also much more actively and targeted. A Berlin-based theatre collective did a "lecture-performance" in 2016 based on director Moritz Riesewick's research on data workers in the Philippines who professionally delete web content. In an interview, he speaks about "people who keep the internet clean for us, a digital waste disposal. They are hired to sort out everything we're not supposed to be confronted with on Twitter, Instagram or Tinder: images of decapitations and mutilations, videos depicting sex with animals, child pornography, or less drastic, things that companies don't want us to see. Most companies aren't transparent about their deletion guidelines, but in order to implement them, software wouldn't do, and instead humans are needed who are capable to perceive images and videos, news and information, in their given context, for instance to determine whether an image is used ironically. The country is right now becoming a global center for such services [...] with currently between half a million and a million employees in this field, mostly women from lower social ranks. It is them who keep the internet clean, pretty, and comfortable. Not too long ago, electronic scrap and toxic waste from the West was shipped to the Philippines, today it is the digital scum that gets disposed of there [...]. Right now, a large-scale traumatization of entire parts of a society is taking place: thousands of people whose daily task is clicking through and looking at shocking images at second intervals many of which are produced on the other side of the world" (Martin Kaul, "Müllentsorger in Sozialen Netzwerken: Sie Berichten Von Depressionen", in *Die Tageszeitung*, last modified April 25th, 2016 [http://www.taz.de/!5295220/], par. 7).

23 | "We ought then to regard the present state of the universe as the effect of its anterior state and as the cause of the one which is to follow. Given for one instant an intelligence which could comprehend all the forces by which nature is animated and the

Imagining the web in the fashion of Laplace's Demon seems on the one hand indebted to theological notions of omnipotence and omniscience (or the resulting paranoia). But on the other hand, it ultimately results in the somewhat anthropocentric construction of an image of the internet as a being (albeit a virtual superbeing), a data hoarding intelligence, which is however still driven by the same desire for imaginary, irretrievable completeness as the human subject. And just like the analogous human "search for truth," i.e. completeness, will always make visible the holes and gaps and cracks and all that it is *not*, the Web-Demon by default will remain unrealized and retain a lack, chasing "the vast intelligence [...] from which it will always remain infinitely removed."[24]

---

respective situation of the beings who compose it – an intelligence sufficiently vast to submit these data to analysis – it would embrace in the same formula the movements of the greatest bodies of the universe and those of the lightest atom; for it, nothing would be uncertain and the future, as the past, would be present to its eyes. The human mind offers, in the perfection which it has been able to give to astronomy, a feeble idea of this intelligence. Its discoveries in mechanics and geometry, added to that of universal gravity, have enabled it to comprehend in the same analytical expressions the past and future states of the system of the world. Applying the same method to some other objects of its knowledge, it has succeeded in referring to general laws observed phenomena and in foreseeing those which given circumstances ought to produce. All these efforts in the search for *truth* tend to lead it back continually to the vast intelligence which we have just mentioned, but *from which it will always remain infinitely removed*" (Pierre Simon Laplace, *A Philosophical Essay on Probabilities* [New York: John Wiley & Sons, 1902], 4).

24 | Ibd. Note that about this intelligence (which is never actually referred to as *Demon* in the text, only later exegetes began to call it that, taking into account the theological dimension of the image) Laplace states that "for it, nothing would be uncertain and the future, as the past, would be present to its eyes." The construction of the image as having eyes and physically *seeing* everything, not only being able to *compute* it, reinforces the assumption of the intelligence's underlying desire. The connection of the gaze – the eyes as a symbol thereof – and (sexual) desire has a long history, examples ranging from the biblical story of "Susanna and the Elders," included in the book of Daniel, or the tale of Greek mythology's Aktaion (or Actaeon) secretly ogling the bathing Artemis/Diana, to Norman Bates spying through his peephole in Alfred Hitchcock's *Psycho* and numerous conceptualizations of desire-driven gazes from Freud's scopophilia to Laura Mulvey's "male gaze" to, again, Lacan: "How can we not see here, immanent in the geometrical dimension – a partial dimension in the field of the gaze, a dimension that has nothing to do with vision as such – something symbolic of the function of the lack, of the appearance of the phallic ghost?" (Lacan, *Book XI*, 88).

Finally

> Information ethics/cyberethics (both since taken)
> Said: Maximize the information flow
> Toward a hypothetical end state in which the cosmos
> Consists entirely of our info,
> And at the highest level possible, not only data
> But data about data dot dot dot
> Or life on top of life on top of life, et cetera;
> Profundity, my mother'd say (I'd not).
> "86 How I Failed Ethics" (The Magnetic Fields, 2016)

If Digital Humanities *really* is a hybrid in its own right, a genuine new mode of 'doing' philology that is neither mainly digital nor mainly humanities, neither 'computer operations that happen to deal with texts' nor 'text operations that happen to be conducted with the help of a computer' but something that actually reshapes our interaction with texts, something that helps rethink and reshuffle agencies, and something that makes us aware that to some extent we have always been hybrid philologists who are not exclusively one individual, dissociated mind, but one that already is deeply entangled in a 'friendly' collaborative co-existence with machines, files, documents, concepts, and many more analog, digital, human and non-human actors: wonderful. If on the other hand DH is mainly an operation that out of a sticky desire-lack-conglomerate chases ideals of totality and completeness via amassing and computing big data, it might get stuck in an infinitely long spiral that is despite its length still rather self-centered: it will surely generate more details and more insights, but not necessarily *new* details and *other* insights. The mere fact that really powerful machines are computing really big amounts of data is neither a guarantee for productive new perspectives nor a promise of salvation in itself, but just a set of new clothes that might prompt us to notice: The Emperor is not wearing anything at all!

But to be fair, she looks very good.

2. Materialities

The Hourglass

Classics and the Dematerialization (or something else) of Philology*

Ádám Rung

As a number of texts point out in this volume, literary studies are more and more intrigued by the physical media of literature: the book, the newspaper, the manuscript and so on. At the same time, as a number of texts here also show, a similar interest has been arising on the effect of evolving digital technologies on literature. While the digital production, editing, dissemination and consumption of literature does happen in the physical realm – and this can actually be studied –[1] often an apparent opposition is perceived between these two tendencies. This is often articulated as the mostly begrudgingly admitted *dematerialization* of literature and literary criticism that is now frequently produced with virtually no physical trace on any traditional writing material,[2] often up

* | I would like to thank Pál Kelemen and Ábel Tamás for initiating me into these, from my then-point of view, remote fields of literary studies; Béla Adamik for bibliographical and technical advice on Roman epigraphy (and drawing my attention to CIL IV. 1173 specifically); and last but not least, Dániel Kozák and Attila Ferenczi for reflecting on my work with classicists' eyes.

1 | See Melinda Vásári's article in this volume.

2 | As a classicist, who does most of his work on the *pre*-paper world, I notice some fascination on the part of modern philologists with *paper* as the only material context of literature (and even some despair about its upstaging by IT – e. g. Wolf Kittler, "Literatur, Edition und Reprographie," *Deusche Vierteljahrsschrift für Literaturwissenschaft und Geistesgeschichte* 65 (1991/2): 235 and Régis Debray, "Dématérialisation et désacralisation. Le livre comme objet symbolique," *Le Débat* 86 (1995/4): 22-30 *passim*). True, for most modern languages, paper is exactly that only material from day one, but when reading passages by, say, Horace on the importance of ruthless, repeated deletion in polishing a text (e. g. *Ars Poetica* 291-294), I cannot help but thinking about the possible similarities between the literary worlds of wax tablets and of digital word processing applications. That could even mean that from the point of view of writers

to the moment of printing – or in the case of e-books, not even then. As both a classicist and a participant of a scholarly project on these two tendencies and their overlap, I decided to (I) take a brief look at the relationship of my own trade to both of these tendencies in general,[3] to (II) introduce an intriguing parallel development to all that in one of the sister/daughter disciplines of Classics, the study of Roman inscriptions (through an, I hope, entertaining case study); and in the end, to (III) see what that case study might imply in relation to the three-sided relationship of Material Criticism, Digital Humanities and our own beloved Classics.

I am afraid here is the place to take a look at the *terms* by which the study of ancient times is conceptualized in differing traditions. The people (including myself) that I call "classicists" (according to the general English meaning of the term) belong to the 19th century tradition of what would be called *Altertumswissenschaft* in German, not to the narrower and older field of Classical Philology *(Klassische Philologie)*. The former differs from the latter in that most of the time it takes the liberty of "blackboxing" the construction and constructedness of editions and prefers to study classical cultures in the wider historical, geographical, and material contexts of the ancient Mediterranean, as opposed to always keeping the textual heritage of the mediaeval Latin West, and to a smaller extent, the Byzantine East, in its focus. This is not as much a real opposition as a functional differentiation (the two subdisciplines are of course interdependent and form a continuum), but the more interpretative and less manuscript-centric tradition has been open in other directions other than philology proper for centuries now, including history, philosophy, anthropology and psychology – but first and foremost, to literary studies.

I

Material literary criticism, as a part of the wider trends of Cultural Studies and Science Studies, explores literary production, distribution and consumption as social and material processes, and their products as concrete objects, so to say, artefacts – as opposed to most 20th century literary studies, based on Russian *Formalism* and Anglophone *New Criticism,* but maybe best described by the

---

having the convenience of deleting and rewriting effortlessly prior to even limited publication, the material history of literature is not in a game-changing crisis, but it has just come full circle after the overlapping episodes of paper and printing (cf. Debray, "Dématérialisation" again, especially 27). But these are just impressions – exploring them properly would probably require a different article.

3 | Similarly to what Dániel Kozák's article does in this collection from another point of view.

German term *Werkimmanenz,* that is, 'staying in the text', which is here understood as an abstract body of meaning.

From another point of view, however, some aspects of a book formerly often disregarded as banal or redundant, like typeface, page layout or paper type, might be just as important as the "text" strictly speaking.[4] The sum of these factors, sometimes called the *bibliographic code,* or, more esoterically, the *aura* of a given book may contribute just as much to the overall meaning of it as the (factual or stylistic) information its sentences contain, let alone the full picture that is painted by the interaction of these two. Some commentators suggest that merely by the mechanical reproduction of books, this *aura* is completely sacrificed, while others say that every specimen of every edition has an aura of its own, which dissolves and replaces the aura of the previous examples only, not that of the whole work, thus making the notion of a given "work" an inherently pluralistic one.[5]

Not even this second definition seems to be satisfactory when I think of either the textual tradition of ancient literary works or the usual attitude of classicists towards it. Benjamin's notion of the *aura* and the ways in which editions' physical properties have been shown as interacting with modern literary texts[6] both suggest that all this has to do something with a quasi-*presence* of the authors and/or their age, which, like a *mana* of some sort, is progressively diminishing with each and every edition. Most people who see or touch a medi-

4 | George Bornstein, "How to Read a Page?" in idem, *Material Modernism: The Politics of the Page,* 5-31 (Cambridge: Cambridge University Press, 2001), 6; cf. Alan Bilansky, "Search, reading and the rise of database," *Digital Scholarship in the Humanities* 32. 3 (September 2017): 518.

5 | Bornstein, "How to," 6-7, citing Walter Benjamin for the concept of an exclusive *aura* and Jerome McGann for that of pluralistic *bibliographic code.* Note that the *aura* Benjamin speaks about is a subjective, maybe even transcendent stand-in for the "ideal text" of other textual theories, and as such, its concept is yet another stage in the tradition of *textual idealism* as opposed to being an early stage of material criticism - for a concise discussion of the former, see Pál Kelemen, Ernő Kulcsár Szabó, and Ábel Tamás, eds., *Kulturtechnik Philologie. Zur Theorie des Umgangs mit Texten* (Heidelberg: Winter 2010), 12-13 (in the foreword by the editors); or Jerome J. McGann, *The Textual Condition* (Princeton N. J.: Princeton University Press, 1991), 5-8 (with citations), where it is followed by much on the latter. When I use the term *aura* here, I use it - quite unlike Benjamin - as a deeply physical one, more or less synonymous with the contingently irreplaceable physicality of a given specimen (cf. McGann, *The Textual Condition,* 8-9). Also of interest is the fact that just as the idea of an ideal text depends on a variable textual tradition, that of the *aura* is dependent on an era of print and mechanical reproduction separating the reader from the "original" manuscript (Kittler, "Literatur," 226).

6 | Bornstein, "How to," 8-31.

aeval codex or an early print of a classical work are likely to perceive an almost tangible aura about it[7] – however, perceiving its bibliographic code as authentically connected to its linguistic code seems just as wrong as denying that it has such an aura. If one does not let go of the figure of the author or even the concept of cultural context (should one do that in these heavily post-New Criticism times?),[8] the joint interpretation of the physicality of a 13th or 16th century book and its, say, 1st or 2nd century textual content does not promise much to someone who is interested in classical antiquity – as opposed to its reception at the time of the book's production. Most Classicists are expected to be and *are* in fact interested in the latter as well to some extent (do we have a choice?), and some of us do fall in love with the middle ages along the way, but in general, the study of mediaeval book culture is just not what we are about.[9] We will not gain any extratextual knowledge about the love poetry of Catullus by looking at the parchment type or the page layout of any of his works' manuscripts:[10] when those were written, his (even near) contemporary readers and editors were just as deaf and blind – and his mistresses were just as unable to seduce anyone[11]– as they are *now*, in their unknown graves.

Already the birth of Classics as a discipline is marked by the Renaissance decision *not* to be too interested in what happened between ancient Rome and the present of the scholar: the most obvious proof is the very concept of the "middle" or even "dark ages", that is, the time between Then and Now, whose contribution to the texts we want to read is nothing but – communicationwise – noise.[12] Now that "noise" is just about *all* of the bibliographic code of our mediaeval codices, when translated to the terms of material philology.

---

7 | Cf. McGann, *The Textual Condition*, 77.

8 | As we shall see, the latter has much more relevance to this article than the former, though.

9 | Again, bear in mind the difference between the concepts of *Altertumswissenschaft* and Classical Philology proper.

10 | For mediaevalists, doing just that makes much sense: see Stephen G. Nichols, "Why Material Philology? Some Thoughts," in *Philologie als Textwissenschaft*, ed. by Helmut Tervooren and Horst Wenzel = *Zeitschrift für deutsche Philologie* 116 (1997): 10-30.

11 | On parallels between erotic relationships and literary production, see Kittler, "Literatur," esp. 205-207 and 215-217; and McGann, *The Textual Condition*, 3-4.

12 | See e. g. Stephen Greenblatt, *The Swerve. How the World Became Modern* (New York - London: W. W. Norton & Company, 2011) *passim* - or for a now-standard account on the birth of Renaissance Humanism, L. D. Reynolds and N. G. Wilson, *Scribes and Scholars. A Guide to the Transmission of Greek and Latin Literature* (Oxford: Clarendon Press 1968-1991), 122-163.

What follows from this with regard to the materiality of texts is overwhelming: from a (literary-minded) classicist's point of view, all the materiality of what we have to read is an obstacle, and the more original, scribal *aura* it has, the faster we want it away from us. As a most striking example, some of us tend to prefer copies by mediaeval scribes who did not even understand what they copied[13] – we do not need them as co-authors.[14] When one is done with the collection, transcription and collation of the extant manuscripts, they are better sent back to their stuffy libraries, while we read and interpret our elegant, standardized editions, splendidly printed on bright white paper with only a scientific looking critical apparatus at the bottom of the pages reminding us of all the codices and possibly, papyri. If a new manuscript is found, a new technology seems to be able to help us "see" the old ones better, or the existing editions simply feel old enough to make a "fresh" look at the manuscripts justifiable, this process is often repeated. But even those of us who are willing to repeat it now and then – and even believe that the attentive reading of its manuscripts is both a means and an end for an expert of a text – still aim at neutral print editions as the end product of their work.

To take and modify the bottleneck metaphor of biology,[15] the lifespan of a text and its philology can be pictured as an *hourglass* (hence my title).[16] The top half of it is the text's production, from the writer's first ideas to the publication (whatever that means), which seems to be analogous to the narrow middle of it, and the lower bulb corresponds to the afterlife of the text, from first publication to all the given reader or interpreter has. The frame of it all is history, with the top cover being the culture of the time of the production, and the bottom one that of the reader's/interpreter's era.[17]

Modern philology often has the means to study both halves of the hourglass – so much so that sometimes it can even question the existence of the clear distinction between them (i.e. a discernible middle); and also, most of the time it has pretty convincing grounds to reconstruct the "top cover", that is, the

13 | Kittler, "Literatur," 218–219 (quoting Lachmann).

14 | Luciano Canfora, *Il copista come autore* (Palermo: Sellerio, 2002) *passim*.

15 | Used to great effect in a philological study by Gregory Nagy, "The Homeric Text and Problems of Multiformity," in idem, *Homer's Text and Language*, 24–39 (Champaign: University of Illinois Press, 2004) *passim*, esp. 27–30, with citations.

16 | One may note here, though, that the version of the hourglass that the Greeks and Romans used (called *clepsydra*) looked nothing like a modern one: I dare not even think of the possible effects of this on my allegory.

17 | Applied to about the same thing, McGann (*The Textual Condition*, 16) uses the metaphor of "the double helix of a work's reception history of and its production history." He reuses that metaphor later on in the same book for the duality of "linguistic" and "bibliographic" codes (77).

cultural background from outside sources (to reflect on its differences to the bottom one). Moreover, with authorial manuscripts, editorial proofs, different authorized editions *et cetera* at hand, the upper bulb can absolutely be its main focus with the advent of cultural/science studies and physical criticism.[18]

Classics have a different hourglass – or at least, *see* a different one. Even if we picture it as a whole, it looks quite like the figure "8" in most typefaces, with the bottom half being significantly larger than the upper half – if not for anything else, because of the time elapsed. But most of the time – that is, virtually always – we have absolutely no access to anything inside the upper half apart from the author's name and a more or less exact timeframe (and theoretically, both can be wrong).[19] Authorial manuscripts of literary works from antiquity are virtually absent, let alone anything from the writers' workshop or personal details concerning the production and publication of a text. The absence almost automatically, raises the value of "the middle", that is, the published text quite a lot – which, given the scarcity of information we have on the publication of any of the texts we have, cannot really be grasped either, and thus has to be substituted by the notion of an "ideal" text, that we think of as the author's post-*ultima manus* version as it entered circulation.[20] This is supposed to be reconstructed

18 | On the rise of (first not particularly material) genetic criticism, see Kittler, "Literatur," esp. 226-232.

19 | For example, the real name of the author we know as Titus Maccius Plautus is, in all likelihood, never to be recovered: the only possibly authentic part of it is Titus, the given name; the other two posing as family name and byname are slightly modified names of stock characters he played - Michael von Albrecht, *A History of Roman Literature* (Leiden - New York - Cologne: Brill, 1997), 163, with citations; and we are still not entirely sure whether the writer Petronius whose (immensely important) *Satyricon* we know is the same Petronius we read about in Tacitus (von Albrecht, *A History,* 1211-1214, with citations).

20 | By the "version" to be reconstructed (of course), we usually mean a body of grammatical structures and meanings down to the "resolution" of a conventional nearly-pho*nemic* transcription, as it might have been understood on the grammatical level by a contemporary reader, and as opposed to either a reconstruction of a text-as-object, or that of a spoken text. No classical edition I am aware of tries to reconstruct the letter forms or the layout of an ancient edition (the latter probably entirely without spacing and punctuation), nor have I seen any that aim to reproduce phon*etic* qualities (sometimes not even phon*emic*, like in the case of Latin vowel length). This is because of both practical and theoretical reasons: the strictly physical formats, spoken or written, however different they might have been to ours, are both lost and considered more or less "transparent" to contemporary readers. An approach of this sort is not limited to Classics: on writing representing grammatical structure iconically or at best phone*mic*ally, instead of spoken language phon*etic*ally, see Sybille Krämer, "Writing, Notaby the highlighted main text of modern editions of the work (as opposed to its own notes or to any manuscript), from Petrarca's famous Livy manuscript[21] to whatever volume came out last of the *Bibiliotheca Teubneriana* or *Oxford Classical Texts* series. The added-up obstacles of the enormous enlargement of the bottom half of the hourglass and that of the remoteness of the upper half makes it impractical or even impossible to think of multiple authorial manuscripts or multiple widely available editions – even if we cannot rule out their existence.[22]

The difference between the two hourglasses of modern and classical literary studies may not be only optical, though: because of the differences in information available, the "middle", that is, the ideal text also tends to be at a somewhat different point on the axis of the hourglass. Modern philologists, encouraged by their comparably good access to the secrets of the trade in the upper bulb, tend to think of the ideal text as something that exists in the author's head, which is corrupted from the moment it touches the perishable physicality of paper.[23] For classicists, on the other hand, the ideal text we may hope to get close to is quite much past that stage: it is not a mental construct in the author's head anymore, but a social one that lives and evolves on the cultural network of its author and its primary readers.[24] A text or version not published is not only inaccessible to us, but it also fails to have participated in the cultural cloud of the era as a published one does – thus, to a classicist, it virtually does not exist.

This importance of the ideal text in Classics leads to two other interesting, if, like some of the above, subjective facts. First, I am not sure whether I would open a box containing wax tablets or papyri with Ovid's sketches on them, even if I could get my hands on it – I cringe at the very thought, even if I know

tional Iconicity, Calculus: On Writing as a Cultural Technique," *MLN* 118. 3 (Apr. 2003): 518-537, *passim*, esp. 518-522 and 526-528.

21 | British Museum, Harley 2493.

22 | (We think) we know, for example, that Ovid selectively abridged his *Amores* for a second edition. It is a legitimate question however, whether one believes him telling us so in the introductory epigram at the beginning of the *Amores*. I mean no offense, though: poets need not tell the truth.

23 | McGann, *The Textual Condition*, 5-8. On the Platonic views of modern philology on itself and on the definition of what a text is, see Kelemen, Kulcsár Szabó, and Tamás, *Kulturtechnik Philologie*, 12-13, again. This idealism, to me, seems to stem from the vision of the "main" text in early Classics, but it has become something quite different in the meantime, something without a consciousness of the inherent virtuality of its "ideal texts" – of which classicists are reminded day by day, willy-nilly, by the much more limited access to "our" texts' production.

24 | On the the notion of text as a social phenomenon – McGann, *The Textual Condition*, 69-87.

what a cheekily curious lot philologists can be (including myself),[25] and that for example, Vergil's *Aeneid,* one of the most definitive texts of Roman literature is widely thought to have been published posthumously, against the wishes of its dying author.[26] I do not think I would be the only classicist who would have a dilemma there[27] – we are so used to the bottom half that the top half seems to be something we are just not supposed to see.[28]

The other result leads us over to the second half of this discussion: from this point of view, dematerialization has long been overdue in classics, or, if we accept standardized, neutral-looking editions as *less material* than one of a kind mediaeval manuscripts, it has already began to happen with printing at the latest, or maybe as early as with Renaissance efforts at producing easily legible and readable handwritten editions from multiple different manuscripts. A digital edition with the alternative readings included as hyperlink in the thus highlighted main text is a logical development on the traditional paper-based edition, the structure of which already foreshadows this division – just as its own "name" and "word indices", and other typical Classics materials like intertextual commentaries or collections like the all-compassing *Thesaurus Linguae*

25 | Cf. Kittler, "Literatur," 233-235.

26 | Suetonius, *Verg.* 39-41. I suppose tradition can constitute an exception for such a subjective rule.

27 | Also, it seems that Horace's *Ars Poetica* suggests something like this by calling attention to the importance of not letting anything subpar out of the workshop (again, remember 291-294), let alone Catullus' notoriously furious *verissima lex* (poem 16), where he (or his narrator) threatens his indiscreet critics with acts of rather crude violence if they insist on peeping into his *life* instead of sticking to his poetry only. One might say that drafts and manuscripts still belong to the category of "poetry", but who would risk messing with 16's truly dangerous Catullus? This also may be mirrored by the pre- and early modern stress put on *ultima manus,* the final/definitive authorial version and the objection of even some modern authors (including Kafka) to philologists' access to their manuscripts (Kittler, "Literatur," 210-214 and 233-235 again, respectively).

28 | Sometimes, one also has the feeling that the works we know of, but do not have were not filtered out accidentally of the tradition: such a text is Cicero's famously dreadful epic *de consulatu suo* i. e. 'On His Own Consulship' (e. g. Quintilian, 11. 1. 24). This would imply that what we have is what we *should* have - we desperately want someone to find Ovid's long lost, but supposedly brilliant *Medea* for us, though (e. g. Quintilian, 10. 1. 98); cf. Canfora, *Il copista,* 76-80 (he quotes and refutes Edward Gibbon on the topic).

Latinae foreshadow digital networks and searchable databases.[29] Such a seemingly immaterial edition is just a logical second step further away from the *aura*-laden, but sometimes very particular and often perishable codex – the first step in the very same direction was the clear-cut, easily readable and universal paper edition, which is, additionally, often part of a series. The editions of different texts in the same series resemble each other physically very much, just as Platonic ideas might be imagined lining up on a shelf in Heaven – they promise to share the feature of being the "ideal state" of the text they contain.[30]

II

To test this model, one might like to look at an alternate history, which also concerns texts composed in antiquity and still read/interpreted nowadays. Not many alternative histories show up at such a wish, but this one actually does. While the mediaeval manuscript tradition is the main source of ancient texts for us, a smaller number of texts have survived the centuries as inscriptions on writing materials other than paper (or its forerunners): walls, tablets of various materials and everyday objects. Most of these are not literary texts, and most of them do not have different variations (that is where the parallel is not quite perfect), but they in fact date from antiquity and are the products of its culture *as physical artefacts* – and as we shall see, there are a lot of literary ones, some of which can even be put into *stemmata* as parts of the same textual family (if not as specimens of the same text).

The traditional models of making these texts available to the public belong to two distinct traditions, or at least, can be grouped into two functional categories. This might be surprising at first sight but it makes quite much sense if one keeps in mind my aforementioned theory on the importance of non-materiality for people studying classical literature. In the following, I take a look at the same epigraphical poems in two collections, one of them aimed at classicists (as readers of literature), and the other mainly at archeologists and historians (or more antiquarian-minded classicists).

The poem I chose is an ancient erotic ditty that seems well-known to residents of Pompeii and Rome, probably a product of folk poetry – and not an

29 | Cf. the article by Dániel Kozák in this volume as well as Hans Ulrich Gumbrecht, *Our Broad Present. Time and Contemporary Culture* (New York: Columbia University Press, 2014), 70.

30 | Editions like that – paradoxically – contribute quite much to notions like Benjamin's *aura* by providing them with perfect foils/antitheses – cf. Kittler, "Literatur," 226, again.

example of *gesunkenes Kulturgut* from "high" elegiac literature, as previously thought:[31]

Fig. 1: Poem 945 in Bücheler's collection, cropped screenshot of the Google Books scan of Franz Bücheler, Anthologia Latina. Pars posterior: Carmina epigraphica II (Leipzig: Teubner, 1897)

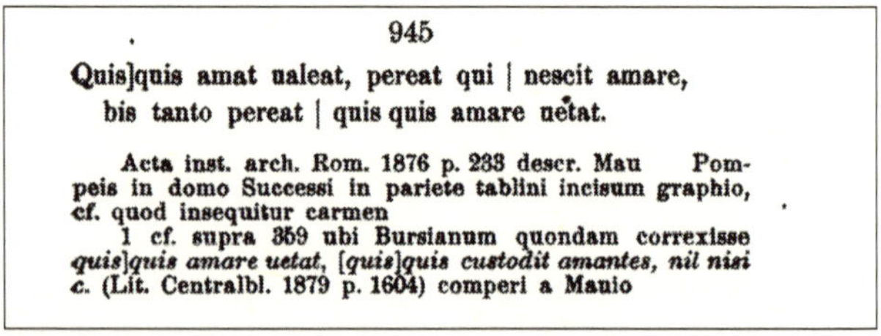

945

Quis]quis amat ualeat, pereat qui | nescit amare,
bis tanto pereat | quis quis amare uetat.

Acta inst. arch. Rom. 1876 p. 233 descr. Mau Pompeis in domo Successi in pariete tablini incisum graphio, cf. quod insequitur carmen
1 cf. supra 359 ubi Bursianum quondam correxisse *quis]quis amare uetat, [quis]quis custodit amantes, nil nisi c.* (Lit. Centralbl. 1879 p. 1604) comperi a Mauio

All the best for those who love, who cannot love should perish;
twice as much should perish whoever impedes love.[32]

The "cutout" is from the fourth volume of the *Anthologia Latina* in the classic Teubner series from 1897, which contains epigraphic poems compiled and edited by Franz Bücheler. This inscription is an archetypical version of a poem (from now on, 945), which has been found in a number of graffiti, in different extensions, abridgements and even parodies in Pompeii and Rome.[33] Here is another version from the same volume (actually from the top of the next page, 436) – painted on a Pompeian wall as part of a fresco and extended into a somewhat obscure love poem, which I need not even translate (my readers shall see why in a minute):

31 | Rudolf Wachter, "'Oral poetry' in ungewohntem Kontext: Hinweise auf mündliche Dichtungstechnik in den pompejanischen Wandinschriften," *Zeitschrift für Papyrologie und Epigraphik* 121 (1998): 73-89, esp. 76-77 and 88-89.

32 | My own raw translation.

33 | See Kristina Milnor, *Graffiti and the Literary Landscape in Roman Pompeii* (Oxford/ New York: Oxford University Press, 2014), 137-189, esp. 184-189 and Wachter, "Oral poetry," 75-79 for discussions of these poems.

Fig. 2: Poem 946 in Bücheler's collection, cropped screenshot of the Google Books scan of Franz Bücheler, Anthologia Latina. Pars posterior: Carmina epigraphica II (Leipzig: Teubner, 1897)

436 DACTYLI

946

Quisquis amat ualeat, pereat qui nescit amare,
 bis tanto pereat quisquis amare uotat.
felices adeas, maneas o Martia, si te
 uidi, dum nobis, maxima cura, placet.

CIL. IV 1173 add. p. 204, tab. 18, 1 in pictura papyri Pompeiana scariphatum exemplum amatoriae epistulae. litterae incertissimae et quae uariis modis legi possint. in secundo disticho quae uerba sibi uisi sunt legere alii, non expedit omnia adscribi, sensum a me recte exploratum esse arbitror

1 *ama ualia peria* et ut Zangemeister testatur *noscit* scriptum est. idem uersus in pariete Pompeiano legitur n. 3199 p. 222 *cuscus amat ualeat, pereat qui noscit amare*, principium etiam 3200 d p. 223 *quis quis amat* et Notizie d. scavi 1891 p. 260, 16 *quisquis amat ua[leat* 2 *bis tantum* Ribbeckius inuenerat mus. rhen. 13 p. 585: *bis tanti* ut uidetur papyrus, deinde *peria*, in fine *uota* quod idem ualet cum *uetat* (Nonius p. 45, Rohde in Ritscheli nouis excurs. Plaut. p. 60 et 129) 3 *adias manea so* ita scriptum ut et *abias* possis legere et *mapupa so.* malo *maneasq. o* quod nescio an per papyrum liceat restituere. in fine *siti.* in carmine Petroniano *dulcis mea Marcia* 4 *dunobis* papyrus, in fine *place* (in quod etiam Zangemeister inciderat) etsi ne *magi(s)* quidem spatio obscurisque reliquiis excluditur. *maxima cura* pro homine amato Vergilianum

These pages, I think, quite neatly demonstrate what I am talking about: there is nothing picturesque about them, the ideal, "cleansed" text is highlighted, even if it is from a medium so overtly physical as a graffito *incisum in pariete,* scratched on a wall. The "main text" is in a larger typeface than the notes referring to its contexts and intertexts, and the whole publication follows the trademark format of all the other Teubner editions, especially of those which publish *traces of texts,* i. e. collections of fragments of lost works found in (codex and papyrus manuscripts of) other authors. As the header DACTYLI of the page in the second cutout shows, the poems are arranged into chapters according to their metrical format: another "ideal" characteristic, very often not indicated by the inscriptions themselves (see the non-metrical line break lines in the main text of 945). The metre of the second version is actually very much spoilt by its many spoken-Latin omissions of word-final consonants (which are edited out of the main text, and only shown in the notes here). Although the scholarly work is as excellent as always on the series, one does not see a lot of interest in textual materiality here, apart from the small type comments under the texts in the author's modern, scholarly Latin (quite likely *not* to be read by a typical university student of Classics, or anyone reading the collection first and foremost as literature).

Let us take a look at these poems in another collection – actually, that is what the Teubner edition's first notes tell us to do, when listing the CIL number of the inscriptions. CIL stands for *Corpus Inscriptionum Latinarum,* a grandiose and still ongoing project started in 1853 by the Nobel Prize-winning German classicist, Theodor Mommsen, aiming to collect *all* the Latin inscriptions of the Roman Empire. The fourth volume of this immense series – along with its later supplements – collects the inscriptions found in Pompeii and Herculaneum. Here is what 946 looks like in CIL IV (1871):[34]

Fig. 3: CIL IV. 1173 (Bücheler's 946) in the main text of the collection, cropped screenshot by Adam Rung of the digitized CIL, arachne.uni-koeln.de

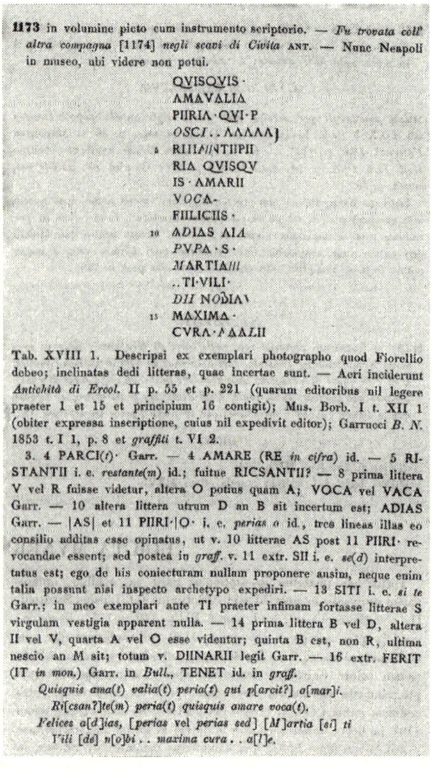

1173 in volumine picto cum instrumento scriptorio. — *Fu trovata coll' altra compagna* [1174] *negli scavi di Civita* ANT. — Nunc Neapoli in museo, ubi videre non potui.

QVISQVIS ·
AMAVALIA
PIIRIA · QVI · P
OSCI . . ΛΛΛΛΛ]
RIIIΛ//NTIIPII
RIΛ QVISQV
IS · AMARII
V*OC*Λ-
FIILICIIS ·
Λ*D*IΛS ΛI*Λ*
*PVP*Λ · S ·
*M*ARTIΛ///
. . TI · VILI ·
DII NO*B*IΛ\
MΛXIMΛ ·
CVRΛ · ΛΛΛ*L*II

Tab. XVIII 1. Descripsi ex exemplari photographo quod Fiorellio debeo; inclinatas dedi litteras, quae incertae sunt. — Aeri inciderunt *Antichità di Ercol.* II p. 55 et p. 221 (quarum editoribus nil legere praeter 1 et 15 et principium 16 contigit); Mus. Borb. I t. XII 1 (obiter expressa inscriptione, cuius nil expedivit editor); Garrucci *B. N.* 1853 t. I 1, p. 8 et *graffiti* t. VI 2.

3. 4 PARCI(*t*)· Garr. — 4 AMARE (RE *in cifra*) id. — 5 RISTANTII i. e. *restante*(*m*) id.; fuitne RICSANTII? — 8 prima littera V vel R fuisse videtur, altera O potius quam A; VOCA vel VACA Garr. — 10 altera littera utrum D an B sit incertum est; ADIAS Garr. — |AS| et 11 PIIRI·|O· i. e. *perias o* id., tres lineas illas eo consilio additas esse opinatus, ut v. 10 litterae AS post 11 PIIRI· revocandae essent; sed postea in *graff.* v. 11 extr. SII i. e. *se*(*d*) interpretatus est; ego de his coniecturam nullam proponere ausim, neque enim talia possunt nisi inspecto archetypo expediri. — 13 SITI i. e. *si te* Garr.; in meo exemplari ante TI praeter infimam fortasse litterae S virgulam vestigia apparent nulla. — 14 prima littera B vel D, altera II vel V, quarta A vel O esse videntur; quinta B est, non R, ultima nescio an M sit; totum v. DIINARII legit Garr. — 16 extr. FERIT (IT *in mon.*) Garr. in *Bull.*, TENET id. in *graff.*

Quisquis ama(*t*) *valia*(*t*) *peria*(*t*) *qui p*[*arcit?*] *a*[*mar*]*i.*
Ri[*csan?*]*te*(*m*) *peria*(*t*) *quisquis amare voca*(*t*).
Felices a[*d*]*ias,* [*perias* vel *perias sed*] [*M*]*artia* [*si*] *ti*
Vili [*de*] *n*[*o*]*bi* . . *maxima cura* . . *a*[*l*]*e.*

In this volume, the neatly numbered lines of the inscription are *actually* the lines of the inscription, not the lines of the ideal poem behind it, and effort is made – through clever typographical means like special glyphs – to reproduce the original layout of the text. All of this is possible thanks to new technology: *videre non potui,* 'I could not see it' in the museum, but *descripsi ex exemplari photographo,* 'I transcribed it from a photograph', says the editor – very much

34 | 945 had not yet been included in the original edition of CIL IV, hence the absence of its CIL number (IV. 4091) in Bücheler's *Anthologia.*

in accordance to what is often said about the connection between the advent of photography and the birth of manuscript philology in general.[35]

Already now, this version strikes the reader as basically *not* the poem we have seen in Bücheler: among others, the pronunciation-induced orthographical problems are not "solved" for the reader (e. g. the t-less, vulgarly vocalised VALIA for *valeat*), let alone the ones caused by the heavily cursive writing (e. g. the glyph || for 'E'). One can find out the first couplet of the poem (i. e. the first 8 lines of the inscription) by knowing 945, especially with a bit of knowledge about ancient handwriting, but I am, for one, deeply puzzled by the second half... in such a case one is to follow the first line of the notes again (Tab. XVIII. 1.), and turn the page to the tables at the back of the book, which have drawings of the inscriptions:

Fig. 4: A line drawing of CIL IV. 1173 in the appendix of the collection, cropped screenshot by Adam Rung of the digitized CIL, arachne.uni-koeln.de

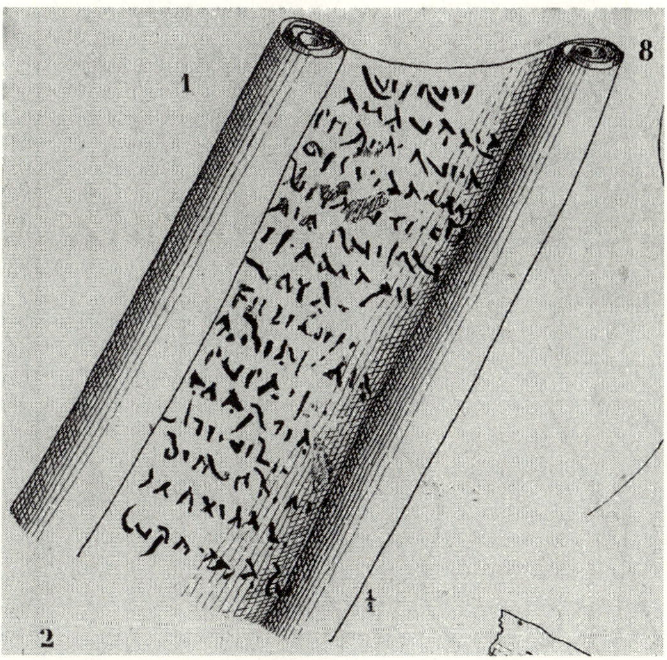

So that is how one should imagine *in volumine picto*, 'in a painted scroll' in the notes here and *in pictura papyri Pompeiana scariphatum exemplum amatoriae epistulae*, 'an example love letter scratched on a Pompeian picture of a papyrus

35 | Kittler, "Literatur," 223-226.

[roll]' in Bücheler. In this picture, the text, especially the bottom of it, looks rather *lorem ipsum*-like: even if a literate Roman could read it if they wanted to, it is quite unlikely that they ever got to the bottom line. It seems that the thing that the unknown artist represented (and that contemporary viewers probably saw) was not exactly a *text*, but much more an *image*,[36] either of a text, or (more probably) the very *medium* of a text. If one looks at a photograph[37] of the wall painting that the scroll is a part of (now peeled off its wall and framed in a museum),[38] this becomes quite clear:

Fig. 5: A photograph of the wall painting containing CIL IV. 1173, downloaded from www.pompeiiinpictures.eu

Still, if we turn the page, or on a screen, scroll back to what the *text* says, it is also obvious that this is no general dummy text: it is a *lorem ipsum* of love letters or love poems.[39] The latter is also supported by what Wachter demonstrates about the relationship between 945's family of inscriptions and "high" elegiac poetry (which is argued *not* to be necessarily earlier, or more *original* than its parietal counterpart) or the literary parallels that Bücheler's notes cite.[40]

36 | On the *instrumentum scriptorium* family of still lifes as a genre of the 4th style of Pompeiian wall painting, see Elizabeth A. Meyer, "Writing Paraphernalia, Tablets, and Muses in Campanian Wall Painting," *American Journal of Archaeology* 113. 4 (2009): 569–597 (here would I like to thank my ELTE colleague Patricia Szikora for calling my attention to this article). Meyer interprets our example as a "tiny painterly joke" of the *non sequitur* type, as papyrus scrolls in paintings of this subgenre usually do *not* seem to have any literary function – as opposed to legal and business functions (Meyer, "Writing Paraphernalia," 575).

37 | The image is from http://www.pompeiiinpictures.eu/r8/8%2002%2028%20p1.htm, accessed 02-03-2018.

38 | Museo Archeologico Nazionale di Napoli, inventory number: 4676.

39 | Milnor, *Graffiti*, 187, cf. 186 (on another member of the *quisquis amat* family).

40 | Wachter, "Oral poetry," 77 and 79, Milnor, *Graffiti*, 137–189.

To sum up, the poem we got to know as Bücheler's 946 or as CIL IV. 1173 is not as much a poem in the strict sense as a *picture*. Even if we do want to read it as a poem, we have to admit that it has quite much of its meaning in its physical, pictorial context, maybe even more than in its last few garbled lines. The general effect – maybe designed so by the artist, maybe constructed by the onlookers, maybe both – is that of a still life with writing materials like wax tablets, pen, papyrus scroll, etc., with the scroll showing a common elegiac formula of inscriptions and maybe a few textual chunks of "high" literary works (the two may overlap),[41] and, of course, a female name. Thus the whole hybrid artefact attributes the meaning of a maybe parodistically generic love letter and/or love poem to the scroll.

It is quite obvious when looking at all this, that this inscription is an exceptionally intriguing one, with an additional metalayer of physicality. Not only is it more meaningful as a physical picture than just a poem, but it is the most meaningful as the picture *on* a piece writing material (the wall) *of* a piece of another writing material (papyrus) which has a text on it – which is itself an artefact in addition to it being a body of meanings, if you will. Moreover, the text gets an additional meaning by the writing material (papyrus) in the picture which is rendered onto another one (the wall).[42] The question thus might arise if the extremely layered story we have just told here can have its implications on both the "stories" of other inscriptions and their presentation in the digital realm.[43]

Even if 946 is something really special, a similar train of thought to mine above might have occurred to the editors of later collections of inscriptions – or maybe traditions like this just evolve in the directions anticipated or even foreshadowed by their early proponents and made possible by evolving technical opportunities. As a logical next step for this particular tradition, and as a return to an old friend to us, here is 945 itself, from the 1909 supplement of CIL IV, which finally added it to the collection:[44]

41 | Bücheler, *Anthologia, ad loc.* (see my second figure again); Wachter, "Oral poetry" *passim*, esp. 88–89.

42 | And we have not even looked at its more general context, its original place in a room of a Pompeiian house (in all likelihood, generously decorated). That would absolutely make sense – but is definitely beyond the scope of this paper (already hijacked to some extent by Classics-specific concerns). All this also brings to mind what Canfora (*Il copista*, 59–67) calls *media archeology*, i. e. detecting a mapping out of earlier writing materials as a set of formal requirements on new writing materials.

43 | Cf. the contributions of Gábor Palkó and Gábor Mezei to this volume.

44 | These cutouts are from the online version of CIL digitized and made searchable by the Arachne project (http://arachne.uni-koeln.de/drupal/?q=en/node/291, accessed 23-06-2018).

Fig. 6: CIL IV. 4091 (Bücheler's 945) in the main text of a later supplement to CIL IV, cropped screenshot by Adam Rung of the digitized CIL, arachne.uni-koeln.de

4091 in exedrae, quae est ad sin. peristylii, pariete dextro, prope ingressum, in tectorio olim minio picto, litteris subtilibus.

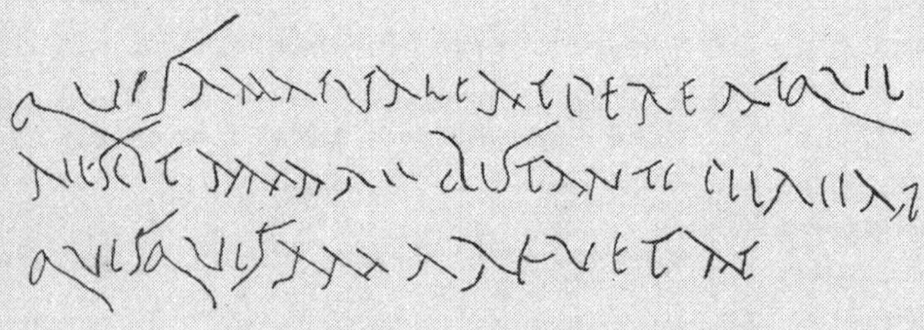

Descripsimus. — Edidi *Bull. Inst.* 1876 p. 233; Viola *Scavi* 1873—78 p. 56 n. 19. Niccolini III, *casa di Cecilio Giocondo* p. 3. Buecheler Anth. n. 945.

(Quis)quis amat valeat, pereat qui nescit amare. Bis tanto pereat quisquis amare vetat.

Here, a *picture* of the text has taken the place of the standardized and yet, by definition, imperfect, realization of the "ideal text" in the *Anthologia*, or the otherwise brilliant "mock handwriting" typesetting of the original CIL.[45] While the text is still not in the form of a photograph, the line drawing of the graffiti represents incomparably more of the inscription's material context than the "poem itself", which is relegated to the small print notes here (following the older CIL tradition already seen on 946 = IV. 1137). It might also be noted that graffiti like this are not artistically planned, intrinsic parts of the surface they are on, so more abstraction in their depiction might be more justifiable even theoretically, than in the case of the painted scroll of the longer version.

Newer collections, of course – *with the advent of digital humanities* – take the tendency even further. The other epigraphical collection I used in exploring the *quisquis amat* minigenre, *Epigraphik-Datenbank Clauss / Slaby*[46] is entirely online, and in addition to its intricate searching system, it does not include any intermediate steps between photograph and deciphered text in publishing an inscription: it leaves criticism or revision of its reconstructed ideal text to its readers, who can now themselves see a photograph,[47] just as the editor of CIL IV

45 | On the inherently pictorial and never truly phonographic nature of writing see, again, Sybille Krämer's article ("Writing" *passim*) on "notational iconicity" ("Schriftbildlichkeit").

46 | http://db.edcs.eu/epigr/epi.php?s_sprache=en, accessed 03-03-2018.

47 | http://db.edcs.eu/epigr/bilder.php?bild=PH0011001, accessed 03-03-2018.

could. And it does not have to be borrowed from a colleague as a favor (see *quod Fiorello debeo* in the notes to our poem in CIL IV), it is now just a click away.[48]

The resources leave nothing to complain about, it seems, for a scholar of classical literature who would engage in the dialogue of material criticism: that is what I have just done. With such databases and search engines both general and specialized at hand, what looks like as if it needed some reconsideration is the attitude of mainstream, especially literary-minded Classics towards them. We have to admit that our own traditional ways of regularizing and "cleansing" literary inscriptions, for all their old-fashioned scholarly excellence, might prove, quite ironically, far less useful than the comparably respectable practices of our historical and archaeological sister disciplines for such a material approach to literature.

I would like to stress here that I in no way regard these traditional ways of, for example, the *Teubner* anthology *passé*, let alone useless. I am merely arguing that CIL, and especially its digital incarnations and successors are suited much better to contemporary material criticism – other, equally valid currents of literary criticism might still benefit from the notion of the "ideal text" – and that these new ways of criticism provide interesting vantage points on our more traditional methods.

III

I think I have proven that one can practice *material literary criticism* in Latin Epigraphy quite relevantly – but what does that have to do with either the broader scope of Classics or with Digital Humanities? As some of my readers might have already noticed when seeing my footnotes, most of my research on literary inscriptions and metaresearch[49] on Classics and Epigraphy has been

48 | Another, more specialized collection, currently being developed in Hungary, catalogues the orthographical peculiarities of inscriptions, and tries to analyze them from the point of view of possible dialectal variation in spoken Latin – http://lldb.elte.hu/en/database/, accessed 03-03-2018, and described by Béla Adamik, "Computerized Historical Linguistic Database of the Latin Inscriptions of the Imperial Age," in *From Polites to Magos: Studia György Németh sexagenario dedicata*, edited by Ádám Szabó (Budapest/Debrecen: University of Debrecen Department of Ancient History, 2016), 13–27. http://real.mtak.hu/37556/1/Adamik%20Bela%20HPS%2022.pdf, accessed 06-27-2018.

49 | It is quite typical of Classics to slip into meta-Classics now and then, right from the beginning: the mediaeval codices we have been trying to figure out since Petrarch or even earlier are nothing but the representation of pre-existent acts of classical scholarship, that is, people's work, who sacrificed their time to passing classical heritage

made much easier by online materials – the materiality of whatever we have of the texts has never been closer to any of my colleagues than it is to us now (sitting in front of our screens anyway).[50]

And that leads to what I wanted to say with this paper: ironically, for classicists, the rise of these opportunities looks like the exact opposite of the *dematerialization* literary scholars have been speaking about for some time now. True, an on-screen photograph of a text on parchment, on papyrus, or on a wall is a *virtual* materiality of it, but for a profession that has spent a good five hundred years now by practicing *virtual* non-materiality in its "ideal" text editions, such a restriction is not much of an obstacle.

While strictly speaking, the resulting changes in our practices often mean the near-total loss of paper-based, on one level, more "material" Classics, they are, on another, *virtual* level, definitely a way up into the upper half of the lower bulb of, and – especially when looking at inscriptions and ancient papyri – maybe even into the upper half of the whole hourglass. While I would still not predict any breakthrough on genetic criticism of ancient authors (inside the upper bulb, if you will), I do think that these digital/quasi-material resources can definitely help us understand the ancient cultural contexts of literature,[51] and maybe even some of the literary practices of antiquity much better (the top wooden plate on my symbolic hourglass).

But how can one transfer all this to more mainstream, codex- and print edition-based Classics? First, literary inscriptions are, well, literary, which means that even if their generic and temporal categories may differ here and there from those of texts from book-based traditions, relationships can be detected between the two timelines. This has already been done a number of times, for example, in Rudolf Wachter's article on (among others) the relationship

on. It is another question if that was always a conscious decision – on that, see e. g. the somewhat pessimistic account by Stephen Greenblatt on monastery copyists (Greenblatt, *The Swerve*, 23–50) in his successful new book on Poggio Bracciolini, cf. Lachman as quoted by Kittler, "Literatur," 218–219 again. From there, it is quite natural that we are sometimes just as interested in earlier classicists' work as we are in the classical authors themselves. Cf. McGann, *The Textual Condition*, 84–85.

50 | "Made easier" is maybe an understatement: using online databases changes the practices of *any* field of literary studies – on that, see Bilansky, "Search" *passim;* on the seemingly immediate "fusion" between human mind and computer and its consequences on physicality (i. e. its loss of function), see Gumbrecht, *Our Broad Present*, 70–71.

51 | Cf. Bilansky, "Search," esp. 515–518, on how the corpus of cited primary texts is broadening in literary studies with the advent of searchable databases – here, "searching" stands for finding information without making use of any classification of content (as in "browsing").

between the *quisquis amat* group of inscriptions and "high" elegiac literature.[52] He argues quite convincingly that these inscriptions tell us about a bilateral relationship between the Roman "street" and "high" traditions of love poetry.[53] Though this is no news in general, if one thinks about the obviously popular nature of Roman comedy (like that of Plautus), conceptualizing Roman love elegy as an *interaction* between a local-popular development and Alexandrian models – as opposed to seeing it as a Late Republican development on Greek models – is certainly something new. This model is supported by the evidence of a version of *quisquis amat* appearing in Pompeii (CIL IV. 4971, among other archaically worded poems on the same wall) maybe as early as the first half of the first century BCE,[54] that is, possibly predating all the Augustan elegiac poets. Although I cannot really devote more time to other solutions to the relationship between this group of texts and "high" elegy here, it does not seem far-fetched to wonder what the physical qualities of CIL IV. 1173 might add to that discourse.[55] Neither am I an expert of Roman art history, but the *lorem ipsum*-ish, possibly sarcastic genericity of the love letter/poem in this wall painting might be as telling as the archeologically possible early date of its oldest version.[56]

These inscriptions are things that might not tell us anything about the life story or particular literary practices of, say, Ovid or Propertius, but certainly stand the chance of giving us a new glance into the literary history and cultural context of the elegiac genre in general. Their increasingly easy availability might remind even literary-minded classicists like me, more than anything before, that literary inscriptions are primary *and* material *and* literary remnants of antiquity, and that we should never turn a blind eye on them as such – now

52 | Wachter, "Oral poetry," 75-79.

53 | Wachter, "Oral poetry," 88-89, cf. Milnor, *Graffiti*, 137-189.

54 | Again, Wachter, "Oral poetry," 79, Milnor, *Graffiti*, 143. These poems are attributed to a hypothetical poet called Tiburtinus, who seems to have signed the wall (see Milnor, *Graffiti*, 141-151 on him).

55 | Cf. Meyer, "Writing Paraphernalia," 575 again.

56 | It also has to be noted here, that 1173's own "papyrus" text contains a verb form (*vota* 'forbids') which is quite curious from the point of view of dating: on the one hand, it does omit the final consonant (as Romance languages do) - on the other hand it has a considerably more archaic vowel than the corresponding, more standard form in 945 *(vetat)*. Although archaizing features were basically never out of fashion in Roman literature, one might consider that even if the very inscription is not as old as, say, the "Tiburtinus" version (4971), the poem itself can still be significantly older than even that one (Wachter, "Oral poetry," 77).

that we might not even have to leave the proverbial armchair to study them *quasi* in person.[57]

It is clear that the exceptionality of literary inscriptions (especially these) makes it an open question whether my reverse dematerialization might happen to scholarship on the textual tradition of "proper" literary texts. Although I see this as a less promising situation than that of Roman epigraphy (the manuscripts we have are still not old enough), some parallel developments might absolutely be possible. The availability of scanned manuscripts on the Internet has already made it much easier to retranscribe and recollate different codices of the same textual material in order to produce new editions, digital or physical.[58] This development belongs to the interface of Classics and Digital Humanities (with some metaclassics thrown in, as always), and does not have much to do with our third topic, Material Criticism. A connection, however, might be established in that direction as well, ironically because of the, I admit, quite old-fashioned fact that the mediaeval manuscripts contain the *same* texts as the coveted authorial manuscripts we are never going to see – even if we stick to the proximity of the author, and do not accept copyists as authors, as some literary critics do, to some extent.[59] For a very theoretical example, comparing different historical layouts of the same poem with a literary scholar's eye might shed light not only on the reception of the poem in different eras, but it can also show possibilities inherent in the text itself – for instance, structures other than either the margin to margin economicality of some codices or the idealized metrical layout of modern editions.[60]

To cut a long and somewhat speculative story short, time will tell – but I doubt if such a smorgasbord of opportunities would prove entirely useless to Classics, let alone the two overlapping smorgasbords of Digital Humanities and Material Criticism. As a first step, one has to admit that by looking at this paper, even on a computer screen, it seems that instead of dematerializing it, the opportunities of the digital world have already made my work on antiquity much more *material* than it had ever been before.

---

57 | Cf. Milnor, *Graffiti*, 145–146 on the dangers of only using the line drawings in CIL.

58 | For example, see a new online edition of Catullus by Hungarian scholar Dániel Kiss: http://www.catullusonline.org/CatullusOnline/index.php?dir=poems&w_apparatus=1, accessed 06-03-2018.

59 | See Canfora, *Il copista* again.

60 | Even though both the texts and the manuscript are mediaeval in Nichols' aforementioned article ("Why Material"), the physical book's relevance to the interpretation of the very texts – along with the considerable time window between the two – looks promising even for classicists (Nichols, "Why Material" *passim*).

Paper Mythology

Extending the Material 'Milieus' of Literature and Philology

Nicolas Pethes

The emergence of a new research topic is not necessarily a symptom of its immediate relevance. On the contrary, sometimes clusters of publications are arranged like the notes of a swan song, saluting the impressive cultural history of an object of study before dismissing it as henceforth irrelevant. This is the way one could describe the simultaneous publication of Ian Samson's *Paper. An Elegy* and Lothar Müller's *Weiße Magie. Die Epoche des Papiers* in 2012 that was anteceded by paper artist Therese Weber's cultural history *The Language of Paper* in 2009 and followed by Lisa Gitelman's monograph *Paper Knowledge. Toward a Media History of Documents* in 2014 as well as Alexander Monro's *Papier: Wie eine chinesische Erfindung die Welt veränderte* in 2015. From an epistemological perspective, Volker Hess and Andrew Mendelsohn edited a special issue on "Paper Technology" in *NTM Journal of the History of Science, Technology and Medicine* in 2013. And most recently, two books were published that combined an interest in paper practices with a presentation of paper art, Irmgard M. Wirtz' and Magnus Wieland's *Paperwork. Literarische und kulturelle Praktiken mit Schere, Leim, Papier* (2017) and Neil Holt's, Nicola van Velsen's, and Stephanie Jacobs' *Papier. Material, Medium und Faszination.*

Of course, these studies were not unprecedented. In Germany, Wilhelm Sandermann already presented a *Kulturgeschichte des Papiers* in 1988, and the media studies approach by Gitelman, the science studies approach by Hess/Mendelsohn as well as the Actor-Network-Theory applied by Gitelman and Wirtz/Wieland could refer to Bruno Latour's concept of "paperwork" from his 1986 essay "Visualization and Cognition: Drawing things together" as well as to Cornelia Vismann's book on *Akten. Medientechnik und Recht* (2000) or Markus Krajewski's history of the slip box *Zettelwirtschaft. Die Geburt der Kartei aus dem Geist der Bibliothek* from 2002.[1] And yet, as both Samson's and Müller's subtitles – *Elegy* and *Epoche* – suggest, this publication cluster was no accident but inspired by a certain notion that the era of paper that had shaped Western culture – with respect to literature, science, and bureaucracy – was about to come to an end in the light of digitization, e-books, open access publication, and social media platforms.

So paper theory may be yet another piece of evidence suggesting that Minerva's owl takes off at dusk, i.e. media technologies become objects of reflection when they are no longer predominantly functional but on the verge of being replaced: in the same way in which cultures observed orality once literacy had been established, they were interested in manuscripts after the printing press had become a mass medium and started to treasure books once digital textuality began to take over.[2] To use McLuhan's metaphor: As we proceed further into the digital sphere, the mediality of paper comes into view in the "rear-view mirror" – e.g. on our computer screens when we organize our digital desktop by filing documents into folders that mimic the shape of a sheet of paper or of a cardboard sheath.[3] Or as Ian Samson puts it: "Paper remains the ghost in our machines".[4]

Therefore, paper is at the same time being removed from and extremely present in today's literature, scholarship, and administration: As in the case of the "paperless office" which, due to easily accessible desktop printing, uses more paper than any previous workplace,[5] the seemingly 'paperless culture' of the digital age has a growing output in print and is, in addition, still shaped by the formats and routines of paper based communication such as desktop folders, PDF documents, e-readers etc.

In what follows I will highlight three aspects of the current interest in paper within a world seemingly dominated by paperless technologies: first, the methodological implications of addressing materialities of communication in

1 | Cf. also Ben Kafka, *The Demon of Writing: Powers and Failures of Paperwork* (New York: Zone Books, 2012), or Hans-Jörg Rheinberger, "Zettelwirtschaft", in *Schreiben als Kulturtechnik*, edited by Sandro Zanetti (Berlin: Suhrkamp, 2012), 441-452.

2 | Cf. Walter Ong, *Orality and Literacy: The Technologzing of the Word* (London: Methuen, 1982); Christian Benne, *Die Erfindung des Manuskripts. Zur Theorie und Geschichte literarischer Gegenständlichkeit* (Berlin: Suhrkamp, 2015); Robert Darnton, *The Case for Books. Past, Present, and Future* (New York: Public Affairs, 2009).

3 | "We look at the present through a rear-view mirror. We march backwards into the future": Marshall McLuhan and Quentin Fiore, *The Medium is the Massage: An Inventory of Effects* (New York: Bantam Books, 1967), 75.

4 | Ian Samson: *Paper. An Elegy* (London: William Morrow, 2012), xvi.

5 | Abigail J. Sellen/Richard Harper, *The Myth of the Paperless Office* (Cambridge MA: The MIT Press, 2002).

literature, media, and science studies; second; the impact that paper has on the processes of storing, distributing, and processing fictional and factual information; and third, the specific, quasi-mythical narrative about paper formats within discourses of cultural theory, literary aesthetics, and philological methodology.

The Methodological Dynamic of Retracing Materiality

The tenuous status of paper is not only observed today but was already reflected more than 200 years ago when, for the first time in history, paper could be produced in quantities that allowed for a mass market of books and journals to emerge. For example, in Jean Paul's novel *Leben Fibels*, first published in 1812, the narrator's quest for biographical material on the title character ends in a used books store where he hopes to retrieve the 40 volumes of a previous account of Fibel's life. But all that is left of this extensive biography are the leather bindings that to the shopkeeper seemed more valuable than the books' "contents" – these contents being, to be sure, not the twisted lifelines of Fibel but the sheer paper of the pages which the bindings 'contained'.[6] In consequence, the books' pages were torn out – but, luckily for the biographer, recycled as household papers for wrapping fish or brewing coffee by the inhabitants of Fibel's hometown. The narrator attempts to retrieve the pages of the 40 volumes from this pragmatic use and re-recycle them back into the realm of literary sources. But what Jean Paul presents as his new biography of Fibel still bears the marks of this temporary (ab)use of print as paper: The novel's chapters are named after the function which the pages they draw on used to have as household papers: Chapter 5 was a "Herring Paper", 9 a "Pepper Bag", and 13 folded into a "Paper Kite" that flew by the narrator's window one morning, where he grabbed it from the sky and transformed it into his own book project.

Jean Paul's ironic metonymy of calling 'paper' the true content of books (which, in consequence, are understood as a binding technology, not as works of science or art) as well as his reference to the manifold uses of paper beyond writing, printing, and reading are quoted here because they illustrate what is at stake when the perspective shifts from the content or the message of a written text to the material that stores these contents and messages. This shift moves from the 'inside' to the 'outside' in two steps: first, metaphorically, from what is 'inside' a book in the sense of a representation of an author's thoughts to the paper that bears the semiotic traces of these thoughts and ideas; and second

6 | Jean Paul, "Leben Fibels, des Verfassers der Bienrodischen Fibel", in *Werke in zwölf Bänden*, edited by Norbert Miller, vol. 11 (München: Hanser, 1975), 365-563; for the following examples, cf. pp. 376, 388, 404, and 425.

from the pages 'inside' a book to the binding framework that holds them together – and the irony within Jean Paul's version of this twofold movement is obviously the fact that a book's value seems to increase the further one moves away from both its mental as well as its material content.

At the beginning of the 19th century, this issue of the 'true value' of books is raised because the book is about to become a mass medium and as such is judged by its success as a market commodity or a bourgeois accessory rather than by the aesthetic complexity of its textual form. But the movement from 'inside' to 'outside' also illustrates a methodological shift that media and science studies take in the digital age today as they become interested in the materiality of paper: in both media and science studies, this interest in paper is guided by an 'anti-hermeneutical' approach against the primacy of meaning in literary aesthetics[7] as well as against theoretical models in what Bruno Latour refers to as "ready made science".[8]

Thus, in the same way as studies of the materiality of communication focus on the asemiotic foundation of semiosis, science studies are interested in preliminary notes and sketches that precede theory. The 'paper turn' in recent media and science studies seems but another step toward a growingly profound analysis of this pre-semiotic and pre-theoretical realm. Jean Paul's scenario illustrates this 'step by step' logic first by retracing the stories told in books to the paper they are written on and then by retracing paper to leather bindings.

But this 'step by step' movement from 'inside' to 'outside' also illustrates a methodological tendency that helped to establish media studies in the first place: abstractly speaking, media studies are driven by the attempt to study communication by addressing the environment of a communicative system, i.e. its sheer and in itself meaningless materiality. Retracing the structure of Homeric epic poems to their initial oral tradition, linear thinking to the structures of literacy, and the rise of a critical public sphere to the printing press means to turn the relation of 'content' and 'framework' upside down by declaring the framework as the determining factor for any given content. Media studies, too, that is to say, have been moving from 'inside' to 'outside'. And the current shift of interest toward paper in recent debates could be considered as a further, but similar step from 'content' to 'framework' that, in this sense, takes

7 | Cf. Hans Ulrich Gumbrecht, "Materialities/The Nonhermeneutic/Presence", in *Production of Presence* (Stanford: Stanford University Press, 2004), 1-20.

8 | Bruno Latour, *Science in Action. How to Follow Scientists and Engineers through Society* (Cambridge MA/London: Harvard University Press, 1987), 4. Cf. my reading of Jean Paul's *Leben Fibels* within a framework of Latourian theory: "Actor Network Philology? Papierarbeit als Schreibszene und Vorgeschichte quantitativer Verfahren bei Jean Paul", in *Medienphilologie. Konturen eines Paradigmas*, edited by Friedrich Balke and Rupert Gaderer (Göttingen: Wallstein, 2017), 199-224.

the epistemological inside-outside dynamic of media studies to the next level. In this sense, pursuing media studies means to expedite the process of reverse blackboxing that Charlotte Jaekel discusses in her contribution to this volume.

This observation and the argument connected with it can be rephrased by the distinction of medium and form as introduced by Niklas Luhmann in *Art as a Social System*. Luhmann introduces this distinction in order to avoid an ontological categorization of technologies as 'media' and ideas as 'contents'. Instead, he suggests a functional and dynamic description of "medium" as a loosely coupled pool of elements and "form" as a specific selection and combination (or "tight coupling") of some of these elements. Accordingly, a literary text or a scientific article would be considered a 'form' insofar as they select and combine (or actualize) elements from a (potential) pool of words or data. But obviously these words and data are also specific forms that can be retraced to previous medial elements and so forth – which means that the distinction of "medium" and "form" is not a stable attribution to objects, but a reversible and functional attribution that results from varying analytical perspectives:

> [M]edia and forms consist of (loosely and tightly) coupled elements. Such elements always also function as forms in another medium. Words and tones, for example, constitute forms in the acoustic medium just as letters function as forms in the optical medium of the visible. This terminology does not allow for the boundary concept of matter as defined by the metaphysical tradition, where matter designates the complete indeterminacy of being regarding its readiness to assume forms. Media are generated from elements that are always already formed. This situation contains possibilities for an evolutionary arrangement of medium/form relationships in steps [...]. In the medium of sound, words are created by constricting the medium into condensable (reiterable) forms that can be employed in the medium of language to create utterances (for the purpose of communication). The potential of forming utterances can again serve as the medium for forms known as myths or narratives, which, at a later stage, when the entire procedure is duplicated in the optical medium of writing, also become known as textual genres or theories. Theories can subsequently be coupled in the medium of the truth code to form a network of consistent truths. [...] How far we can push this kind of stacking depends on the evolutionary processes that lead to the discovery of forms.[9]

That is to say that tightly coupled forms are established from loosely coupled media, but as forms may serve as media for subsequent selections of forms and so forth. But Luhmann's perspective on the process of production of artworks or theories can also be reversed with respect to the analytical reconstruction of this process in literary, media, and science studies – 'analytical reconstruc-

9 | Niklas Luhmann, *Art as a Social System* (Stanford: Stanford University Press, 2000), 160.

tion' meaning to retrace each form to the medium it was selected from. This is precisely what happens when media studies suggest shifting the scope of analysis from 'literature' to 'texts', from 'texts' to alphabetic systems, from alphabetic systems to technologies of writing, and so forth. And it is also the way by which paper comes into play: Retracing the mediality of texts may also result in describing the book as a medium, which in turn can be considered a form that was selected from the medial potential of paper (or leather bindings, for that matter) – and obviously one could keep going further backwards.

But even when we stop at the level of paper as a basic medium for printing books, the epistemological dynamic of media studies is obvious: This dynamic is based on the paradoxical strategy to include all previously excluded aspects of communication in the process of analysis – and this paradoxical strategy is a highly productive one, to be sure, because it ensures that academic debates do not reach a dead end where everything seems said and done and can therefore only be repeated over and over. On the contrary: Scholarly research remains innovative and dynamic as long as it is able to declare that something is of interest that so far had seemed to be simply the framework or material foundation of its object of study, but in itself without any informational or aesthetic value.

To return from this theoretical digression back to the topic of paper, the discovery of paper is in fact a very vivid example of this dynamic research strategy: Following Harold Innis' distinction of 'heavy' and 'light' materials of communication, one may question Elizabeth Eisenstein's theory of the *Printing Press as an Agent of Change*, published in 1979, and claim that print could only become a mass medium (as well as the foundation of modern science and literature) when there were sufficient supplies of cheap printing material: Had Gutenberg and his followers been dependent on expensive parchment, books could have never become a mass medium for the modern public sphere and network society:

> Media that emphasize time are those durable in character such as parchment, clay and stone. The heavy materials are suited to the development of architecture and sculpture. Media that emphasize space are apt to be less durable and light in character such as papyrus and paper. The latter are suited to wide areas in administration and trade.[10]

Innis also quotes 19th century literary historian Henry Hallam who allegedly speaks of paper as the "universal substance" of the cultural revolution in the late middle ages.[11] Upon looking into Hallam's *View of the State of Europe During*

10 | Harold Innis, *Empire and Communication* (Oxford: Clarendon Press, 1950), 7.

11 | I am following Lothar Müller, *White Magic. The Age of Paper* (Cambridge UK: Polity Press, 2014), 63.

the Middle Ages, first published in 1818, however, the term "universal substance" rather seems to refer to metaphysical debates of the time in Hallam's work. But elsewhere, Hallam in fact speaks of "the happy invention of paper", which "seems to have naturally preceded those of engraving and printing".[12]

I cannot discuss in detail here whether paper was the actual precondition for the take-off of the Gutenberg Galaxy but will merely focus on the observation that there is a specific discourse within media studies that establishes the very notion of the invention of paper as the insurmountable origin – or, better maybe, primeval scene – of modern culture, including more or less accidental misquotations that further support this claim such as the one by Innis. And this discourse is one of the basic – and as such at the same time: tacit – practices of establishing a media theoretical perspective within writing the history of culture.

Referring to the terms 'origin', 'primeval scene', and 'myth' within this contexts hints at the fact that the evolutionary model of medium and form, abstract as it may be, implies the possibility to return *ad fontes* when it is turned upside down by the methodological approach of media studies: studying media means to study the *milieus* of communication,[13] to move from an analysis of meaning to the study of the material of its production, i.e. from information to noise, or from what Luhmann calls the "marked space" of a system's observation to the "unmarked space" of everything beyond the system. Of course, these movements do not all take place on the same level – in fact, one will have to distinguish the materiality of signs from the materiality of paper precisely because they result in different forms ('texts' vs. 'books'). But the direction of study toward the more general and less tightly coupled elements connects them, and 'paper' seems to be a basic one of these elements.

The Formatting Aspect of Paper

According to the argument so far, the interest in paper in current media and science studies is not only caused by the advent of digital technologies and their alleged replacement of paper, that is to say: it is not only a phenomenon of crisis or nostalgia. It also results, systematically, from the inherent drive of media studies to extend its scope of research further and further into the realm of what had so far been considered as an insignificant precondition of meaning.

12 | Henry Hallam, *View of the State of Europe During the Middle Ages* (London: John Murray, 1846), vol. II, 489 and 528f.

13 | I elaborated the epistemological paradoxes of this concept in my article: "Milieu. Zur Exploration selbstgenerierter Umwelten in Wissenschaft und Ästhetik des 19. Jahrhunderts", in: *Archiv für Begriffsgeschichte* 59 (2017), 139-156.

Paper is 'insignificant' insofar as, being a continuous and more or less white surface, it bears no marks, traces, or other distinctions which, as such, are the necessary precondition for any observation or communication. Paper can be distinguished from an environment, e.g. as a 'sheet' or a 'page', and as such, it is a form. But apart from its material boundaries, it is merely the necessary background for the basic operation of 'drawing a distinction' in the sense of theorists of science such as Gregory Bateson and George Spencer Brown. That is also to say: In Luhmann's sense, paper is a medium with respect to the form of books and other technologies of binding; but with respect to the forms of letters, words, sentences, and texts, paper is not the medium from which elements are selected, but simply the background against which these elements become visible. It is, to use the concept Gábor Mezei elaborates on in his contribution to this volume, the grid against which information becomes discernable.

From this point of view, the epistemological theorem that "we cannot make an indication without drawing a distinction" (in the sense of a "difference that makes a difference")[14] has a strictly material dimension: Bruno Latour alluded to this double meaning of "drawing" in his article on "Visualization and Cognition" when he traced back scientific models to practices of 'drawing things together' – "things" being data from various sources as well as objects or theories; and "drawing" being the metaphorical process of combining them for the sake of an argument as well as the literal one of designing graphs, tables, diagrams, lists, formulas, etc.

It is in this sense that Latour refers the entire practice of science back to "paperwork", i.e. first to the transformation of three-dimensional observations from the outside world into the two-dimensional space of the page and the lines inscribed on it; and second to the ability of paper to serve as the foundation for standardized representations that can travel to other places and thus be shared through time and space – a quality that Latour calls "immutable mobile".[15]

But obviously, because of his interest in diagrammatic forms such as graphs and tables, Latour's theory is not interested in paper as such but rather in its ability to store, distribute, and transport graphic representations such as maps or scientific 'papers'. Therefore, it seems necessary to further differentiate between, on the one hand, "paper technologies" such as drawing or writing and "paper formats" such as graphs or texts and, on the other hand, actual "paper tools" such as sheets, files, or staplers as well as "paper practices" such

14 | Cf. George Spencer Brown, *Laws of Form* (London: Julia Press, 1969), 1; Gregory Bateson: *Steps to an Ecology of Mind* (Nortvale NJ/London: Jason Aronson, 1972), 315.

15 | Bruno Latour, "Visualization and Cognition: Drawing Things Together", in *Knowledge and Society. Studies in the Sociology of Culture Past and Present*, Vol. 6, edited by H. Kuklik, 1-40. Greenwich, CT: JAI, 1986, 25 and 7.

as turning, stacking, filing, ripping – as well as including folding and gluing household papers or paper toys.[16]

Not all of these technologies, formats, and practices may be equally relevant if it comes to the question how paper participates in encoding and decoding information. But even if one does not want to go as far as to attribute an active agency to the basic materiality of written communication for the process of communicating, paper displays what ecological psychologists refer to as "affordance", i.e. the faculty of an object that prompts and favors specific modes of its use.[17] In the case of paper, this affordance may result in practices such as writing within columns that are oriented according to the margins of the sheet, turning the page over and using its back side, stacking and storing packs, folding as well as in the opposite of these practices (i.e. writing crisscross and on one side only, crumpling and throwing paper out, tearing it up etc.). And as Björn Sonnenberg-Schrank demonstrates in his contribution to this volume, true philologists do not consider gestures of tearing up and throwing out as final, on the contrary: the waste basket is the true key to reconstructing further previous stages of textual production.

That is to say: paper neither determines what is written on it nor how this information is processed, remembered, or forgotten. But it promotes and shapes certain ways to go about these basic operations of cultural production and tradition according to its material features and faculties. And only if we move to this basic level of paper tools and practices are we actually approaching the cultural function of paper *as such* as opposed to paper as a background or surface for 'drawing distinctions' or 'drawing things together'. Because only with respect to 'paper' as tool or practice are we able to consider the material in question as a 'distinction' by its own means: Paper, in the form of the page, has physical boundaries that distinguish it from its environment, and stacking, folding, or gluing paper are subsequent formative procedures.

Although these paper tools and paper practices seem detached from the actual process of signification by drawing, writing, and reading that Latour and other science studies scholars are interested in, they, too, have an immediate influence on 'secondary' paper technologies that are usually in the focus of analysis instead of paper itself. Katherine Hayles, e.g., argues that the materiality of the page printed on paper prompts a different reading process than the one usually applied when reading a web page: it is precisely because empirical

16 | Cf. Volker Hess/Andrew Mendelsohn, "Paper Technology und Wissensgeschichte", in *NTM. Zeitschrift für Geschichte der Wissenschaften, Technik und Medizin* 21 (2013), 1-10, as well as Wirtz/Wieland, *Paperwork*, 25ff., who refer to the artistic dimension of "cut & paste" by which the traditional notion of the author's brain work is replaced by material "pratiques du papier".

17 | Cf. Benne, *Die Erfindung des Manuskripts*, 130f.

evidence shows that reading on digital screens tends to be limited to scrolling down the left margins of a text and only focuses on the introductory paragraph that the cultural technique and philological method of 'close reading' emerged during the 'paper age' of literary communication.[18] Markus Krajewski, to name another example (that is further elaborated in Charlotte Coch's contribution to this volume), argues that it was the practice of arranging loose slips of papers in wooden boxes (*Zettelkasten*) that helped establishing modern scientific and literary authorship by, first, providing a tool to take notes and excerpts from previous writings in libraries and then, second, combining and rearranging them for the production of new texts: paper serves as the lubricant for a cybernetic "scholarly machine" which produces new text from old by transferring the old ones into loose fragments that are mobile and combinable.[19] And finally, to refer to a third and last illustration of the epistemological function of paper as such, Lisa Gitelman argues that in 19th and 20th century bureaucratic culture the authority of documents did not derive from their content but from the performative gesture of 'showing', i.e. being framed and distributed in paper formats. Therefore, Gitelman argues, even in the digital age with its PDF formats, "[t]he ways that paper works have become part of what documents are for, and vice versa".[20]

Latour, Hayles, Krajewski, and Gitelman all refer to the paper formats of scholarly writing or bureaucratic knowledge management. But similar functions can be discussed with respect to the influence of paper practices on literary writing – e.g. by analyzing "scenes of writing" within fictional scenarios that reflect the material preconditions of literature.[21] But in fact, the entire modern "Paper Age" (as Thomas Carlyle entitled the second part of his *The French Revolution: A History* in 1837) is omnipresent in literary fiction: In *Illusions perdues*, e.g., that Balzac started writing in the same year in which Carlyle published his work, the tendency toward light, short, and ephemeral prose narrations significant for the feuilleton culture that Lucien tries to become part of is not only connected to the rise of the periodical press, but also to the basic faculties of the

18 | N. Katherine Hayles, "How we Read: Close, Hyper, Machine", in: *ADE Bulletin* no. 150 (2010), 62-79.

19 | Markus Krajewski, *Zettelwirtschaft. Die Geburt der Kartei aus dem Geiste der Bibliothek* (Berlin: Kadmos, 2002), 66.

20 | Lisa Gitelman, *Paper Knowledge. Toward a Media History of Documents* (Durham/London: Duke University Press, 2014), 3.

21 | Cf. Rüdiger Campe, "Die Schreibszene. Schreiben", in *Schreiben als Kulturtechnik*, edited by Sandro Zanetti, (Berlin: Suhrkamp, 2012), 269-282., as well as the three volumes on *Schreibszenen* in manuscript, typoscript, and digital cultures, edited by Martin Stingelin, Davide Giuriato, and Sandro Zanetti in 2004, 2005, and 2006 (München: Fink).

materiality of paper: Lucien comes from a family that owned a paper mill in the countryside and thus, as Lothar Müller puts it, "the question of what literature was made from was placed on an equal footing with the poetological question of how it was made".[22]

Müller's second example of this convergence of the production of paper and novels are scenarios in Charles Dickens' *Bleak House* or Hermann Melville's *Bartleby* that depict judicial "paper worlds overshadowed by masses of paper sinking in the realm of rags and decay" as well as the modern paper mill industry by using the vocabulary of ancient myths that establishes a "paper mythology" which resembles a "cult of the dead".[23] On a less dramatic note, the transfer between paper and "rubbish" (in the sense of Michael Thompson's *Rubbish Theory*) is also significant for the scenario of recycling waste-paper as we encounter it in Jean Paul's *Leben Fibels*: as Torsten Hahn argues, the sheer materiality of media is always considered rubbish compared with the alleged value of immaterial meaning – and yet medial rubbish remains the only manifest aspect within any process of communication.[24]

But besides these mythological or satirical reflections on the poetological value of paper in 19th century literary fiction, there is another aspect of paper formats and practices that accounts for the modern concept of literature in general: Practices of writing such as crossing out, overwriting, underlining etc. that are significant for 19th century manuscript culture are also based on the extensive availability and use of paper: *Before* the "Paper Age", literary tradition is grounded in handwritten copies or prints that may result in mistakes, but do not produce variants – so that there is no notion of previous versions or editing stages that become part of modern philological archiving in the way the articles by Livia Kleinwächter and Júlia Tóth-Czifra analyze it within this volume. *After* the "Paper Age", computer programs delete all traces of revisions and, although mimicking the paper format, exclude most paper practices – so that philology has to adopt methods of digital forensic in order to reconstruct the contents of computer storages, as Melinda Vásári argues in this volume. Therefore, the procedural notion of modern textuality as represented in facsimile editions of the writings of Hölderlin or Kafka, for instance, derives from genuine paper practices and is part of the "Paper Age".[25] Modern literature, that is to say, is

22 | Müller, *White Magic*, 233.

23 | Ibd., 235.

24 | Cf. Torsten Hahn, "Im Absturz. Kafkas Beobachtung der Gegenseite oder Von Resten und Medien", in *The Parallax View. Zur Mediologie der Verschwörung*, edited by Marcus Krause and Arno Meteling (München: Fink 2011), 105-121.

25 | Cf. again Benne, *Die Erfindung des Manuskripts* as well as Almuth Grésillon, Éléments de critique génétique. Lire les manuscripts modernes (Paris: PUF 1994); for the examples see Wolfgang Groddeck/D.E. Sattler, "Frankfurter Hödlerlin-Ausgabe.

not only written on paper as an exchangeable surface for marking traces. Its notion of text as something that evolves from bodily gestures of marking and its recursive movements, subsequent revisions, corrections, new beginnings, and transcriptions is shaped by the affordance of paper, i.e. the practices of writing that it favors over possible others.

That is to say that paper is by no means simply an insignificant and interchangeable carrier of literary production and distribution. Rather, the basic aesthetic tendency of modern literary writing since the late 18th century – i.e. to growingly conceptualize the literary artwork by modes of digression, fragmentation and perpetual rewritings of texts – is founded not only on the possibilities granted by the availability and flexibility of paper but also on the traceability of all the revisions applied. It is only by the lasting traces of the revisions that the procedural notion of modern textuality can be perceived, and paper is the medium that stores these traces – in a way similar to the one in which Sigmund Freud described his *Wunderblock*.

The "Work" on the Paper Myth

In spite of these last remarks that hint at the basic significance of paper formats and paper practices for our notion of literary aesthetics, my argument is not meant as a deterministic one. In the same way that turning to paper means to address the medium of literary writing as the previously unmarked space for future distinctions and couplings, the interrelation between the materiality of paper and the aesthetic concept of modern literature is based on the realm of possibilities that resides on the white page – a notion that is often reflected within the history of literature, e.g. in the works of Melville, Mallarmé, or George Perec.[26] But as we have seen in the remarks made above on the 'backward' dynamics of media and science studies as well as through the examples of Innis and others, the attempt to trace back literary communication

---

Editionsbericht", in *Le Pauvre Holterling. Blätter zur Frankfurter Hölderlin-Ausgabe* no. 2 (1979), 5-19 and Gerhard Neumann, "Schreiben und Edieren", in *Literaturwissenschaft. Einführung in ein Sprachspiel*, edited by Heinrich Bosse and Ursula Renner (Freiburg: Rombach, 2010), 339-358. Cf. also Thomas Wortmann, *Literatur als Prozess. Annette von Droste-Hülshoffs "Geistliches Jahr" als Schreibzyklus* (Konstanz: Konstanz University Press, 2014).

26 | Cf. Lars Schneider: *Die* page blanche *in der Literatur und bildenden Kunst der Moderne* (München: Fink, 2016) and Andreas Langbacher, "Das große Leuchten. Unterwegs zu einer kleinen Poetik der leeren Seite. Eine Lektürebericht", in *Paperwork. Literarische und kulturelle Praktiken mit Schere, Leim, Papier*, edited by Irmgard M. Wirtz and Magnus Wieland (Göttingen: Wallstein, 2017), 107-121.

to ever more fundamental materialities not only results in the empirical study of material objects, but as a methodological imperative (*ad fontes!*) rather leads to the narrative construction of material origins, the design of a primeval scene of mediality, a *mythologie blanche,* as it were.

This is why I suggest to contextualize the possibly deterministic "paper mythology" in current media studies with approaches to paper practices in science studies: the praxeological approach in science studies favors micro-analytic and non-systematic concepts that describe inconsistent operational networks instead of a causal relation between medium and message. In the same way, I suggest to describe the "Paper Age" not as a period in time determined by the materiality of paper that is now on the verge of disappearing gone and in consequence to be mourned, but rather as a historical period in which paper formats were used and criticized, commented and experimented on, mimicked and rejected etc. – i.e., a historical period in which paper was the main reference for discursive and material practices, practices which at the same time defined and altered what was considered as paper in terms of its cultural function. Paper, in other words, is not simply a material that is unchangeably 'out there', but a phenomenon *produced* by technological, cultural, scientific and literary practices.

This praxeological approach also helps us to avoid the mythological understanding of paper as an origin or primeval scene of culture during the Gutenberg Galaxy. In the same way that the materiality of paper formats is shaped by paper practices, the myth of paper as the basic medium is the result of mythological practices in the sense of Hans Blumenberg's *Work on Myth:* According to Blumenberg, mythological narratives may claim to tell the story of the world from its very beginning, but as narratives they are never actually able to represent the original nature of the world but are always already part of the cultural practice reconstructing it.[27] And this becomes especially obvious when we remember that paper has by no means always been subject to mythological praise. Instead, already in the early days of print culture, paper was criticised for its volatility, lack of durability, as well as its sheer quantity by which it flooded the eyes and minds of readers.[28] Thus, cultural criticism of paper is also part of modern paper mythology.

In the same way, paper mythology is not to be considered as an actual account of our culture's and literature's roots in the unmarked space of the white page. What makes the unmarked space unmarked is that it cannot be observed as such and therefore cannot become part of mythological narratives. Rather, according to Blumenberg, every myth constructs the idea of the origin

27 | Cf. Hans Blumenberg, *Work on Myth* (Cambridge MA: The MIT Press, 1985), 34-58.

28 | Cf. Ann Blair, *Too Much to Know. Managing Scholarly Information Before the Modern Age* (New Haven: Yale University Press, 2010).

by working on and continually reworking its narrative. That is to say: There are narratives of origins, but no insights into the origin itself. Every mythological account of an origin is part of the "work on myth" – as are the paper-shaped icons of files and documents on our computer screens that suggest the ongoing validity of paper formats in digital times.

Blumenberg's anthropological argument is useful because it also sheds light on the tendency within media studies to identify certain technological inventions and shifts as the starting point for subsequent processes of cultural transformation. Retracing the material foundations of scholarly or literary communication, therefore, is another variation of the "work on myth", contributing to our notion of paper as one of the foundations of the history of literature and science. In the same way, the so-called 'material turn' in philology carries out the same work when it engages in a sociology of individual texts or the reauratization of manuscripts.[29] At the same time, philology is also one of the central fields that uses paper technologies and paper practices and thus contributes to a understanding of paper that results from this use.

Finally, literature itself partakes in the work on paper myths – I have already hinted at authors such as Lawrence Sterne and Jean Paul or Honoré de Balzac and Charles Dickens, a list that could easily be continued by the various paper formats, paper archives, and paper stacks in Goethe, Stifter, Raabe, or Kafka within the context of German literary history.[30] In these texts, paper can both be subject to praise and admiration with respect to its durability and easy storability or an object of cultural criticism in the light of the ever growing 'paper floods' of 19th century print culture and 20th century bureaucracy.[31] Because this is the downside of the positive paper mythology of recent media studies: the nightmare of paper stacks collapsing on readers who, as Nietzsche once put it in his famous critique of archival historicism in 1874, "devour with pleasure even the dust of bibliographical quisquilia."[32]

Instead of elaborating on this multifaceted history of literary, philosophical, and scientific reflections on the qualities and dangers of paper, I will hint at only one further example of the work on paper mythology in 19th century German

29 | Cf. Stephen Nichols, "Why Material Philology? Some Thoughts", in *Philologie als Textwissenschaft. Alte und neue Horizonte,* edited by Helmut Tervooren and Horst Wenzel, *Zeitschrift für deutsche Philologie* (2016), 10-30; Douglas F. McKenzie, *Bibliography and the Sociology of Texts* (Cambridge: Cambridge University Press, 1999).

30 | Cf. Daniela Gretz/Nicolas Pethes (eds.), *Archiv/Fiktionen. Verfahren des Archivierens in Literatur und Kultur des langen 19. Jahrhunderts* (Freiburg: Rombach, 2016).

31 | Cf. Alex Ciszar: "Seriality and the Search for Order. Scientific Print and its Problems During the Late Nineteenth Century", in *History of Science* 48 (2012), 399-434.

32 | Friedrich Nietzsche, *On the Advantage and Disadvantage of History for Life* (Indianapolis/Cambridge: Hackett Publishing Company, 1980), 21.

literature, Heinrich von Kleist's *Michael Kohlhaas,* first published in 1810.[33] This story of a 16th century horse trader who initiates a feud after customs officers of Saxony kept two of his horses as a tax deposit and subsequently mistreated them to the verge of being worthless refers to the use of paper in manifold ways: Kohlhaas is asked to present his papers at the border, he writes letters to his sovereign, recruits a private army through broadsheets, is denounced by a public poster authored by Martin Luther who condemns his attempt of self-administered justice, etc. In sum, all legal and anti-legal procedures that drive the story forward are almost overexplicitly paper-based. And so is the strange ending that Kleist chose for his story: Kohlhaas, who is condemned to death by the Elector of Saxony, receives a capsule with a sealed paper slip from a gipsy woman that contains predictions on the future of the electoral dynasty. Upon learning about this important content, the Elector attempts to retrieve the paper and decides to take hold of it after Kohlhaas is executed. But in order to fulfill his quest for revenge, in the story's final scene Kohlhaas, already on the scaffold, swallows the paper slip after briefly reading the prophecy, so that its contents are forever lost to the Elector and his Family.

Thus, it is various papers that govern – and not only mitigate but continuously complicate – the proceedings of Kleist's story, and one final piece that mediates its ending – by eventually disappearing and dissolving completely. The little paper slip presented to Michael Kohlhaas by the mysterious gipsy (who has a *Doppelgänger* and in addition resembles his wife who died in the course of the conflict) is a particularly small object of desire that as such contains a secret of utmost importance – but in order to fulfill its structural function for the narrative, this desire and this secret must not be fulfilled and solved. Rather, paper displays an affordance so far neglected here, the possibility to eat it, which in this case also includes annihilating the key for a possible understanding of the gipsy woman's strange role, Michael Kohlhaas's possible justification, and the Elector's uncertain future.

Thus, Kleist's *Kohlhaas* emphasizes the essential role of paper as an agent within networks of communication by simultaneously questioning its accessibility, readability, and hermeneutic closure. And it is precisely the double notion of omnipresence and permanent withdrawal that is at the heart of modern culture's basic paper myth: by swallowing the paper slip, Kohlhaas contributes to the work on this myth by making its basic object disappear.

33 | Heinrich von Kleist, "Michael Kohlhaas", in *Erzählungen* (Berlin: Realschulbuchhandlung, 1810), 1-215.

The Literary Manuscript

A Challenge for Philological Knowledge Production

Livia Kleinwächter

At a conference in 2007, the prominent literary theorist Friedrich Kittler pointed at the weak spot of current literary criticism and its contrast to traditional medieval or classical philology in Germany when he polemically stated:

> Wenn [...] die Neuphilologie vor lauter Liebe zum Dichtergenie ihre Bücher zuschlägt und statt dessen nur mehr Autorenhandschriften feiert, herausgibt oder gar - wie im Fall Nietzsche - am Computer simuliert, vergißt sie einen ihrer eigenen mediengeschichtlichen Gründe. So schön und traurig es ist, daß dem alten Goethe beim Wiederlesen von Versen, die sein Bleistift am 7. September 1780 im Jagdhaus auf dem Kickelhahn bei Ilmenau gekritzelt hat, die Tränen geflossen sind, so unerheblich ist es auch.[1]

Even if not taken for a fact, one can still use this statement as a starting point for the reflection of the state of the handwritten manuscript in recent literary studies as well as for problematizing it with regard to its critical examination in today's philological research. These manuscripts themselves are not considered as silent witnesses but rather as implicit observations of their own production process as well as their position within the milieu of literary history. This autoreferential status of manuscripts aroused interest in the last century and

1 | "When the philologists of modern literature close their books as an act of love for the genius of the poet and instead celebrate and publish the author's handwriting or even simulate it on the computer screen, as happened in the case of Nietzsche, then they forget their own media historical background. As lovely and sad it is, that tears ran down old Goethe's face when he reread the own verses his pen scribbled down on the 7th of September in 1780 in his hunting lodge on the Kickelhahn near Ilmenau, as insignificant it is, too.", Friedrich Kittler, "Philologische und Homerische Frage," in *Was ist eine philologische Frage? Beiträge zur Erkundung einer theoretischen Einstellung*, ed. Jürgen Paul Schwindt (Frankfurt/M.: Suhrkamp, 2009), 288-303, here 292, my translation.

led to the formation of research areas such as the French *Critique Génétique* that switched from analyzing the product of the creative process to this process itself or the German *Schreibszenenforschung* – an area of research that examines self-reflective scenes of writing in their twofold appearance of physical materiality and semiotic utterance. The latter formed around the question how to describe the relation between the intransitive process of writing – meaning that in the production of aesthetic texts in contrast to scientific ones the act of writing is not directed at a specific purpose but rather a self-sufficient operation in itself[2] – and the product of writing – the text to be analyzed – in literary scenes that reflect on just this act itself. Rüdiger Campe, whose essay on the "Schreibszene, Schreiben" ('Writing Scene, Writing', 1991) initiated said research area, describes those scenes as an instable ensemble of language, instrumentality and gesture and locates the characteristics of literature in its ability to mediate (or rather: irritate the distinction) between the praxeological dimension of the act of writing and the communicative semiotic operation it performs.[3] To observe the praxeological dimension of the staged descriptions of the performances of writing, the documents that accompany a literary work – the manuscripts – are assigned a crucial role.

In 2015, Christian Benne published an extensive work on the topic of the 'emergence' of the literary manuscript and its different phases in European literature and literary studies. In a series of case studies from the forgeries of Ossian to Schlegel's term of the fragment, Jean Paul's method of excerpting, and Balzac's sociological observations on the material prerequisites of literary production, Benne exemplifies the recursive relation between the development of the system of literature and the media technological prerequisites that are connected with the distinction of printed publication and handwritten manuscript. In demarcating the latter from the medium of the book, the crucial distinction is the one between the publication and replication of a text in contrast to the unpublished and singular manuscript. The criterion of being handwritten is explicitly excluded so that the typescript can also become subject of examination. Thus, the perspective on manuscripts spans a wide range and includes formats such as the letter, the diary, as well as genres of the literary production process like the note, the excerpt, the workbook or the proof sheet. These genres, Benne asserts, are subject to a profound historical change that in the course of the 18th and 19th century transforms autographs into literary manuscripts that in consequence become the venture point of a self-observant

2 | Cf. Roland Barthes, "To Write: An Intransitive Verb?," in *The Structuralist Controversy: The Languages of Criticism and the Sciences of Man*, ed. Richard Macksey and Eugenio Donato (Baltimore: Johns Hopkins University Press, 1970), 134-145.

3 | Cf. Rüdiger Campe, "Die Schreibszene, Schreiben," in *Schreiben als Kulturtechnik*, ed. Sandro Zanetti (Frankfurt/M.: Suhrkamp, 2012), 269-282, here 270f.

écriture. Benne describes the process of this change in a series of stages that begin around 1750 with the emergence of a new significance of the manuscript[4], which then becomes self-reflective in early German romanticism. The foundation of this observation is the argument by media historians according to which the printing press does not supersede the handwritten manuscript but, on the contrary, even proliferates its production. This process of a functional differentiation of the manuscript in the print age is also part of Lothar Müller's history of paper:

Für das Verständnis dieser Gefährdung der Autorität des Gedruckten ist es entscheidend, sich den Doppelsinn der Formel 'from manuscript to print' zu vergegenwärtigen. Sie ist nicht lediglich als diachronische Abbreviatur des faktischen Prozesses zu lesen, in dem in der Frühen Neuzeit die Drucktechnologie die mittelalterliche Manuskriptkultur ablöst. Sie beschreibt zugleich den optionalen Horizont, der auf der synchronen Ebene jedes - auf welchem Träger auch immer niedergelegte - Schriftstück umgibt, wenn die Druckerpresse einmal in der Welt ist. Mit der Druckerpresse, so lässt sich diese zweite Lesart formulieren, kommt nicht nur das Gedruckte in die Welt, sondern auch das Ungedruckte.[5]

This tension between the printed and the handwritten texts serves as a motor for the development to which the origin of our modern understanding of literature can be traced back. Freed from the basic tasks of storing and publishing, the success story of the manuscript only begins with the advent of print, and each autograph is measured according to the logic of the production process. Following Benne and Müller, one will have to argue that the logic of unprinted matter spawned through print initiates a writing process that transforms the published literary work into an accidental moment within an overall endless writing procedure: "Die Drucklegung wird zum Moment eines übergeordneten Schreibprozesses, der erst mit dem Tod des Autors endet; in einigen Fällen nicht

4 | Cf. Christian Benne, *Die Erfindung des Manuskripts. Zur Theorie und Geschichte literarischer Gegenständlichkeit* (Frankfurt/M.: Suhrkamp, 2015), 2.

5 | "To understand the threat to the authority of the printed matter it is crucial to realize the twofold sense of the formula 'from manuscript to print': It should not simply be read as the diachronic abbreviation of the actual process in which in the Early Modern Age the technology of printing supersedes the culture of the medieval manuscript but rather as a description of the optional horizon that surrounds each writ on the synchronic level at the moment the printing press enters the stage of history. To phrase this second reading one could say that together with the printing press not only the printed matter enters the world but the unprinted matter as well.", Lothar Müller, "Das Ungedruckte autorisieren. Wie die Wahrheit zu Papier kommt," *Zeitschrift für Ideengeschichte* IV, no. 4 (Winter 2010): 14-22, here 17, my translation.

einmal dann."[6] What Benne calls 'the invention of the manuscript' describes the development that leads to the formation of a specific understanding of the literary autograph that manages to transform the system of literature itself insofar as that the distinction between handwritten document and published book becomes blurred once again[7]. This perspective is illuminating insofar as it allows to observe a wide range of feedback effects that occur for instance between private correspondences, the genre of the epistolary novel and literary criticism or between the diary, autobiographies and autographs that suddenly become sought-after collector's items.

In the following, I want to trace some questions raised by Benne in highlighting three historical constellations that concern the distinctions mentioned so far: Firstly, I will look at some of the effects of the printing technology and its relation to what could be referred to as 'the birth of the modern figure of the author' in 18th century England; secondly, I will show how this new figure is challenged by what Benne calls 'the emergence of the manuscript' with the example of Goethe's 'file management'; thirdly, I will add the question how these transformations as well as the historicist race for autographs affected the institutionalization process of German philology. In closing, I will return to the question of the manuscript as an object of study that keeps haunting the process of self-reflection in today's philology.

PRINT AND THE 'AGE OF THE AUTHOR'

In 18th century London, the printing technology is not an unknown quantity anymore. Its impact had fully struck society and the older literary system of courtly letters. In consequence, the system of literature became divided into the two extremes of aristocratic circles depending on patronage on the one side and 'Grub Street' where aspiring poets became impoverished 'hack writers' on the other. In his study on printing technology in early 18th century England, Alvin Kernan gives some insight on the effects that the booming book market had on the theoretical concept as well as the actual conditions of authorship when he describes Samuel Johnson as one of the first writers who supposedly fully understood the new economic and technological principles emerging. He points at the peculiarity of the case of Johnson as an author who embodies the "transition between two cultural worlds, one dying and one trying to be

6 | "Printing becomes the moment in a superordinated process of writing that does not end bevor the death of the author, in some cases not even then.", Benne, *Erfindung des Manuskripts*, 28, my translation.

7 | Cf. Benne, *Erfindung des Manuskripts*, 32.

born"[8] – one being the old literary system of patronage, the other the new one that was adapting to the literary market and thus created new affordances of visibility for the author. Thus, the author was born anew "in the romantic system of literature that gradually developed after him, [where] the authorial personality had to be, and continued in fact to be, like Johnson, in the respect of being strange and interesting enough to impart to writers and writing a psychological dignity and meaning they could no longer derive from a place and function in the social world of palace, great house, and cathedral."[9] It is the logic of the market that demands to be fed by an exponentially growing number of deliverers of texts. But these deliverers were by no means mere laborers for the factorylike publishing system but influenced through both pictures of the gentlemen writer and the rare economically successful examples of their co-writers. As Kernan argues, this situation lead to inventive self-depictions that would even culminate in forgeries like the one of the Scottish national bard Ossian whose creator James McPherson was rightfully challenged by Johnson's request to see the manuscripts.[10]

Johnson depicted the peculiar situation of the ever increasing number of writers in proclaiming his time as "The Age of the Author" in the periodical *The Adventurer*:

They who have attentively considered the history of mankind, know that every age has its peculiar character. At one time, no desire is felt but for military honours; every summer affords battles and sieges, and the world is filled with ravage, bloodshed, and devastation [...]. The present age, if we consider chiefly the state of our own country, may be styled, with great propriety, *The Age of Authors*; for, perhaps, there never was a time in which men of all degrees of ability, of every kind of education, of every profession and employment, were posting with ardour so general to the press. [...] It may be observed, that of this, as of other evils, complaints have been made by every generation: but though it may, perhaps, be true, that at all times more have been willing than have been able to write, yet there is no reason for believing, that the dogmatical legions of the present race were ever equalled in number by any former period: for so widely is spread the itch of literary praise, that almost every man is an author, either in act or in purpose: has either bestowed his favours on the publick, or withholds them, that they may be more seasonably offered, or made more worthy of acceptance.[11]

8 | Alvin Kernan, *Printing Technology, Letters & Samuel Johnson* (Princeton: Princeton University Press, 1987), 22.

9 | Kernan, *Printing Technnology*, 21.

10 | Cf. Kernan, *Printing Technology*, 88f.

11 | Samuel Johnson "The itch of writing universal," *The Adventurer,* December 11, 1753, accessed April 2, 2018, http://www.johnsonessays.com/the-adventurer/no-115-the-itch-of-writing-universal/.

In this poignant description Johnson presents society as honeycombed with the desire to be renowned for one's personal literary production and the desire of everyone to educate everyone else. Thus, being an author becomes meaningless as a tool for exclusiveness if used by everybody to distinguish themselves from all others. Johnson basically displays the logic of fashion here, only on a larger scale. The distinction between exclusion and inclusion is instructive for understanding the role of printing in the process of the valorization of literature: The main difference between a printed book and a manuscript is attributed to the difference between publicity and exclusiveness. Thus, the printed text turns into a stigma for its author who is exposed as one of the despised aspirants writing for a living. Especially poetry seemed unprintable to its creators as the publication history of Thomas Gray's famous *Elegy Written in a Country Churchyard* demonstrates: When Gray learned that his poem was about to be pirated for a periodical, he felt forced to arrange its publication even though it seemed to him a tasteless act altogether. He refused salary and pleaded the publisher to claim that the poem had come into his hands 'by accident'.[12] "It is impossible to predict on social grounds exactly who would and who would not print in the late sixteenth and seventeenth centuries, but it is nonetheless clear that there was till during this time a fashionable and long-continuing, though not universally observed, antipathy to a medium that perverted the primary courtly literary values of privacy and rarity."[13] Again the shift in the literary system becomes evident: in the dawning realm of courtly letters where poetic texts circulated within a manuscript audience being printed would be a stigma that initiated different strategies when it occurred nonetheless – such as the author's name being disguised behind pseudonyms or anonymity or deploying friends who would be alleged as a pretext for the 'lack of control'[14] – whereas economic necessities in the 18th century proofed to render the avoidance of print impossible.

Earlier in the century – around 1700 – the dispute about the risks and opportunities of the printing technology traversed another famous conflict at the turn of the 18th century: the *Querelle des Anciens et des Modernes*. In England, the protagonist's names of this *querelle* are Sir William Temple, the employer of Jonathan Swift – who would allegorize the conflict in his *Battle of the Books* –, on the one side and William Wotton and Richard Bentley on the other, the latter

12 | Cf. Kernan, *Printing Technology*, 64f.

13 | Kernan, *Printing Technology*, 42.

14 | Cf. J.W. Saunders, "The Stigma of Print," *Essays in Criticism* 1 (1951), 139-163, here 143 and 145.

being a classical scholar and philologist who would later serve as a role model for German philologists in the 19th century.[15]

In his "Essay upon Ancient and Modern Learning" Temple declared: "The Invention of Printing has not, perhaps, multiplied Books, but only the Copies of them [...]. For the Scribblers are infinite, that like Mushrooms or Flys are born and dye in small circles of time; whereas Books, like Proverbs, receive their Chief Value from the Stamp and Esteem of Ages through which they have passed."[16] Temple points at the core of the problem: The printing technology produces masses of text that inundate the reading parts of society and destroy any ability to distinguish valuable texts from trivial ones. This argument is transformed into a larger narrative of cultural criticism within which the intellectual force that was strongest during Greek and Roman antiquity fades together with the number of geniuses the further history develops. Temple speculates if this decline can be attributed to the availability and indistinguishability of knowledge that, by piling up in the heads of the disciples, extinguish possible strokes of genius:

> Besides, who can tell whether Learning may not even weaken Invention in a man that has great Advantages from Nature and Birth, whether the weight and number of so many other men's thoughts and notions may not suppress his own, or hinder the motion and agitation of them from which all Invention arises; As heaping on Wood, or too many Sticks, or too close together, suppresses and sometimes quite extinguishes a little spark that would otherwise have grown up to a noble Flame.[17]

Education is one central issue of the demonization of print because it poses the question how to differentiate between good and bad books. In addition, by making available and accessible a multitude of contradicting opinions and texts, print blurs what can be recognized as truth. Part of the topological critique of print is therefore the differentiation between pedantic (philological) teaching of texts and valuable moral and cultural education. Roughly one century later, a similar demarcation line will be drawn within the process of establishing philology as an autonomous discipline at German universities: On the one side, there were the Classical philologists that strived for a pedagogical connection between idealized antiquity and their own present – protagonists

---

15 | Cf. for instance August Boeckh, "Über die kritische Behandlung der Pindarischen Gedichte [1822]," in *Gesammelte kleine Schriften* V, ed. Paul Eichholtz and Ernst Bratuschek (Hildesheim/Zürich/New York: Georg Olms, 2005), 248-396, here 263.

16 | William Temple, "An Essay upon Ancient and Modern Learning [1690]," in *Essays On Ancient & Modern Learning and On Poetry*, ed. J.E. Spingarn (Oxford: Clarendon Press, 1909), 2-42, here 3f.

17 | Temple, *Essay*, 18.

of this approach include Friedrich Wolf, Friedrich Schlegel, and Friedrich Nietzsche. On the other side, there was the school of strict editorial criticism that evolved around Karl Lachmann, whose goal was to objectify philological methods through historical exactness – an approach that would repeatedly be referred to as 'pedantry' by Lachmann's critics.

Contrary to this discursive tradition, Temple's opponent within the English *querelle,* William Wotton, defined the advantages of the printing technology by arguing that modern times owe almost everything they excel in to the use of print:[18] the increasing distribution enables more people to partake in knowledge acquiring and production; standardization saves time in the process of deciphering the texts; the possibility to add indexes and other layout options help organize the matter and the preservation of texts that are therefore less liable to be corrupted by transcribers.[19] The tertium comparationis which for Wotton guarantees the victory of the 'Moderns' in the *querelle* is historical "Exactness"[20] – which was again countered by the accusation of pedantry as an opposite of true learning from 'Ancients' such as Temple. Wotton gave two answers to this objection: one by referring to knowledge in general in contrast to the single subject working on its realization, i.e. the "Commonwealth of Learning"[21]; the other by redeeming the critical subject that in its labor of conjecturing would require "great Sagacity, as well as great Industry".[22]

Within this framework, the true centerpiece of the English *querelle* is a rather philological one: the controversy over the *Epistles of Phalaris.* William Temple used the Sicilian tyrant Phalaris as an example for the superiority of the Ancients regarding their rhetoric abilities. But Richard Bentley, upon being asked by his friend William Wotton, identified them as a fictive epistolography descending from medieval times and thus ridiculed Swift's employer. This was the turning point in favor of the modernists – out of the spirit of 'pedantry' so to say.

With respect to the problem of criticism, we have to go back to Johnson one last time to see how he already connected the question of criticism with a phenomenological view on the effects of printing. In the periodical *The Rambler* he points at the different reading practices toward the printed text and the more draftlike manuscript:

18 | Cf. William Wotton, *Reflections upon Ancient and Modern Learning* (London: J. Leake, 1694), 170.

19 | Cf. Wotton, *Reflections*, 171f.

20 | Wotton, *Reflections*, 316.

21 | Wotton, *Reflections*, 321.

22 | Wotton, *Reflections*, 318.

I have had occasion to observe [...] the different temper with which the same man reads a printed and manuscript performance. When a book is once in the hands of the publick, it is considered as permanent and unalterable; and the reader, if he be free from personal prejudices, takes it up with no other intention than of pleasing or instructing himself: [...]. But if the same man be called to consider the merit of a production yet unpublished, he brings an imagination heated with objections to passages which he has yet never heard; he invokes all the powers of criticism, and stores his memory with Taste and Grace, Purity and Delicacy, Manners and Unities [...].[23]

Johnson points at the different reading manners of printed and of handwritten texts and describes how the inalterability of the text leads to a passive (or 'readerly') reception whereas the character of the draft that is implemented in handwritten documents by means of its contraposition to its printed counterparts evokes a critical (or 'writerly') attitude. In what Alvin Kernan refers to as the "platonizing power of print"[24] when he links Johnson's reflections to the argument of standardization through comparability – an argument we encountered with Wotton – we can observe the recurrence of the logic of the medium of print: by overtaking functions of the older medium the printed text leads to the implementation of new functions for the manuscript. According to Benne this yields effects on a large scale in the literary system – most crucially concerning the ideas of authenticity and originality[25]: The 'individualized' manuscript becomes a valuable source ready to be exploited by individual or philological research and the upsurge of historicization of the figure of the writer – by himself or others – is a stringent consequence.[26]

The Author and the 'Age of the Manuscript'

The author who in Kernan's depiction became 'real to himself' now appears as a guarantee and origin of the imagined unity of his work. As such he has to react to the mass of paper he produces. He has to destroy what ought not to be part of the construction of his poetic image. He has to keep trace which of his works belongs to which period of his poetic production, has to complete what seems

23 | Samuel Johnson, "The contrariety of criticism. The vanity of objection. An author obliged to depend upon his own judgment," *The Rambler*, June 5, 1750, accessed April 2, 2018, http://www.johnsonessays.com/the-rambler/no-23-the-contrariety-of-criticism-the-vanity-of-objection-an-author-obliged-to-depend-upon-his-own-judgment/.

24 | Kernan, *Printing Technology*, 165.

25 | Cf. Benne, *Erfindung des Manuskripts*, 162-168.

26 | Cf. Benne, *Erfindung des Manuskripts*, 168.

important, and to sort out all other texts of 'minor' significance. Finally, he has to rework texts that do not fit into this developmental scheme. All these problems were already reflected on extensively by Johann Wolfgang Goethe, to name an early example from the German canon, as can be deduced from his letters and statements as well as from a vast number of research literature. Carlos Spoerhase and Kai Sina tagged this emerging demeanor with the term "Nachlassbewusstsein" – legacy awareness[27]. They observe how a number of different memory practices simultaneously address the handwritten document around 1800. Using the example of Schiller, Spoerhase and Sina point out how cutting up Schiller's handwritten documents and using them as souvenirs seemed no big deal at the time – even though it seems to contradict the practice of archival collections in the 19th century that emphasize the importance of completeness and exactness of the collected documents. In contrast, it seems that Goethe already internalized the philological and administrative occupation with his work. According to Müller, for Goethe working on his own legacy served as the verification of the unity of his œuvre.[28] Ernst Robert Curtius demonstrated as early as 1951 how Goethe's administrative occupations would become a model for the writer to organize his life and writing in general and he shows how that generated a personal 'paper technology' that could capture and mediatize every single experience. Curtius cites a letter to Schiller that shows how this system works. Goethe describes here how he processes new 'data' when travelling: Firstly, he collects, selects, and files public papers such as newspapers or play bills; secondly, he probes his new insights in society; and thirdly, he would file away his broadened and revised experiences, too.[29] Following Curtius who thus presented the first and fundamental observation of Goethes 'File Management', Cornelia Vismann produced additional insights into Goethe's interaction with his personal archive. Vismann describes the aging Goethe as a redactor and philologist who spent his remaining time mainly on organizing and preserving his files instead of beginning new projects in order to secure the image of himself he had created. The idea of the poet as a mirror of his era (which is called 'Goethezeit' accordingly in German literary criticism) was to be ensured by two parallel projects: Firstly, the legacy had to be processed which included autodafés, rewritings, and juridical administration. Vismann

27 | Carlos Spoerhase and Kai Sina: "Nachlassbewusstsein. Zur literaturwissenschaftlichen Erforschung seiner Entstehung und Entwicklung," *Zeitschrift für Germanistik* 23, no. 3 (2013), 607-623.

28 | Cf. Lothar Müller, *Weiße Magie. Die Epoche des Papiers* (München: dtv, 2014), 284.

29 | Cf. Ernst Robert Curtius, "Goethes Aktenführung [1951]," in *Grundlagen der Literaturwissenschaft. Exemplarische Texte*, ed. Bernhard J. Dotzler (Köln/Weimar/Wien: Böhlau, 1999), 158-167.

describes how a transparent arrangement of his files should defend the dead poet against possible posthumous distortions and serve as a reading script for coming recipients to ensure the intended equity of his œuvre.[30] Secondly, Goethe's autobiographical writings were supposed to support the reintegration of œuvre and life. To this end, these writings also explain possible lacunas – for instance when certain works remained unfinished and unpublished. Goethe explains this by picturing himself as an author whose interests were manifold and whose development therefore suffered from diffusion:

Die *Goethe*schen Arbeiten hingegen sind Erzeugnisse eines Talents, das sich nicht stufenweis' entwikkelt und auch nicht umherschwärmt, sondern gleichzeitig, aus einem gewissen Mittelpunkte, sich nach allen Seiten hin versucht, und in der Nähe sowol als in der Ferne zu wirken strebt, manchen eingeschlagnen Weg für immer verlässt, auf andern lange beharrt. Wer sieht nicht, daß hier das wunderlichste Gemisch entspringen würde, wenn man das, was den Verfasser gleichzeitig beschäftigte, in Einen Band zusammenbringen wollte, wenn es auch möglich wäre, die verschiedensten Produktionen dergestalt zu sondern, daß sie sich alsdann wieder, der Zeit ihres Ursprungs nach, neben einander stellen liessen.[31]

Goethe answers to the edition of Schiller's works here as well as to the question whether a chronological edition would also be suitable for editing his collected works. The answer is negative because Goethe sees a contrast between his own writing practice and the supposedly gradual and linear development of the talent and writing of his friend Schiller. Goethe places himself within a tradition of universality (of talents and interests) that does not require a chronological presentation and narration. Rather, the narrative of Goethe's career shall be accomplished by autobiographical and authorized biographical writings and is supposed to create an 'organic' order of the published and unpublished mass of texts delivered to posterity.

30 | Cf. Cornelia Vismann, *Akten. Medientechnik und Recht* (Frankfurt/M.: Fischer, 2000), 238.

31 | "The works of Goethe in contrast are productions of a talent that does neither develop itself gradually nor swarm around, but that probes simultaneously from a certain center to all directions and that attempts to operate near and far, that leaves some chosen tracks for good while persisting on others for a long time. Who cannot see that the most curious mélange would emanate here when what held the authors attentions simultaneously should be brought together in one volume even if it was possible to differentiate the various products so that they would again - in the order of their origins - be positioned next to each other.", Johann Wolfgang von Goethe, "Über die neue Ausgabe der Goethe'schen Werke", *Morgenblatt für gebildete Stände*, April 26, 1814, 2-3, here 3, my translation.

For this seems to be the main object of Biography, to exhibit the man in relation to the features of his time; and to show to what extent they have opposed or favoured his progress; what view of mankind and the world he has formed from them, and how far he himself, if an artist, poet, or author, may externally reflect them.[32]

The advent of the younger German philology that evolves from the classical and medieval studies will find its starting point here: it departs from the attempt to restore the wholistic context of an author's life from the remnants of written texts. In accordance to the self-constructed imago of Goethe as an 'être collectif'[33] or a 'natural' genius born into modernity, his life will become a model for the capabilities of individual development. As such, it was exploited by 19th century national philology and, as an object of study, helped to create new hermeneutical practices such as 'Nacherleben' – the idea of understanding literature through emphasizing with the author that got more or less institutionalized by Wilhelm Dilthey.

What these approaches to literature miss is that if the author (as a function so to say) may guarantee the unity of a work – this does not guarantee the unity of the subject itself.

As can be seen with the example of Goethe the process of becoming a writer, the model of an administrative life management and the emphasis on individual development ("Bildung") around 1800 become inseparable. Despite Goethe's precise plans for posterity, academic and private collectors hungered for every piece and bit that left traces of his life and writing in the mid-19th century. The periodical *Jahrbücher für wissenschaftliche Kritik* ('Yearbooks for Academic Criticism') as an example regularly tried to urge living contemporaries of the poet to deliver every piece of information they could provide and asked proprietors of possible written remains to gather and publish them – combined with instructions how to redact them correctly.[34] Around the manuscript as a fetish object – I want to argue – evolves a large complex of con-

32 | Johann Wolfgang von Goethe, *Truth and Poetry: From my own Life*, translated by John Oxenford (London: Henry G. Bohn, 1848), vii.

33 | Johann Wolfgang von Goethe talking to Frédéric Soret (February 17, 1832), in *Goethes Gespräche. Eine Sammlung zeitgenössischer Berichte aus seinem Umgang*, vol. 3.2 (Zürich/Stuttgart: dtv 1987), 839: "Que suis - je moi - même? Qu'ai-je fait? J'ai recueilli, utilisé tout ce que j'ai entendu, observé. Mes œuvres sont nourries par des milliers d'individus divers, des ignorants et des sages, des gens d'esprit et des sots. L'enfance, l'âge mûr, la vieillesse, tous sont venus m'offrir leurs pensées, leurs facultés, leur manière d'être, j'ai recueilli souvent la moisson que d'autres avaient semée. Mon œuvre est celle d'un être collectif et elle porte le nom de Goethe."

34 | Cf. Wilhelm Danzel, "Goethiana", *Jahrbücher für wissenschaftliche Kritik*, no. 44-46 (September 1846), 345-363.

flicting interests in the 19th century: between writers and philologists, between amateurs and professionals and between private collectors and new founded institutions. I would like to present in the following pages three short examples for this situation: Jacob Grimm and his contemporaries from German romanticism, the case of Gerstenbergk, and Dilthey's call for the installation of literature archives at the end of the century.

The Historicist Race for the Manuscript

Lothar Müller outlines one of the main characteristics of 19th century's historicism: the professionalizing of handling manuscripts that he labels as a "paper machine." Müller describes this machine as a mechanism that feeds manuscripts into the universities where they get transformed into historic-critical editions. Between archives, libraries, and universities handwritten texts are constantly translated into printed matter.[35] If one takes into consideration what Cornelia Vismann wrote on the Prussian machinery of administration that took off from the paradigm of the self-governing subject, this becomes visible as another element of the same paper machine. Through the necessity to control the growing mountain of files, the system produces feedback effects and even more paper that threatens to incapacitate it. Vismann points out how in Prussia, where files where maintained on everyone and everything, every citizen became a civil servant so that the distinction between private and official records was blurred.[36] Analogously Johnson's description of the 'urge' for literary praise gives way to a system of self-writing imperatives that can be referred to as just another formation of the 'Age of the Author'.

Reichsfreiherr von Stein – a Prussian minister and reformer – urged to replace the type of the dull copyist by the autonomous civil servant that was able to manage the threatening mass of files.[37] At the same time, the academic figure of the philologist is questioned in a similar manner. Nikolaus Wegmann argues that in the case of Karl Lachmann theoretical reflection was substituted by his reputation and his 'moralism of professionality'[38]. And similar to the deep sighs of post-Goethian poets that they were mere epigones of the Golden Age of Weimar Classicism some philologists in the mid-19th century addressed

35 | Cf. Müller, *Weiße Magie*, 280.

36 | Cf. Vismann, *Akten*, 236.

37 | Cf. Vismann, *Akten*, 234.

38 | Cf. Nikolaus Wegmann, "Was heißt einen 'klassischen Text' lesen? Philologische Selbstreflexion zwischen Wissenschaft und Bildung," in *Wissenschaftsgeschichte der Germanistik im 19. Jahrhundert*, ed. Jürgen Fohrmann and Wilhelm Voßkamp (Stuttgart/Weimar: Metzler, 1994), 334-450, here 408.

themselves as epigones of the early, supposedly more productive *Altertumswissenschaften* that evolved around the figure of Friedrich August Wolf.[39] The process of philology's emancipation from its rank as an ancillary discipline is based on the one hand on the reform-oriented Prussian state and on the other on German literature and its newly awakened interest for its own past. This includes philhellenism and the romantic interest for the Germanic and medieval heritage. From this starting point, Classical Philology was established quickly – and along with it the purified text-critical method as *sine qua non* of philological practices. In contrast to the Anglo-American sphere, in 19th century Prussia the state and the humanities were closely linked. The state took a huge effort of modernizing the universities which in return payed the price that their research was closely linked to politics. Within philology, the first effect of this constellation was the construction of the authority of the specialized critic. Whereas the dividing line between professional literature studies and literary criticism stayed blurred in other nations, in Germany the styles of criticism and philological research drifted apart.[40]

There is a letter by the brothers Grimm that illustrates this drifting apart of the two paradigms both between the literary system and the academic one as well as within 19th century Classical philology itself. Even though the romantic writers and newly founded German philology shared the same interest – if not to say enthusiasm – for their cultural past in combination with a vigorous passion for collecting what came with it, differences in the handling of the collected material emerge. In the letter Jacob Grimm writes to his brother on their mutual friends within the Romantic Movement Clemens Brentano and Achim von Arnim and complains about their ideal of collecting and distributing old texts. For even though he acknowledges their splendid selection and their witty connections that should be pleasant for the audience, he criticizes the lack of historical exact observations and the carelessness of publication. Jacob Grimm contrasts his friend's idea to connect the past to the presence with the insistence on letting the past speak for itself and highlights his argument with a zoological metaphor:

> Sowenig sich fremde edele Tiere aus einem natürlichen Boden in einen anderen verbreiten lassen, ohne zu leiden und zu sterben, sowenig kann die Herrlichkeit alter Poesie wieder allgemein aufleben, d. h. poetisch; allein historisch kann sie unberührt genossen werden, und wer die unglückseligen Känguruhs kennenlernen will, der muß zu ihnen

39 | Cf. Wegmann, "Philologische Selbstreflexion," 399.

40 | Cf. Hans-Harald Müller and Sandra Richter, "Nationale Philologien – europäische Zeitschriften," in Christoph König (ed.), *Das Potential Europäischer Philologien. Geschichte, Leistung, Funktion*, ed. Christoph König, (Göttingen: Wallstein, 2009), 81-93.

nach Australien reisen, die gefangenen Löwen und Tigertiere müssen immer vergittert sein und gehen ewig in einem traurigen ∞ herum.[41]

Again, the main dispute evolving around the philological object concerns its significance for education: In the case of Classical Philology it is the question of 'classic' that is up for discussion. One can attribute the benefit of studying it to the project of bridging the gap between idealized antiquity and deficient present, which can be called the pedagogical way. Or one has to treat ancient objects 'neutrally' and maintain the study of the past as a goal in itself. In the latter case, the term 'classic' becomes a mere indicator of age.

In German literature studies at the end of the nineteenth century, the link between autographs – that are irrelevant for Classical philology since they are not part of the transmission of texts – and the author's life generates the rather unfortunate tradition of psychological readings on the one hand and its even more problematic conjuncture with nationalist ambitions to handle the products of 'German talents' as holy relics on the other. The latter demeanor seems to transcend different circles of interest – academic as well as non-academic areas – as the example of a *Handbook for Collectors of Autographs* and an attempted coup of forgery clearly demonstrate: In 1856, the county court in Weimar sits over the case Gerstenbergk. During the past years, a mysterious growth of circulating documents by Schiller's own hand was noticed by professional collectors. A professor and a trader of autographs eyed this development suspiciously. Through considerable philological rigor, it is determined that these writings lacked the 'curvature' and 'verve' of the poet's handwriting and that all the documents in question were united by the circumstance that they consisted of the same type of paper. Additionally, they displayed similar deviations in spelling as well as signatures on documents that usually were not signed. Three different surveyors find the delinquent guilty. The authors of the handbook are settled: These manufactory products debunked themselves quickly, since the quantity, the material identity, and the conspicuous frequency of signatures reveal the artificial fabrication. They conclude: Ideally the collector disposes of enough philological abilities to discern the original

41 | "As little as foreign, noble animals can be shifted from their natural habitat to another without suffering and dying, as little can the splendor of old poetry be revived in general. In other - poetic - words; only historically can old poetry be savored unspoiled and who wants to get to know the poor kangaroos should travel to Australia. The captured lions and tigers have to stay behind bars and forever walk around in a sad ∞.", Letter from Jacob to Wilhelm Grimm (May 17, 1809), in *Briefwechsel zwischen Jacob und Wilhelm Grimm aus der Jugendzeit*, ed. Herman Grimm and Gustav Hinrichs (Weimar: Böhlau, 1963), 100-102, here 101, my translation.

and the forgery himself. This example shows how intensely autographs were sought after as collectables inside and outside the context of academia.

In contrast to the academic processing of the collected material that aimed for the extraction of the insights of a culture or an individual's life and the preservation in verified editions, the materiality of the objects here becomes a priority and even can be economically measured. A handwriting containing a signature increases by value as does a rare hand or, naturally, stains of Goethe's tears. Here the literary handwriting nurtures the hope to get an unmediated relation to the spirited past. These manuscripts become "visible relics of the ideas, the spirit's outflow, the telltale daguerrotypes of the inner life of famous and most outstanding persons in their personal writings that most often rather can be characterized through one line here than through a whole biography."[42]

Handwritings are collected and worshipped in order to make present what is long gone, and here again the private and academic conceptions converge in the idea of being able to recover the poet's spirit through his material legacy. The manuscript seemingly hovers between the condition of a fetish object with small information value and that of a vital deliverer of knowledge.

That the so-called historicism was a broad social-cultural phenomenon is documented by publications such as the handbook for collectors of autographs which creates a nexus between private passion and a market that already observes the tendencies in question: "Der commerzielle Werth der Autographen, je nach den Verhältnissen der Wichtigkeit der Person und des Inhaltes, ist mit jedem Jahre gestiegen, da sich die Vorliebe für diese historischen Dokumente über alle Länder und alle Klassen der Gesellschaft verbreitet hat."[43] One can observe the different functions and applications that manuscripts are charged with here: In the academic world, the nation as a 'cultural unity' constructs its own glorious past and the discipline(s) of philology thus

42 | My own translation, full quote: "Wenn nun auch theilweise zugegeben werden muss, dass die Autographie eine Liebhaberei zu nennen ist, so möchte sie doch unter allen eine der edelsten und geistreichsten sein , da sie sich die hohe Aufgabe stellt und ihr Vergnügen, sowie ihren Reiz darin findet, die sichtbaren Reliquien der Gedanken, den Ausfluss des Geistes, die sprechendsten Daguerreotypen des Seelenlebens berühmter, in jeder Beziehung hervorragender Menschen in ihren Selbstschriften, worin oft eine Zeile treffender charakterisirt als eine umfangreiche Biographie, zu sammeln, zu ordnen und für die Nachwelt als selbstredende Denkmale aufzubewahren.", in: Johann Günther and Otto August Schulz, *Handbuch für Autographensammler* (Leipzig: Otto August Schulz, 1856), III.

43 | "The commercial value of autographs increases - depending on the importance of the individual and the content - with every year because the penchant for historical documents spread through all nations and all social classes.", Günther/Schulz, *Handbuch*, 201, my translation.

acquires its autonomy. Meanwhile, the market generates its own principles and classifies manuscripts according to criteria such as rareness, prominence, and significance. In consequence, they are converted into an exchange value. In the area of literature itself, the manuscript is transformed into the essential work: According to Benne, the literary remains now constitute an author's œuvre whereas the published single work is considered a mere tip of the iceberg. In addition, the self-reflective writing scenes grow exponentially at the same time, i.e. the process of writing growingly addresses itself. These self-reflections also refer to philological practices as a necessary competence for writers that seems, in a sense, required by the manuscript itself.

The competition over manuscripts leaves no doubt about their increasing significance in the context of writing projects. The network between private collectors, legacy aware writers, and heirs that fear for the reputation of their ancestors induces Wilhelm Dilthey in 1889 to demand the formation of archives for literature that should be modeled after the already established national archives. To serve his purpose, he depicts 'helpless paper piles' that are constantly threatened by decomposition, conflagrations, and sloppy heirs.[44] On the one hand, Dilthey asks for the extensive access to documents for academic purposes, on the other hand, he aims at preserving the heirs' right to look out for the reputation of their ancestors. He imagines an archivist who takes over the role of an intermediary and becomes a posthumous constructor of the writer's image. Interestingly enough he seems to nourish the hope to escape the hermeneutic circle with the help of the handwritten manuscript:

> Wir verstehen ein Werk aus dem Zusammenhang, in welchem es in der Seele seines Verfassers entstand, und wir verstehen diesen lebendigen, seelischen Zusammenhang aus den einzelnen Werken. Diesem Zirkel in der hermeneutischen Operation entrinnen wir völlig nur da, wo Entwürfe und Briefe zwischen den vereinzelt und kühl dastehenden Druckwerken einen inneren lebensvollen Zusammenhang herstellen. Ohne solche handschriftliche Hilfsmittel kann die Beziehung von Werken aufeinander in dem Kopfe des Autors immer nur hypothetisch und in vielen Fällen gar nicht verstanden werden.[45]

---

44 | Cf. Wilhelm Dilthey, "Archive für Literatur," in *Zur Geistesgeschichte des 19. Jahrhunderts*, ed. Ulrich Hermann (Göttingen: Vandenhoek & Ruprecht, 1970), 1-16, here 9.

45 | "We understand a work of literature contextually, that is the context of the mind of its composer and we understand this vivid, spiritual nexus out of these single pieces of writing. We are able to get out of this circle of the hermeneutic operation only there, where drafts and letters can be found between the cold line-up of printed works and create an inner, vital coherence. Without these handwritten tools we can only hypothetically connect the single works with each other and the writers' mind – if at all.", Dilthey, "Archive für Literatur", 5, my translation.

Dilthey here links the possibility of successful philological knowledge production to the condition of available autographs that ought to restitute what he imagines as an organic nexus between a writer's œuvre (as the totality of available texts) and his (or her) life.

The Object(s) of Philology

Since Dilthey, the zeal for text-critical processing and editing has spread out further. At the same time, the 20th century added a plurality of theories and turns and topoi to this process on the side of interpretation and self-reflection – such as 'the crisis of literature studies', 'the crisis of the crisis of literature studies', 'the end of theory', etc. The significance of the autograph varies strongly within these different speculations on philological knowledge production. Peter Szondi, who wrote an essay on the question of the production of philological knowledge, describes the autograph as a tool that stabilizes (or, in contrast, destabilizes) the prior understanding of a text but nonetheless cannot escape the hermeneutical circle the way Dilthey had hoped. But rather than problematizing the circle one could point at its function for the proliferation of literature studies. It continuously renders it possible to reactualize critical understanding, to proliferate the debate and challenge the ongoing reflection of philology itself – its objects, its practices, its objectives. What is crucial within this context – also for processing marginalia – is the moment of self-reflection within philological practice, or as Szondi puts it: to stay on the same level as the object and the theoretical framework one applies. In the light of the most recent developments within the field – the challenge of Digital Humanities – the question is how to position them in this scheme: Are they part of the turns that proliferate our discipline or do they threaten or promise (depending on the point of view) to *over*turn it?

One observation with regard to this question concerns the valorization of the studied object. In theoretical reflections as conjectured by Friedrich Schlegel or Nietzsche, but also by Peter Szondi, the object has a crucial role in its ability to permanently raise questions and engage the observer in reattempts of understanding the text and his own observation[46]. Here, the poetic quality is positioned at the center of a text's faculty to provoke critical reflection that results in a canon in consequence, no matter how little it is trusted. In contrast, there

46 | Cf. Peter Szondi, "Über philologische Erkenntnis," in *Schriften I*, ed. Jean Bollack et al. (Frankfurt/M.: Suhrkamp, 1978), 263-286, on the relation between the ambiguity of the literary text and the self-reflective nature of philological knowledge production. (264, 282f.) He states that the assignment of the material already indicates the direction for the interpretation (278).

exist approaches like the 'pure' text criticism in the sense of the methodological positivism of 19th century philology as well as some current Digital Humanities projects that aim at the 'great unread' that explicitly treat texts as pure historical data. Therefore parts of the Digital Humanities use rhetoric strategies that can be parallelized with the argumentations of the advocates of a positivistic philology in the 19th century who relocated the question of their discipline's unity to the material alone by emphasizing the importance of exploiting the material on hand with help of new technological possibilities but at the same time withhold proposals how to read it or how to reflect on their own theoretical assumptions. Again the manuscript seems to become either an idealized object of a forlorn past that needs to be reconnected to the (post)modern world via study and pedagogy – or else, it threatens to become sheer 'data'.

Szondi argues that the seemingly big divide between objective facts and subjective commentary is an illusion to both – positivist and interpreter. The interpreter who ignores facts also ignores the rules of understanding whereas the positivist who refrains from subjective insights would not be able to investigate the positive facts.[47] The autograph in Szondi's sense is a deliverer of facts that ought to be taken neither to light nor too seriously. It delivers information that needs to enter the process of understanding without replacing it. Likewise James Mussell argues convincingly that there is no unmediated engagement with historical objects and any disacknowledgement of theory leads to a naturalization of the idea of "raw data" or to the concept of authentic witnesses of a forlorn past.[48] Mussell here makes an argument in favor of Digital Humanities when confronted with criticism directed against the problem of representing historical objects by digitizing printed texts: "If the purpose of digital resources is only to reproduce print objects, then we remain trapped in the logic of deficiency. A more productive approach is to rethink digital resources as offering representations of whatever it is that the archival object *also* represents."[49]

It is this emphasized '*also*' that may show a way out of the strict dichotomy of new quantifying approaches toward literature and hopes for a return to a more 'classic' philology as a threshold without relinquishing literature's ambiguities. If print creates the unalterable, readerly text, the manuscript can be a reminder of its other exposed side – but only if we consider it as the open and self-reflective fragment in Friedrich Schlegel's sense and not the truer, more authentic version of the work.

47 | Cf. Szondi, "Über philologische Erkenntnis", 268.

48 | James Mussell, "Repetition: Or, 'In Our Last'," *Victorian Periodicals Review* 48, no. 3 (Fall 2015), 343-358, here 343f.

49 | Mussell, "Repetition", 354.

From Abstraction to Inscription and Back Again

(Reverse) Blackboxing described by Aaron Bernstein and Bruno Latour

Charlotte Jaekel

Around 1800, in literature and in the still unsystematic awareness of what will later – in a scientific form – lead to the subject of 'folklore', a change emerged that would mark a new epoch: the hitherto despised, the void (with a quotation from Friedrich Theodor Vischer's 'thing novel': "das recht eigentliche Bagatell, das des Nennens nicht wert ist" [the quite real trivial, which is not worth mentioning]),[1] begins, initially hesitantly, to come to the fore. In this "erste[n] Verdichtungsphase des Bagatelldiskurses" [first compaction phase of the discourse about the trivial],[2] as the folklorist Martin Scharfe described the beginnings of his subject, there is an unprecedented interest in the interrelation of things, a new kind of attention to everyday life, that is – not least – based on the dismantling of divine providence in favor of dealing with issues of coincidence.[3]

The starting point of the essay is a phenomenon that coincides with the institutionalization of the subject of folklore in the middle of the 19th century, in the second compaction phase of the trivial discourse, and, thus, also with the increased observation of everyday and popular culture. This phenomenon is based on Aaron Bernstein's observations of entering cultural and scientific achievements into everyday life and becomes describable with a term of one of the co-founders of "Völkerpsychologie", Moritz Lazarus, as "Verdichtung"

1 | Friedrich Theodor Vischer: *Auch Einer. Eine Reisebekanntschaft.* Mit einem Nachwort von Otto Borst (Frankfurt a.M.: Fischer, 1987), 550. In the following translations of shorter German quotes are given directly in the continuous text, longer quotes in the footnotes.

2 | Martin Scharfe: "Bagatellen. Zu einer Pathognomik der Kultur", *Zeitschrift für Volkskunde* 91 (1995), 1-26, here 8.

3 | Cf. ibid., 9-13.

[compaction].[4] In this respect, compaction is meant in a double sense – on the one hand, one can observe what Bernstein practices as the 'real prose' of things, on the other hand, and this is the side of the term that interests me in the following, as a law of cultural-historical development, which basically describes an abstraction process of not only immaterial, but also material objectifications:[5] it is, according to Bernstein, a "Kulturgesetz" [cultural law] that thoughts and things circulate which were originally "mühsam [...] erarbeitet" [laboriously worked out], that thoughts and things are taken over by culture and are finally used even "ohne Gedanken-Operation" [without thought operation] to become "alltäglich und gedankenlos" [commonplace and thoughtless].[6]

With his reflections, Bernstein wants to open the eyes for the "Wunder der Alltäglichkeit" [miracles of everyday life] (AG 81), and this, ultimately, means giving historicity and genealogy back to innocently used things, meaning a reappropriation of their repressed genesis and the involved actors behind it, who are connected in networks.

The same phenomenon of compaction echoes, secondly, in the recent theory in Bruno Laotur's notion of *blackboxing*. In this respect, a historical deep dimension of the actor-network theory (ANT) can be found at the beginnings of folkloric debates about the trivial. I would like to illustrate this exemplarily on the basis of a text by Latour, which is less present in the German debate about the ANT, but has caused a sensation, especially in the, so-called, *Science Wars* in the late 80s/early 90s: Latour's socio-semiological analysis *A Relativistic Account of Einstein's Relativity* (1988), which is based on Albert Einstein's popular science book *Relativity: The Special and the General Theory* (1917).[7] I

---

4 | Moritz Lazarus: *Grundzüge der Völkerpsychologie und Kulturwissenschaft* (Hamburg: Meiner, 2003), 27.

5 | Rudolf Helmstetter notes that compaction should be characterized as a "kulturgeschichtliches Entwicklungsprinzip" [principle of cultural-historical development], as a "Komplement zu den ungleich prominenteren Konzepten 'Rationalisierung' und Abstraktion" [complement to unequally more prominent concepts of 'rationalization' and abstraction]: Rudolf Helmstetter: "Verlorene Dinge, die Poesie der Siebensachen und der Realismus der Requisiten (Gottfried Keller, Aaron Bernstein, Theodor Fontane)." In: *Die Dinge (in) der Romantik*, edited by Christiane Holm, Günter Oesterle, Dagmar von Wietersheim (Würzburg: Königshausen&Neumann, 2010), 213-41, here 231.

6 | Aaron Bernstein: "Ein alltägliches Gespräch". In: Idem: *Naturkraft und Geisteswalten*. Neue Ausgabe (Stuttgart: Verlag von Carl Krabbe, 1876), 89-11, here 90. In the following, citations are given directly in the continuous text with the outline AG and the page number.

7 | In the selected texts, all three authors, Bernstein, Einstein and Latour, do have in common their interest in watches as gauges, the effort for concretion instead of abstraction and – last not least – a dialogical style through which the reader is sought to

will not go into a detailed interpretation of the text, but will – possibly in an illegitimate shortening – pick out individual elements of the text to illustrate my understanding of *reverse blackboxing*, which Latour (as well as Bernstein), in my opinion, pursue. I want to show how Latour, on a metatheoretical level, observed how Einstein traced conceptual abstractions back to inscriptions, mainly to inscriptions of technical things and apparatuses or experimental setups.

By looking at inscriptions in the sense of *reverse blackboxing*, thus the argument, the black box of scientific activity is opened, its individual components become visible and the hiatus between words and reality can be overcome by circulating reference (Latour). Thirdly, on the basis of these concepts and practices, a completely different form of writing practice can be pursued than the classic literary scenes offer: writing scenes of technical things in the laboratory and their inscription into the scientific text.[8]

be involved in requests/instructions (what Latour emphasizes in his semiotic analysis of Einstein's text and takes over as a principle of style for the own text). The latter may be related to the fact that the three authors are not least connected by mutual reading: Einstein reads Bernstein, Latour in turn reads Einstein. Albert Einstein was a faithful reader of Bernstein's texts; he wrote in reference to Bernstein's texts, that he "hatte [...] das Glück, die wesentlichen Ergebnisse und Methoden der gesamten Naturwissenschaft in einer vortrefflichen populären, fast durchweg aufs Qualitative sich beschränkenden Darstellung kennen zu lernen (Bernsteins naturwissenschaftliche Volksbücher, ein Werk von 5 oder 6 Bänden), ein Werk, das ich mit atemloser Spannung las." [he had the fortune to get to know the essential results and methods of the entire natural science in one presentation that is admirable, popular, almost entirely limited to the quantitative (Bernstein's scientific folkbooks, a work of 5 or 6 volumes), a work I read with breathless suspense.] (Albert Einstein: Autobiographical Notes [1949], edited by Paul Arthur Schilpp [Illinois: Open Court Publishing Co., 1991], 12-14). What is at least striking is the style: again and again, all three of them apply to the reader with reading instructions, which, as a consequence, creates an author within the text – driven to the extreme, one can find this in Latour's door-closer text *Mixing Humans with Non-Humans: Sociology of a Door-Closer*, written under the pseudonym of an American scientist named Jim Johnson, whom he then reveals in a footnote on the grounds that American scientists do not read texts by French sociologists.

8 | The used 'Begriffskonturierung' [term contouring] of the writing scene is based on works of Rüdiger Campe, who coined the term for a "nicht-stabiles Ensemble von Sprache, Instrumentalität und Geste" [non-stable ensemble of language, instrumentality and gesture] of the heterogeneous moments involved in the writing act (Rüdiger Campe: "Die Schreibszene, Schreiben." In: *Paradoxien, Dissonanzen, Zusammenbrüche. Situationen offener Epistemologie*, edited by Hans Ulrich Gumbrecht, K. Ludwig Pfeiffer (Frankfurt a.M.: Suhrkamp, 1991), 759-72, here 760.

Aaron Bernstein and the Breaking Up of the Ordinariness

Aaron Bernstein, writer, publicist with a wide-ranging interest in contemporary science, wrote first and foremost in the middle of the 19th century. He is particularly known for the popularization of scientific and technical discoveries and inventions, but best remembered for the popular scientific *Naturwissenschaftliche Volksbücher* (*Scientific Folk Books*), which were published in the years 1855–1856 in 21 volumes. In particular, I am interested in two shorter texts by Bernstein: On the one hand, I want to focus on the contemporary cultural diagnosis *Ein Alltägliches Gespräch* (*An Everyday Conversation*), published in Auerbach's *Volkskalender für 1861*, in which he discusses the principle of compaction as the principle of cultural progress, as described above, and, on the other hand, I want to concentrate on his essay *Verlorene Dinge* (1862) (*Lost Things*), which exposes technical, social and economic human-thing relations. In this essay, Bernstein describes the millions of lost needles that nobody misses:

Campe is particularly keen to highlight the heterogeneity and processuality of the writing act. Writing is thus composed of the three factors language/semiotics, corporeality/gesture and instrumentality/technology, whose respective weighting is rearranged in each individual writing scene. With regard to such 'non-stable ensembles', the view of the writing act as a cultural technique in the sense of ANT seems particularly fruitful, as Harun Maye has shown. Cultural techniques in the discourse about media, in the minimum definition determined as "Praktiken und Verfahren der Erzeugung von Kultur, die an der Schnittstelle von Geistes- und Technikwissenschaft ansetzen und als Bedingung der Möglichkeit von Kultur überhaupt" [practices and processes of the production of culture that begins at the interface of Humanities and technical sciences and as condition of the possibility of culture at all] (Harun Maye: "Was ist eine Kulturtechnik?" Zeitschrift für Medien- und Kulturforschung 1 (2010), 121-35, here 121) receive – from the point of view of ANT – an added value insofar as that they can be described as networks and therefore, hierarchical issues can be circumvented. With the help of ANT, the question of a prioritization of technology or culture can be resolved in favor of "rekursiver Operationsketten" [recursive chains of operations] (Ibid., 127). Maye concisely summarizes in this sense: "In solchen Operationsketten wird weder dem Kulturellen noch dem Technischen ein Vorrang eingeräumt, sondern erst deren Interaktion erlaubt die Rede von 'kulturellen Praktiken'. In der Terminologie der ANT sind Kulturtechniken also Operationen, die als Netzwerke verteilter Handlungsmacht beschrieben werden können und an denen menschliche und nichtmenschliche Akteure beteiligt sind." [In such chains of operation, neither the cultural nor the technical priority is given, but only their interaction allows the talk of 'cultural practices'. Thus, in the terminology of ANT, cultural techniques are operations that can be described as networks of distributed agency in which human and non-human actors are involved.] (Ibid., 121)

Es gehen tagtäglich so viele andere Dinge in der Welt verloren, daß all die verlorenen Nadeln sich wiederum verlieren in den Millionen verlorener Dinge! – Alle Menschen in der Welt schaffen oder machen oder fabrizieren oder fördern tagtäglich, jahraus, jahrein immerfort lauter neue Dinge.[9]

Thereby, he denoted a rather simple model of recycling, the lost needle, designated by Bernstein as "kleine[s] unbeachtete[s] eiserne[s] Kunstwerk unserer Industrie" [a small unnoticed iron artifact of our industries] (VD 32)[10] which

9 | Aaron Bernstein: "Verlorene Dinge". In: Idem: *Naturkraft und Geisteswalten*. Neue Ausgabe, (Stuttgart: Verlag von Carl Krabbe, 1876), 8-32, here 8. In the following, citations are given directly in the continuous text with the outline AG and the page number. [Every day so many other things are getting lost in the world that all the lost needles in turn are lost in the millions of lost things! – All people in the world create or make or fabricate or promote new things every day, year after year, all the time.]

10 | In this respect and from Bernstein's perspective, the progressive industrialization does not pose a threat to contemporary art, as one of his contemporaries, aesthetics professor Friedrich Theodor Vischer, consistently stated: For contemporary art, the reality of modernity is destructive, "jeder Fortschritt der Kultur [ist] ein Rückschritt der Schöhnheit" [every progress in culture is a step backwards in terms of beauty] (Friedrich Theodor Vischer: Ästhetik *oder Wissenschaft vom Schönen. Zum Gebrauche für Vorlesungen. Das Schöne in einseitiger Existenz*, Vol. II, edited by Robert Vischer (Munich: Meyer & Jessen, ^{2}1922), § 365, 320). In a review of Anton Hallmann's *Kunstbestrebungen der Gegenwart*, Vischer writes in 1843 that, in addition to traffic – for example the transition from riders in rough terrain to carriages on paved roads – and, in particular, the letterpress printing of modernity, indeed reached ,"das unschätzbare Gut einer blitzschnellen Zirkulation aller Kenntnisse und Ideen, einer geflügelten Verbreitung des elektrischen Gedankenstoffes durch alle Stände" [the invaluable asset of a circulation with lightning speed of all knowledge and ideas, a winged dissemination of electrical thought material through all ranks]; modernity has won "rein geistig" [purely spiritually] and also "praktisch, politisch, demokratisch unendlich gewonnen" [practically, politically, endlessly democratically], "ästhetisch" [aesthetically], however, "unendlich verloren" [lost infinitely] (Friedrich Theodor Vischer: "Kunstbestrebungen der Gegenwart." In: Kritische Gänge, Vol. 5, edited by Robert Vischer (Munich: Meyer & Jessen, ^{2}1922), 56-87, here 73). Newer media – whose constructive factors are missjudged by Vischer – such as the "Reliefkopiermaschine" [relief copying machine], the "Diagraph" [diagraph], the "Daguerreotype" [daguerreotype] or the "Öl- und Farbendruck" [oil and color print] would endanger the artistic design; although they are of great benefit to social education, they are by no means "Beförderungsmittel der produktiven Kunst." [means of transport of productive art] (Ibid., 73) Thus, through the "fortschreitenden Mechanismus im engern und weitern Sinne eine um die andere poetische Form [aufgehoben]." [progressive mechanism in the narrower and wider sense, one poetic

delivers – transferred to the field, iron for spinach, which the farmer's wife and former owner of the needle then prepares in her kitchen (VD 32). Bernstein's discussion about the loss is by no means characterized by melancholy – in a more or less unbroken euphoria in progress, he continued to welcome the consumer, and also the throwaway society created by industry and new machines and the division of labor. The demise of things is the condition of possibility of a technical as well as a spiritual progress:

> [E]s erginge uns herzlich schlecht, wenn alle gemachten Dinge gar nicht untergehen wollten; denn dieser unausgesetzte Untergang der alten Dinge ist die Grundquelle der Arbeit aller neuen Dinge, und all die Arbeit der neuen Dinge ist die Grundsäule unseres Kulturlebens. (VD 9)[11]

The focus on material culture then leads Bernstein to the observation of the infrastructure of writing: Thereby, another trivial thing provides the transition from material and everyday practical development to cultural development: the steel spring, which replaced the goosequill and which prevailed against various resistances, such as the contemporary commonly used iron gall ink, which led to the corrosion of steel springs, and the too fibrous, unsatinized paper, on which one could not write (VD 26). "[F]ür unser Thema hat jedoch der Sieg

---

form after the other would be repealed] (Ibid., 73) Bernstein, on the contrary, considers industrial products themselves as small pieces of art. This also shows his unconditional euphoria for the rise of photography, which leads to a "Verallgemeinerung des Genusses" [generalization of enjoyment] (VD 29) – art can now also 'move' into the home of the "in Dürftigkeit lebenden Fabrik-Arbeiters" [factory worker living in poverty]: Rafael and Correggio, Rubens and Rembrandt, Dürer, and Holbein would "die unglaublich große Verbreitung ihrer eigenen Meisterwerke in photographischen Abdrücken, und in viel größerer Treue, als sie selber je im Stande gewesen wären sie zu copiren, als ein Merkzeichen des höchst gesteigerten und verfeinerten Kunstsinnes betrachten." [regard the unbelievably large spread of their own masterpieces in photographic prints, and in much greater fidelity than they themselves would ever have been able to copy, as a mark of the most intensified and refined artistic sense] From this point of view, photography has catered for the "ungeheure Wachstum des Kunstsinns und die Verallgemeinerung des Kunst-Bedürfnisses seit der Zeit, daß eine Erfindung aufgetreten, welche für die Befriedigung dieses Bedürfnisses in der Weise der Industrie zu sorgen im Stande ist" [tremendous growth of the appreciation of art and for the generalization of the artistic demand since an invention has arisen, which is capable to satisfy this need in the same manner industry does] (VD 30).

11 | [We felt very bad, when all things made did not want to perish; because this perpetual downfall of the old things is the basic source of all new things, and all the work of new things is the basic pillar of our cultural life.]

der Fabrikation nicht nur in volkswirthschaftlicher, sondern auch in rein intellektueller Beziehung eine unendlich hohe Bedeutung. [...] [E]s bedeutet, daß in unserem Zeitalter unvergleichlich viel mehr geschrieben wird als früher." (VD 27)[12]

The invention of the steel spring triggers – along with other developments that Bernstein designates, such as the expansion of the postal system – the release of intellectual potential, because this is not least evident in Niklas Luhmann's statements on literature in his reflection on the achievements of his slip box: "Ohne zu schreiben, kann man nicht denken; jedenfalls nicht in anspruchsvoller, anschlußfähiger Weise." [Without writing you cannot think; at least not in a demanding way that leads to connectivity.][13] Bernstein had already come to this conclusion: Merely the increase of the written form, which is also reflected in newspapers, leads to a content related concentration of what is written in relation to what has been said, and to a "größeren und Bestimmtheit und Sammlung des Geistes" [greater certainty and collection of the mind] (VD 27). To have to take "Zuflucht im Gänsekiel" [refuge in the goose quill] (VD 27) again, would simply be impossible, according to Bernstein. Bernstein's considerations also draw attention to the manifold branches and heterogeneous actors of those networks that make it possible to produce such a banal thing as the steel spring:

> Wer die tausendfachen Fäden verfolgt, die auf den verschiedensten und scheinbar fernstliegenden Zweigen der Arbeit durcheinandergehen müssen, um mir die Möglichkeit der Stahlfeder-Fabrikation zu gewähren, der wird erkennen, wie die Stahlfeder, wenn sie die Repräsentantin der sehr gesteigerten Intelligenz ist, in ihrem Denkthätigkeits-Geschäft eine Unmasse stiller Theilnehmer hat, die scheinbar gar nichts mit der Schreiberei [...] zu thun hat, die aber gleichwohl an dem großen Verdienste theilnehmen, mit der Steigerung und Verallgemeinerung der sogenannten materiellen Arbeits-Erzeugnisse zugleich auch intellektuell der Welt dienen. (VD 28)[14]

12 | [For our topic, however, the victory of fabrication has an infinitely great significance, not only in economic but also in purely intellectual terms. It means that incomparably more is written in our age than before.]

13 | Niklas Luhmann: "Kommunikation mit Zettelkästen. Ein Erfahrungsbericht." In: Öffentliche Meinung und sozialer Wandel, edited by Horst Baier u.a. (Opladen: Westdeutscher Verlag 1981), 222-28, here 222. Cf. the Essay by Charlotte Coch in this volume.

14 | [The one who follows the thousandfold threads, which must get confused through the most diverse and seemingly most remote branches of labor, in order to grant me the possibility of the fabrication of steel-springs, will recognize how the steel spring, if it is the representative of the greatly increased intelligence, has a mass of quiet participants within its business of thinking in the field of intellectual activity, participants

Bernstein's text, which traced these 'tausendfache Fäden' to the various actors and their entanglements into a net, fundamentally disturbs the process of cultural compaction (which aims at a simple merge of things in the context of use, abstracting from the manifold factors of its genesis) by evoking the manifold actors of the genesis of everyday things. The text makes obvious that things are conditioned by an infinite number of mental as well as material conditions and technical dispositifs. Everyday things, which are degraded to dumb servants, are overlooked and not noticed. Bernstein relieved things of their notorious bleakness and invisibility.

Apart from the fact that he remarkably kept his eye on the networks behind intellectual progress, which, as it were, made this progress possible, the place where he situated this progress is of particular interest. In *Ein Alltägliches Gespräch,* he writes:

> Wir sind so sehr geneigt, zu glauben, daß unsere Gedanken in den Büchern stecken, die die Wissenschaft repräsentiren; aber das ist ein Irrthum. Die Wissenschaften, wie sie auch heißen mögen, stellen nur zum *allerkleinsten Theil* die Entstehung, die Genesis solcher Reihen dar, die uns methodisch übersichtlich gemacht werden können. Das große Gedanken-Dasein jedoch, in dem wir wirklich leben, liegt unmethodisch durcheinander versteckt in *den tausendfältigen Dingen*, unter denen wir uns von frühe auf bewegen [...]. (AG 108f., second emphasis C.J.)[15]

One object that assembles more thought and culture than any other is the clock. In the same text, Bernstein invited the reader (here the dialogical structure of the text becomes clear, see footnote 7) to a thought experiment – he let a clock owner meet an astronomer and a philosopher, who speak to him about a "wissenschaftlichen Kunstwerk" [scientific work of art] (AG 93), which, without a telescope and measurement, is able to determine the position of the sun, and so the philosopher is likewise able to make clear "unsichtbare Abschnitte der Ewigkeit, die man 'Zeit' nennt, in Theile der Unendlichkeit zu verdeutlichen, die man mit dem Wort 'Raum' bezeichnet" [invisible sections of eternity, which are called 'time', in part of the infinite, which one calls 'space'] (AG 94). Of course, the watch owner considered this wondrous work of art far too precious

---

that seem to have nothing whatever to do with writing, but nevertheless participate in the great merit of serving the world both with the growths and generalization of the so-called material labor products and in an intellectual way.]

15 | [We are so inclined to believe that our thoughts are in the books that represent science; but that is a mistake. The sciences, however they may be called, represent only in the *smallest part* the genesis of such series, which can be made methodically clear to us. However, the presence of great thoughts, in which we truly live is unmethodically confused in the *thousandfold things*, on which we move from early on.]

as to possess it as a private citizen, and was informed that he already carried it in his vest pocket. The clock acts as an approver of what the concentration of spiritual achievements on an everyday thing is about: astronomical and philosophical knowledge about space and time of millennia is sedimented and concentrated in this watch. Compaction, in this sense, means – completely uncritically – materialization, the materialization of thought. Bernstein, thus, explained the principle of civilizational progress: compaction of intellectual achievements on the trivial objects only establishes the possibility for its enhancement. At the same time, with a transformation of the view from intellectual to material production, there is a revaluation of trite everyday objects, which are regarded as constitutive for the design of society. The fact that the ordinary watch wearer is unaware of the cultural achievements and the potential of the watch, that the meaning has flowed off, that the watch has sunk to a simple everyday thing, is indeed described by Bernstein with a slight sorrow, but – once more – without any melancholy or nostalgia. On the contrary, this compaction or blackboxing – as I would like to phrase it in the light of the following part – is the necessary principle of any progress. And Bernstein concludes with the following plea:

Wir *müssen* und *dürfen* nicht nur alle geistigen Vorarbeiten der Geschlechter, die vor uns lebten, als ererbtes Eigenthum hinnehmen, sondern unsere eigentliche Kulturaufgabe besteht darin: Alles, was wir etwa auf dem schweren Wege der Gedanken erinnern, erfinden oder schaffen, so ins Leben hineinzutragen, daß es so bald wie möglich *alltäglich* und von allen, die nach uns kommen, eben so ohne selbstschöpferische Gedanken-Operationen benutzt, genossen und aufgenommen werde, wie wir es mit der Uhr in der Westentasche, mit dem Wochenmarkt und der Briefpost und nicht minder und in gleicher Berechtigung mit dem Lehrsatz des Pythagoras machen. (AG 108f.)[16]

16 | [We *must* and *shall* not accept all intellectual preliminary works of the sexes that lived before our times as inherited property, but our real cultural task consists in: everything that we remember, invent, or create on the difficult path of thought must be carried into life so that it will be *ordinary* as soon as possible and used and enjoyed and absorbed by all people who come after us; without self-creative thought operations, as we do with the clock in the vest pocket, with the weekly market and with the letter post, and no less and with the same justification with the theorem of Pythagoras.]
Bernstein goes on: "Aber hiermit *müssen* wir nicht nur zufrieden sein, sondern wir *dürfen* es auch. Ja, es ist ein Kulturgesetz, das für die Wissenschaft ebenso wie für das Leben gilt. Wir können ebensowenig alle geistigen Vorarbeiten durchmachen, die den großen Pythagoras auf die Erfindung seines berühmten Lehrsatzes leiten, so wenig wir mit dem Frühstück warten können, bis wir uns selber etwa Thee aus China oder Kaffee aus Mokka geholt haben werden!" [But we do not just *have to* be satisfied with that, we also *can* be. Yes, it is a cultural law that applies to science as well as to life as such. Neither can we

Compaction is, as this quote points out, a central component of technical and intellectual development, it is downright a condition for the success of new ideas. Although Bernstein so emphatically welcomed the trivialization and compaction of cultural achievements, his texts are characterized by a significant ambiguity: paradoxically, it was Bernstein himself who gave things their history, who referred to the threads of the networks behind them, and, thus, counteracted their thoughtless use by confronting the "Ordnung der Alltäglichkeit" [order of the everyday] (AG 140) with its complexity created by human and non-human actors – and thereby opened the blackbox.

Reverse Blackboxing 2.0 – Abstraction and Inscription

About 200 years later, things are – and this may not be surprising in view of how far modernity has progressed – quite different: Bruno Latour, with the help of strong arguments, vehemently refuses to be called an enemy of technology. However, there is no talk about an unconditional affirmation of and a euphoria for the advancement and development of new technologies. Rather, Latour argues for the other side of what Bernstein had in mind – the visualization of actors involved in new technologies. The hybrids or monsters, as Latour calls them with reference to Shelley's *Frankenstein*, must be socialized, and this means, first of all, to be made observable. He declares himself not least in favor of ecological reasons, as one can see especially in his programmatic and at the same time political text *Politics of Nature – How to bring the sciences into democracy* (2004) (and perhaps Bernstein would have reconsidered his findings of an increase in spiritual achievements due to an increased correspondence, if he had followed a conversation on *WhatsApp, wechat, iMessage* or the tweets of US President Donald Trump). Latour, however, does not observe the everyday, but the scientific everyday life and develops an idea commensurable to Bernstein (even though he draws exactly opposite conclusions from Bernstein's findings). But according to him, a form of compaction, more precisely: blackboxing, guarantees scientific success. With blackboxing, an

> expression from the sociology of science that refers to the way scientific and technical work is made invisible by its own success. When a machine runs efficiently, when a matter of fact is settled, one need focus only on its inputs and outputs and not on its

---

undergo all the spiritual preparation which guides the great Pythagoras in the invention of his famous theorem, nor can we wait for breakfast until we have brought tea from China or coffee from Mocha!] (AG 108)

internal complexity. Thus, paradoxically, the more science and technology succeed, the more opaque and obscure they become.[17]

As an example of this kind of blackboxing, Latour draws on the example of the overhead projector, which suddenly "breaks down": Only its "crisis reminds us of the projector's existence",[18] and only the malfunction that brings technicians, who examine the device, into the arena, makes the individual elements that the blackbox overhead projector consists of beyond its operational capability visible. Latour is willing – unlike Bernstein, who opted for *more* darkening on the same basis – to bring light into the darkness of science: For example, if he goes to the laboratory, when he analyzes studies of Pasteur or Einstein, his attitude towards observation can be designated as *reverse blackboxing*. This means that he looks at the processes and the actors involved in these processes, which lead to the production of, so-called, scientific facts. He points at the operational chains behind this production and directs the view in such a way – basically analogous to Bernstein, but more detailed and with a more contrastive program – to all actors involved, the scientists, but also the apparatuses, documents, texts; in the end, to everything that produces inscriptions, under which he not only subsumes letters with a broader scriptural concept borrowed from Derrida, but also "traces, spots, points, histograms, recorded numbers, spectra, peaks, and so on."[19] The aim is – of course – not to make science less successful by breaking up the blackbox (whereas a deceleration in the sense of a shift from modernization to greening is an important part of the aim of the ANT Latourian provenance), but with the epistemological interest in a science of science.

This program can particularly be illustrated by a short example from Latour's text *A Relativistic Account of Einstein's Relativity*, in which Latour explores Einstein's account of the special and general relativity theory of 1920.[20]

17 | Bruno Latour: *Pandora's Hope. Essays on the Reality of Science* (Cambridge et.al.: Harvard University Press 1999), 304.

18 | Ibid., 183.

19 | Bruno Latour/Steve Woolgar: *Laboratory Life. The Construction of Scientific Facts* (Princeton: Princeton University Press, 1986), 88.

20 | This text was – as mentioned at the beginning – a stumbling block in the so-called Science Wars. Latour's essay became a target for the harshest criticism, especially in the polemic text against postmodern thinking *Fashionable Nonsense: Postmodern Intellectuals' Abuse of Science* from 1999, written by the physicists Alan Sokal and Jean Bricmont. In a polemical style, they state that Latour's essay "illustrates perfectly the problems encountered by a sociologist who aims to analyze the content of a scientific theory he does not understand very well." Jean Bricmont/Alan Sokal: *Fashionable Nonsense: Postmodern Intellectuals' Abuse of Science* (New York: Picador 1998), 124.

In the following, I am interested in Latour's reading of Einstein's treatment with abstract concepts in his semi-popular writing. What he emphasizes is that the physicist does not want to be content with vague general terms. Einstein writes: "In the first place, we entirely shun the vague word 'space', of which, we must honestly acknowledge, we cannot form the slightest conception".[21] What follows then is a process by which these concepts are put into a meaningful context so that a concrete meaning is assigned to them. On the basis of a thought experiment on the simultaneous impact of two flashes, Einstein notes:

> The concept does not exist for the physicist until he has the possibility of discovering whether or not it is fulfilled in an actual case. We thus require a definition of simultaneity such that this definition supplies us with the method by means of which, in the present case, he can decide by experiment whether or not both the lightning strokes occurred simultaneously. As long as this requirement is not satisfied, I allow myself to be deceived as a physicist (and of course the same applies if I am not a physicist), when I imagine that I am able to attach a meaning to the statement of simultaneity. (I would ask the reader not to proceed farther until he is fully convinced on this point.)[22]

It is only through using clocks – and here a significant congruence with Bernstein's statements can be established – that an operational concept of time can be generated: "Under these conditions we understand by the 'time' of an event the reading (position of the hands) of that one of these clocks which is in the immediate vicinity (in space) of the event. In this manner a time-value is associated with every event which is essentially capable of observation."[23] According to Latour's understanding, Einstein replaced the fuzzy term 'time' with a dynamic network of observers and clocks. Hence, time is not an absolute quantity, but something that can be deduced from the process of measuring and comparing. Conceptual abstractions – and this applies not only to the concept of space or time, but also to terms like society, the social and the social context, because it is Latour's aim to draw conclusions on the constitution of

---

However, it is equally polemical to discover the problems a physicist has to face, who wants to criticize a scientific-sociological text whose formation he did not understand very well. Sokol and Bricmont, in turn, are not interested in the true interest of Latour's text: "For the sake of brevity, we won't enter into the sociological conclusions Latour purports to draw from his study of relativity, but shall simply point out that his argument is undermined by several fundamental misunderstandings about the theory of relativity itself." (ibid.)

21 | Albert Einstein: *Relativity. The Special and General Theory.* Translated by Robert W. Lawson (New York: Pi Press, 2005), 13f.

22 | Ibid., 30.

23 | Ibid., 32.

the social based on Einstein's text – must be substituted by observation and an accurate description of actor networks, which is what Latour observes in Einstein's approach: "Einstein takes the instruments to be what *generates* space and and time. [...] Einstein's first move in this text is to bring the abstractions back to the inscriptions and to the hard work of producing them."[24]

'Bring the abstractions back to the inscriptions' – this is what Latour is all about (and in his reading, Einstein too). Thus, writing scenes are created in which human and non-human actors work together – which will be discussed later.

For Latour, space and time are not only relevant with regards to inscriptions and conceptual work. Likewise, what has to be analyzed becomes the analytical instrument. Latour uses a semiotic approach to represent the operational chains of textual semiotics by Algirdas Julien Greimas. This model, among others, has the advantage that it comes from actants, which can be both human and non-human, and this is the reason why it is, as a model, so attractive for the ANT since it already conceptually undermines the *a priori* distinction between subject and object. Based on a semiotic analysis, one can track how the different actors or actants, human or non-human, inscribe themselves in the text. In Latour's exploration of *Einstein's Relativity*, he reveals his analytical tools more clearly than anywhere else, making the various actors in the text traceable through the practices of *shifting in* and *out*.

The *shifting* operation is constitutive for any kind of text – literary as well as scientific – because it can transport *enunciator* as well as *enunciatee*, which are stuck in space and time, into other times and to other places:

> The shifting operations, and the building up of reality that ensues, have another important effect on the reader. While the enunciator and the reader (also called 'enunciatee') are both stuck to one portion of space and time and to one character [...], the effect of the shifting-out operation is to delegate them elsewhere, and then, thanks to the shifting-characters back. If there were no shifting, there would be no way of ever escaping from the narrow confines of *hic et nunc*, and no way of ever defining who the enunciator is. There would be utter silence. No science, no politics, no art would be possible. The delegation provided by the triple shifting – actorial, spatial and temporal – is the basis of every discourse. These simple semiotic tools allow us to follow precisely practices usually subsumed under the names of 'power', 'institution' and 'domination', as well as others such as 'instruments' and 'equations' [...].[25]

24 | Bruno Latour: "A relativistic Account of Einstein's Relativity." *Social Studies of Science* 18, no. 1 (1988), 3-44, here 11.

25 | Ibid., 8f. A more detailed analysis of the relationship between fictional and scientific genres can be found in Latour's recent study *An Inquiry into Modes of Existence.*

The difference between fictional and scientific texts is merely that the latter – in contrast to the 'savaged' actants of fiction (no reader would seriously expect to find evidences about the stories of Hercule Poirot in Agatha Christie's desk, thus Latour's example)[26] – domesticates their actants and charges them to come back from these places and from these times with documents, information, etc., with which they can give an account of their findings.

This proximity between fictional and scientific text production exposes Latour very vividly in his own works – if one does not retrace the program behind this procedure, one can easily get the impression that one must deal with 'elegant non-sense'. Because Latour always resorts to literary genres, he draws attention to a transgression of boundaries between genres on the relations between the different disciplines: be it that he connects Pasteur's 'discovery' of lactic acid to the fairy tale of Cinderella,[27] that he investigatively tracks the story of ARAMIS, which he describes as *scientifiction*, as a detective novel to clarify the circumstances of the death of a fully automatic, track-guided transport system, that he authors his explanations of the *humanités scientifiques* as an epistolary novel or that he writes his scientific historical study *Laboratory Life* in the style of the *Lettres Persanes* written by Montesquieu.

Writing Scenes in the Lab – of Traces, Spots, Points and Histograms

For the latter study *Laboratory Life*, Latour resided at the Salk Institute in California between 1975 and 1977. Along with Steve Woolgar, he participated in observations that are considered groundbreaking in the field of scientific anthropology. However, both amusingly and paradoxically, it is precisely the lack of training as a sociologist and an anthropologist that enabled him to conduct the study, as a quote from the epilogue of the second issue of *Laboratory Life* makes clear:

> Professor Latour's knowledge of science was non-existent; his mastery of English was very poor; and he was completely unaware of the existence of the social studies of science. Apart from (or perhaps even because of) this last feature, he was thus in the classic position of the ethnographer.[28]

An Anthropology of the Moderns (published in French in 2012). There he pleads for assigning an ontological status to the 'beings of fiction'.

26 | Cf. ibid., 12f.

27 | Cf. Latour, *Pandora's Hope*, 175.

28 | Latour, *Laboratory Life*, 273.

The fact that this characterization of Latour's (highly questionable) qualification for the study was written by himself is far more than an ironic twist or a modest gesture of unpretentious understatement: To break up the blackboxes – as the example with the defective overhead projector showed – a disruption/ interference is required for his laboratory studies; the supposedly dilettante sociologist Latour generated this disruption himself so that the study could produce results precisely because of the precarious 'ethnographer's' prerequisites.

The quite ambitious goal of Latour and Woolgar's anthropological research is "to show through empirical investigation how […] craft practices [scientific skills and techniques, C.J.] are organized into a systematic and *tidied* research report".[29] The term *tidied* research report plays a considerable role; the observations of Latour's *We have never been modern* (1991) as well as basically all texts were about visualizing the two modern levels of translation, i.e. the production of hybrids and purification, i.e. the invisibilization of this production of hybrids on a theoretical level, the 'modern constitution'. The question at this point, however, is: From *what* exactly should the research report be rectified? Here, Latour comes to a very interesting conclusion: Roger Guillemin, the head of the study at the Salk Institute, whose invitation Latour had followed, was in search of an evidence of the hormone TRF, the Thyrotrophin-Releasing-Factor. A gigantic network with a monstrous apparatus of living things, instruments and scientists was served up. Latour opened the blackbox of scientific inscriptions by focusing on the inscription devices – a whole amalgam of instruments, analogous to Bernstein's description of the conditions of possibility for the development of an inconspicuous steel spring, is responsible for scientific innovations in the 20th century: At the beginning of the chain of operations, there are laboratory rats, from which laboratory samples are taken. The samples undergo a radical transformation; they are converted into digits by an apparatus, which are then translated into numbers, graphs and texts, whereby the samples are worthless and become waste. Now, the focus is on the paper with the digits – which in turn is used as an input for the PC – from which a datasheet is created, which is basically the most important product of the entire procedure.[30] From this, in turn, a graph is created, the curve is then discussed and changed, from which – at best – a publication is created, which, in turn,

29 | Ibid., 29, my emphasis.

30 | One wonders what happens to the elements of blackboxes that are not available for further coordination of interests, that is, what leaves the operational chains and the assembly of human and non-human beings. These things are dropped; their path will not be pursued any further. Notably, Latour does not address the wastebasket in the computer room in this context, which symbolically materializes the process of cleaning and the path of the waste. Cf. Latour, *Laboratory Life*, 100, Photograph 11.

can actuate a new cycle, if appreciated by the scientific world. The goal of the scientist, and, at the same time, the basis of research success is to come up with statements in a factlike status, preferably without any modality – ideally A = B, without quotation marks and without footnote.

From what the text is being cleaned up of becomes evident with regards to the translation- and abstraction processes: The general intention of authors of scientific publications is to let their results, achieved with the help of instruments, *speak for themselves*, i.e. the human factor within the "construction" of a scientific fact is spread out. According to Latour, the device makes it "easy to get that impression that substances directly provide their own 'signatures'".[31] The writing scenes with shared agency that Latour tracks down are thus scriptures of the 'real', a 'real' that works its way to the surface via inscription instruments, thus leading to 'objective' scientific facts in the finally produced text.

With Latour's approach, it is possible to trace how scientific facts are constructed in the laboratory so that they are not only real, but at the same time always socially and constructively observable. Once the final product – the curve – is created, the entire process/individuals/apparatus can be forgotten, the act of producing can be spread out and the traces of authorship can be blurred.[32] The laboratory is translated into statements, its existence then no longer plays a role – instead there are ideas, theories and reasons, which subsequently, (may) lead to a stabilization of the obtained knowledge.

The question that I would like to add to my remarks is whether the reflection of *Digital Humanities* enables a similar analysis of inscription instruments and operational practices, such as the one Latour does in the laboratory. One might think of Moretti's *Graphs Maps Trees* (2005), whose *distant reading* techniques are translated into diagrams and graphs and which are very similar to the final products of the Salk Institute. Possibly and with the material of the *digital humanities*, a blackbox could be opened, by making knowledge available again to a large extent, which itself has sedimented and condensed over centuries. However, this would then be a double farewell – not only a farewell from the goose quill, but also from conventional writing scenes, not in literature, but in the field of literary studies.

This observation leads me back to the beginning of my exposition, namely to Aaron Bernstein. He anticipates – once more completely non-melancholic – the fate of his text, which will get lost like the millions of needles: "Und nun

31 | Ibid., 51.

32 | The approach of classical philology in the sense of Karl Lachmann shows a counter-development: For the creation of a stem, all text documents are collected to reconstruct a preferably gapless text genealogy (the procedure also produces exclusions – such as in the form of *eliminatio*). The textual criticism is – in this way – interested in the return of the history, in the archiving of the individual genesis of the texts.

mag denn auch diese Betrachtung ihren Weg hinaus in die Lesewelt nehmen, um auch wieder verloren zu gehen in dem großen unübersehbar gewordenen Strome der Betrachtungen, die der Zeitenlauf an unserm reichen Zeitalter vorüberführt." (VD 32)[33]

What he is not able to see in his little pretentious vision is that new techniques of digitization are used to break up the compaction again, and that the sedimented knowledge can, thus, be revisited at its source and can be subject to a *reversed blackboxing*. However, the question then is whether the accumulation of digital documents must be understood as a progress or a retarding moment.

33 | [And now even this consideration may take its way out into the world of reading in order to get lost again in the large unmissable streams of reflections, which the course of time drives past our rich age.]

On-the-Table

Text Curating in the Electronic Age

Júlia Tóth-Czifra

For Hermes

This is not the first and, *God only knows*, may not be the last time I refer to Friedrich Kittler's text from 2007 entitled "Philologische und Homerische Frage".[1] In his lecture Kittler evokes Hermes without calling him by name, referring to him with the meaningful and suggestive expression, "a technically very talented God". A technically very talented God, of whom we, philologists, should remind ourselves as often as possible. Therefore, I would like this essay to be referred to as a memo: a short, rough, and fallible note that, as a slip on the table, might warn of something we tend to forget[2] during our everyday practices, and help us speculate over the issues we *will* face in the future as consequences of our exercises and decisions today.

As a "philologically educated factory worker," as I prefer to call myself,[3] I am concerned about digital humanities in two ways. Firstly: I am curious to see how the recently improved methods (standards of digitizing, the use of databases, creating visualizations, etc.) will cope with the past. I mean how they process, archive and create access to the documents of bygone centuries. In this regard, I think, success is a question of time and money. With the countless related digital projects underway, we are on the right path to a genuine "broad-

1 | Friedrich Kittler, "Philologische und Homerische Frage," in *Was ist eine philologische Frage?*, ed. Jürgen Paul Schwindt (Frankfurt am Main: Suhrkamp, 2009), 288-289.

2 | In the sense in which the articles by Charlotte Jaekel and Gábor Palkó in this volume describe the blackboxing of material practices of textual editing or scholarly research as 'forgetting'.

3 | I am a full-time editor of Kalligram Publishing House (Budapest), but, on the other hand, I try to remain active in the field of literary studies as well.

ening of our present", as Gumbrecht would put it,[4] with the accessible past. But in the meantime, the present itself tends to slip by.

That would be my second point: how digital philology *today* could prevent or solve in advance problems that will crop up in a few decades. One of the causes of the difficulties future generations will face is the partial separation of technology and everyday practice. Let there be no doubt: our technological environment would already make it possible to produce all the documents in a standardized, always already identified digital way, so as "born-digitals". But totally standardized and tracked digital production is for the moment only a theoretical possibility. It exists, ironically enough, only on paper.[5] The truth is that the everyday practices involved in the production of texts are much more conservative and highly habitual. On the one hand, the habitual nature of these practices derives from the private routines of the authors. You cannot and should not persuade someone who used pen and paper throughout his/her life of the advantages of a word processor, nor should you force someone to upload manuscripts to Google Docs instead of sending Word documents. On the other hand, the book industry also has its long-running production habits, partly as protocol, partly as unwritten routine.[6] But then the question arises: at which stage of production could the latest achievements of digital humanities enter the process in order to do their job *real-time?* That is, in what way could the simultaneity of the production of the text and of its philological processing come true?

In the following my aim is to share observations concerning some of the practical phenomena I face every day as an editor, and I will attempt to link these observations to questions I face as a philologist, or – sticking to this expression – as a philologically educated factory worker.

The collaborative nature of literary production is not a novelty, and this aspect has been part of textual criticism for decades. Think of the so called *social* orientated approaches of, for example, D. F. McKenzie, Dino Buzzetti, or Jerome J. McGann, and of *social textual criticism* "[...] which denies the automatic priority given to author's intentions and sees textual creation as a collaborative, social act."[7] It suffices here to recall Jerome J. McGann's famous expression of a "continuous production text," certainly with the restriction that

4 | Cf. Hans Ulrich Gumbrecht, *Our Broad Present: Time and Contemporary Culture* (New York: Columbia Unversity Press, 2014).

5 | Cf. the articles by Nicolas Pethes and Melinda Vásári in this volume.

6 | It would be, thus, interesting to examine to what extent publishing houses resembles the "laboratory", and to what extend the "factory". See: Bruno Latour and Steve Woolgar, *Laboratory Life: The Construction of Scientific Facts* (Beverly Hills: Sage Publications, 1979); Hans-Jörg Rheinberger, *Toward a History of Epistemic Things: Synthesizing Proteins in the Test Tube* (Stanford: Stanford University Press, 1997).

7 | David C. Greetham, *Theories of the Text* (Oxford: Oxford University Press, 1999), 9.

he mainly focused on editions, i.e. the published versions of a book, on the bibliographical codes of cultural practices, and on the traces of the different participants. Nevertheless, the statement is true: “more authorities sit at the textual table than the author”.[8] And the question of authority is not the only one at this table. Another one precedes all the deliberations, namely: who was the *archivist* among the authorities?[9]

Correspondences between publishers and authors or the handwritten notes of a typesetter in the margins are often found in the literary estates [*Nachlässe*] of 19th or 20th century authors. One can potentially find all the related traces of editorial collaboration, though with a significant restriction: these literary estates provide only the documents the author possessed. Many others (letters, contracts, manuscripts and proofs, even plates) became part of the archives of the publishing and printing house itself. The problem – at least in Hungary – is the hard fate of the editorial estates of the same period. It is also due partly to historical events (the two world wars), partly to the not less historical author-centered and manuscript-fetishized approach[10] of institutional literary archives (which have been based and focused predominantly on the authorial estates), as well as – and this is of crucial importance, considering the present aspect – partly to the neglect of the publishing houses themselves.

A couple of years ago I presented a few examples of archiving forms concerning the literary production of the early 20th century.[11] I referred to institutional forms, but my train of thought focused on the private archiving methods of the authors. But, turning back to the textual table of McGann, the question comes up: during the process of textual production, especially speaking of the non-published working material, who else has the duty and the responsibility of archiving? Who has the authority today to do so, when the fast and various forms of written communication make the collaborative nature of literary production even more prominent, as well as complicated, and, of course, much harder to trace?

E-mails and chat conversations, shared digital documents, and online word processors like Google Docs are natural parts of the editing process nowadays, but the basic structure is as simple as it was a hundred years ago. It's the triangle of the author, the publisher, and the editor. The agreement concerning the terms and conditions of publication (financial questions, dates, the format

8 | Dino Buzzetti and Jerome McGann, *Electronic Textual Editing: Critical Editing in a Digital Horizon*, accesed July 1, 2018, http://www.tei-c.org/About/Archive_new/ETE/Preview/mcgann.xml.

9 | Cf. Björn Sonnenberg-Schrank's description of philological hoarding in this volume.

10 | Cf. the article by Livia Kleinwächter in this volume.

11 | Júlia Tóth-Czifra, “Kivágás - mentés - beillesztés - mentés másként,” [Cut - Save - Paste - Save as] *Kalligram* 23, no. 9 (September 2014): 80-85.

of the book, the number of copies etc.) is reached by the author and the publisher. Then the publisher assigns an editor to the task and supervises his or her work from the beginning to the end. Then the author and the editor start to work together on the text, and the editor mediates between the author and the publisher, as well as between the proofreader and the author and, if needed, between the maker-up and the author.[12] The editing process at my publishing house has at least eleven stages with different textual qualities:

1. The author sends the publishing house the manuscript in the form of a text file.
2. The editor gets a printed version of that.
3. After reading the printed version, the editor proposes modifications and corrections, marked on the printed manuscript.
4. The author goes through the proposals and accepts or refuses them, and makes his or her own proposals. (These two phases can be repeated.)
5. The editor produces the digital text file for making-up. (It is also an interesting question here, who designs the book: who chooses the format, the font types, the font area etc.)
6. After the making-up, the publisher gets a PDF file.
7. The PDF it printed in two (or three) copies as proofs: for the author, for the editor, and for the proofreader.
8. After the proofreading has been done, the editor gathers the three versions. At first, he or she interleaves his or her own corrections with the ones made by the proofreader, then he or she discusses them all with the author (who, again, accepts or refuses them), and adds the author's own alterations after examining his or her proof.
9. The editor adds all the corrections as proof marks to the PDF file and sends it back to the maker-up.
10. The maker-up sends a new, revised PDF file.
11. The editor double-checks to be sure the corrections have been made,[13] and asks for them again, if needed. Then he or she passes the proofs on to the press.

The process, thus, produces at least nine different versions, several of which are not even digital. It is worth stopping here for a moment. There seems to be no real need of paper-based material in the digital age. One could easily do the proof-reading on screen, why not? What is the sense of troubling oneself with

12 | The word "maker-up" [*Umbrecher* in German] itself implies the factory character of literary production: its other meaning is "an assembler or packer of manufactured goods."

13 | Unfortunately with McLeod's so-called "Wimbledon Method"...

printed stuff? Since the 1980s, scholars in many fields, including psychology, media studies, computer engineering, and information and library sciences, have published extensive studies investigating one question: how does reading on screens differ from reading text on printed paper?[14] They observed the differences in terms of speed, accuracy, fatigue, and comprehension on the basis of eye movements, visual angles, etc. "By the early 1990s, most studies concluded that people read more slowly, less accurately, and less comprehensively when reading from screens than when reading from the printed page. Research since then, however, has produced mixed results. Some studies have confirmed previous conclusions, while many more have found few significant differences in reading speed, accuracy of recall, or comprehension between paper and screen."[15] As far as I know, one of the most recent study on the subject was published in February 2017 in the journal *Computers in Human Behavior* with the title "Cognitive map or medium materiality? Reading on paper and screen." The authors, Jinghui Hou, Justin Rashid, and Kwan Min Lee, investigated the two most widespread mechanisms which were held responsible for the different reading outcomes, and they tried to isolate the effects of these two mechanisms.

> The first mechanism is concerned with the psychological aspects of reading behavior. It contends that screens make it difficult for readers to construct an effective cognitive map, or a spatial representation, of the text (Li, Chen, & Yang, 2013; Payne & Reader, 2006). This weak efficiency for constructing cognitive maps, in turn, impairs navigational performance (i.e., searching for or locating a piece of textual information), reading speed, content recall, and reading comprehension (Li et al., 2013; Payne & Reader, 2006). The second mechanism focuses on the material characteristics of the presentation medium (screen or paper), and it suggests that the materiality of the reading medium influences text processing (Mangen & Schilhab, 2012; Mangen, 2008). Text on

14 | Only three examples of the early reflections: J. D. Gould and N. Grischkowsky, "Doing the Same Work with Hard Copy and with Cathode-Ray Tube (CRT) Computer Terminals," *Human Factors: The Journal of the Human Factors and Ergonomics Society*, no. 26 (1984): 323-337; Paul Muter et al., "Extended Reading of Continuous Text on Television Screens," *Human Factors* 24, no. 5 (1982): 501-508; Pat Wright and Ann Lickorish, "Proof-reading texts on screen and paper," *Behaviour and Information Technology* 3, no. 2 (1983): 227-235.

15 | See the rich summary and bibliography of the former studies in: Jinghui Hou, Justin Rashid, and Kwan Min Lee, "Cognitive map or medium materiality? Reading on paper and screen," *Computers in Human Behavior* 67, (February 2017): 84-94. Further literature: Baha Makhoul, Thuraia Copti-Mshael, "Reading Comprehension as a Function of Text Genre and Presentation Environment: Comprehension of Narrative and Informational Texts in a Computer-Assisted Environment vs. Print," *Psychology* 6, No. 8 (June 26, 2015): 1001-1112.

paper is touchable and tangible, whereas text on screens is intangible, mediated, and detached from the physical support of the reading medium. The haptic interactions with paper text afford readers richer sensorimotor engagement with the text compared to screen text, which enhances information encoding and comprehension.[16]

After reviewing the earlier direct tests, the research employed a three-group between-subject comparison design. The three subjects were: paper vs. digital equivalent vs. digital disrupted view. The reading material used in this study was a comic book. The digital equivalent means that one full page of the comic is displayed. The digital disrupted view zoomed in on each individual panel. The "results indicated that reading a paper book was similar to reading its digital equivalent, both of which were better than reading the digital disrupted view version in terms of reading comprehension, feelings of fatigue, and immersion."[17] In general, the inquiry provided support for hypotheses based on the cognitive map mechanism, but not for the hypotheses following the medium materiality mechanism.[18] Problems, as the article itself admits, may arise when, instead of comics, other, exclusively narrative types come into the picture.

Word for word: into the picture. On my 15,6-inch laptop display, a proof page of a book with the dimensions of 132 and 208 mm looks like this (see Fig. 1, p. 153).

It's not hard to see that if I try to keep the page as a whole, the text becomes illegibly small, impossible to read. It's not much better with my 25-inch desktop display as well, which is not portable. The readable size on screen, on the other hand, means the disruption of the page. And then I immediately face the differences between the paper and the digital disrupted view mentioned above.[19]

16 | Jinghui Hou, Justin Rashid and Kwan Min Lee, "Cognitive map or medium materiality? Reading on paper and screen," 84.

17 | Jinghui Hou, Justin Rashid, and Kwan Min Lee, "Cognitive map or medium materiality? Reading on paper and screen," 92.

18 | The findings implied that reading on a screen could match that of reading from paper if the representation of the document on electronic reading devices resemble that of the printed book.

19 | See Dániel Kozák's argument on the segmentation of semantic and non-semantic elements in this volume.

Fig. 1: A proof page of a book with the dimensions of 132 and 208 mm on a 15,6 inch laptop display. Collected Poems of Walther von der Vogelweide, trasl. László Márton (Budapest: Kalligram, 2017), p. 400, screenshot by Júlia Tóth-Cifra

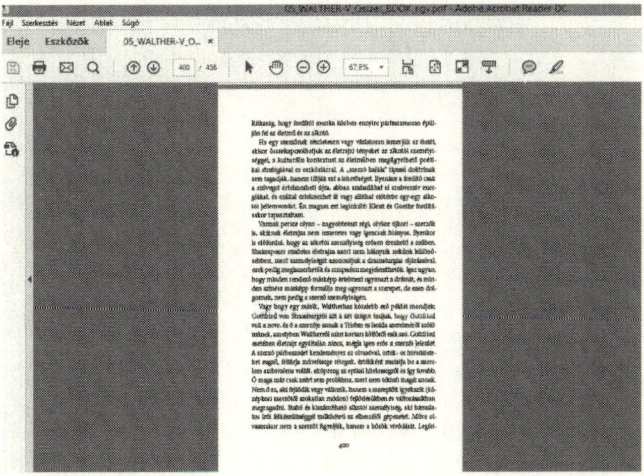

Fig. 2: The readable size on screen means the disruption of the page. Collected Poems of Walther von der Vogelweide, trasl. László Márton (Budapest: Kalligram, 2017), p. 400, screenshot by Júlia Tóth-Czifra

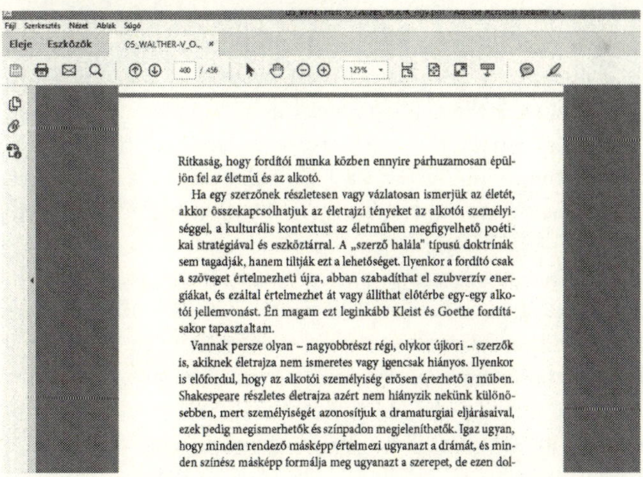

Ritkaság, hogy fordítói munka közben ennyire párhuzamosan épül-jön fel az életmű és az alkotó.

Ha egy szerzőnek részletesen vagy vázlatosan ismerjük az életét, akkor összekapcsolhatjuk az életrajzi tényeket az alkotói személyi-séggel, a kulturális kontextust az életműben megfigyelhető poéti-kai stratégiával és eszköztárral. A „szerző halála" típusú doktrínák sem tagadják, hanem tiltják ezt a lehetőséget. Ilyenkor a fordító csak a szöveget értelmezheti újra, abban szabadíthat el szubverzív ener-giákat, és ezáltal értelmezhet át vagy állíthat előtérbe egy-egy alko-tói jellemvonást. Én magam ezt leginkább Kleist és Goethe fordítá-sakor tapasztaltam.

Vannak persze olyan – nagyobbrészt régi, olykor újkori – szerzők is, akiknek életrajza nem ismeretes vagy igencsak hiányos. Ilyenkor is előfordul, hogy az alkotói személyiség erősen érezhető a műben. Shakespeare részletes életrajza azért nem hiányzik nekünk különö-sebben, mert személyiségét azonosítjuk a dramaturgiai eljárásaival, ezek pedig megismerhetők és színpadon megjeleníthetők. Igaz ugyan, hogy minden rendező másképp értelmezi ugyanazt a drámát, és min-den színész másképp formálja meg ugyanazt a szerepet, de ezen dol-

Thus, paper-stages seem to be unavoidable during the process of editing. I do not rule out the possibility that, in addition to the mental mechanisms described above, private habits also play roles in people's preferences for paper-based proofs. (Personally, I find twice as many mistakes when using a printed

Fig. 3: The limited space of an editor's archive. Part of a bookshelf at the authors home. Photo: Tóth-Czifra Júlia

copy than when using a digital display.) And it might be only a question of time and training to make the difference disappear.[20]

In the end, we must consider the following consequences: After the process of editing, we end up with a bunch of mixed type variants which could be of importance concerning both a future critical edition, both the editorial administration. Archiving the born-digital material appears to be easy (and to some extent automatic). The systematic archiving is usually done by the editor. Neither the author nor the maker-up receives all the files, only the editor does, and only the editor can put all of them in a folder and keep them on the HDD or upload them to the cloud. But is that really all? Does it make the digital stages secure? The responsibility and authority of the editor tends to be disproportionately large here.

And it is even more disproportionate in the case of paper-based materials. The authors quite often do not keep the printed versions with their handwritten revisions and remarks. Usually, the editor keeps them in order to add all the notes and corrections to the proofs and in order to be able to follow and check them during the making-up of the present and the following editions. So the editor becomes the archivist. Then he or she can decide whether to keep the

20 | See: Christian Benne, *Erfindung des Manuskripts: Zu Theorie und Geschichte literarischer Gegenständlichkeit* (Berlin: Suhrkamp, 2015), 600-614. The emergence of "Literarische Handschriften" is not bound to the very moment of the investment of printing itself – but to the change of reading habits.

papers at home, where he/she usually works, or take them to the publishing house. After a while, space becomes limited in any case.

The publishing house, thus, faces the choice of whether to accept responsibility for the *longue durée*-archiving, or, as was done in the 19th and early 20th centuries, simply sort out and get rid of the 'unnecessary' mass of paper after a period of time. The difference, as far as I can judge, is that, thanks to changes in technology, we do not need to make this choice today. My suggestion would be that publishers scan all the paper-based versions, archive them as digital objects (with appropriate IDs), and create datasets of them along with born-digital versions. This is not intended as a humanitarian or noble gesture towards the scholars. It is in the best interests of the publisher itself to make the process through which the work came into being verifiable and retrievable. Again: it's a question of time and money. Various services are available for publishing houses, but in terms of cooperative effort, the publisher is mostly the content provider who makes its digital books and articles available on a certain surface for sale (CEEOL, Ingenta, EBSCO, etc.), or it pays to have the publications indexed (Crossref, ScienceOpen). On the one hand, these opportunities serve most of all the academic field.[21] On the other, these services aim to establish readerships that are as broad as possible, or rather, as numerous as possible, in other words, to make the publisher's (or the author's) titles public and widely familiar. But what about the private, so called pro domo materials of a publisher? What kind of business services are available in terms of archiving and organizing?

If a service of this kind were available and affordable, then the papers could be given back to the authors, who could decide whether to keep and reuse them or to throw them away. Thus, the responsibility and authority of archiving would be well (or at least better) balanced. The publishing house, without having to address problems involving storage capacity, would only keep and store the data that concerns the publisher. And it would be kept in a way that consists and records, for example, the basic temporal information on the process of editing, in a way that makes it decisively harder to manipulate the documents subsequently without any digital traces of the manipulation. It does not mean a duplication of the sources then, because the digitized version in the estate [*Nachlass*, or rather the *Vorlass*] of the publisher is fixed and joined with the data concerning its temporal and authorial peculiarity, while the paper-based source in the *Vorlass* of the author is not, and is open for manipulation.

Speaking of which: the fairy tale of the future philologists and textual scholars will turn into a nightmare at a certain point. Everyday editorial practices will make it extremely hard to do justice around the table of McGann. If

21 | The differences between publishing academic and literary works and the things philology could learn from the best practices of the former would be worth another essay.

the editorial archiving method outlined above (or one resembling it) is adopted, significantly more sources will be available for a critical edition or for research than today. And the handwriting of the author will not always help scholars decide in questions of authority or authenticity. For example, the combining process of the author's and the editor's proof often takes place in person, as does the discussion of the editor's proposals. On such occasions, it is usually the author who dictates the new variants and the editor who notes them down. Even if the new variant was suggested by the author, one will only find the handwriting of the editor on the pages, without any chance to distinguish the accepted editorial proposals from the author's newly made additions.

It will put textual criticism in a difficult position, but, I hope, in the long run it will set it free, demonstrating that the search for the clear intentions of the author is a hopeless pursuit – especially when the authors themselves accept the collaborative nature of literary production. This is what early 20th century authors did when they applied newspaper clippings as part of a new manuscript without proofreading them properly. And this is what contemporary authors do when they dictate personally or send their alterations via SMS, Messenger, and Skype to the editor without signing the particular proof pages. On the other hand, we should not simply throw in the towel. There are new text formats, for example Google Docs, which try to fix different text layers in a detailed way.[22] We, as it seems, will have to work within controversial bounds.

In order to get to the point I am most interested in, let me deconstruct the bottom line of my essay with the question: is that *really* that important to archive these documents? Are they interesting at all? Who cares what the maker-up did? Does a proof really have philological relevance? I'm not sure, I would say. But then I think of the fact how glad I would be to have more sources of this kind from the 19th and early 20th century, supporting my researches on the working methods of the authors in that age. But I do not have them, because the publishers and editors of that time had the same answers to the above mentioned questions – and threw the mass of paper away. I do not blame them. Speaking of our own simplest and most frequent everyday practices it is natural not to find any particular interests or specialty in them. That is why, actually, they are "everyday practices".

Therefore, the archiving of the documents in question seems absolutely redundant today. But what's wrong with redundancy as such? In his study "Scripts and Scribbles", Hans-Jörg Rheinberger illustrates his considerations on laboratory writing with the example of German botanist Carl Correns. Correns was able to make discoveries he did not even aim at, because his notes consisted

22 | Future textual scholars will have opportunities to detect the non-handwritten, digital traces of partial authorities when working with born-digital material, but only if they gain skills in the very technical side of digital philology as well.

not only of the data that had relevance to the original research subject. "His notes were drafted in such a way that *enough redundancy* and *excess of possible information* existed so as to allow for reorientation of the experimenter's gaze at a later stage."[23]

Archiving is a practice of storing for later use. The problem is that we cannot predict properly what could be useful later. Careful (or frightened) archiving is, therefore, inevitably redundant. Redundant to be open to possibilities. The question is how to distinguish between possibly productive redundancy and unmanageable, opaque redundancy. That is what we should consider, and particularly now, when storing capacity appears to be no problem anymore, we should consider it *radically*. Or should we just resign ourselves to the fact that negligence towards certain document, our selective storing habits, are also part of our everyday practices, and therefore the lack of information itself will inform us about the literary habits and character of a given age. Like the lack of early 20th century editorial estates, or like the author's missing handwriting on the proof pages today.

23 | Hans-Jörg Rheinberger, "Scripts and Scribbles," *MLN*, no. 3 (April 2003): 627-631.

3. Practices

Opening, Turning, Closing

The Cultural Technology of Browsing and the Differences between the Book as an Object and Digital Texts

Matthias Bickenbach

One of the practices often neglected within discourses on the future of the book in the digital age is browsing in books. For a long time, this discourse was dominated by the catchy phrase of "The End of the Book" – inspired by Marshall McLuhan's euphoric welcoming of the dissolution of the alleged linearity of the book within the Gutenberg galaxy. Over the past years, more elaborated arguments were developed in the light of a new generation of reading devices such as e-books and tablets as well as in the light of the growing number of digitalized text within Open Access repositories. These arguments facilitate a more thorough differentiation between practices of reading on the one hand and the necessity of reading both on screens and in books on the other.[1] Basic distinctions such as 'good vs. bad' or 'focused vs. dispersed' that had dominated cultural criticism for the longest time and had attributed good reading to books and superficial titbits to digital media,[2] seem no longer feasible with respect to

1 | Cf. Michael Hagner: *Zur Sache des Buches* (2. ed. Göttingen: Wallstein, 2015); Axel Kuhn/Christoph Bläsi: "Lesen auf mobilen Lesegeräten 2011. Ergebnisse einer Studie zum Lesen digitaler Texte". In: *Media Perspektiven* 12 (2011), 583-591; Katherine N. Hayles: "How We Read: Close, Hyper, Machine". In: *ADE Bulletin* 150 (2010), 62-79; Andrew Piper: *Book was there. Reading in Electronic Times* (Chicago, London: University of Chicago Press, 2012), Barbara Herrnstein-Smith: "What was "Close Reading"? A Century of Method in Literary Studies". In: *Minnesota Review* 87 (2016), 57-75.

2 | As a contemporary view, cf. Sebastian Böck/Julia Ingelmann e.a. (eds.): *Lesen X.0. Rezeptionsprozesse in der digitalen Gegenwart* (Göttingen: Vandenhoek & Ruprecht 2017). On the critical view oft he decay of reading cultures through electronic media cf. Sven Birkerts: *Die Gutenberg-Elegien: Lesen im elektronischen Zeitalter* (Frankfurt/M.: Fischer 1997) and more recently Nicolas Carr: *Wer bin ich, wenn ich online bin und was macht mein Gehirn solange? Wie das Internet unser Denken verändert* (München: Blessing 2010).

the fact that different motivations of reading (i.e. entertainment vs. information or analysis) or varying reading techniques apply for both, digital and bookish, media.

In the following browsing in books will be highlighted as a hardly noted but basic condition of reading books from a praxeological point of view: Browsing does not reduce the use of textual media to the process of decoding and understanding of contents but reflects on the various uses of the materiality and mediality of texts as cultural technologies of appropriation.[3] My key question is going to be in which way this cultural technology cannot be reduced by the gestures and techniques applied when reading digital texts. Or to put it in other words: The deprivation of browsing within digital reading practices will be considered as a challenge that sheds light on the specific qualities of the printed book. The hand that leafs through the pages is replaced by clicks and hyperlinks, wiping and searching.[4] But no matter how efficient navigating digital texts may seem, extensive browsing in digitalized texts turns out to be extremely tedious. What, then, is the quality of browsing in books that the immediate access to digital data cannot compensate?

Medial differences are relevant for answering this question mostly with respect to the forms of using different devices and less with respect to the technical dimension of encoding visual data. The printed book as a material object of stacked pages allows for different ways of navigating and accessing texts compared to scrolling digital documents – a metaphor that refers to the medium that preceded print, rolls (or scrolls) of parchment. With respect to the different practices and applications facilitated and modelled by reading devices, there is no bibliophile apotheosis of 'good old books' at stake here. Rather, the question is which advantages and disadvantages old and new technologies of culture imply when we use texts, and how they influence our understanding and analyzing of these texts. As Robert Darnton put it: "[T]hanks to a new source of energy, the electronic book, wich will act as a supplement to, not a substitute for Gutenberg's great machine."[5]

Nevertheless, the medial changes of the past decades have been breathtaking. In 2004, Google started its scanning project Google Books. In 2005,

---

3 | Cf. Steffen Martus/Carlos Spoerhase: "Historische Praxeologie. Quellen zur Geschichte philologischer Praxisformen 1800-2000". In: *Zeitschrift für Germantistik* 23 (2013), 221-404.

4 | Cf. Adrian van der Weel: *Changing our textual minds. Toward a digital order of knowledge* (Manchester: Manchester University Press, 2011), Christine Grond-Rigler: "Der literarische Text als Buch und E-Book", in: Christine Grond-Rigler/Wolfgang Straub (ed.): *Literatur und Digitalisierung* (Berlin/Boston: de Gruyter, 2013), 7-20.

5 | Robert Darnton: "E-Books and old Books", in: ibd.: *The Case for Books. Past, Present, and Future.* (Philadelphia: PublicAffairs, 2009), 67-78, 77.

the first generation of e-Books was already extinct. In 2007, Apple established smartphones and tablets as reading devices. And since 2010, with Amazon's *Kindle,* a third generation of e-Books has become a significant part of the book market. Ever since, stereotypical arguments about the advantage of reading on paper have become obsolete. Recent neurological studies already emphasize the advantages of reading on a tablet, since it it seems to require less brainwork. Tablets are also used as a motivation device for students in teaching enviroments. And the former days when people read short texts online while printing longer ones to read in on paper seem to be over. In 1999, even Bill Gates still argued:

> Reading off the screen is still vastly inferior to reading off paper. Even I, who have these expensive screens and fancy myself als a pioneer of this Web Lifestyle, when it comes to something over about four or five pages, I print it out an I like to have it to carry around with me and annotate. And it's quite a hurdle for technology to achieve to match that level of usability.[6]

This "hurdle for technology" has been softened by second screens such as tablets, e-books and smartphones, but it is not completely suspended. On the contrary: It has become even more important to distinguish between reading on a screen and reading in a book. We find ourselves in a complex situation where one can neither be sure that 'good' literature requires printed books nor that everything will be available in digitalized archives soon. Even when Hilmar Schmundt summons the "joy of digital reading" in Germany's news magazine *Der Spiegel,* this does not have to be the last word.[7] Instead, the concept of reading has to be extended in a praxeological sense. Reading, then, is not reduced to activities of the eye and the contents of a text, but to a cultural technology that is based on the body of the reader and on physical activities such as turning pages. These bodily dimensions influence the experience and the effects of texts so that a digital text is not simply to be considerd a different version of the printed one but rather something that changes the relation between hand and text.

6 | Bill Gates, quote from ibd., 69.

7 | Hilmar Schmundt: *Gutenbergs neue Galaxis: Vom Glück des digitalen Lesens* (Hamburg: Spiegel E-Book, 2013). Cf. also Jeff Gomez: *Print is dead. Books in Our Digital Age* (New York: Palgrave Macmillan, 2007).

The Return to Materiality

Due to the growing distribution of digital texts the printed book, no longer a matter of course, is once more recognized as a complex three-dimensional paper machine and even labeled the "perfect reading machine".[8] Digitalization reminds us of the materiality of the book. This is not only true for the academic discussion. Literary texts also refer to this materiality and emphasize both the form of the codex and the practice of browsing.

In Mark Z. Danielewski's *House of Leaves*, browsing is promtep by pagelong footnotes that force the reader to decide which text to read.[9] Other footnotes refer to various appendices that are equally voluminous so that the reader will not return to the main text for a considerable amount of time.[10] Furthermore, presenting footnote references as a disruption of the text, this corresponds to the novel's plot of roaming through a house that continuously creates new rooms. In the chapter that introduces the maze as a model for this house, the text is split up into several columns. In the middle of the page, there is a box with mirror writing on its back as if there was a duct driven through the pages into the debt of the book. On the left and right, names and references are listed in columns one of which is presented upside down.[11] Further back, footnotes are printed not at the end but in the middle of the page, albeit in a 90-degree angle. The reader's hand has to turn the pages back and forth, turn the book around, turn it upside down, and look at a page repeatedly from different angles. On other pages, letters become scarce, until merely a few words remain scattered across the page.[12] Turning the pages becomes faster and corresponds to the panic the novel talks about. This is not a traditional layout issue but a performative order of text that connects reading and processing information with the form of communication so that the page and turning it become acknowledged as a part of reading. Browsing is recognized as a basic part of the practice and pleasure of the reader who has to follow the textual arrangement or make an attempt to escape it.

8 | Roland Reuß: *Die perfekte Lesemaschine. Zur Ergonomie des Buches* (Göttingen: Wallstein, 2014). Cf. Christan Benne: *Die Erfindung des Manuskripts. Zur Theorie und Geschichte literarischer Gegenständlichkeit* (Frankfurt/M.: Suhrkamp, 2015), Carlos Spoerhase: *Linie, Fläche, Raum. Die drei Dimensionen des Buches in der Diskussion der Gegenwart und der Moderne* (Göttingen: Wallstein, 2016).

9 | Mark Z. Danielewski: *Das Haus. House of Leaves* (Stuttgart: Klett-Cotta, 2007). Cf. Hanjo Berressem's article in this volume.

10 | Cf. ibd., 121.

11 | Ibd., 158 ff.

12 | Ibd., 263 ff.

In 2015, J. J. Abrams and Doug Dorsts published the novel *Theseus' ship* that was presented as a library copy with a shelf mark from 1949 and mildew on yellowish pages.[13] The cover and the typography resemble books from the 1950s. Its alleged author is one V.M. Straka. The book appears to be used and includes a stamped index of checkout entries from the library in the rear. Comments in two different handwritings are placed on the margins and there are passages in the text that are underlined. A female student and a PhD-candidate discuss the book. They wonder about the mysterious author and do research about the strange novel. Therefore, there are two seperate readings that defer and multiply the text of the novel. The reader has to decide whether to read the actual novel first and then the commentaries or whether it is possible to do both at a time. In between the pages, there are photocopies, photographs, index cards, a napkin with a drawing, postcards and letters – i.e. various papers and prints beyond the book that present additional information and as such are part of the book. Abram's und Dost's novel is based on digital printing technology that facilitates an inexpensive simulation of all these papers.

Thus, this product of digital media specifically refers to the materiality of the book – something that otherwise escapes the reading eye and the general concept of the text.

The problematic concept of 'text' and the theory of affordance

Is there a difference whether you would read this text on a laptop, a smartphone, or an e-book or whether you read it from a hardcopy or in a book? You might say no, there is none, and in a certain sense you would be right. Obviously there are medial differences – the ink of my printer is not identical with the one a book is printed with, its paper is not the same used by publishing houses, and there may be different layouts and typographies between printed and electronic texts on screen – but even if they were identical: What is the difference between the text that is read from a paper during a lecture and the one that students see projected on a screen by a beamer? The reading eye does not operate differently in both cases. According to the law of invariance as introduced by the leading neurological expert for reading, Stanislas Dehaene, the eye and the brain do not distinguish different typographical featres such as lower case or upper case letters, or different textual media in general. Reading is reading, regardless of the medium.

13 | Cf. J.J. Abrams/Doug Dorst: *Das Schiff des Theseus* (Köln: Kiepenheuer & Witsch, 2015).

Thus, the question of difference seems to refer only to the contextual framework of texts. Scholarly theories define 'text' by abstract categories such as structure, coherence, or closure instead of its materiality. Whether it's a computer print or book and whether this book is a paperback or a hardcover seems irrelevant. And yet, digital texts provoke the difficult question how a scholarly theory of text is able to reflect the status of text as an object. Christian Benne talks in his *Invention of the Manuscript. History and Theory of Literary Objects.* about the "ontological anxiety" of literary studies with respect to the manifold differences within the concept of text. How can we account for the different effects of the same text in its various medial appearances? Benne refers to the psychological category of affordance that addresses the implicit prompt of certain objects or media to use them in a specific way. This approach implies a functional notion, but is not reduced to it: one can use a door to close a room, but also slam it – i.e. use it as a means of communication. Voluminous books can serve as paperweights, and browsing through books can also be used for other purposes than the initially intended ones: "Flip through the pages and feel the breeze on your face."[14] The theory of affordance also enables to understand the different implications of a commodity – for instance of a paperback, an E-book, a hardcover or of a first edition – as well as to comprehend that practices are shaped by materialities. In Benne's words:

> As an alternative to studying the 'materiality' of texts that emerged from the philology of manuscripts, I treat texts also as objects regardless of their textuality. The concreteness of a book, for instance, would be, roughly speaking, its affordance as an artifact (a folio disposes of a different affordance compared to a paperback), its actual 'material' configuration (e.g., its typography) that seems subordinate to most users and readers, but nevertheless influences the practical use of each 'text' through its resistance, insofar texts never appear in an abstract way, but always as a concrete object, even when they are digitalized. [...] The ways actual readers experience concrete literary objects or the way groups of readers experience elements of a genre, include the prerequisites to acknowledge a specific object as a book and to attribute it with a specific cultural and symbolic status. That is core issue of the debate about e-books - not its status as a text but its materiality.[15]

The affordance of first editions may require a more thorough and careful treatment compared to paperbacks. Digital texts always appear as if unread, and in addition, the reading devices they are presented on serve as distinctive features within social discourse and call for additional communication beyond reading.

14 | Keith Houston: *Book. A Cover-to-Cover exploration of the most powerful object of our time* (New York/London: W. W. Norton & Company, 2016), S. XVI.

15 | Benne: *Die Erfindung des Manuskripts*, 132 f.

The affordance of a text is therefore structured in various ways by its material representation.

So the reduplication of texts in printed and digital variants raises the question of usage. What are books able to offer that digital texts cannot – and vice versa? The answer seems simple: Leafing through a book is different to the way one scrolls through a digital document. This simple observation refers to a basic distinction of practices and its implications for the concepts of book, text, and reading. The differences between *close* vs. *deep reading* or *hyper* vs. *machine reading* as introduced by Katherine Hayles are not sufficient in this context.[16] Important it to distinguish different modes of reading, a praxeological approach changes the concept of reading as such. Reading can no longer be understood with respect to seeing and understanding. Instead, the scene of reading implies the threefold relation of materiality, cognotion, and body in the same way Rüdiger Campe described this constellation for the scene of writing.[17] Thus, the hand that browses or clicks are different technologies of the body and of cultural techniques. In his fascinating study on *Manipulating and Grasping. Handling and Visualization in Early Modern Leaflets,* Jörn Münker hinted at the significance of the hand within the reading process.[18] By treating technologies of culture as technologies of the body, Münkler analyzes leaflets with respect to the symbolic and graphical representation of hands in texts. Münker claims "cognitive processes cannot be understood without the assistance of the hand. [...] The grasping, directing, leading, and manipulating role of the hand [...] deserves to be within the focus of attention."[19] Or, as Andrew Piper puts it with respect to current media: "To think about the future of reading means, first and foremost, to think about the relationship between reading and hands".[20]

Christoph Benjamin Schulz was the first one to extensively tackle browsing through books in his bok on the *Poetics of Browsing* from 2015: "Reading books means browsing", Schulz states, and describes it as an interaction with books as material objects:

16 | Hayles: "How We Read", 62 ff.

17 | Cf. Rüdiger Campe: "Die Schreibszene. Schreiben". In: *Paradoxien, Dissonanzen, Zusammenbrüche*, eds. Hans Ulrich Gumbrecht/Karl Ludwig Pfeiffer (Frankfurt/M.:-Suhrkamp, 1991), 759-772.

18 | Cf. Jörn Münker: *Eingreifen und Begreifen. Handhabungen und Visualisierungen in Flugblättern der Frühen Neuzeit* (Berlin: Erich Schmidt, 2008).

19 | Cf., 85, my translation. The landmark publication from an anthropological point of view is Frank Wilson: *The Hand. How its Use Shapes the Brain, Language, and Human Culture* (New York, Vintage, 1999). For the more recent media evolution, cf. Oliver Ruf: *Die Hand. Eine Medienästhetik* (Wien: Passagen, 2014).

20 | Piper: Book was there, 3.

The code sequentializes the texture of the text regardless of possible innertextual dispositions such as paragraphs or chapters. It spatializes the text, turns it into a palpable object stacked by various layers that require browsing. If the book is the main medium of our culture, than this culture not only consists in the history of the codex but also in the culture and history of browsing.[21]

To explain all features between digital and digital text would go beyond the scope of discussion here, but the advantages of keyword searches in digital texts immediately hints at one difference: Within digital media, exact findings are presented together with extensive lists, whereas browsing in printed texts is based on a context sensitive and general mode of perception. The effect is widely known: While looking for a specific passage, one misses it but finds another one of interest. Browsing and stumbling over new findings coincide whereas digital keyword searches will only result in the same character strings that one had initially entered.

Furthermore, browsing in books can take on a number of functions. The initial opening of a book has to be distinguished from opening the book to a random page. Turning the page in the process of reading differs from looking up a specific passage or going back to it. Therefore the cultral technology of browsing has to be considered a form of use with a number of internal differences.

If one looks up digitally possible traditions or modes that tell us more about browsing than a classic encyclopedia, you also learn something about the philological use of digital media. Keywords such as "turning the page", opening up a book" or "book pages" in the *Deutsches Text-Archiv* (DTA), in the *Bayerische Landesbibliothek*, the *Staatsbibliothek Berlin* or the *Herzog August Bibliothek* in Wolfenbüttel display two basic results: Firstly, there is only very little to be found (two findings within 120.000 online texts in the *Bayerische Landesbibliothek*, three in the DTA). Secondly, you may still discover a forgotten tradition – for instance historical instructions about the art of browsing through the Bible. That is no accident: The Bible uses the codex ever since late antiquity and has been accompanied by commentaries and indexes since the times of Alexandrine philology. The *Privilegirte Ordentliche und Vermehrte Dreßdnische Gesang-Buch* from 1774 includes a biblical register of those passages of the Holy Scripture "from which hymns were made" and announces this as especially "convenient for opening up at home prayer".[22] Johann Gotthilf Lorenz' *Versuch eines Lehrbuchs für Landschullehrerseminarien* (Berlin 1790) even

21 | Christoph Benjamin Schulz: *Poetiken des Blätterns* (Hildesheim, Zürich, New York: Olms, 2015), 26, my translation.

22 | *Das Privilegirte Ordentliche und Vermehrte Dreßdnische Gesang-Buch* (Dresden/Leipzig: Michael Gröll, 1774), no pagination, view http://digital.staatsbibliothek-be

contains an entire chapter on opening up the Bible and the Hymn Book.[23] The first sentence reads: "Opening up the Bible and the Hymn Book is not to be neglected, because both books are needed in school and in church." But besides these references to a tradition of browsing through books that has so far hardly attracted any scholarly attention at all, the concept of reading is also altered, if not deconstructed, in literary texts.

Browsing Through Literary Texts

Browsing through books is usually labeled superficial reading. "Do read thoroughly, there is no use in browsing", Grimm's dictionary tells us shortly.[24] This degradation of browsing in books as an opposition to mindful reading is a narrow perspective that deserves widening. There are a lot of different functions of browsing: opening up a book, deliberately looking for a passage, or comparing different passages in the process of reading. All these different functions affect different books and thus refer to the notion of an overflow of books that has posed the problem of orientation long before the twentieth century. "It's not the book that is the problemaic aspect of his life but the books, their abundance, their masses,"[25] Paul Raabe writes on Gotthold Ephraim Lessing's use of the library in Wolfenbüttel that he had directed for eleven years.

In the face of the evergrowing flood of books since the eighteenth century, browsing qualifies as a sophisticated way to deal with the quantities of printed matter as well as the necessity to select relevant writings and passages. As Johann Gottfried Herder remarks:

> Through which bulks of little writings we have to work through, before getting to the few sheats that contained something Lessing said" and on which the truth was expressed that all good things within bourgeois society cannot be commanded but must result

rlin.de/werkansicht?PPN=PPN664491618&PHYSID=PHYS_0675&DMDID=DMDLOG_0001); my translation.

23 | Johann Gotthilf Lorenz: *Versuch eines Lehrbuchs für Landschullehrerseminarien* (Berlin: Friedrich Maurer, 1790), 23 ff., view http://digital.staatsbibliothek-berlin.de/werkansicht?PPN=PPN856474940&PHYSID=PHYS_0028&DMDID=DMDLOG_0012. (last access 21.6.2018); my translation.

24 | Cf. Harun Maye: "Blättern". In: *Historisches Wörterbuch des Mediengebrauchs*, eds. Heiko Christians/Matthias Bickenbach/Nikolaus Wegmann (Köln/Weimar/Wien: Böhlau, 2015), 135-148.

25 | Paul Raabe: "Der Bibliothekar und die Bücher". In: *Wolfenbütteler Beiträge. Aus den Schätzen der Herzog August Bibliothek* 2 (1973), 131-146.

from a free enlightened will. How many large volumes did we have to browse through before stumpling upon [Garve's] *On Solitude*.[26]

Finding good literature requires acknowledging many books – and therefore browsing. As Friedrich Schlegel wrote on the status quo of reading at the turn oft he nineteenth century in his *Discourse on Poetry*: "In this age of books, it is impossible not to browse through, if not read, many, very many bad books."[27] This should also remind us of the literal meaning of calling somebody well versed: The term refers to the Latin *velum versare*, i.e. turning the page.

The topic can also be addressed critically as Joseph von Eichendorff did in his *History of Poetic Literature* in Germany: "Through printing, the entire literature became a book in which anybody can browse at their own pleasure. This results in a general dilettantism of producers and consumers."[28] But instead of following the path of cultural criticism, browsing should be accepted and studied as a basic technology of culture. For example, already the first mentioning of a codex in Western literature refers to the hand. In Martial's *Epigrams* the poet advertises his book as follows:

If you would choose a book to be Your travelling comrade, I remind you To buy a handy one like me, And leave your heavy tomes behind you. One that a single hand can hold Is best of all.[29]

Martial distances himself from scriptural norms here – the scroll – and favors what we came to call a book: the codex. The statement makes the book talk for itself, as a friend or *vademecum*. Thus, quick and easy accesibility are brought into position against the heavy tomes and convoluted scrolls. The reader can open the book anywhere at anytime – whereas a scroll has to be unfolded in a complicated manner.

Therefore, opening up a book has become part of what may be the most famous reading scene of Western literature. St. Augustine's *Confessions* connect the conversion to code with opening up the Bible at a random passage –

26 | Johann Gottfried Herder: *Briefe zur Beförderung der Humanität*. Ed. Heinz Stolpe. vol. 1 (Berlin, Weimar: Aufbau, 1971), 409, my translation.

27 | Friedrich Schlegel: "Gespräch über die Poesie". In: *Kritische Friedrich-Schlegel-Ausgabe*, ed. Ernst Behler, Bd. 2 (München/Paderborn/Wien: Schoeningh, 1958), 332.

28 | Joseph von Eichendorff: *Geschichte der poetischen Literatur Deutschlands*. Ibd.: *Werke. Nach den Ausgaben letzter Hand*. Ed. Ansgar Hillach. Bd. 3 (München: Winkler, 1970), 605 f.

29 | Cf. Martial: *Epigramme*. Lateinisch-deutsch. Hrsg. v. Paul Barié, Werner Schindler (3. ed. Berlin: de Gruyter, 2013). Book I, No. 2, my translation.

a practice that is only possible when using a codex. Beginnig with this practice which was connected with oracles at the time, continuing with Pliny's *Praefatio* in his *Historia Naturalis* (where the reader is informed that he does not have to read all 35 volumes, for he first time in Latin literature he provided a table of contents so that he can look up specific passages) and ending with the introduction of page numbers one could tell an entire media history of the book page up to the days of the pdf file.[30]

But sometimes one will also come accross a passage as this:

> The first thirty pages, said my father, turning over the leaves, - are a little dry; and as they are not closely connected with the subject, - for the present we'll pass them by [...].[31]

What seems to be a parody of unprofessional, fragmentary reading is, in the light of a topic that refers to nothing less than the genesis of humanity, in fact a game Sterne plays with his readers who are supposed to browse forward and backwards. This is exemplified in a passage that addresses a female reader in order to remind her of her inattentiveness:

> How could you, Madam, be so inattentive in reading the last chapter? I told you in it, That my mother was not a Papist. --- Papist! You told me no such thing, Sir. - Madam, I beg leave to repeat it over again, That I told you as plain, at least, as words, by direct inference, could tell you such a thing. - Then, Sir, I must have missed a page. - No, Madam, - you have not missed a word. - Then I was asleep, Sir. - My pride, Madam, cannot allow you that refuge. - Then, I declare, I know nothing at all about the matter. - That, Madam, is the very fault I lay to your charge; and as a punishment for it, I do insist upon it that you immediately turn back, that is as soon as you get to the next full stop, and read the whole chapter over again.[32]

The end of this period thus becomes the starting point for its rereading. The text is performative and ties in its reader by a hyperlink *avant la lettre*. As Benjamin Schulz concludes: "Insofar browsing is implied by literature and signaled at by

30 | Cf. Bonnie Mak: *How Page Matters* (Toronto e.a.: University of Toronto Press, 2011). For Augustines practice of silent reading and the bookish evolution in a grammar or reading see Matthias Bickenbach: Von den Möglichkeiten einer 'inneren' Geschichte des Lesens (Tübingen: Niemeyer, 1999. Reprint Berlin: de Gruyter 2017), 76 ff.

31 | Laurence Sterne: *The Life and Opinions of Tristram Shandy, Gentleman* (New York: Modern Library, 1995), vol. 1, 64.

32 | Ibd., vol. 5, 412.

the text, it becomes a literary event."[33] Browsing becomes part of the narrative structure of texts.

This also implies a decentralization of the concept of reading as it implies materializing the ideal of a hermeneutically focused study of a text. The interplay between 'part' and 'whole' is also reflected in the act of browsing, as Reger puts in in Thomas Bernhards novel *Ancient Masters*:

> I am rather a browser than a reader, you have to know, and I love browsing as much as I love reading, all my live I have turned pages a billion times more than I have read a page, but I always enjoyed turning the page just as much as I enjoyed reading.[34]

This statement seems to satirically emphasize the difference between professional and unprofessional practices of reading. Reger continues:

> Never in my life have I ever finished a book. My way of reading is the way of a highly talented browser, of a man who prefers browsing to reading, who turns dozens and if need be hundreds of pages before reading a single one.[35]

Thus, browsing may turn out to be true reading. Before a single page is read, there has to be browsing in order find it: "When a man reads a page, he reads it more thoroughly than anybody else and with a much greater passion of reading as one may imagine."[36] Reading trough a book becomes reading from it, a practice that, as Reger emphasizes, is not a random one but the only way to find the right page. This reader is, according to Reger, "a thousand times more thorough than a regular reader who reads everything, but not a single page in a thorough way." Which means: "It is better to read twelve lines of a book with the highest intensity and thus to grasp it completely than to read the entire book in the manner of a *regular reader*".[37]

However, to authors, random browsing may also appear as a horror vision, if it threatens to replace careful reading in the means of recognizing the whole of a text. With respect to the implicite and explicite directions for reading and browsing in novels by Laurence Sternes and Jean Paul, Schulz remarks:

> Browsing is permitted and, as a paraliterary practice also desired, if it is motivated by explicit or implicit hints within the text, i.e. when it is, as in the case of Laurence Sterne's

33 | Schulz: *Poetiken des Blätterns*, 244.

34 | Thomas Bernhard: *Alte Meister. Eine Komödie* (Frankfurt/M.: Suhrkamp, 1985), 39. All translations from German sources are my own.

35 | Ibd., 38 f.

36 | Ibd., 39.

37 | Ibd.

Tristram Shandy, legitimized by the authority of the narrator. But it is not permissible as an autonomous gesture of appropriating a text. In this case, the case of Jean Paul, it unfolds it destructive energy.[38]

But the critical perspective on browsing as a superficial use of books is not inevitable. Schulz adds:

> But besides labeling browsing as gambling with the aesthetics and materialities of literary fiction, Jean Paul also reflects on turning pages and introduces a general notion of browsing as a procedural approach of unfolding, exfoliating, and defoliating that applies to everything that is subject to the process of understandig.[39]

The cultural technology of browsing is moved to a symbolic dimension that is connected to Blumenberg's notion of a legible world.[40] Natural phenomena have to be unfold in order to be understood, the book of nature is opened up, and revolutions are considered as turning over a new leaf of history. Thus, "browsing becomes the basic notion of the process of knowing and understanding even beyond reading."[41] This result is remarkable because it shows that browsing and understanding are not categories that necessarily contradict each other but form a recursive connection. That is not only true for the ostensive (but unbookish) notion of defoliation as a way to reach the essence of a natural phenomenon, but also for any intense contact with knowledge and information. As mentioned before, people who know much about a certain field are called 'well versed' which means literally that they have turned many pages. In Heinrich von Kleist's *Käthchen von Heilbronn* the count Wetter vom Strahl exclaims: "Truly and really! I will browse through my mother tongue and look up the entire rich chapter entitled: sentimentality in a way that no maker of verse will henceforth be able to say in a new way: I am sad."[42] Browsing through the mind and through language describes the mode of finding the right expression, a new expression that will express more precisely what used to be the conventional metaphors of melancholia.

Other reflections on browsing highlight flexible relations with reading. In his *Preschool to Aesthetics,* Jean Paul talks about the creative process of browsing

38 | Schulz: *Poetik des Blätterns*, 227.

39 | Ibd.

40 | Hans Blumenberg: *Die Lesbarkeit der Welt* (Frankfurt/M.: Suhrkamp, 1981).

41 | Schulz: *Poetik des Blätterns*, 228. Due to growing technologization and general acceleration, however, since the twentieth century browsing is considered an outdated practice.

42 | Heinrich von Kleist: "Das Käthchen von Heilbronn". In: Ibd.: *Sämtliche Werke und Briefe*. Ed. Helmut Sembner, Bd. 1 (4. ed., München: Hanser, 1965), 453 f.

as it connects individual passages from a text. Jean Paul presents a manual for a learned book here that contains a genuine literary aesthetics as well as a critical evaluation of contemporary philosophy by Kant and Fichte. The *Preschool* is structured by so called "programms" that refer to irony. But at the same time Jean Paul writes:

> But I tell about the programms of the laughable, humor, irony, and wit so that researching critics may browse through them attentively and calmly, and consequentyl because of the interconnections I wish the same for the programs that precede and follow them.[43]

Jean Paul's sentences are notoriously dark. But what they seem to suggest is that each chapter of his *Preschool* should be read thoroughly as well as with respect to its connection to all other chapters, i.e. both with respect to its overarching topic and in comparison to chapters before and after. Or to put in differently: All chapters and topics are interconnected. Mindful browsing will discover connections that linear reading will miss, no matter how thoroughly it is conducted. Reading requires repetition, browsing forward and backward, so that elements that are dispersed and articulated differently within a linear text can be compared and connected. Naturally, this calls for an elaborate way of reading and an intense study of a book. By demanding such a reading, Jean Paul extends the ideal of reading from a standard model of continual studying to the mode of interconnected browsing.

These few findings from the history of German literature thus demonstrate that browsing in books highlights highly differntiated literary and philolgical practices. And they remind us that digital texts, too, should not simply be considered as stored away in a stable way forever, but have to be kept open for flexible approaches.

43 | Jean Paul: *Vorschule der Ästhetik*. In: Ibd.: *Werke*. Ed. Norbert Miller. Bd. 5 (München: Hanser, 1963), 25.

Combination of Order and Disorder

The Slip Box as a Medium for Second Order Communication

Charlotte Coch

In 2002, Friedrich Kittler held lectures on the philosophies of literature in Berlin. In these twelve lectures, which have later been published by the Merve publishing house, he does not only present different philosophies of literature from Plato and Aristotle to Sartre and Lacan, but he also talks about the changing relationship between philosophy and literature, in other words about the mere possibility of a philosophy of literature. On the one hand, his main historical thesis concerning modernity is that philosophical thinking after 1800 needs to be considered as philosophy of literature. On the other hand, literary studies in their origins are based on the philosophical institutions that are already established in the 19th century, both in a material and in a communicative way.

To be more exact, Kittler claims that the interpretation of literature and the process of institutionalizing certain ways of scientific communication about literature are based on a distinct kind of philosophy: namely, the philosophy of idealism emerging in the 19th century. Many literary scholars, like Rüdiger Campe and others, however, would argue that we owe the possibility of communicating about literature the way we do to the literary and especially theoretical developments in Early romanticism, for example to the texts and fragments published in the famous journal *Athenäum*, by Friedrich Schlegel and others.

For Kittler, this is obviously not true. For him, it is Hegel who finally shapes the room for an ordered – in Hegel's words 'concrete' – communication about literature and can thus be rightfully called the founder of our discipline: "Friedrich Schlegel hat einmal postuliert, erst seine Philosophie könne eine 'Theorie des (möglichen) Inhalts' von Dichtung liefern. Aber erst Hegel, dürfen wir jetzt ergänzen, hat dieses Postulat verwirklicht."[1]

---

1 | Friedrich A. Kittler: *Philosophien der Literatur. Berliner Vorlesung 2002* (Berlin: Merve, 2013), 179.

How can Kittler come to such a definite conclusion? He does not make a clear statement here, but there are clear hints in his lectures on philosophies of literature as well as in his other texts, such as in his talk "Nacht der Substanz". Out of curiosity, I want to follow his opinion here as it provides me with the opportunity to look at philosophical, or theoretical, communication in the 'making' as opposed to theory or philosophy as such.

Upon approaching the 'making' of communication or text, I am proposing that Hegel's simultaneous developments in the field of philosophy and literary studies can be attributed to a certain way of making, hence to a certain media technology: the slip box: "Wenn Hegel interpretiert, liest er eben nicht seine jugendlichen Lieblingsdichter ein zweitesmal wieder, sondern deren bereits in Philosophie überführten Extrakt oder Zettelkasten."[2]

Slip boxes, as we can learn from Marcus Krajewski's book on *Zettelwirtschaft*, have been developed for private and public libraries, as an important instrument to connect title and content of a book to its location within the library. However, since libraries and science have, at least concerning the actual protagonists, been separated during the 18th century, there is a second kind of slip box, which is not of public but only of private use. Krajewski calls this kind of slip box an idiosyncratic 'workstation philosophy'[3], which is only accessible – both physically and hermeneutically – to one person, in contrast to a library slip box, which must be accessible to all users.

Already in 1689, the German scholar Vincent Placcius published an inventory of educated knowledge management, which contains the chapter *De scrinio litterato*. This chapter on the educated box also presents a detailed instruction on how to build this early slip box.

In Pictures 1 and 2 one can observe how this educated box was supposed to look like. It is a box with two leaf doors, with transverse wooden sticks to hold the square cards labelled with loci (*Amor, Deus, Fides, Vita, Deus, Virtus, Voluptas*) as the main pattern for ordering the slips.

Here, we have the first 'machina', which is how Placcius calls his slip box; or, how Krajewski calls it, the first universal discrete machine.

2 | Ibd., 166.

3 | Cf. Markus Krajewski: *ZettelWirtschaft. Die Geburt der Kartei aus dem Geiste der Bibliothek* (Berlin: Kadmos, ²2017), 11.

Fig. 1: The slip box of Vincent Placcius in Vincent Placcius, De Arte Excerpendi. Vom Gelahrten Buchhalten liber singularis, (Hamburg/Stockholm 1689), 138.

Fig. 2: The framework of the slip box of Vincent Placcius with appliances to attach excerpt slips in Vincent Placcius, De Arte Excerpendi. Vom Gelahrten Buchhalten liber singularis, (Hamburg/Stockholm 1689), 140.

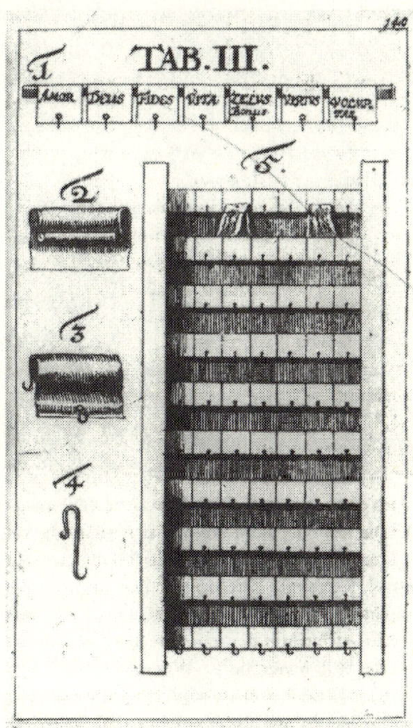

> Zettelkästen genügen einem strengen Begriff der 'theoretischen Kinematik': Die Möglichkeit, ihre Elemente umzuordnen, macht die Kartei zur Maschine: Wenn die Lageänderung eines Zettels und das anschließende Einordnen an anderer Stelle dazu führt, damit unmittelbar auch die anderen Zettel zu verschieben, so läßt sich dieser Vorgang als verketteter Mechanismus beschreiben. Dieser hingegen kommt in Bewegung, wenn auf eines seiner beweglichen Glieder eine Kraft, welche die Lage desselben zu ändern im Stande ist, einwirkt. Die Kraft verrichtet dabei eine mechanische Arbeit, die unter bestimmten Bewegungen vor sich geht. Das Ganze ist also dann eine Maschine. Die einwirkende Kraft wird von der ordnenden Hand des später so genannten 'Kartei-Führers' oder einem anderen Benutzer ausgeübt.[4]

For Kittler, it is this specific media technology that makes Hegel both the greatest philosopher and literary scholar. Hegel's famous spirit turns out to be the slip box itself: "Denn wenn der Buchstabe von Autoren, philosophischen oder auch poetischen, schon im Zettelkasten verschwunden ist, trifft der Geist des Interpreten, streng nach Fichte, ja immer nur auf andere Geister."[5]

Here, Kittler plays with the different semantics of 'Geist' (ghost). First as a mind with the individual capacity to think; second as spirit, which is a transcendent concept of the absolute, and third as ghost, to encapsulate the non-sensual remains of a human being. In the slip box, letters are then transformed into being 'Geister' (ghosts) in all three proposed dimensions.

Hegel, in other words, transforms the world into a slip box and thus abstract data into, more or less, concrete ghosts. Due to this transformation, Hegel's philosophy does not remain a local philosophy among other possible systems, but rather the prima philosophia, and thus a universal machine for interpretation. A short remark by Hegel in the *Enyzklopädie der philosophischen Wissenschaften* (1830) shows how he conceptualizes his philosophical project: "Die der Zeit nach letzte Philosophie ist das Resultat aller vorhergehenden Philosophien und muß daher die Prinzipien aller enthalten: sie ist darum, wenn sie anders Philosophie ist, die entfaltetste, reichste und konkreteste."[6]

In relation to the slip box as a material encyclopedia, Hegel's philosophy is the most concrete as it is not only communication itself, but it also contains and absorbs all the communicative acts; in other words, all philosophical texts that have been written before being rendered into paper slips and thus into ghosts

---

4 | Ebd., 14f.

5 | Kittler: *Philosophien der Literatur*, 166f.

6 | Georg Wilhelm Friedrich Hegel: *Enzyklopädie der philosophischen Wissenschaften im Grundrisse. Erster Teil: Die Wissenschaft der Logik*. Mit den mündlichen Zusätzen. In: ibd.: *Werke in 20 Bänden*. Hrsg. von Eva Moldenhauer und Karl Markus Michel, Bd. 8 (Frankfurt am Main: Suhrkamp, ^{2}1989), 58.

by Hegel's ordering hands. Therefore, I argue that the Hegelian philosophy of the spirit is a first version of second-order communication.

Unfortunately, Hegel's slip box is no longer available to us. The only mentioning of its appearance and system comes from one of Hegel's first biographers, Karl Rosenkranz, who describes the Hegelian procedure as follows:

> Bei seiner Lektüre ging er nun folgendermaßen zu Werke. Alles, was ihm bemerkenswerth schien – und was schien es ihm nicht! – schrieb er auf ein einzelnes Blatt, welches er oberhalb mit der allgemeinen Rubrik bezeichnete, unter welche der besondere Inhalt subsumirt werden mußte. In die Mitte des oberen Randes schrieb er dann mit großen Buchstaben, nicht selten mit Fracturschrift das Stichwort des Artikels. Diese Blätter selbst ordnete er für sich wieder nach dem Alphabet und war mittels dieser einfachen Vorrichtung im Stande, seine Excerpte jeden Augenblick zu benutzen. Bei allem Umherziehen hat er diese Incunabeln seiner Bildung immer aufbewahrt. Sie liegen theils in Mappen, theils in Schiebfutteralen, denen auf dem Rücken eine orientierende Etikette aufgeklebt ist.[7]

This detailed description in Rosenkranz's biography is one of the few hints we have concerning the actual materiality of Hegel's slip box. There is, however, another figure in German intellectual history who has become famous for his slip box: Niklas Luhmann. His slip box is in fact available to us.[8] "Serendipity – About the Joy of Finding"[9], a recent exhibition of works of art in the Kunsthalle Bielefeld, combines the display of many Luhmannian paper slips with the concept of a slip box. In contrast to Hegel, Luhmann is eager to reflect the specific kind of relationship between him and his educated machine, which Marcus Krajewski refers to as 'intimate communication'. A short text called "Kommunikation mit Zettelkästen. Ein Erfahrungsbericht" functions as an instructive source for the question how Luhmann views his 'making' of theory, including his cooperation with the slip box. He describes and recommends the slip box as a communication partner:

---

7 | Karl Rosenkranz: *Georg Wilhelm Friedrich Hegels Leben* (Darmstadt: WBG, 1963), 13f.

8 | A long-term project at the University of Bielefeld (2015-2030) called 'Niklas Luhmann – Theorie als Passion; Wissenschaftliche Erschließung und Edition des Nachlasses' supported by the Centre for eHumanities in Cologne aims at securing, exploiting and publishing valuable materials of Luhmann's estate. Cf. http://www.uni-bielefeld.de/soz/luhmann-archiv/ (09.10.2017).

9 | Vgl. Friedrich Meschede e.a. (ed.): *Serendipity. Vom Glück des Findens: Niklas Luhmann, Ulrich Rückriem, Jörg Sasse. Kunsthalle Bielefeld* (Köln: Snoeck, 2015).

Dass Zettelkästen als Kommunikationspartner empfohlen werden können, hat zunächst einen einfachen Grund in technisch-ökonomischen Problemen wissenschaftlichen Arbeitens. Ohne zu schreiben, kann man nicht denken; jedenfalls nicht in anspruchsvoller, anschlussfähiger Weise. Irgendwie muss man Differenzen markieren, Distinktionen entweder explizit oder in Begriffen impliziert festhalten; nur die so gesicherte Konstanz des Schemas, das Informationen erzeugt, garantiert den Zusammenhalt der anschließenden Informationsverarbeitungsprozesse. Wenn man aber sowieso schreiben muss, ist es zweckmäßig, diese Aktivität zugleich auszunutzen, um sich im System der Notizen einen kompetenten Kommunikationspartner zu schaffen.[10]

For Luhmann, the slip box is not just an archive or a collection of data, but it is a communication partner. It does not only provide information based on a common pattern of comparison, but it can surprise its human communication partner due to a different pattern of comparison on the one hand, and thus due to the element of chance on the other hand. Still, in order to earn trust from its communication partner, the slip box has to be structured in a certain way which Luhmann describes in a very detailed fashion.

Zur technischen Ausstattung des Zettelkastens gehören hölzerne Kästen mit nach vorne ausziehbaren Fächern und Zettel im Oktav-Format. Diese Zettel sollten nur einseitig beschrieben werden, damit man beim Suchen von vorne lesen kann, ohne den Zettel herauszunehmen. Das verdoppelt zwar den Raumbedarf (aber doch nicht ganz, weil ja nicht alle Zettel auch hinten beschrieben werden würden), und das ist nicht unbedenklich, da nach einigen Jahrzehnten der Benutzung die Kastenanlage so groß werden kann, daß man sie von einem Sitzplatz aus nicht mehr leicht bedienen kann. Um dem entgegenzuwirken, empfiehlt es sich, auf Karteikarten zu verzichten und Papier zu nehmen.
Das sind jedoch Äußerlichkeiten, die nur die Bequemlichkeit und nicht die Leistung betreffen. Für das Innere des Zettelkastens, für das Arrangement der Notizen, für sein geistiges Leben ist entscheidend, daß man sich gegen eine systematische Ordnung nach Themen und Unterthemen und statt dessen für eine feste Stellordnung entscheidet. Ein inhaltliches System (nach Art einer Buchgliederung) würde bedeuten, daß man sich ein für allemal (für Jahrzehnte im voraus!) auf eine bestimmte Sequenz festlegt. Das muß, wenn man das Kommunikationssystem und sich selbst als entwicklungsfähig einschätzt, sehr rasch zu unlösbaren Einordnungsproblemen führen. Die feste Stellordnung braucht kein System. Es genügt für sie, daß man jedem Zettel eine Nummer gibt, sie gut sichtbar (bei uns links oben) anbringt und diese Nummer und damit den Standort niemals ändert.[11]

---

10 | Niklas Luhmann: "Kommunikation mit Zettelkästen. Ein Erfahrungsbericht". In: ders.: *Universität als Milieu* (Bielefeld: Haux, 1992), 53-62, 53.

11 | Ibd., 55.

For Luhmann, this system has enormous value for the internal organization of notes and he considers the possibility of endless and arbitrary capacity for bifurcations, as a slip with the number 57/12, can be complemented by numerous other slips, either 57/13 or 57/12a etc. Hence, there is the possibility for internal growth without a systematic pre-programming and without having to order thoughts in a linear way and one slip can also contain numerous references to other slips or groups of slips. Following this logic, the static order can be complemented by a registry of tags, listing important topics and the respective slips, rather than their ordinal number.

To visualize this rather abstract description, picture 3 functions as another example.

Fig. 3: Niklas Luhmann's slip "536/15 Conferences", www.uni-bielefeld.de/soz/luhmann-archiv

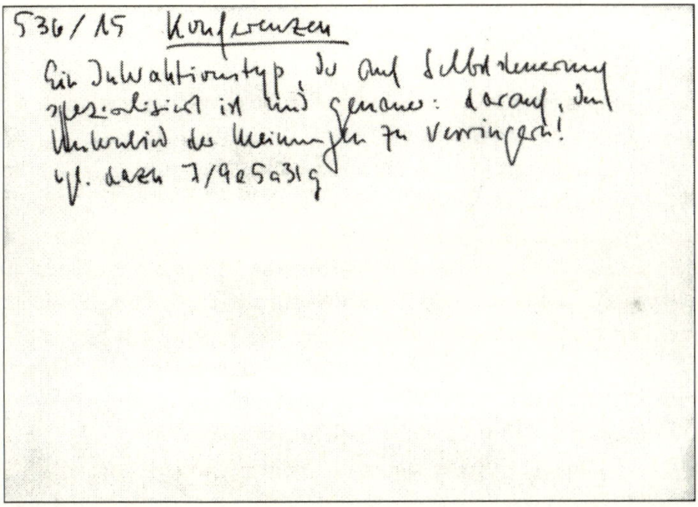

The slip in question has the number 536/15 and its main topics are conferences, with a slip that reads: "Ein Interaktionstyp, der auf Selbststeuerung spezialisiert ist und genauer: darauf, den Unterschied der Meinungen zu verringern."

The reference to another slip with the number 7/9c5a31g shows the very complex system of add-ons which has already established. Interestingly enough, there is also a massive difference in the respective first numbers: 536 and 7, which is due to the static order of the slip box, where similar topics tend to find themselves in different spots.

In short, Luhmann claims that this technique he describes here ensures that the developed order does not turn into a handcuff, but rather adjusts to the development of thoughts. Doing so, every note is just an element that gains its importance by the network of references and recursions. Structured in this way, a slip box can gain independence after a few years of working with it.

> Der Zettelkasten braucht einige Jahre, um genügend kritische Masse zu gewinnen. Bis dahin arbeitet er nur als Behälter, aus dem man das herausholt, was man hineingetan hat. Mit zunehmender Größe und Komplexität wird dies anders. Einerseits vermehrt sich die Zahl der Zugänge und Abfragemöglichkeiten. Er wird zum Universalinstrument. Fast alles kann man unterbringen, und zwar nicht nur ad hoc und isoliert, sondern mit internen Anschlußmöglichkeiten. Er wird ein sensibles System, das auf vielerlei Einfälle, sofern sie nur notierbar sind, intern anspricht.[12]

The communication with the slip box supports something that Luhmann calls 'relating relations', a technique that evokes order and chance at the same time and can thus be called a combination of order and disorder – the heading of this essay. This technique of relating relations in the medium of the slip box then is, compared to Hegel's slip box, another version of second order communication.

I want to conclude with some preliminary thoughts on these two different versions of second order communication, and thus two different kinds of media usage. As Krajewski and Kittler both point out, Hegel tries to make his slip box invisible. His conception of the spirit is, as Krajewski calls it, a 'hidden slip box'. Hegel's educated slip box must, again with Krajewski, hide its own discursive power; the slip box and the whole process of writing must disappear to make room for the concrete world which is actually being evoked in Hegel's philosophy: "Die verschwiegene Finsternis hütet eifrig das Betriebsgeheimnis genialer Texte. Die Rede vom Zettelkasten als Produktionsmaschine muss verstummen."[13] Instead of being examined for signatures of its medium, the collection of data that is provided by the slip box must be reinterpreted as the thoughts of a mind and of a spirit, which are both absorbing the ghosts of the other authors into one absolute universe.

Luhmann, however, constantly treats the slips in his box not as data, but as communicative acts, which can only be – in their mediality – the object of a second order communication, which always first and foremost speaks about its own way of being.

With a conscious anachronism, one could relate these two different kinds of media use with the distinction of print and electronical medias presented in Luhmann's Gesellschaft der Gesellschaft. Here, Luhmann writes about electronical media:

12 | Ibd., 60.

13 | Krajewski: *ZettelWirtschaft*, 76f.

Im Ergebnis führen diese Erfindungen dazu, daß die gesamte Welt kommunikabel wird. An die Stelle der Phänomenologie des Seins tritt die Phänomenologie der Kommunikation. Man sieht die Welt so, wie die Bildkommunikation es einem suggeriert – wenn auch nicht so dramatisch, nicht so kontrastscharf, nicht so lupenrein, nicht so farbig und vor allem: nicht so ausgesucht.[14]

I am aware that this comparison is very far-stretched. Hegel's slip box is of course not a pictorial medium in the material sense, and it is far from being electronical. Yet I still think you can say that his concept of a slip box makes the whole world communicable, in the form of a philosophy of the spirit which is presented by Hegel himself.

Finally, I would like to summarize with the following description of the two different slip boxes: Hegel's slip box can structurally be compared to an electronical medium which provides information and is a small version of the world, a virtual reality. On the contrary, Luhmann's slip box is a communication partner, and can thus be related to the print medium where the distinction between message and information must be made for every single element as it is being provoked by every single communicative step. This difference in the use of media technology is also reflected by the difference between Luhmann's and Hegel's respective theories, both in the making of theory and in theory as such. An elaboration on this difference would strain the reader's patience way too much. What I tried to point out is that there is not one single way to incorporate a slip box into the writing of theory, but that there are important differences in the use and in the reflection of media technologies that have to be considered when describing theories and other texts from the perspective of their 'making-of'.

14 | Niklas Luhmann: *Die Gesellschaft der Gesellschaft*. Bd. 1 (Frankfurt am Main: Suhrkamp, 1992), 306. It is interesting to notice Luhmann's choice of words here. The 'phenomenology of being' and the 'phenomenology of communication' seem to hint not only at Husserl of course, but also at Hegel's famous work.

Fractures of Writing

Space Production and Graphic Surfaces

Gábor Mezei

> Beyond the inscription of pure geometry on the terrestrial globe, the Apollonian gaze inscribes its surface with elemental division of earth and water.
> Denis Cosgrove: Apollo's Eye

Topography and cartography always embody a double spatiality; the graphic space of the page and the space constituted by its operations. To understand how these operations occur, I will raise the question of the relation between the two: the space of the graphic surface in the case of maps and texts, and the space produced by them. Space is necessarily constituted by these surfaces, because topographical knowledge as *techné* precedes any spatial accessibility;[1] we cannot reach any spaces without topo/cartography. And as the fundamental operations of writing – as it appears on a surface in its spatiality – are in many respects analogous with the operations of topography, we also have to take it into consideration that these mutual operations may determine the way we can get access to spatial arrangements.

Thus, to answer the question towards the relation between literary texts and the map, or even the landscape, "the answer is not the semantics of space, that can be accessed through the map or the text, that is, not the poetics of space (Bachelard), or the category of '*Landschaft*' (Ritter)."[2] Instead, it is more about the way writing and cartography play a role in the production of spatiality. The human gaze constructing the "prevailing individuality" of thc landscape, making it an aesthetic entity as understood by Simmel or Ritter cannot be the basis of a possible explanation at this point anymore, because we have to pay

1 | Sigrid Weigel, "Zum 'topographical turn'. Kartographie, Topographie und Raumkonzepte in den Kulturwissenschaften". *KulturPoetik* 2 (2002), 151-165, 163.

2 | Robert Stockhammer, *Kartierung der Erde. Macht und Lust in Karten und Literatur* (München: Fink, 2007), 68.

attention to technical operations as the presence of these makes it understandable that it is never the space in itself we are dealing with.

Fig. 1: An Australian map that shows how the graphic arrangement of a map determines the way we get access to different territories. David Turnbull, Maps are Territories. Science is an Atlas (Chicago: The University of Chicago Press, 1993), 32.

To provide an example that may serve as a starting point, let us take a look at an Australian map that shows the homeland (Biranybirany) of the Gumatj clan, which resembles the figure of a crocodile.[3] The map (used by aboriginal Australians) may point at the basic interrelations between the graphic and the landscape: the figure of the crocodile helps the user to locate him/herself. The names of the parts of the crocodile are areas of land. The coast is where the crocodile's rear legs are, the mouth of the river is where the tail joins the body. We could say that in the case of this map, the figure *is* the landscape and we can suppose, that we generally need the graphic to locate ourselves in a territory, and it is always in operation when we are moving within space. But how does it happen? How is the graphic surface that is present in writing is at the same time in operation in cartography as well?

Speaking about graphic surfaces in general my starting point is to figure out what mutual operations writing, and maps share. Or, from another perspective, how the structures of writing are in operation when we are dealing with space either through topography, or cartography. I will try to show that the graphic surface itself provides and determines fractures in both cases, that proves to be a decisive feature here. But the aspect of writing cannot be for-

3 | David Turnbull, *Maps are Territorries. Science is an Atlas* (Chicago: University of Chicago Press, 1993), 32.

gotten here either, so we have to take a look at how writing is present in these operations.

Graphic Surfaces

The role of the page is far from being passive both in the case of writing and cartography. Considering how the page takes part in graphic operations, we can say that "[t]erms like "ground" and "support" also reinforce a hierarchy in which the base is subservient to the presumably more substantive text and graphical elements that will be placed "on" it."[4] But why is it that we cannot accept this subservient role of the graphic surface, besides the fact that its material presence is a necessarily determining factor in all graphic operations?[5] I suppose, because we need units and fractures to create space, but there is no fracture without a graphic surface, and no text without the surface of the page. And as the graphic surface provides the possibility of fractures, everything that happens *in* it, happens in its spatiality; fractures, gaps (interspaces, line endings, laying-out, space between stanzas) are the results of the two-dimensional space of the graphic surface. Trying to follow the analogy between writing and cartography it is crucial to examine what function fractures have in the case of topography.

Fractures and Topography

Discussing the role of fractures in writing or topography, first we have to take into consideration Heidegger's notion of the 'rift' *('Riß')*; he understands it as a line that makes a path joining one place to another. At the same time, it is a fissure dividing this side from that in an uncrossable abyss. As he announces it in the *Origin of the Work of Art,* the rift provides a basic design, an outline sketch,[6] it is a 'trait' or carved line that engraves the earth, making its surface into a sign. Such paths give the world edges and measures which holds the potentiality to join places.[7] That is why the rift is always there, always in operation, establishing spatiality as an active foundation. The geometrical arrangement Heidegger is talking about here is not only present with its dividing lines in topography, but it is continuously emphasized as well that these lines are

4 | Johanna Drucker, *Speclab. Digital Aesthetics and Projects in Speculative Computing* (Chicago/London: University of Chicago Press, 2009), 161.

5 | Cf. the article by Nicolas Pethes in this volume.

6 | Martin Heidegger, *Poetry, Language, Thought.* Translated by Albert Hofstadter. (New York: HarperCollins, 2001), 63.

7 | Joseph Hillis Miller, *Topographies* (Stanford: Stanford University Press, 1995), 14.

inscriptionlike and that they are creating signs; they are based on the spatiality of writing.

It is not only Heidegger's notion of the rift that can be used in this respect. Fractures are very crucial parts of Georg Simmel's topography as well. Considerably, in *The Philosophy of Landscape,* he raises the question what decides the identity of a landscape and how it is possible to look at something as a landscape. To get access to a landscape according to him we need to circumscribe it, highlight a part of it, make a unit with its own center and divide its elements. This way fractures are necessary for Simmel to make divisions and to create something that can be understood or seen as a landscape.

Unlike in the case of Heidegger and Simmel, de Certeau in *Practice of Everyday Life* does not start out of geometrical grounds, though divisions themselves are crucial for him as well. Practices of space are understood here through rhetoric – there is a rhetoric of walking based on synecdoche that is providing density, and asyndeton with the suppression of links, cutting out of connecting elements resulting in unconnectedness. Space, this way, is made up of enlarged singularities, separate islands as "walking selects and fragments the space traversed; it skips over links and whole parts it omits."[8] This way we could say that everyday spatial practices are creating fragments, using fractures, just like writing does and though de Certeau develops his notion of these practices in terms of rhetoric, walking as an everyday practice situates them in a spatial presence.

These three concepts are based on how we can be, and how we in fact are determined to make distinctions between spatial units in topography. And as they are all referring to dividing lines, fissures or fragments, it can be said that it is the empty space between spatial units that matters here. The structure of graphic surfaces is in operation as it is the surface itself that makes the empty space possible at all. Altogether it shows that space is the product of these fractures in topography.

Fractures in Writing

In a next step we should examine how fractures are present in different determining concepts of writing. Starting out with Flusser, it seems to be obvious that fragmentedness is a basic feature of writing as well, though he refers to it from the perspective of productivity: "Quills must be removed again and again to dip them into the inkwell. Even a typewriter, technically relatively advanced, must have its ribbon changed from time to time." That is why "[i]ntervals must be inserted between words, sentences, paragraphs, and chapters. The gesture

8 | Michel de Certeau, *Practice of Everyday Life.* Translated by Steven Rendall. (Berkley/Los Angeles/London: University of California Press, 1988), 101.

of notation is staccato because the code of writing itself is particulate (discrete)."[9] According to Flusser's concept, we are continuously forced to interrupt our writing process, and these interruptions provide the fractures that are necessarily there in the structure of writing. This is the reason why writing has to use a discrete system of letters, where particularity is a basic principle. The place of a letter is designated by the graphic surface itself, and it is just the particularity and discreteness of writing that makes the interruptions and fractures necessary, and to make writing two-dimensional. Fractures, in the Flusserian notion of notation serve as a basis for the way codes are formulated.

It is this two-dimensionality that will serve as a common ground for contemporary writing concepts as well. Sybille Krämer, following Nelson Goodman and Friedrich Kittler, states that finite differentiation and disjointness are the basic principles of writing. As written signs are always arranged discretely, there is always a gap between two bordering signs. This is the foundation of her notion of interspatiality as well, which is determined as: "spatial modality that depends on spacing and gaps."[10] From this point of view it seems to be obvious that as only discrete units can build the structure, the two-dimensionality of surfaces and interspatiality are necessary preconditions of writing as an – in Krämer's concept – primarily spatial phenomenon.

Talking about gaps and interspatiality as basic principles of writing, we have to consider a cartographical technique as well: the structure of the grid. It was Bernhard Siegert who understood it as a cultural technique and he determines the notion of the grid in the following way: "cultural technique which considers that something may be missing from its place. In other words, it encompasses the notion of an empty space", which means, the grid provides "the ability to write absence".[11] Even digital systems may serve as an analogy here, as they need empty spaces just like writing and – according to Siegert – cartography. This way writing holds the basic distinctions of digital systems (positive/non-positive; 1/0) in as much as they always need a 'zero', a 'non-letter' to work, even though programming languages (or programmers) do not need interspaces, only lines.

As we have earlier seen from the perspective of writing, in the grid's case it is the graphic surface itself that provides the possibility of an empty space, gap or fracture. That is why Siegert can state that "the grid precedes the object

9 | Vilém Flusser, *Does Writing have a Future?* Translated by Nancy N. Roth. (Minneapolis/London: University of Minnesota Press, 2011), 19.

10 | Sybille Krämer, "Writing, Notational Iconicity, Calculus: On Writing as a Cultural Technique", *Modern Language Notes* 118 (2003), no. 3, 518-537, 523.

11 | Bernhard Siegert, *Cultural Techniques. Grids, Filters, Doors and other Articulations of the Real.* Transl. Geoffrey Winthrop-Young. (New York: Fordham University Press, 2015), 97.

located therein".[12] The grid is presupposed by the surface of the (cartographic) page, and just like the fractures of writing themselves they both need empty spaces. This is the point where writing and cartography show analogous operations that are fundamental for both of them; fractures and empty spaces are the bases of creating any kind of spatial units in the case of writing and cartography as cultural techniques.

Writing and Topo/Cartography

There are two examples for the interrelations of writing and topography to discuss here. Starting with the notion of the grid, I would like to shortly refer to Ptolemy's *Geography* which is an early example of maps using the technique of the grid. Not being the first, however, it dates back to a Chinese grid map carved into stone from the first century.[13] Ptolemy's work (considered a treatise on cartography) contains ten regional grid maps of Europe and he creates captions for each of his maps with a list of the principal cities and basic data concerning their whereabouts. The question that may be important for us here from the perspective of the interrelations between writing and cartography then is how these captions relate to the maps themselves?

Fig. 2: The first map using the grid, inscribed into stone. Turnbull, Maps are Territorries, 26.

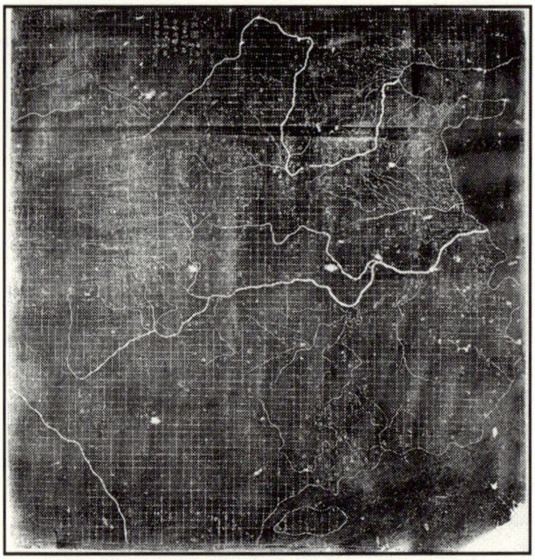

12 | Siegert, "Cultural Techniques," 100.

13 | Turnbull, "Maps are Territorries," 26.

In cartography, the grid is made up of the lines of longitudes and latitudes determining position. In Ptolemy's case, the captions on the left-hand side tables indicate that they can point at longitudinal positions only, which is the only direction that can be determined by the page. It is because of the list structure that the elements of the list are arranged under one another on the caption in the same order as on the map. That is why on this list only the latitudes must be added as a distance from Alexandria (the meridian at the time), e.g. in the last but one line: "Vienna has a longest day of 15 ½ equinoctial hours and is 2 ½ equinoctial hours west of Alexandria."[14] This way we could say that lists can determine the longitudinal order provided by the page and by extension, by the graphic surface. Thus, it is enough to say, "west of Alexandria", because the list structure shows the whereabouts on the north-south axis. The caption uses the grid structure necessarily provided by the page, by the spatiality of writing, because of its lines, empty spaces, fractures and list elements to fill up the grid.[15]

The interrelations of Ptolemy's map and list show that the map inherited the grid structure from writing, meaning from the spatiality of the page and its two-dimensional surface. And as such, it is determined by gaps, empty spaces and its structure based on fractures. Hence, writing decides on topography and the structure of writing provides the basis for cartography and determines how we access space. That is why we do not have to accept S. Y. Edgerton's interpretation of this map who claims that this way "Romans turn all Europe into one vast sheet of graph paper".[16] This logic covers a crucial feature of cartography, which is: the graphic surface and writing are always in operation when dealing with spatial relations.

Trying to understand the interrelations between writing and cartography I would like to focus on the next examples that may hopefully show what new perspectives the reading of literary texts can add to the presented insights, and what the possible poetical functions of cartographical operations in literature are. I will shortly mention a few prose poems written by the Hungarian poet and essayist Ágnes Nemes Nagy that may show how the grid structure works and how the structures of writing are present in topographical operations. The prose poems of Nemes Nagy very often refer to the technique of the grid and to the experience that one can get access to urban (or any kind of) spaces through the structure of the grid. It very often happens in a self-reflexive way, like in the

14 | J. Lennart Bergrren; Alexander Jones, *Ptolemy's Geography. An Annotated Translation of the Theoretical Chapters* (Princeton/Oxford: Princeton University Press, 2000), 124.

15 | Cf., in the level of the technological device, the function of the "static order" of Luhmann's slip box in as described i the article by Charlotte Coch in this volume.

16 | Turnbull, "Maps are Territorries," 26.

case of her poem, *Tram – Final Station,* where she identifies grid and poetry: "Iron grid, painted yellow; fin de siécle cast-iron poetry."[17]

This self-reflexivity in the presence of the grid considered in the following step can be a part of the poem's material operations as well. Another Nemes' Nagy poem I would like to discuss in a more detailed way is *The Transformation of a Railway Station,* where the grid appears not only thematically, but as a preliminary structure as well:

[...] Exhausted trams lurch down ligatured veins, connections tacked together over a shortage of subsiding stones, swollen stitches of rail. [...]

[...] Here, we will establish an institutional headquarters. Here, the main hall. Asparagus goes here, notice board there. Look...can you see? Up there, among all those vacant cubic metres, there, yes there, that is where we shall put whatever does not yet exist. It's still transparent, still negotiable. [...][18]

The text is focusing on the construction site of a station where the station building is still transparent and invisible though the grid's structure is already in operation. And it does not only happen thematically through the presence of such main motives as the cobblestones (producing a grid), "stitches of rail" or "vacant cubic meters". The technique of the grid seems to be functioning on the graphic surface of the page and the fractures of the text as well. Though there are differences between the different text versions as far as the layout is concerned, these prose poems are structured following the graphic arrangement of the grid. The lines of the texts are justified, the margins are wide, and the section breaks between the stanzas are ordered in a rhythm that results in cubelike (or cobblestonelike) stanzas, which are producing the grid structure. The texts – just like the station – are filling up an invisible grid structure created by empty spaces and breaks and made possible by the graphic surface of the page. What we have here is the grid of the text that is accessible and precedes the still invisible grid of the station. Though the English edition does not follow this arrangement as the margins here are not especially wide, the layout of the following text version follows a definite cube structure. This structure makes it possible to get access to the poem simultaneously, using the whole page at the same time, that is, the graphic space of the text. Reading in this case happens together with this simultaneous, spatial accessibility.

17 | Ágnes Nemes Nagy, *Nemes Nagy Ágnes összegyűjtött versei.* (Budapest: Osiris, 1997), 124. (my translation)

18 | Ágnes Nemes Nagy, *The Night of Akhenaton.* Translated by George Szirtes. (Newcastle: Bloodaxe, 2004), 62.

Fig. 3: The text of this poem is filling up the grid in a peculiar way, even though this technique is always in operation, whenever a graphic space is used. Ágnes Nemes Nagy, Összegyűjtött versei [Collected Poems of Ágnes Nemes Nagy] (Budapest: Osiris, 1997), 119.

vények, a végképp védtelenek, akiknek szárát szemétvödörbe-dobáskor eltörik, mint Jézus lábát (szinte) keresztről-levétel után, a növények poros rémületükben.

Középen pedig a működés. Az exkavátorok, a fix-platósok. A gépkezelő odafent, mint egy függőben maradt pilóta. Citromsárga gumiruhában gödrökbe mászó űrhajósok. A lárma tűrhetetlen torlaszai közt katasztrófák nyugalma, fejvesztett közöny. Egy drótcsomón plasztikszatyor. (Az ételcsomagok a világon. Papír, műanyag, egy-egy kendervászon-darab. A textúrák, a bogok és kötések. Bizony, feleim, emitt, amott.) És milyen különös sapkák! Talán bálnavadászok fejfedői, egy szertartás álarcai. S az óriási munkakesztyűk, e kézutánzó, absztrahált kezek.

Itt lesz a központi létesítmény. Itt lesz a csarnok. Itt aszparágusz, információk. Itt lesz a... látod? Fent, ahol még üresek most a légköbméterek, fent, fent a nem-levő. Még átlátszó, még elvitatható. Túlságosan sok szél fúj rajta át. De egy jó lencse már rögzítené. A kellő fényerőnél. Hiszen oly keskeny réteg zárja el, oly keskeny réteg attól, hogy legyen. Így már-már látni éleit fent, a biztos és a kétes közti térben, így már-már elbeszélhető, amint beúszik a képbe e visszájára fordult csökkenés (homályos, nagy hajótest), lételőtti, beláthatatlan emeleteivel.

Te emlékszel még, ugye, a mozdonyforgató dobra? Terméskő-ellipszisben végződött akkor a pályaudvar, az ellipszis fejében ott volt az acéldob. A mozdony ráállt és megfordult vele, mint egy táncoló elefánt. Még ott a régi, sárga állomásépület, avult, de működő nosztalgiákkal. A gőzbodor mögötti lámpák, esőben a hajnal. És a

119

The Transformation of a Railway Station points at this process again in a self-reflexive line; there is an empty space within the text, an unfinished sentence as a part of a future time description: “Look...can you see?” In the spatiality of writing we can see the structure of the "vacant cubic" arrangement as an empty, still continuous line. The grid as a foundation is working even if there is nothing to fill it up with yet. This sentence is pointing not only at the materiality of the text, but at the same time it makes the operation of the grid visible. This way, we could say that in this poem the empty grid, the transparent building of the station, is present on the textual level. At the same time, neither the description nor the line is visible even though the grid is in operation. The fracture of the empty space is present and is in operation both in writing and cartography, even when it is still not filled up. Here the text stops working but the grid is still functioning; in *The Transformation of a Railway Station* the grid is present through writing and it is made possible by the graphic surface and the opportunity to write absence. Grid as a cultural technique of cartography seems to have common roots with writing and with a possibility of the literary text, where the poetics of emptiness within empty structures present itself on a material basis.

The graphic surface of writing works in a similar fashion, which I will briefly refer to here. In *The Proportions of the Street,* the space is geometrically determined: "[...] proportions, interdependencies, coefficients. This is what you see in the street." (Nemes Nagy 2004, 64) And what happens when the buildings of this geometrical space are deconstructed is shown at the end of the second stanza: "If I were to strip the house down, if I were to strip it to the bone [...] then lines would remain, inflexions, webs." In this poem, stripping down and destroying the house does not mean the disappearance of the grid, as it has always been there: "The world is simply transparent. House and tarmac are transparent: behind them the metallic framework of the scales."

Therefore, we could say that this framework is the basis of spatial units in these two Ágnes Nemes Nagy poems, as they do not only point at the grid arranging topographical units, they at the same time show that there is a grid as well in textual operations as the poems are filling up. To write absence is necessary in any textual and topographical processes, and the absence of any units in space is probable only within the graphic surface. Writing absence, thus, in the spatiality of writing can become the poetics of emptiness in poems where fundamental materiality is at the core of textual operations.

If we take a look at the woodcut picture of Paul Pfintzing from *Methodus Geometrica,* showing a cartographer at work,[19] what may first come to our attention is that the ongoing cartographical process – that is covering something from the outside world – happens inside. Behind blind windows the cartographer is drawing a map with quills only on the ground of the page's geometrical surface. Mapping, as it seems to be obvious looking at this scene, starts with the operations of writing, and the foundation of the cartographical operations is the spatiality of the graphic surface. To come to a conclusion we could say that

19 | Turnbull, "Maps are Territorries," title page.

everything written is written *in*to a(n active) two-dimensional surface, which is why topography or cartography follows the structure of writing and uses the spatiality of the graphic surface as well. Fractures of writing are always in operation when we are dealing with space that is necessarily graphic, because we need gaps, empty spaces and spatial units to get access to it. And this is the point that topography and cartography, literature and poetry seem to share: an operation that may become central when literature begins to produce space.

Fig. 4: An early illustration of a cartographer at work, 1598. Turnbull, Maps are Territorries, title page.

New Practices = New Conditions?

Interrelations of Practical Approaches, Methodologies, and Theoretical Concepts in Digital Literary Studies

Julia Nantke

1. Theory and Practice in Scholarly Editing and Literary Analysis

Digital techniques and methods have significantly changed the field of research in literary studies in the recent years and it can be assumed that their impact will continue to increase. Fundamental changes are mainly due to the fact that the access to literary texts and related forms of (re)presentation of literary objects in the Digital Literary Studies (DLS) differ substantially from those in the 'analogue' literary studies. The establishment of digital methods and techniques for editing and analysing literary texts not only changes the possibilities for what can be observed in a text, but also the *modus operandi* of the philological discourse as a whole. This applies in particular because changes in different areas of research superimpose in the course of digitization.

In scholarly editing and analysis as the two central 'stages' of philological work, new procedures have been established in the course of digitization which are to be described primarily as practices, as modes of working with texts because beyond theoretical localisations they take literary documents resp. published texts as empirical 'material' which is to be processed and manipulated during the research process.

Scholarly editing represents a genuinely practice-oriented field anyway since it is primarily concerned with the representation of (mainly historical) documents. The wide variance of editorial concepts, applied in the different disciplines and in a historical perspective, but also within one discipline in a synchronic perspective, however, indicates that these different practices go along with miscellaneous theoretical concepts, e. g. with regard to the relationship of author and work, material and linguistic text etc. The mutual relation of theory, methodology, practice and the edited object is a complex one and it is not always possible to decide which perspective is dominant in the design of the edition. Often it can be assumed to be a mixture of the different contributing factors. This counts for digital scholarly editions as well as for printed ones. But given this intertwining of theory, methods and practice, it is necessary to ask whether the changed practices in the course of the shift to digital research environments result in a conceptual realignment as well.[1]

In contrast to the inevitable practice-orientation of scholarly editing, analytical contributions in literary studies can refer predominantly or totally to the field of theory or methods. This applies to contributions reflecting on methodological aspects as well as to those that elaborate theoretical models and only quote literary examples as evidence punctually. Therefore, the rupture between analogue and digital approaches appears to be greater, because for the former even in practice-oriented studies specific theoretical-methodological presumptions build the scaffold for the practical analysis at least in the display of results. Whereas in DLS this relation is reversed in such a way that the practice of modelling related to a specific literary text or corpus becomes the primacy and centre of scientific activity,[2] from which further steps of interpretation, editing, and reflection are derived. However, the activity of modelling itself is already characterized by certain theoretical assumptions, which are implicitly reflected in the models resp. the modelled results. Conversely, it can also be assumed that the textual practices of digital analysis and editing have an impact on the theoretical reflection of fundamental parameters of literary discourse.

This paper attempts to describe in more concrete terms the influence of digitization on philological practice and the interrelations between digital practices and the concepts of philological theory. Due to the brevity of the paper, this can only be done by means of exemplary selected characteristics of digital edition and analysis, which in this context are regarded as fundamental. Theoretical concepts and methods based on them, however, are difficult to clearly distinguish from each other, since they are mutually related in philological practice. The same applies to the methods and practices of literary studies. Certain philological practices are associated with specific methods of literary studies. Nevertheless, a differentiation shall be attempted in the following. This is based on the assumption that it is precisely at the junction of traditional concepts and new practices that the relations between object, theory, and practice can be grasped. This applies firstly when comparing different practices to reveal their

1 | Cf. Patrick Sahle, "Digitales Archiv – Digitale Edition. Anmerkungen zur Begriffsklärung," in *Literatur und Literaturwissenschaft auf dem Weg zu den neuen Medien*, eds. Michael Stolz, Lucas Marco Gisi and Jan Loop (Bern: germanistik.ch, 2005), 64-84, cited here at 65.

2 | See for this for instance the activities of the project "Modelling between Digital and Humanities: Thinking in Practice" http://modellingdh.eu.

respective determinant potential with regard to the processed objects, secondly when changed practices imply new methods and suggest new theoretical conceptualizations, thirdly when these practices appear equally influenced by existing concepts, and fourthly when established methods undergo significant changes in their practical implementation, which in turn have an impact on the methods and their theoretical foundation. The following considerations lie at the intersection of these four perspectives.

2. Characteristics of the Practices of Digital Scholarly Editing and Digital Analysis

In principle, all current editions, irrespective of the media form in which they appear, can be described as digital, since they are created and produced on the computer. In the following, however, I will deal with those editions that are not only digitally produced, but also presented and received digitally and that make use of the specific digital possibilities for the processing and presentation of their objects.[3] In addition, the digitization of literary studies has led to a large number of new analytical methods that cannot be evaluated in detail in this article. As already mentioned, I will therefore confine myself to highlighting two basic characteristics that become apparent from the digital textual practices. They serve as a basis for the exemplary discussion of the displayed questions.

2.1 Increase in Capacity

A central feature of digital (research) environments, when compared to analogue conditions, is their much higher capacity, both in terms of storage and processing of texts. This is a very general observation, but it has very specific implications for the practices of edition and analysis. In contrast to analogue editions, which mainly focus on *one* constituted text due to the limited space in the medium of the printed book, the number of texts presented in digital editions can be extended practically indefinitely. This is exemplified by the *Faustedition* currently being developed in Frankfurt am Main, Weimar, and Würzburg.[4] The portal, which is still under construction and is currently available in the beta 3 version, offers various accesses to the edited documents,

3 | Cf. Sahle, Patrick, *Digitale Editionsformen. Zum Umgang mit der Überlieferung unter den Bedingungen des Medienwandels. Teil 2: Befunde, Theore und Methodik* (Norderstedt: BoD, 2013), 148.

4 | Cf. http://beta.faustedition.net.

which open up different perspectives on the objects.[5] Thus, the recipient has the possibility to view the different stages of processing of the material by the author Goethe individually and/or within one stage of processing. The variants existing for the respective text passages in other versions can be displayed in the current version. In contrast to the *Faustedition*, the aim of the *Samuel Beckett Digital Manuscript Project* (BDMP), which has not yet been completed as well and is developed at the Universities of Antwerp, Reading and Austin/Texas, is to produce a complete scholarly edition of Beckett's works.[6] Here it is again possible to switch between different views. The starting point in both editions is mainly the manuscripts of the authors. Each document is represented by a facsimile, a "documentary" (Faust) or "topographic" (Beckett) and a "textual" (Faust) or "linear" (Beckett) transcription. In a further view, the BDMP also aims to make the transformation process of Beckett's notebooks into printed publications comprehensible by mapping manuscripts, publications and "reading traces" in the digitally reconstructed Beckett library.[7]

The practices of digital analysis are based centrally on the increase in capacity, too, which is facilitated by large literary corpora that are provided in machine-readable form by digital libraries and editions. While analogous analyses inevitably rely on the limitation of their research corpora to a few exemplary cases, computer-aided analysis also enables the investigation of unmanageable amounts of text and the systematic recording of the results generated. A canonical example of this is the study of literary history described in detail by Matthew Jockers in *Macroanalysis*.[8]

5 | Multiple forms of representation can also be found in print editions such as Büchner's *Woyzeck* or Hölderlin's texts. But this is mainly due to complex conditions that are characterized by the incompleteness of the works themselves (cf. Georg Büchner, *Sämtliche Werke und Schriften [Marburger Ausgabe], vol. 7.1 and 7.2 Woyzeck*. Ed. by Burghard Dedner (Darmstadt: WBG, 2005) and Friedrich Hölderlin, *Sämtliche Werke [Frankfurter Ausgabe]*. Ed. by. Dietrich E. Sattler (Frankfurt/Basel: Roter Stern/Stroemfeld, 1976-2008).

6 | Cf. http://www.beckettarchive.org. While the *Faustedition* is accessible in Open Access, a password is required for the main sections of the BDMP, which must be purchased.

7 | Cf. the demo version of *L'innomable/The Unnamable*. http://www.beckettarchive.org/writingsequenceofinnommable.jsp as well as the remarks on the *Beckett Digital Library* http://www.beckettarchive.org/library/home/welcome.

8 | Mathew Jockers, *Macroanalysis. Digital Methods & Literary History* (Urbana/Chicago/Springfield: University of Illinois Press, 2013). Cf. the contribution by Gábor Vaderna to this volume.

2.2 Texts as Data

The second central aspect that characterizes DLS's practices and marks a fundamental difference to analogue philological practice is the transformation of texts into data and their enrichment with metadata, where "[d]ata in the humanities could be considered a digital, selectively constructed, machine-actionable abstraction representing some aspects of a given object of humanistic inquiry".[9] This abstraction is achieved by capturing literary structures in formalized descriptions as a basis for the automatic processing of texts. Different degrees of abstraction and forms of enrichment with metadata make it possible to perform different operations, from full text search and structured presentation of the texts in a digital edition to the establishment of certain sorting and linking rules as well as the corresponding query categories for interpretation. Here, two main issues can be distinguished on the basis of the keywords 'big data' and 'smart data', which are to be understood rather as poles of a gradual scaling and finally converge in the goal of 'big smart data'.[10] The two approaches imply different techniques of creating those data in the field of tension between human activities and machine-based operations. For the creation of 'big data', large literary corpora are compiled according to certain criteria and pre-structured mostly only preliminary, which can be partially automated. These data form the basis for quantitative analyses, in which algorithms filter the texts according to certain parameters, whereby within the corpora linguistic or structural patterns and shifts in these patterns can be detected depending on the respective instructions. In the 'smart data' approach as pursued by digital editions and in an extended form in projects in the context of the Semantic Web, however, the focus is initially on the systematic 'deep' annotation of literary texts according to certain criteria, which due to the complexity of literary structures is usually carried out manually on the basis of existing ontologies or specially designed annotation guidelines.[11] The systematic recording of text

9 | Christof Schöch: "Big? Smart? Clean? Messy? Data in the Humanities," *JHD: Journal of Digital Humanities* 2, no. 3 (2013), 2-13, cited here at 4.

10 | Cf. Schöch: "Big? Smart? Clean? Messy? Data in the Humanities", 10.

11 | Here, TEI or XML schemes and RDF schemes differ in terms of their (semantic) 'range': "Both an XML schema and an RDF schema can assign a data model to a document, but in the first case the model depends on internal relations between different portions of the document, whereas in the second case it consists in an external structure independent of the structure of the document. In this context, XML documents act 'as a transfer mechanism for structured data'" (Jerome McGann/Dino Buzzetti: "Electronic Textual Editing: Critical Editing in a Digital Horizon" [2007] http://www.tei-c.org/About/Archive_new/ETE/Preview/mcgann.xml).

structures enables the linking of documents as well as the automated retrieval of common patterns.

3. Practical Implications: Changed Conditions of Perception and Research

The changes outlined here on the basis of two central features which are related to the procedures of the digital edition and analysis have decisive consequences for philological practice. The digital paradigm-oriented edition, when compared to the print edition, provides a changed basis for philological follow-up operations and the practices of digital analysis allow changed approaches to literature as an object of investigation, but also require them. Initially, the increase in capacity provides new possibilities in the choice of materials for scientific research. Jockers' *Macroanalysis* illustrates this for the case of literary analysis. When the human capacity to read and systematically capture the content of literary texts is no longer the limiting criterion for scientific research, corpora can be investigated and texts can be compared with each other on a large scale and, due to their technically supported structurability, characteristics can be systematically recorded.

Likewise, the variety of text views and correlations presented in digital editions makes it possible to choose between the different accesses to the text or to combine and compare several views with each other. Due to the network structure of digital editions, the increasing establishment of bibliographic, personal and location-related authority data and metadata standards[12] as well as the availability of further media resources in digital form, the recipient can also explore further connections on the basis of the edition. This is exemplified by the link between the Beckett Edition and the author's library, which, in addition to his own texts, shall make it possible to trace the 'conditions of production' of Beckett's writings in the form of potential intertexts. Instead of presenting the singular result of an editing process, the edition offers various components created on the basis of a range of scientific parameters to the recipient for selection and comparison. Thus, the different transcriptions of the two editions used as examples each exhibit a different understanding of the text: while the document/topographical view focuses on the "bibliographic code" of the texts, the textual/linear transcription emphasizes their "linguistic code".[13]

---

12 | See for this for instance the remarks on "standardisation" on the website of the Deutsche Nationalbibliothek http://www.dnb.de/EN/Standardisierung/standardisierung_node.html.

13 | Cf. Jerome McGann, *The Textual Condition* (Princeton: Princeton University Press, 1991), 77.

At the same time, this multiplication of perspectives goes along with the increased need for recipients to make their own decisions on the selection of texts and to make them plausible in the research process. The historical-critical print edition served to establish a scientifically sound basis on which further literary research could be based, without questioning the emergence of the text presented in the edition. Instead, the edition, which is committed to the digital paradigm, corresponds in its potentiality to a hybrid of edition and archive in which the reader has to orientate himself/herself: "A digital edition is more like a workspace or a laboratory where the user is invited to work with the texts and documents more actively."[14] Whereas the increase in capacity thus contributes to reducing the normative character of scholarly editions, while at the same time shifting responsibility to the user's side, digital methods of analysis as well require heightened strategies of validation on the part of the scholars due to the increase in capacity: The general possibility to include as many texts as desired in an analysis increases the necessity of clarifying the plausibility of corpus boundaries and – especially for (partially) automated quantitative analyses – of research hypotheses. For here, the impossibility of reading all of the analysed texts requires the development of research hypotheses before or instead of the actual reading process or the derivation of such hypotheses from the selective reading of smaller corpora.[15]

The conditions of perception therefore also change due to the increase in capacity. By storing the contents as machine-readable data, a mode of reception in the form of search queries and "zapping" from one view to another replaces the complete, exact reading of self-contained structures.[16] Though

14 | Patrick Sahle, "What is a Scholarly Digital Edition?," in *Digital Scholarly Editing. Theory and Practice*, eds. Matthew James Driscoll and Elena Pierazzo (Cambridge: Open Book Publishers 2016), 19–39, cited here at 30, cf. also ibd., 34. Cf. for this tendency also the remarks in the editorial of the BDMP: "Usually, digital 'archives' are distinguished from 'editions' because the latter offer a critical apparatus. An interoperable tool such as CollateX can enable any user – not necessarily an editor – to transform a digital archive into an electronic edition. As a consequence of these developments in scholarly editing, the strict boundary between digital archives and electronic editions is becoming increasingly permeable, resulting in a continuum rather than a dichotomy." (http://www.beckettarchive.org/editorial.jsp)

15 | For hypotheses as a prerequisite for big data analyses, see Martin Frické, "Big data and its epistemology," *Journal of the Association for Information Science and Technology* 66, no. 4 (2015), 651-661, cited here at 656.

16 | This does not necessarily have to be a linear reading, which is probably not the primary mode of perception even for analogue editions with their apparatus and register structures. Nevertheless, there are significant differences compared to the "traditional bibliographic methods". Cf. Adriaan van der Weel, *Changing our textual minds. Towards*

digital editions facilitate such a mode of perception, there is also the possibility of a 'closed' reading, while the fragmented perception in the form of lists and database queries is indispensable when evaluating the results of digital analyses.

In connection with this, the change in perception conditions is also caused by the fact that the presentation modes of the textual relations resp. the generated analysis results in DLS publications differ significantly from the analogous flow text-based presentation mode. As a result of the increase in capacity and enabled by the conversion of texts into data, relationships between texts in the DLS are increasingly presented in the form of diagrams. The *Faustedition*, for example, visualizes the various versions on display and their relations with each other in a series of bar charts from which the texts can be accessed.[17] The visualizations of research results of digital analyses as diagrams, networks or graphs that follow mathematical description conventions, are considerably more complex as the figures in *Macroanalysis* show.[18] The visual forms allow a neat representation of the otherwise unmanageable amounts of text and of their relations. This at the same time holds a heuristic potential that should not be underestimated. 'Representation' therefore means a "presentation in the sense of a production, a production in which the depicted itself takes shape in the first place".[19] The graphics thus are specific "tools of thought" that represent concrete operations in relation to universal arithmetic rules in a way that is not defined in principle.[20] They are therefore to be understood as new discursive practices, the 'operating modes' of which must be acquired. Besides the underlying mathematical rules, this also applies to the argumentative and aesthetic

---

a digital order of knowledge (Manchester/New York: Manchester University Press, 2011), 154. Weel ibid., 168 establishes the word "zapping" for the digital mode of perception which "as a concept may derive from television, but [...] is highly applicable too to the world of digital text". Cf. the article by Dániel Kozák on reading databases and by Hanjo Berressem on reading television in this volume.

17 | Cf. http://beta.faustedition.net/genesis. See for this in detail also the review by Gengnagel, Tessa, "The 'Beta Dilemma' – A Review of the *Faust* Edition," *ride* 7 (2017) http://ride.i-d-e.de/issues/issue-7/faustedition/.

18 | Cf. e. g. 84n. and 101-103.

19 | Rheinberger, Hans-Jörg, *Experiment, Differenz, Schrift. Zur Geschichte epistemischer Dinge* (Marburg: Basilisken-Presse, 1992), 73, my translation. See also ibid. 81.

20 | Cf. Krämer, Sybille: "Punkt, Strich, Fläche. Von der Schriftbildlichkeit zur Diagrammatik," in *Schriftbildlichkeit. Wahrnehmbarkeit, Materialität und Operativität von Notationen*, eds. Sybille Krämer/Eva Cancik-Kirschbaum/Rainer Trotzke (Berlin: Akademie, 2012), 79-100, cited here at 81, my translation.

aspects, i. e. the operational potential of graphic representation, which has to be taken into account in production as well as in perception of visualizations.

4. Methodological Implications

4.1 'Reverse Blackboxing' and Philological Positivism

Digital practices of edition and analysis draw increased attention to processes of authorial production, editorial text constitution and the canonization of works in literary discourse that tend to be out of reach of scientific (and private) observation within the framework of analogous practices. Based on Bruno Latour's science studies this process can be described as 'reverse blackboxing'.[21] But here this procedure does not refer to the rendering visible of the transition from the "world of things" to that of "sign[s]".[22] In contrast to the processes of scientific research examined by Latour, in literary analysis signs are already the origin point of departure. It is them that are subject to "a regulated series of transformations, transmutations, and translations" within the course of philological processing.[23]

In the two editions presented, the philological operations and the theoretical perspectives influencing them previously only presented in summarized form in the guidelines of the edition and otherwise largely invisible or opaque, are made comprehensible to the recipient in the comparative examination of facsimile and different types of document representation. Therefore, the alternative transcriptions illustrate the effects of differing understandings of 'text' on the design of a scholarly edition. Not only the literary text, but also the edition itself thus is presented as a product of a specific scholarly perspective.

The digital methods of analysis also make visible scholarly selection processes at various levels. On the one hand, the direct coupling of primary texts and analytical access leads to an 'empiricization' of the relationship between theory and practice: neither individual texts nor individual sections of texts are selected as examples for the analysis, but a large number of texts are filtered indiscriminately by the respective programs and the results serve as the basis of scholarly statements. Semantic annotations, e. g., of narratological categories or intertextual references must furthermore be linked directly to the respective text passages to which they relate. This requires a concretization of the relationship between literary practice and the theoretical framework referred to in the

21 | Cf. for this in detail the articles by Charlotte Jaeckel and Gábor Palkó in this volume.

22 | Latour, Bruno, *Pandora's hope: Essays on the Reality of Science Studies* (Cambridge/London: Harvard University Press, 1999), 48.

23 | Latour, *Pandora's Hope*, 58.

context of the analysis. Therefore, uncertainties become evident in the respective theoretical concepts, which either remain undiscovered in the context of a purely argumentative and exemplary investigation or can be obscured by a clever choice of examples.[24]

On the other hand, a central argument for the application of quantitative analytical methods is that the expansion of observation units makes it possible to examine literary texts beyond the canon.[25] Processes of canon formation can thus be observed with regard to their attachment to concrete text structures and literary historical paradigms can be explored beyond the small circle of established literary works.

The research and presentation modes of DLS are thus increasingly oriented towards the positivist perspective of scientific and social research practices.[26] Literary texts as 'data' contain quantifiable features that can be counted, catalogued, queried and visualized. These features can refer to the "bibliographic code" in terms of letters, the arrangement of graphic characters on a manuscript or in a collection, as well as to the "linguistic code" in terms of words, text structures and entities contained in the text. The term "data mining", taken from statistics and used in quantitative analysis, refers to this idea of extracting or "harvesting" textual data.[27]

This positivistic perspective is also reflected in the publication ethos of DLS. Comparable to the new presentation modes of the digital edition, in this case as well the presentation of experimental 'test series' tends to replace 'round' nar-

---

24 | Thus, e. g., a review of systematic representations of intertextuality reveals how often the studies cite the same literary examples and, at the same time, only refer to certain, very definite elements. For an attempt to close the gap between theoretical concepts and practical textual analysis on the basis of a formalised description of intertextual phenomena see Nantke, Julia and Frederik Schlupkothen, "Zwischen Polysemie und Formalisierung: Mehrstufige Modellierung komplexer intertextueller Relationen als Annäherung an ein 'literarisches' Semantic Web," *DHd 2018: Kritik der Digitalen Vernunft Konferenzabstracts*, 345-349 (http://dhd2018.uni-koeln.de/wp-content/uploads/boa-DHd2018-web-ISBN.pdf). For the detection of fuzziness in the narratological taxonomy of Genette, which is significantly shaped by one single literary work, see Evelyn Gius and Janina Jacke, "The Hermeneutic Profit of Annotation: On Preventing and Fostering Disagreement in Literary Analysis," *International Journal of Humanities and Arts Computing* 11, no. 2 (2017), 233-254, cited here at 243n.

25 | Cf. Moretti, Franco, *Distant Reading* (London/Brooklyn: Verso 2013), 48; Jockers, *Macroanalysis*, 8.

26 | Cf. for this explicitly Moretti, Franco, *Graphs, Maps, Trees: Abstract Models for Literary History* (London: Verso 2005), 2.

27 | See for these terms e. g. Jockers, *Macroanalysis*, 9, 35.

ratives.[28] This goes along with the replacement of the traditional monographic form in literary studies by the publication of abstracts, blog posts, shorter papers or posters.[29] Furthermore, technical data and structures in the form of TEI schemata and encoding guidelines are documented for example in the course of analysis projects and in editorial paratexts in addition to the usual documentation of the philological work steps, and they are frequently made available for reuse in Open Access.[30] This practice, like the versioned publication of digital editions, contributes to increased transparency and observability of the research process by the community.[31]

4.2 The Enhancement of the 'Intelligent Text'

As Adriaan van der Weel rightly points out, the DLS' central concept of "making a text intelligent" via markup is based on a traditional method of philological text processing that has been mainly developed in the course of scholarly editions:

> Though the processing possibilities are greatly broadened by the computer, the concept of the creation and publication of an authoritative text enriched with interpretive expert knowledge by an appropriately skilled person is thus not new. In that sense, the practice

28 | See for this e. g. the remarks regarding the experimental nature of the contributions to the volume in Thomas Weitin, "Scalabe Reading" *LiLi Zeitschrift für Literaturwissenschaft und Linguistik* 47, no. 1 (2017), 1-6, cited here at 6.

29 | Cf. e. g. the research blog of Matthew Jockers (http://www.matthewjockers.net/). Another example of this is the fact that usually no subsequent proceedings are produced after Digital Humanities conferences, but instead the 'raw' abstracts of the contributions are made available.

30 | Cf. for the BDMP the links "Technical Documentation" and "Encoding Guidelines" under "Documentation". The *Faustedition* provides the code of the web application on Github and the editors state that they are going to publish the TEI-XML codings of the transcriptions in "one of the further beta versions" (http://beta.faustedition.net/beta-release). For projects on annotation see e.g. Evelyn Gius and Janina Jacke, "Zur Annotation narratologischer Kategorien der Zeit. Guidelines zur Nutzung des CATMA-Tagsets. Version 2.0 (November 2016)" http://heureclea.de/wp-content/uploads/2016/11/guidelinesV2.pdf.

31 | On the other hand, though, this practice goes along with a decrease in reliability and refereability, as Gengnagel points out with regard to the *Faustedition* (cf. Gengnagel, "The 'Beta Dilemma'", sec. 37). This hints back to the aforementioned shift of responsibility to the user's side.

of what I have called 'making text intelligent' is still strongly motivated by a notion of scholarship that was fully determined by the Order of Books.[32]

However, not only are their technical "processing possibilities" being expanded within the framework of DLS, but also the performance spectrum of the method has been enhanced within the scope of digital use. This applies on the one hand to the practice of annotation of digital corpora in editions and as preparation for digital analysis. Here, the additions no longer serve in the main as explanations addressed to the reader, but rather represent the formal and linguistic structure of the text. In this function, they are initially destined for a machine addressee and build the basis for possible human-readable formats.

On the other hand, the method is being broadened specifically in the domain of analysis and interpretation of literature. While the enrichment of the text with annotations from an editorial perspective is primarily intended to support the reading process, which means it is prior to the actual literary analysis, in DLS the semantic annotation itself can become a heuristic tool of analysis. In that the markup, as well as the ontologies and annotation guidelines on which it is based, bare a high epistemic potential in that they determine the criteria according to which literary corpora are filtered, how they can be looked at and, accordingly, how they can be received. This is illustrated e.g. by projects in which the methods of narratological analysis are transformed into annotation guidelines. These thus become the 'grid' of the analytical comprehension of narrative texts.[33] In this way, the interpretative impact of explanatory commentary, which is discussed as a problem from an editorial perspective,[34] is turned productively into a means of actual analysis. This way, not only the methods of narratological analysis but also the associated terminologies and taxonomies are incorporated into the markup structures of the projects. The reference to concepts of structuralism is no coincidence here. Rather, the corresponding perspectives on literature are the precondition for this convergence, by accommodating the formalization conditions of the machine-readable semantic annotation. Due to the great influence of markup structures on the perception of literature in the research process, it is therefore appropriate to speak of a strengthening of the methods and the related theoretical postulates

32 | Weel, *Changing our textual minds*, 157.

33 | See for example the projects heureCLÉA (http://heureclea.de) and SANTA (https://sharedtasksinthedh.github.io/overview/).

34 | Cf. Gunther Martens, "Kommentar – Hilfestellung oder Bevormundung des Lesers?," in *Kommentierungsverfahren und Kommentarformen*, ed. Gunter Martens (Tübingen: Niemeyer, 1993) 36-50; Sigurd Paul Scheichl, "Grenzen des Kommentars," in *Probleme des Kommentierens. Beiträge eines Innsbrucker Workshops*, ed. Wolfgang Wiesmüller (Innsbruck: Innsbruck University Press, 2014), 29-37.

of structuralism within DLS. Through the formalisation and 'empiricization' associated with digital practices, their methods undergo productive developments that substantiate the relationship between theory and practice.

4.3 Blurs and New Black Boxes

The oversight that can be obtained in the course of digital practices, both over large amounts of text and literary trends, at the same time and in the double meaning that Latour has established for scientific abstraction processes, is accompanied by the fact that certain things have to be ignored.[35] Thus, the described perception mode of zapping leads to the effect that the corpus under examination in its entirety becomes a black box, which can only be captured by the human recipient in excerpts in form of the predefined parameters and the output data. However, the transformation of literary texts into data requires that the texts must adapt to the conditions of their machinability. In this way, the 'text world' is changing in its superposition with digital inscription techniques.[36] This is precisely because the textual data collected in the framework of digital methods are "selectively constructed",[37] i. e. they do not represent given facts, but are always "sublata".[38] As Latour describes it for the plants in biological research texts and textual elements in the DLS are "detached, separated, classified, and tagged. They are then reassembled, reunited, redistributed according to entirely new principles that depend on the researcher".[39] The zapping as a basis for further interpretations is therefore already based on specific transformations.

However, the condition of the data cannot be read off from the results of a query, but must be actively accessed with considerable effort. If the interaction of input and output functions smoothly, which means the researcher receives satisfying results on the basis of the given translations, fragmentations and contextualizations by means of zapping and querying, hence there is a risk that the various procedures of 'recoding' the literary objects tend to be blanked out just as much as the conditions of text constitution in the use of printed

35 | Latour, *Pandora's Hope*, 38.

36 | See for this Latour's question with regard to the natural sciences: "For here we must ask how much the world needs to change in order for one kind of paper to be *superposed* on a geometry of another kind without suffering too much distortion." (Latour, *Pandora's Hope*, 54)

37 | Schöch, "Data in the Humanities," 4.

38 | "One should never speak of 'data' – what is given – but rather of *sublata*, that is, of 'achievements.'" (Latour, *Pandora's Hope*, 42) See also McGann and Buzzetti, "Electronic Textual Editing".

39 | Latour, *Pandora's Hope*, 39.

editions. Their influence on the 'originals' and philological follow-up operations becomes invisible in this way.

This already applies to the digital representation of a manuscript or a printed page of a book in the form of a digital facsimile, which is juxtaposed in the editorial of the BDMP as a neutral "record" with the philological "interpretation" in form of a transcription.[40] Although digital facsimiles can transport certain, especially visually recognizable properties of the represented objects, this does not apply to their haptic qualities. In addition, segmentations, contextualizations and – due to the dependency on the respective output device – size and colour are variables in the representation.

To a greater extent, this applies to the results of quantitative analyses which, together with the methodological approach, adopt a certain vagueness from the statistically working disciplines. The measured data obtained are highly dependent on the predefined parameters and the subsequent operations of normalization and standardization of values. Depending on the design of the procedure, it is difficult even for the executing scholars to comprehend the exact functioning of the algorithmic survey. This is because only a large number of measurements provide meaningful results in relating the data, which is why randomly selected textual fragments are included by the algorithm in several passes, and the results are combined in the output.[41] Dieter Mersch describes this statistical procedure as "patterns that generate patterns". The result is therefore a "metagraph", "whose content is not data, but structures".[42]

The effect of "blackboxing"[43] therefore increases significantly if technical documentation is incomplete or if the recipient lacks expertise, especially in understanding the technical aspects of the transformations. Technical documentation, actually a means of reverse blackboxing, can itself become a black box if it is not read or understood properly. This points out that the effect of blackboxing does not necessarily depend on the objective possibilities of visibility. It is also dependent on the active reconstruction of certain aspects of the research process that the actors of knowledge production and reception consider relevant.[44] Therefore, in this sense, too, the methods of DLS exert a

---

40 | Cf. http://www.beckettarchive.org/editorial.jsp.

41 | See for this in detail Frické, "Big Data", 655.

42 | Dieter Mersch, Dieter, "Schrift/Bild – Zeichnung/Graph – Linie/Markierung. Bildepisteme und Strukturen des ikonischen 'Als'", in *Schriftbildlichkeit. Wahrnehmbarkeit, Materialität und Operativität von Notationen*, eds. Sybille Krämer/Eva Cancik-Kirschbaum/Rainer Trotzke (Berlin: Akademie, 2012), 306-327, cited here at 323, my translation.

43 | Cf. Latour, *Pandora's Hope*, 304.

44 | Cf. Bruno Latour, *Science in Action. How to follow scientists and engineers through society* (Cambridge: Harvard University Press, 1987), 29.

great influence on philological practice by demanding knowledge, that was previously completely unrelated to the discipline, in order to comprehend crucial work processes.

5. Interrelations of Digital Practices and Philological Concepts

5.1 Influences of Digital Practices on the Conception of Literature

In contrast to the analogous paradigm of the materially and ideally closed literary work, the digital practices of decentralizing the individual text convey the perspective of works as networks of writings. The space expansion on the Internet is used in the two scholarly editions presented to 'destabilize' the already canonized texts by Goethe and Beckett. The different text views provided by the digital editions (re)construct the production processes of the texts, different stages of the work can be classified historically and compared or perceived as singular manifestations of a work status at a certain time. The texts thus appear less as auratic works than as dynamic 'works in progress'. In contrast to cases such as Büchner's *Woyzeck* or Hölderlin's texts, with regard to the digital examples presented above one can literally speak of a redynamization of an actually completed production process within the editions.

In a comparable way, the analysis of literary texts by means of a computational approach also focuses on a network of works instead of an individual text. This causes a shift in perspective: it is not the peculiarities of a specific literary work that are explored in a detailed analysis, but fundamental structures of concordance and deviation in a large corpus that become the focus of literary scholarly observation. This changed view, which is provided by the DLS, is of great heuristic benefit, especially for objects where the application of a stable author-work scaffold is equivalent to a reduction or narrowing of perspective. This applies, for example, to the medieval and early modern texts, which are often available in large quantities of different versions and without any clearly identifiable authors, or to literary montages, which in this way become better understandable as 'intersections of dialogue'.[45] However, the examples cited have shown that the shift of scope in DLS refers to all literary objects. Similar to the way in which printed books and human reading capacities imply a restriction and peculiar forms of ordering and hierarchizing contents, the media conditions of the Internet and mechanical processing are shaping a new paradigm in dealing with literature in general. Accordingly, Franco Moretti postulates

45 | See for this also the remarks on editing Shakespeare in McGann and Buzzetti, "Electronic Textual Editing".

a fundamental change in the literary scholar's attitude towards his subject matter:

"Distant reading: where distance, let me repeat it, *is a condition of knowledge*: it allows you to focus on units that are much smaller or much larger than the text: devices, themes, tropes – or genres and systems. [...] If we want to understand the system in its entirety, we must accept losing something."[46]

By means of this statement it becomes clear that not only does the attitude towards the subject matter change in DLS, but potentially the subject matter itself is a different one. Because the "something", that is lost by Moretti, is the text as a unit. The resulting new "condition of knowledge" can be expressed using Weel's formula of the "end of the document":

"Documents that were originally physically separately published [and perceived; J. N.] now form a de facto unit in digital information space or 'docuverse'. The continuity of this textual space represents a fundamental difference in relation to the world of material documents, where physical separation also means logical separation."[47]

In the DLS, the "logic separation" addressed by Weel has no longer to be provided by material structures, instead immaterial ontologies and guidelines for annotation provide separation because of their grid structure. This changes the perspective on what can be considered exemplary in philological practices. If the abstraction in the analogue practices consists primarily of using a singular text or the insights gained from it as an exemplary basis for extrapolating general literary trends and developments,[48] the digital practices are based on the recontextualization of data that originates from a large number of texts. This abstraction of another kind then serves as well as the foundation for the investigation of processes in literary history. The singular text here appears as a small cog in an overarching system of continuous progression and rewriting.

5.2 Influences of Philological Concepts on Digital Practices

Despite the discursive shifts described above, DLS's practices cannot be conceived in terms of a complete reorientation of literary research. As the case of the 'intelligent text' already suggested, the digitization of textual practices is taking place in front of the background of a centuries-long philological theory building, whose established concepts influence the design of digital practices.

46 | Moretti, *Distant Reading*, 48n.

47 | Weel, *Changing our textual minds*, 155.

48 | Cf. Jockers, *Macroanalysis*, 47.

Hence, the semantic grids and tools that are used to process texts as data "are constructed or adopted in the light of what we know, or theories we have, about what we are measuring and what the instruments are telling us about some kind of reality beyond themselves and their apparent surface indications".[49] The Moretti quote from the previous section with its focus on "genres and systems", too, gives a hint to this. Literary genres or systems are concepts that have emerged from analogue philological practice and are hence based on the practices of editing and analysing individual (more or less) canonical works. These practices have shaped the heuristic horizon to which the quantitative observation of literature refers. Although the digital edition and computer-supported analysis offer considerably expanded possibilities for the presentation and investigation of large corpora that allow canonical and material boundaries to be crossed, the described increased necessity of clarifying the plausibility of corpus boundaries and the incomprehensibility of the exact content of the texts promote an orientation towards established philological categories.

Here, the analogous concept of authorship is also a central point of reference.[50] Even though the digital editions destabilize the text as a closed unit the singular author remains the central only few category of reference, since only his writings – or in the case of the BDMP, also the writings read by the author – are included in the intertextual network presented by the editions. Beyond the examples, it can also be stated that the category of the author remains central to the editorial practice in the DLS, since there are major editorial efforts beyond this scope. In contrast to the stated dynamization, this alignment also strengthens the function of the work as an author-related stabilizing factor. This is illustrated on the one hand by the *Faustedition,* which deals exclusively with *Goethe's* adaption of the story of Faust. On the other hand, this tendency is also reflected in the arrangements of digital analyses. Here, a concrete text is used as the basis for annotations and queries. However, since the relation to a concrete edition rarely plays a role in the interpretation of the results, in most

---

49 | Frické, "Big Data", 652. Frické refers primarily to data collection in the natural sciences. Regarding the "autopoietic aspect" of epistemic things in literary studies cf. Steffen Martus, "Epistemische Dinge in den Literaturwissenschaften?" in *Theorien, Methoden und Praktiken des Interpretierens*, eds. Andrea Albrecht, Lutz Danneberg and Carlos Spoerhase (Berlin: De Gruyter, 2015), 23-51, cited here at 28 and 39, my translation.

50 | Cf. for an orientation towards the categories genre and authorship e.g. Christof Schöch, "Corneille, Molière et les autres. Stilometrische Analysen zu Autorschaft und Gattungszugehörigkeit im französischen Theater der Klassik," *Philologie im Netz, Beiheft 7: Literaturwissenschaft im digitalen Medienwandel* (2014), 130-157 http://web.fu-berlin.de/phin/beiheft7/b7t08.pdf.

cases the text serves as a representative for an abstract work.[51] The described dynamization of textual relations thus takes place to a large extent within the boundaries drawn by genre, authorship and work.

The traditional concepts partly seem to be even strengthened in DLS practices. This is illustrated by the method of stylometry, the subject of which mainly is the attribution of authorship on the basis of linguistic characteristics of texts. In this context, the potential of computer-assisted analyses to link scholarly concepts more closely to concrete textual phenomena, shows again.[52] At the same time, the traces of individual writing instead of the text become the focus of attention. Parallel to this, in the digital edition, the 'writing scene', i. e. the process of writing as an authorial practice, displaces the text from the core of representation. This is demonstrated by the title *Beckett Digital* Manuscript *Project* as well as by the two objectives of the BDMP announced in the editorial section: "The BDMP tries to accomplish genetic criticism's double task by (1) making Samuel Beckett's manuscripts accessible and (2) analysing the composition process in order to open the manuscripts' hermeneutic potential."[53] The practical implementation of the theoretical ideas of the Critique Génétique[54] in the digital edition underlines exactly the stated tension between dynamic and stabilizing tendencies. The Critique Génétique is concerned with the redynamization of consolidated works on the basis of the poststructuralist actualization of the metaphor of text as a weave, whereby – contradictory to the again poststructuralist concept of unlimited intertextuality – the concept of authorship remains a fixed point. The example thus points out that the DLS' reference to the concepts of (post-)structuralism not only leads to productive sharpening of the theory-practice-relationship of the respective methods, but also results in the reproduction of some of their contradictions and aporias.

The definite edition of the text is in this concept of the work replaced by the author's original writings as authentic proof of his creative process, of which

51 | However, this can be partly attributed to the collections of digital repositories, which are often unsatisfactory from a text-critical point of view. The current copyright amendment (in Germany) and the increasing number of digital editions contribute to improving this situation. In turn, the above mentioned challenges of corpus foundation on the part of DLS could become even more acute if, as the basis for a digital analysis, not only a selection from a large number of works has to be made, but also a large number of versions in machine-readable form would be available for each work.

52 | Cf. Fotis Jannidis, "Dem Autor ganz nah. Autorstil in Stilistik und Stilometrie," in *Theorien und Praktiken der Autorschaft*, eds. Matthias Schaffrick/Marcus Willand (Berlin/Boston: de Gruyter, 2014), 169-195, cited here at 190.

53 | http://www.beckettarchive.org/editorial

54 | Cf. Almuth Grésillon, Éléments de critique génétique: Lire les manuscrits modernes (Paris: Presses Universitaires de France, 1994).

the various transcriptions represent only stages of diminution due to usability. The new media possibilities thus convey a return to the 'manuscript fetish' of historicism,[55] in that the manuscripts no longer only form the archival basis of the edition, but rather become its structuring element. This orientation stands in a certain tension to Weel's postulated "end of the document", as it is precisely the documents in their authoritative value, their material limits and their reciprocal references that are the basis of the "docuverse" of the edition.

6. Digital Literary Studies between Innovation and Tradition

The preceding sections at least exemplified the complexity of the interrelations arising in the course of digitization between philological practices, methods and theoretical concepts of accessing and processing literature. Although the DLS are characterized by a strong practical orientation, their practices are based on a variety of established theoretical concepts and methodological structures, which are maintained, updated and modified. This is not only true for literary concepts, as has been shown. Rather, the DLS are essentially oriented towards methods of social and natural science research, for which a "close relationship, even a fusion of technology and science" was already characteristic in the 20th century due to the lack of direct observability.[56] In this situation literary texts are superimposed with a new kind of 'technoscientific structures'[57] that differ significantly from the structures of print culture. Digital practices therefore imply changed perspectives on literary objects and their historical contexts. Though a bit exaggerated, it can be said that in contrast to analogous literary studies, in DLS the text itself, which must first and foremost be described in its form and meaning in the course of its interpretation, does not represent the central 'epistemic thing'.[58] Rather, the text is captured by two opposing dynamics that, on the one hand, dissolve the text into smaller units and, on the other hand, locate it as a small unit in a network. Writing itself as a procedural act and as a socio-historical process becomes the focus of interest as an actual research object, whereas the work as a strategic unit for defining and limiting corpora remains a decisive factor.

Within the scope of these dynamics, the digital practices themselves are embedded in theoretical and methodological concepts such as "macroanalysis" and "distant reading", which emphasise in particular the innovative potential

55 | See for this in detail the article by Livia Kleinwaechter in this volume.

56 | Rheinberger, *Experiment, Differenz, Schrift*, 67, my translation.

57 | On "technoscience" cf. Latour, *Science in Action*, especially 174.

58 | Cf. Rheinberger, *Experiment, Differenz, Schrift*, 70.

of digital textual practices. However, the normative character of such paradigmatic settings has been highlighted in the consideration of editing and analysis practices. On the one hand, the new digital practices call into question traditional philological concepts of literary objects and thus emphasize their determining effects. On the other hand, they themselves are to a considerable extent shaped by certain traditional philological concepts. The notions of a documentless textual universe beyond traditional heuristic boundaries are not fulfilled seamlessly within the framework of digital practices, too.

In particular, the links to traditional concepts and the translation of existing methodological approaches into digital structures point out that the changes brought about by the practices of DLS should not be understood as absolute, but rather in the sense of movements. These are expressions of a literary discourse in constant change and expansion of perspectives.[59] Observing its dynamics and the resulting interferences between theoretical, methodological and praxeological approaches – which means *constructing* them[60] – can help to become aware of the heuristic and epistemic potential of the different textual practices.

59 | Approaches that seek to overcome "the polemical front lines of close and distant reading" also point in this direction (Weitin, "Scalable Reading", 2, my translation).
60 | Cf. Latour, *Pandora's Hope*, 39.

4. Technologies

Sites of Digital Humanities

About Virtual Research Environments

Gábor Palkó

> "The depth of our ignorance about techniques is unfathomable."
> Bruno Latour

In his infamous analysis of the history of history writing entitled "The Writing of History", Michel de Certeau lays heavy emphasis on parameters falling out of the scope of the self-reflection of humanities-specific research that should have been as true forty years earlier as today. Elaborating on the twofold function of the "place", he states that on the one hand places enable a particular form of research along the common problems, while on the other, the place works as a censor, closing out other starting points (and the reflection of this closing itself) from the discussion.

> Such is the double function of the place. It makes possible certain researches through the fact of common conjunctures and problematics. But it makes others impossible; it excludes from discourse, what is its basis at a given moment; it plays the role of a censor with, respect to current - social, economic, political - postulates of analysis. This combination of permission and interdiction is doubtless the blind spot of historical research [...][1]

According to de Certeau, history and humanities research are often overlapping terms, such as in the passage where he describes "place" as a condition defining the limits and scope of the research, connecting the possible to the impossible. The specifically unique place where the historian, or the humanities scholar in general, speaks is just as important as the place that is the subject of the

1 | Michel de Certeau, *The Writing of History*, trans. Tom Conley (New York: Columbia UP, 1988), 68.

research.[2] But if the place where the scholar speaks, or as in the present reasoning the place in subject, is virtual, can we in that case talk about a physical, social, or any other type of place at all? To be more precise: when analyzing the circumstances affecting the research, does de Certeau take the possibility of a digital environment into account? The question may seem anachronistic in the context of a text that precedes not only eScience, but also the emergence of what Manuel Castells calls "network society". This makes the fact that de Certeau holds the role of computers in high regard when it comes to the entirety of humanities research even more surprising. When he analyzes the practice of the "university" excluding the non-interpretative practices from its reflection space by declaring them "auxiliary science", he mentions computer science, after codicology, paleography, and others as not reflected, but reflectable practices, with an emphasis on computer science as well.[3]

In the aforementioned quoted essay, the computer is discussed as a phenomenon that completely changes research in at least one more context. De Certeau states that a research can be considered "scientific" only if it creates its "resources", and the "documents" of the research in another way compared to how they were given before. Referring to new relevance, humanistic work transforms tools, recipes, songs, the location of soil, or the topology of a city to documents, also altering their function. Research, if it is scientific, redistributes the space by institutionalization acts and transforming techniques. De Certeau uses the term "apparatus" to describe the latter, which is, at the same time the prerequisite and/or the instrument, and the result of the moving or rearrangement that is a property of researches. The segment of the apparatus highlighted by de Certeau is the archive, which as an institutionalized technology determines whether it is possible to give new answers to other types of questions. In other words: only a new type of apparatus makes it possible to form new questions and answers. De Certeau takes the computer as an example for a change that defines the research to its very core: the digital storage as an archive comes with an array of changes, it restricts the scope of the research to what can be formalized prior to the programming procedure. An important footnote that draws a parallel between computers and traditional libraries introduces the term "information space", making it clear that the place of the research gains a new meaning in the space of information science between the "input" and the "output".[4]

This means that not only did de Certeau predict that using the computer would become a common practice in scientific research, but he also saw that the computer as technology was an entirely new apparatus to also define the

2 | De Certeau, *The Writing of History*, 68.

3 | De Certeau, *The Writing of History*, 69.

4 | De Certeau, *The Writing of History*, 107.

place of research and the places that can be subject to research at the same time: namely, the subject and mode of discussion in the humanities. This may be the most obvious in the case of practices ironically called "auxiliary sciences" by de Certeau. The history of writing, the codicology, and the history of books are all fields that have been radically rewritten in the last decade, as their everyday practices and correspondences were being placed into the digital space. The digitization of the philological apparatus and the wide range of metaphilological reflections on it are an outstanding example for this. Bernard Cerquiglini in his work *In Praise of the Variant* (1989), which is rightfully called the fundamental reading of "New Philology",[5] considers the change of the (scientific) space essential for the entirety of scientific research as the "booklike arrangement" is replaced by a "screenlike arrangement". The digital apparatus radically rearranges the spaces of research, in the twofold sense of de Certeau: in the case of both the document representing the research and the document being the subject of the research. Moreover, Cerquiglini goes even further when he connects – after Michael Foucault – the change that can be described as the migration from the reality of ink to the world of substanceless electronic impulses to the change in the author function.

> What the screen provides the reader is an always instantaneous grasp, the ephemeral visualization of different and mobile textual spaces, of texts that are no longer that palpable reality of ink on a page but are only the immateriality of a few electrical pulses. The two-dimensional stability of the text, attributed to an originating and controlling subject, no longer seems the basis for this new technology of the written world. Computer inscription is variance.[6]

Of course, de Certeau and Cerquiglini are not the only ones to attribute such a fundamental role to the digital technologies of the apparatus in the mechanism of humanities research and culture in general, but they surely are among the first ones who realized its substantial significance. Not taking the computer in particular, but observing the correlation between research and the apparatus, de Certeau refers to the fact that this interplay is not necessarily transparent. The apparatus defines where the blind spots of the research lay, but it does not come clear in the essay how and from where it becomes possible to discover these blind spots. The theories of archives, or more precisely, media archaeologist point of view pays special attention to the digital migration of archives

5 | Balázs Déri, Pál Kelemen, József Krupp, and Ábel Tamás, "Előszó" in *Metafilológia 1.*, ed. Balázs Déri, Pál Kelemen, József Krupp, and Ábel Tamás (Budapest: Ráció Kiadó, 2011), http://digiphil.hu/o:metafilologia1.01.

6 | Bernard Cerquiglini, *In Praise of the Variant: A Critical History of Philology*, trans. Betsy Wing (Baltimore: Johns Hopkins UP, 1999), 81.

and the apparatus of data spaces with special care for the limitations of understanding and of the transparency of the medium, in other words "the shadow side" of the archive.[7]

For the interpretation of this question in the context of today's virtual environments, there are two other authors to help us: According to de Certeau, research creates its own documents in the space of its apparatus, which is also transformed by the scholar. The practices of forming the document change in the digital environment, but it is not certain whether the language and the perspective that enables us to see through the changes are available for us. We can refer to the twofold meaning of the document again: there is a duality of the sources documenting something (according to the rhetoric of the research) and documents being created through the processes of publication.[8]

Cornelia Vismann's *Akten. Medientechnik und Recht* originally published in 2000, is as much cited in English as in German. The book's title in English translation shows an ambiguity in media technology that is no stranger to the reasoning of the book, and that also bears special significance in the present reasoning: *Files*. As an explanation of why it is worth studying the history of bureaucratic systems of record offices digging down as deep as its technical details Vismann writes about the – only now grasping the full scope of how illusionary it was – promise of paperless offices,[9] the current opposition of paper files and computer files, as well as today's demands for free access. However, in this study electronic files are only mentioned in the short closing section. Files become icons on the screen of the computer as referred to by the section title: *Files into Icons*.

> The very terminology of computer surfaces is designed to remind users seated before screens of the familiar world of files. The menu tab offering options like 'list,' 'format,' 'thesaurus,' 'table' and the instructions copy, delete, save turn users into virtual chanceries or chancellors. By condensing an entire administrative office, the computer implements the basic law of bureaucracy according to which administrative techniques are transferred from the state to the individual: from the specialized governmental prac-

7 | The topic of to what extent the theoretical works of Wolfgang Ernst or Jussi Parikka unfold the limitations and possibilities provided by the apparatus in the functioning of institutional digital archives is attempted to be described in Gábor Palkó, "Media Archaeology of Institutional Archives?" *Studia UBB Digitalia* 62, no. 1 (June 2017): 75-82.

8 | De Certeau also states that the different pasts are not merely preserved in their documents, but also in the historical work as an "archive". (De Certeau, *The Writing of History*, 46.)

9 | On the same illusion, cf. the articles by Júlia Tóth-Czifra and Nicolas Pethes in this volume.

tices of early modern chanceries to the 'common style,' from absolutist administrative centers to individual work desks, from the first mainframe computers in defense ministries to the desktop at home.[10]

If Vismann is right, and the "surface" of computers and the user interface are designed to resemble the familiar world of material file management, while the language in which it communicates with us translates digital commands to analogue practices, it means that the difference between the analogue and digital way of managing files that also defines the difference between analogue and digital archives can hardly be brought to the surface. The fact that the windows of Microsoft Windows enable us to see a virtual office "desktop" thus creates a familiar environment for the interaction with the computer, while the processes in the background ('under the hood') stays out of sight.

The phenomenon of thinking about the separation of the display medium and the computer, in other words the digital apparatus as a somewhat different argumentation, has been described by Luhmann as the opposition of the surface and the depth in his media history summary chapter from *Die Gesellschaft der Gesellschaft*. The machine is connected to the user through the surface of the display and what happens in the background remains blurred out.

Die Oberfläche ist jetzt der Bildschirm mit extrem beschränkter Inanspruchnahme menschlicher Sinne, die Tiefe dagegen die unsichtbare Maschine, die heute in der Lage ist, sich selbst von Moment zu Moment umzukonstruieren, zum Beispiel in Reaktion auf Benutzung. Die Verbindung von Oberfläche und Tiefe kann über Befehle hergestellt werden, die die Maschine anweisen, etwas auf dem Bildschirm oder durch Ausdruck sichtbar zu machen. Sie selbst bleibt unsichtbar.[11]

The computer – just like a black box – can never be opened according to Luhmann, which comes clear in the concept of double contingency[12] even more than in the descriptions of digital media above. The inner world of computers, similarly to the psychic system, always remains unreachable. If we observe the digital research environments from this perspective, there is hardly any chance for us to understand the operations of the apparatus since they remain unobservable.

10 | Cornelia Vismann, *Files, Law and Media Technology*, trans. Geoffrey Winthrop-Young (Stanford: Stanford University Press, 2008), 163.

11 | Niklas Luhmann, *Die Gesellschaft der Gesellschaft* (Frankfurt am Main: Suhrkamp, 1998), 304.

12 | Detlef Krause, *Luhmann-Lexikon* (Stuttgart: Lucius & Lucius, 2005), 17.

The interaction between human and not human is always subject to obscurity and opacity in the reading of Bruno Latour, similarly to Luhmann. Latour's term, the 'black box' seemingly stands close to the invisibility that hides the continuous self-reconstruction of the computer's functioning in the terms of Luhmann. But in fact, as the main difference in the relation of computers and humanities, it is not impossible for Latour to open the black box to see what is inside underneath the surface. To emphasize this notion, he refers to the overhead projector as an example which exists while it is working but once it breaks its individual parts begin to exist smaller black boxes as well (Latour 1999: 183). The closed black box is divided into functional parts, also functioning as black boxes on their own, but the connections between them can become transparent. What is uncovered by the insight to this black box is not a homogeneous object or the functioning of a machine; rather, the interaction of human and non-human actors that can be close or distant to each other. This uncovering is labeled by the adjective 'technical' leading to an important question in the relation between the technical apparatus and the research:

> 'Technical' applies, first of all, to a subprogram, or a series of nested subprograms, like the ones discussed earlier. When we say 'this is a technical point', it means that we have to deviate for a moment from the main task and that we will eventually resume our normal course of action, which is the only focus worth our attention. A black box opens momentarily, and will soon be closed again, becoming completely invisible in the main sequence of action.[13]

In Latour's reasoning, technical malfunctioning is a precondition to this uncovering which could also mean the failure to achieve the initial goal, namely that we find ourselves elsewhere compared to where we were headed. Put differently, the malfunctioning of the apparatus can lead to its transformation.

> 'There is a technical problem to solve first.' Here the deviation may not lead us back to the main road, as with the first meaning, but may threaten the original goal entirely. Technical is no longer a mere detour but an obstacle, a roadblock, the beginning of a detour of a long translation, maybe of a whole new labyrinth.[14]

So far, we considered conclusions from Michel de Certeau, Cornelia Vismann, and Bruno Latour with desired goal to understand to what extent they can be used in the context of humanities research and the digital environment. Taking the risk of serious oversimplification, we can summarize these contexts

13 | Bruno Latour, *Pandora's Hope. Essays on the Reality of Science Studies* (Cambridge: Harvard University Press, 1999), 191.

14 | Latour, *Pandora's Hope*, 191.

as follows: de Certeau's argumentation allowed us to see the "place" of the research and that the apparatus determines the scope of questions a researcher can ask. The digital transformation of the research environment radically rewrites the set of research problems and their answers (while being a scientific research) must also undertake the rearrangement of the apparatus. Vismann's parallel between paper-based and digital files reflected on the fact that we should approach the familiar interfaces carefully, as they imitate the world of analogue offices while working with digital technologies which can also be considered as a relocation of authority technique practices themselves. Last but not least, Latour's argumentation about what technical means came with the possibility of observing the interplay of human and non-human, as well as close and distant in space and time when opening the black box during the time gap created by the malfunctioning of complex technologies. He also describes this as the cooperation of subroutines that prevent the option of purely human control, as the control of human over non-human. The question is how these theoretical conclusions can be utilized in the digital practices of humanities research. Let me hence use two specific examples as an illustration. One of them comes from the field of digital philology, while the other one comes from practice of *distant reading*.

The first example comes from the Petőfi Literary Museum in Budapest, where the Institute for Literary Studies of the Hungarian Academy of Sciences undertook the digital transcription and publication for research purposes of the five printed critical editions the correspondence of János Arany as part of the DigiPhil project.[15] A graphical user interface imitating an office software environment has been developed for the editors.[16] It is worth mentioning that an interface like this does not allow the user to see the content of the black box. Furthermore, the editor making the markup transcript of the volume does not see the code and the complicated workflow behind the familiar interface, essentially being a workflow with a specification that has been developed by digital philologists and Arany experts. In the sense how Latour understands this matter, this is an example where actors are involved in a non-simultaneous cooperation, in which the creation of the place of research, in other words the creation of and reflection on the interconnected black boxes of the digital environment as a scientific research activity in a de Certeauian sense, become separated from the work done "blindly" within the environment.

15 | http://digiphil.hu.

16 | Cf. the contribution by Júlia Tóth-Czifra in this volume.

Fig. 1: A letter written to János Arany displayed in the virtual research environment of the DigiPhil project, digiphil.hu, screenshot by Gábor Palkó

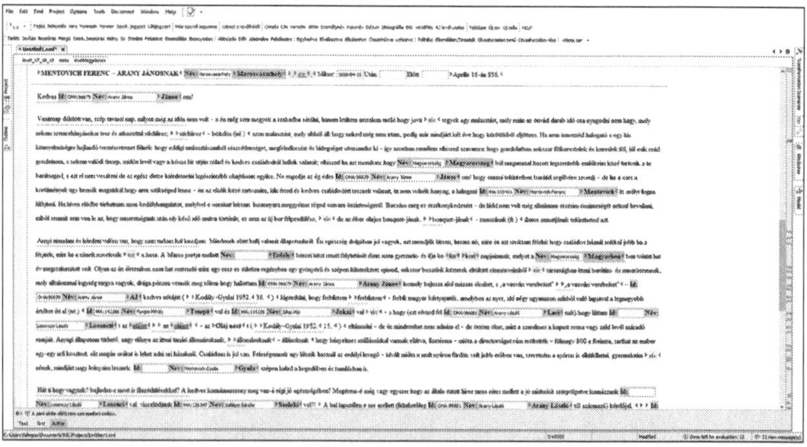

If we interrupt the workflow and open the black box to take a look at how the research environment as our apparatus works we will indeed find an unparalleled complexity in the interaction of human and non-human, near and distant, past and present. The first of the time layers is obvious: the postal lifespan of the correspondence of Arany from the writing of messages through their posting until their arrival, as well as the second one, a decade-long creation process of the printed critical edition (already taking a century of cultural context and reception into consideration) in the second half of the 20th century. The transformation process into the digital realm has a complex system of time layers on its own. In the first phase, digital philologists and literary historians create a model that can accommodate about 3000 letters to form a data network, also involving decisions about building a specific markup language encoding that includes the structure of the encoded textual features and the connection of data and metadata, while considering markup language recommendations (e. g. TEI XML) and metadata standards (e. g. MARC) as best practices in use. With the specifications having been set, other digital humanities specialists can create a user interface in a specified software environment (Oxygen XML Editor) imitating the interface of other popular office software (naming conventions and placement of buttons, menu structure), but in fact using the specified encoding standards for the transcription process, in a way that they are hidden from the end users. Doing so, the editor using the interface see the checking algorithms running on the encoded text, for example the ones warning the users about typical errors or syntactical defects such as wrong date format or missing required metadata. In the text of the correspondence and the critical notes, the editor marks the names and the interface provides suggestions on names for an easier identification based on a list of names previously collected by others. Finally, the system sends the encoded document to a server thoroughly logging all committed changes on the document. Further processing, checking and publishing of the document is done in another environment.

The second example is a stylometric service, which has been tested by the Wrocław University of Science and Technology, the Digital Literary Academy hosted by the Petőfi Literary Museum, and Eötvös Loránd University Centre for Digital Humanities in cooperation. This service, called Multilingual WebSty, compares texts processed by natural language processing algorithms to search for similarities. This service, as opposed to fully automated solutions lacking any user interaction, makes it impossible for us to not see the fact that a set of embedded subroutines work together to create the text similarity statistics and their visualization. Therefore, the service does not hide the technical apparatus, it rather highlights it. The apparatus involves the interaction of human and non-human, near and distant actors, and can also be influenced using a large set of parameters, meaning its results are always highly relative so that they assume interpretations by researchers, and provoke reinterpretations.

Fig. 2: Text similarity analysis of Péter Esterházy's works. A visualization of the "Text similarity analysis system", ws.clarin-pl.eu/websty.shtml, screenshot by Gábor Palkó

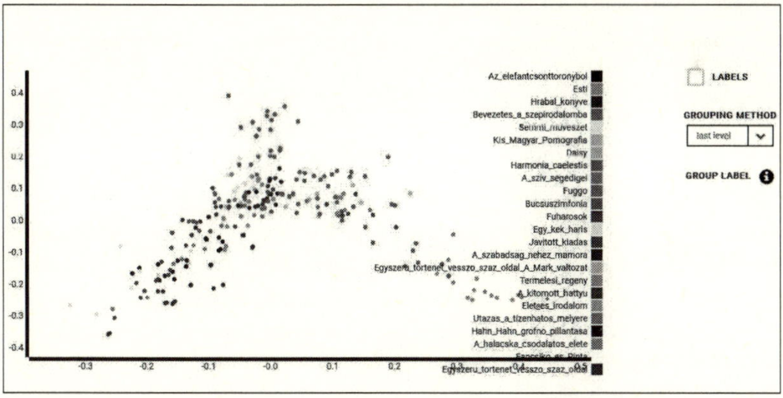

Having analyzed the prose of Péter Esterházy as a test of the service using the corpus provided by the Digital Literary Academy, the statistical quantification had been preceded by the morphological analysis of the texts. In sum, the results depend on external tools of varying effectiveness, which are developed by computational linguistics researches. It is an important fact that the faults of automatic analysis – as NLP or OCR technology – do not necessarily decrease the success rate of text comparison, such as author identification.[17] The service randomly broke the text into segments of equal length and grouped them using a method that involves the results of the linguistic analysis. The system then delivered spectacular results even using the default settings and it grouped segments from the same text effectively, while on a higher level of abstraction, it produced visualizations supporting literary historical interpretations as well as language use and stylistic tendencies of an entire oeuvre.

It is of utmost importance that a stylometric service as complex as this one, a black box in the Latourian sense, cannot be made sense of without assuming a cooperation among heterogeneous human and non-human actors, radically differing in space, time, and competence. The process involves a set of participants including the computational linguists training, the analytics software on corpora, the statisticians using mathematical models, the literary researchers encoding and interpreting the texts, as well as the algorithms of the analytics software, which are rapidly getting distanced from their creators and their original functional environment.

Without the analysis of the heterogeneous technological apparatus it is impossible to analyze and reflect on the more and more widespread virtual research environments. Hence, the ability to see through the new apparatus which creates a new form of unity among the diverging competences indicates that it is getting harder and harder to obtain for the solitary researcher with its limited insight.

17 | Greta Franzini, Mike Kestemont, Gabriela Rotari, Melina Jander, Jeremi K. Ochab, Emily Franzini, Joanna Byszuk, and Jan Rybicki, "Attributing Authorship in the Noisy Digitized Correspondence of Jacob and Wilhelm Grimm," *Frontiers in Digital Humanities* (05. April 2018), https://doi.org/10.3389/fdigh.2018.00004.

The Intertextual Frontiers of Vergil's "Empire without Limit"

Digital Comments on *Aeneid* 1.278-9

Dániel Kozák

Although not unknown in other disciplines, commentary as a philological genre has always played an especially important role in classical philology, and received much attention in the last twenty years, from both historical and theoretical perspectives.*[1] In an early document of this renewed interest, Don Fowler discussed the role of commentary in the digital age.[2] In his view, this seemingly old-fashioned and conservative scholarly genre may turn out to be particularly timely for the digital age, not only in the practical sense of allowing, for example, to selectively display just particular types of comments at a time. More importantly for Fowler (writing in the era of some overoptimism with

* | This paper was written with support by the ÚNKP-17-4 New National Excellence Program of the Ministry of Human Capacities (Hungary). I am grateful for Attila Ferenczi, Ábel Tamás, and the editors of this volume for their comments and suggestions regarding various versions of this paper. I also express my thanks to the Library of the Central European University for providing access to the *LLT* database. Translations of Latin passages are my own.

1 | See most importanly the edited volumes: G. W. Most (ed.), *Commentaries – Kommentare* (Göttingen: Vandenhoeck & Ruprecht, 1999); R. K. Gibson and C. S. Kraus (eds.), *The Classical Commentary: Histories, Practices, Theory* (Leiden/Boston: Brill, 2002); C. S. Kraus and C. Stray (eds.), *Classical Commentaries: Explorations in a Scholarly Genre* (Oxford: Oxford University Press, 2016); and J. Henderson (ed.), *'Oxford Reds': Classic Commentaries on Latin Classics. R. G. Austin on Cicero and Virgil, C. J. Fordyce on Catullus, R. G. and R. G. M. Nisbet on Cicero* (London: Duckworth, 2006).

2 | D. Fowler, "Criticism as Commentary and Commentary as Criticism in the Age of Electronic Media", in Most (ed.), *Commentaries*, 426-42; cf. W. McCarty, "A Network with a Thousand Entrances: Commentary in an Electronic Age?", in Gibson and Kraus (eds.), *The Classical Commentary*, 359-402 for a more theoretical and less classics-oriented approach.

regard to hypertext), digital media offer better and faster means of communication, and thus allow scholars to collaborate more easily in the (public) discussion of particular passages, and to produce multi-authored and constantly evolving notes as, to use Fowler's favorite term, postmodern equivalents of the traditional *variorum* commentary. Such collaborative notes may also promote a view of philology as a never ending process of explanation and interpretation, as a practice of selecting, putting on show and discussing objects of interest rather than (or least, in addition to) offering "solutions" to exegetical "problems". These collaborative notes, however, being "under construction" and growing forever, may easily tip up the balance between copiousness and constraint, the drive to include as much information as possible in the limited space "on the margins of the text", discussed by Gumbrecht as the double characteristics of commentary.[3] Two decades have passed since the publication of the volume containing both Fowler's and Gumbrecht's papers, but commentaries still tend to be written for print: the balance between copiousness and constraint has been given some respite. Even so, however, recent commentaries present the results of research conducted with a constantly growing use of digital tools. In this paper, I am going to discuss this aspect of the relationship between commentary and the digital, concentrating on the large-scale digital *corpora* of ancient Greek and Latin texts and their search engines.

Commentaries "atomize" texts by selecting for explanation – and making up, in the first place – segments such as words, expressions, sentences, passages which are "problematic" and/or "interesting". Classical philologists usually mobilize a huge amount of other ancient texts in the process of explaining such a segment in commentary notes. To interpret texts – and even to make sense of them, in the most basic sense of the world – so distant from us both culturally and linguistically, we have to use every available bit of comparative evidence. Two texts, even if far from each other in any narrative of literary history (like a tiny fragment of a Greek medical text from the fifth century B. C. and a line in Vergil's *Aeneid*), are directly compared to each other if we think that "linking" the two helps solving a problem of textual criticism, provides an answer to a question regarding language or content, or advances interpretation in any way. We do not necessarily imply, of course, that the two texts are in an intertextual relationship with each other in the literary sense of the word; still, in a very general sense, we are discovering-and-constructing intertextual connections between the texts and their segments as part of our philological activity. Typical commentary notes are partially – sometimes, for the most part – made up by lists of such "parallel passages" *(loci paralleli/similes)*. These lists are frequently introduced only by the (in)famous formula "cf. e. g." as a substitute for

3 | H. U. Gumbrecht, "Fill up Your Margins! About Commentary and *Copia*", in Most (ed.), *Commentaries*, 443-53, here 446-8, 452-3.

a detailed explanation by the author.[4] This formula and the standard, (mostly) edition-independent abbreviations marking particular passages in ancient texts (e. g. Cic. *Rep.* 3.24 = Cicero, *De re publica* Book 3, Chapter 24 – a passage which will play an important role later in this paper) act like pre-digital links, inviting the reader to surf from one text to the other and back, or even – consulting the commentary on the second text as well – to a third one and so on, *ad infinitum*. Thus, in the process of doing research on ancient literature, classicists have constructed an infinitely dense and complex network of connections between the texts they study, ranging from "mere" similarities of language or topic on one end of the spectrum to more specific and interpretable examples of intertextuality (like allusions and quotations) on the other. This network is just a virtual one, of course: no one has ever drawn it in its entirety. It would probably be impossible to do so, anyway. Still, it might tell much about the scholarly reception of ancient texts if we could see which texts or segments are the central nodes of this network: which are the ones cited frequently to explain something in other texts, or, *vice versa*, which are surrounded by an above average number of parallels in commentaries.[5]

This network model of the *corpus* of ancient literary texts is realized to the fullest (as far as we can currently imagine) by digital *corpora:* databases in which all (or most) extant texts are stored for fast and easy access of particular passages for various purposes (typically, reading or quoting by copy-paste). Many of these databases also allow direct access to passages, employing the above mentioned standard citation scheme in the construction of URL's.[6] Even more importantly, these digital *corpora* offer *corpus*-wide search. Having run a query for a word or expression found in the text we are studying, we are presented with a list of results: passages of text linked together by the search terms we have chosen. The list might contain false positives and irrelevant results as well; but after careful selection and categorization, we might end up with a

4 | More on this by R. K. Gibson, "'Cf. e. g.': A Typology of 'Parallels' and the Role of Commentaries on Latin Poetry", in Gibson and Kraus (eds.), *The Classical Commentary*, 331-57, who also develops a possible typology of parallels, concentrating on the commentary tradition of poetic texts (333-46).

5 | On the digital analysis of some "citation networks" linking passages of ancient texts in scholarly publications, see M. Romanello, "Exploring Citation Networks to Study Intertextuality in Classics", in *Digital Humanities Quarterly* 10/2 (2016), [www.digitalhumanities.org/dhq/vol/10/2/000255/000255.html], 21-39.

6 | E. g. *Classical Latin Texts. A Resource Prepared by The Packard Humanities Institute (PHI)*, latin.packhum.org/cit/Cic/Rep/3.24 (accessed 06-27-2018) for the above-mentioned example. The *Classical Works Knowledge Base* (cwkb.org, accessed 06-27-2018) allows access to a given passage in several different databases using Linked Open Data technologies.

list of lexical parallels to be included in a commentary note. The list of results thus may form the basis of drawing a more detailed version of a small section of the full textual network – more detailed in at least two senses. First, digital *corpora* allow us to find more parallels. However, extending the list of parallels – already too long, in some cases – would not in itself advance our understanding of a given passage.[7] Representativity and variety of the results seem to be more important. The *corpus* of ancient literary texts is too vast to be held in the natural memory of any philologist, and even the most detailed scholarly dictionaries (also used as pre-digital "search engines") cite only examples rather than all occurrences of a given word, except for especially rare ones; with digital search engines we can quickly scan even those texts and passages which we have never read or do not remember, and those which are not cited in dictionaries or in any publication we have consulted. By their greater degree of representativity, moreover, digital queries may also reveal a greater variety of parallels from more authors, genres, periods, including those which we might have thought to be irrelevant. Such unexpected parallels allow us, in many cases, to reevaluate interpretations which had become more or less canonized in the course of (scholarly or non-scholarly) reception.

It is no surprise, given classicists' traditional practice of collecting parallels (as outlined above), that the development of digital *corpora* of ancient Greek and Latin such as *TLG (Thesaurus Linguae Graecae)* and *PHI* (the *corpus* of Latin texts by the Packard Humanities Institute) had begun very early, in the 1970s.[8]

7 | Some negative aspects of hunting for parallels are discussed by Gibson, "'Cf. e.g.'", 347-53.

8 | On the development and history of these digital *corpora*, see T. F. Brunner, "Classics and the Computer: The History of a Relationship", in *Accessing Antiquity: The Computerization of Classical Databases*, edited by J. Solomon, 10-33. Tucson: University of Arizona Press 2004 and G. Crane, "Classics and the Computer: An End of the History", in *A Companion to Digital Humanities*, edited by S. Schreibman *et al.*, 46-55. Malden: Wiley-Blackwell, 2004, [also online: www.digitalhumanities.org/companion]. *TLG* and *PHI* (and similar databases) include only literary texts (literary in the wider sense of having been produced for public circulation and surviving typically in manuscript traditions) as opposed to documentary papyri and inscriptions, which have their own special digital *corpora* such as papyri.info (papyri.info, accessed 06-27-2018) and the Epigraphik-Datenbank Clauss/Slaby (db.edcs.eu, accessed 06-27-2018); for a case study involving the latter, and on the digitalization and materiality of inscriptions, see Ádám Rung's contribution to this volume. This strict separation of literary texts, documents and inscriptions (and the lack of at least a metasearch engine accessing all of them) is, of course, a very problematic philological practice (one not started, but perhaps made more apparent, by digitalization); but I cannot discuss that in this paper. Another insufficiency of *TLG*, *PHI* etc., not to be discussed here, is that the texts have

Made widely available on CD-ROM in the 1990s and then online, they have become today's standard tools used by most classicists. Scholarly reflection on the widespread use of such digital *corpora*, however, seems to be lacking to a large degree in classical philology. They are not regularly reviewed in classical journals like print publications,[9] and the acknowledgment of their use is frequently limited to general statements to this effect in footnotes or prefaces instead of a detailed documentation on particular queries and the analysis of the results. Thus, the practice of how digital *corpora* are actually used by classicists remains, in many ways, "blackboxed".[10] The presentation of the results of research hides the method by which they have been obtained, which seems problematic in particular because this method – running digital queries – is a relatively novel one in the long history of (classical) philology; without discussing the method itself, we will be less able to understand how our everyday philological practices are changing. My aim in this paper is to start opening the blackbox through detailed documentation of a case study. I have chosen a passage of Vergil's *Aeneid*, an epic at the center of the canon of Roman literature, to interpret. As I will try to show in the first part of the paper, a rather one-sided (but by no means wrong) interpretation of an important expression in this passage had become canonized in commentaries; this detailed review of reception, I feel, is necessary before I can discuss, in the second part, how digital search engines can be used to arrive at a hopefully more balanced interpretation. Finally, I will offer a few points on the methodology of "digital classics".

"Empire without Limit"

The main narrative of the *Aeneid* begins with the Trojans' shipwreck on the shores of Carthage. Venus, Aeneas' mother, then approaches Jupiter to remind him that he had promised safety and power for the Trojan survivors. In his

been digitized without the *apparatus criticus* of the base print editions (counter-examples, if few, do exist: see e. g. *Musisque Deoque, A Digital Archive of Latin Poetry* (mqdq.it., accessed 06-27-2018).

9 | Some reviews have been published recently on scholarly blogs and non-classicist journals: see e. g. M. Loar, "Review: The Packard Humanities Institute (PHI) – Classical Latin Texts", in *Society for Classical Studies Blog*, [classicalstudies.org/scs-blog/matthew-loar/review-packard-humanities-institute-phi%E2%80%94classical-latin-texts] and D. Kozák, "PHI Latin Texts" (Review), in *RIDE. A Review Journal for Digital Editions and Resources* 8, [ride.i-d-e.de/issues/issue-8/phi].

10 | On blackboxing, see the contributions by Charlotte Jaekel and Gábor Palkó in this volume.

reply the king of the gods assures Venus that he did not change his mind. He reveals in a prophecy (1.223–96) that the descendants of Aeneas will have unlimited power, culminating in the age of Caesar/Augustus,[11] when wars will give way to peace:

His ego nec metas rerum nec tempora pono:
imperium sine fine dedi.
...
Nascetur pulchra Troianus origine Caesar,
imperium Oceano, famam qui terminet astris.
...
Aspera tum positis mitescent saecula bellis;
...
dirae ferro et compagibus artis
claudentur Belli portae.

(Verg. *Aen.* 1.278-9, 286-7, 291, 293-4)

For them [i. e. the Romans] I have set neither a turning point or a span of time: I have given them power/empire[12] without end. ... Caesar will be born, of noble Trojan ancestry, who will extend his power / the empire to the Ocean, his fame to the stars. ... In that age wars will end and harsh centuries will soften; ... the dreadful gates of War will be closed with strong locks of iron.

The first line quoted above (1.278) is characterized by a clear distinction between space and time: *meta* ('cone', 'turning-post') is inherently spatial, *tempus* by definition temporal. Jupiter's next statement, apparently a paraphrase of the previous line,[13] lacks such a distinction: *finis* ('end', 'limit') can be either spatial or temporal, or both at the same time.[14] What kind(s) of infinity the expression *imperium sine fine* implies is a problem typically treated (and created in the first

11 | It is not possible here, nor needed, to examine the much discussed problem whether lines 286ff. refer to Julius Caesar or Augustus, or both; see in more detail the discussions by J. J. O'Hara, *Death and the Optimistic Prophecy in Vergil's* Aeneid (Princeton: Princeton University Press, 1990), 155-61 and E. Kraggerud, "Which Julius Caesar? On *Aen.* 1.286-96.", in *Symbolae Osloenses* 67 (1992), 103-12.

12 | On these two meanings of *imperium*, see note 32 below.

13 | Cf. e. g. R. D. Williams, "The Opening Scenes of the *Aeneid*", in *Proceedings of the Vergil Society* 5 (1965-1966), 14-23, here 21.

14 | *Thesaurus Linguae Latinae*, the most detailed dictionary of classical Latin, quotes *Aen.* 1.279 as an example for the spatial meaning of *finis*, but adds a comment that in this particular passage the word is used with reference "to both space and time" *(et de*

place, probably) in a commentary, and is in large part a consequence of segmentation (as discussed above): authors of papers and monographs may safely write something like "in this episode Jupiter sets no limits in space or time for the Roman Empire", without indicating if this statement is based on *his ... pono* (278) only or *imperium ... dedi* (279) as well.[15]

The spatial sense of the expression is, of course, inherently more exaggerating. Even if the Roman Empire will never collapse (at least a possibility for Vergil and his contemporary readers), the Ocean will constitute a natural boundary. Jupiter himself states so a few lines later (1.286). The acknowledgment of this limitation, however, also emphasizes that as far as political geography is concerned, there will be no limit to Roman expansion: no nation in the world will be powerful enough to withstand Rome's armies. Similar statements about Rome's world-wide empire return from time to time in the *Aeneid*.[16] It might be argued that the intratextual context provided by these passages is enough to make us accept that *imperium sine fine* itself may have at least some spatial significance, too; but the traditions of classical philology encourage (if not require) commentators to look for intertextual parallels as well.

Jupiter's prophecy is obviously of great importance for any reading of the *Aeneid* as a whole. Along with Anchises' speech about future Roman heroes in the Underworld (*Aen.* 6.756-892) and the *ekphrasis* of Aeneas' shield, exhibiting scenes from Roman history (*Aen.* 8.608-31), this passage is one of the cornerstones upon which 'optimistic' or 'Augustan' readings of the epic are based; but even 'ambivalent', 'pessimistic' or 'anti-Augustan' interpretations require them to be set in contrast with various other passages in which 'further voices' are raised, emphasizing personal loss and the perspectives of the defeated instead of the glory of Roman expansion.[17] The synthesis of these two inter-

loco et de tempore; TLL s.v. *finis* 1.a). The *Oxford Latin Dictionary* – as a sign of reluctance to decide the question? – does not quote the Vergilian passage at all under *finis*.

15 | On occasion it is explicitly stated that *sine fine* also refers to both time and space: F. Christ, *Die römische Weltherrschaft in der antiken Dichtung* (Stuttgart: W. Kohlhammer, 1938), 10, 58, 62; A. Mehl, "*Imperium sine fine dedi*: Die augusteische Vorstellung von der Grenzenlosigkeit des Römischen Reiches", in *Stuttgarter Kolloquium zur historischen Geographie des Altertums 4, 1990*, edited by E. Olshausen and H. Sonnabend, 431-464. Amsterdam: Hakkert, 1994, 436; C. Nicolet, *Space, Geography, and Politics in the Early Roman Empire* (Ann Arbor: University of Michigan Press, 1991), 29.

16 | *Aen.* 3.97, 6.781-782, 7.99-101. Cf. G. Binder, *Aeneas und Augustus: Interpretationen zum 8. Buch der* Aeneis (Meisenheim am Glan: A. Hain, 1971), 41 n. 129, collecting less explicit instances as well.

17 | The scholarly reception of the *Aeneid* in the 20th century is summarized e. g. by S. J. Harrison, "Some Views of the *Aeneid* in the Twentieth Century", in *Oxford Readings*

pretations is also possible. We encounter such a reading, for example, in T. S. Eliot's essay *Virgil and the Christian World*, predating most of the fierce scholarly debates over the meaning of the *Aeneid* in the second half of the twentieth century.[18] Eliot quotes the passage under discussion here, along with Anchises' (in)famous advice at *Aeneid* 6.851-3, to grasp an element of European/Christian identity in the Vergilian lines:

I think that he [Vergil] had few illusions and that he saw clearly both sides of every question – the case for the loser as well as the case for the winner. Nevertheless, even those who have as little Latin as I must remember and thrill at the lines:

His ego nec metas rerum, nec tempora pono:
Imperium sine fine dedi...

Tu regere imperio populos, Romane, memento
(hae tibi erunt artes) pacique imponere morem,
parcere subiectis et debellare superbos...[19]

I say that it was all the end of history that Virgil could be asked to find, and that it was a worthy end. And do you really think that Virgil was mistaken? You must remember that the Roman Empire was transformed into the Holy Roman Empire. What Virgil proposed to his contemporaries was the highest ideal even for an unholy Roman Empire, for any merely temporal empire. We are all, so far as we inherit the civilization of Europe, still citizens of the Roman Empire, and time has not yet proved Virgil wrong when he wrote *nec tempora pono: imperium sine fine dedi.* But, of course, the Roman Empire which Virgil imagined and for which Aeneas worked out his destiny was not exactly the same as the Roman Empire of the legionaries, the pro-consuls and governors, the business men and speculators, the demagogues and generals. It was something greater, but some-

in Vergil's Aeneid, edited by S. J. Harrison, 1-20. Oxford: Oxford University Press, 1990 and P. Hardie, *Virgil.* Greece & Rome New Surveys in the Classics 28 (Oxford: Oxford University Press, 1998), 94-101. On "further voices", see R. O. A. M. Lyne, *Further Voices in Vergil's* Aeneid (Oxford: Clarendon Press, 1987).

18 | T. S. Eliot, *On Poetry and Poets* (New York: Noonday Press, 1961), 145-46; the essay was originally delivered in 1951 as a BBC radio speech. I cannot discuss here the vast topic of Christian appropriations of Vergilian poetry, from antiquity to the present. A good summary, as far as the *Aeneid* is concerned, is offered by P. Hardie, *The Last Trojan Hero. A Cultural History of Virgil's* Aeneid (London/New York: I. B. Tauris, 2014), 127-47, a chapter itself titled "Imperium sine fine" (see esp. 128 and 134 on how Prudentius and Augustine "recycle" *Aen.* 1.278-279).

19 | "Remember, Roman, that your duty is to rule over peoples – these will be your forms of art – and to impose rules on peace; to spare the vanquished and defeat the proud."

thing which exists because Virgil imagined it. It remains an ideal, but one which Virgil passed on to Christianity to develop and to cherish.

For Eliot, Vergil's vision of *imperium sine fine* contributes to his being "our classic, the classic of all Europe", as he had famously expressed in *What is a classic?*[20] This *imperium* is not, primarily, the actual political entity expanding spatially but only temporarily, with the help of "legionaries ... and generals;" rather, it is an idealized cultural entity in the first place which may continue to exist even after the political entity had fallen.

The Commentary Tradition

I quoted Eliot – self-professedly, a non-professional classicist[21] – at some length because his reading reflects a certain tendency in the long commentary tradition on the *Aeneid* passage. Just like Eliot, commentators tend to focus almost exclusively on the temporal interpretation of *imperium sine fine.* This can be seen already in the extant late antique commentaries. Servius, working at the turn of the 4th and 5th centuries A. D., writes:[22]

***metas** ad terras rettulit, **tempora** ad annos; Lavinio enim et Albae finem statuit, Romanis tribuit aeternitatem, {quia subiunxit **imperium sine fine dedi**}.*
(Servius ad *Aen.* 1.278)

By the word *metas* [Jupiter] refers to the countries [they will conquer], by *tempora* to the years [of their rule], since for the cities of Lavinium and Alba he allotted an end, but for the Romans he granted eternity, {because he adds ***imperium sine fine dedi***}.

20 | Eliot, *On Poetry and Poets*, 73, originally delivered in 1944 as the presidential address to the Virgil Society, one year after its foundation. On Eliot's interpretation of the *Aeneid* passage, esp. with regard to time/timelessness, cf. F. Kermode, *The Classic* (London: Faber and Faber, 1975), 25-8; D. Kennedy, "Tradition and Appropriation: T. S. Eliot and Virgil's *Aeneid*", in *Hermathena* 158 (1995), 73-94, here 81–2.

21 | See Eliot's reference to his "little Latin". As noted e. g. by Hardie, *The Last Trojan Hero*, 144, Eliot in this essay draws heavily but without acknowledgment on the Christianizing interpretation of Vergil in T. Haecker, *Vergil, Vater des Abendlandes* (München: Hegner, 1931).

22 | On Servius' commentary in general, see e. g. D. Fowler, "The Virgil Commentary of Servius", in *Cambridge Companion to Virgil*, edited by C. Martindale, 73-78. Cambridge: Cambridge University Press, 1997.

Servius starts with acknowledging that line 278 refers to both space and time; but he continues by focusing on the latter aspect exclusively. Jupiter has, indeed, told Venus in the previous section of his speech (264-77) that Aeneas will rule for three years in Lavinium, his son for thirty in Alba Longa, and his descendants for three hundred until the foundation of Rome. Servius is summarizing this climactic series of ever longer periods, culminating in the eternal power of Rome; and as part of this summary, he also uses the word *finis,* clearly in a temporal sense. In the "original" version of Servius' commentary, the note ends here; but in the so-called "Servius *auctus*" variant, containing additional comments, the note also includes the quotation of the first half of line 279 (quoted above in curly brackets). In this expanded version of Servius' note, *imperium sine fine* serves to further illustrate the point made by *nec tempora pono* in 278: this is made clear by the use of the causal conjunction *quia*. It follows, then, that the author of the expanded note (probably in agreement with Servius himself) interprets the Vergilian *sine fine* in a temporal sense, and treats it as a paraphrase of only the second half of line 278.[23]

The word *aeternitas,* already present in Servius' note, is foregrounded in later commentaries as critics try to grasp the cultural and intertextual context of the Vergilian expression. Let us see first the commentary by the Spanish Jesuit Juan Luis de la Cerda, originally published in 1617 (Fig. 1). His note on line 279[24] consists entirely of parallels, the first of them being a passage in Vergil's contemporary elegist Tibullus: *Romulus aeternae nondum formaverat urbis moenia* ("Romulus [at the time of Aeneas' flight from Troy] had not yet established the walls of the eternal city", Tib. 2.5.23-4). The proposed connection between *imperium sine fine* and the idea of *Roma aeterna*[25] is reinforced by

23 | We find a similar interpretation in Servius' contemporary, Tiberius Claudius Donatus (*Interpretationes Vergilianae* ad loc.) and in a rather vague parallel drawn with Horace by pseudo-Acro (*ad Carmen Saeculare* 25).

24 | J. L. La Cerda (1642), *P. Virgilii Maronis* Aeneidos *libri sex priores argumentis, explicationibus et notis illustrata. Cologne: Joannes Kinchius* [online: sceti.library.upenn.edu/sceti/printedbooksNew/index.cfm?TextID=virgil1647_2), 56. The structure of la Cerda's commentary differs from the practice more familiar today: instead of numbering his notes according to the line numbers of the *Aeneid*, he prints the Latin text in sections, followed by a short summary (*argumentum*), interpretation *(explicatio)* and then the individual notes *(notae)* numbered consecutively (cf. Barthes' similar notation in *S/Z*). On la Cerda's commentary in general, see A. Laird, "Juan Luis de La Cerda and the Predicament of Commentary", in Gibson and Kraus (eds.), *The Classical Commentary*, 171-203.

25 | On the *Roma aeterna* tradition, see F. G. Moore, "On *Urbs Aeterna* and *Urbs Sacra*", in *Transactions of the American Philological Association* 25 (1894), 34-60; C. Koch, "Roma aeterna", in *Religio. Studien zu Kult und Glauben der Römer*, 142-175. Nürnberg: Hans Carl 1960; K. J. Pratt, "Rome as Eternal", in *Journal of the History of Ideas* 26

the label *Roma urbs aeterna* ("Rome, the eternal city") printed on the margin. La Cerda then lists a number of other parallels from imperial and late antique Roman and Greek literature. Finally, he calls attention to the use of *aeternitas* in Roman imperial titulature. No examples are cited this time; La Cerda refers his readers to Johannes Smetius' (1591–1651) work on the subject. The comment with which he ends his note – and also the page – is a fine example of the commentator's feeling of constraint, as discussed by Gumbrecht: *omitto, ne impleam paginam* ("I omit [citing examples] in order not to fill up the page").

Fig. 1: La Cerda, P. Virgilii Maronis Aeneidos libri, 56 (cropped screenshot), ad Aen. 1.279 (sceti.library.upenn.edu/sceti/printedbooksNew/index.cfm?TextID=virgil1647_2).

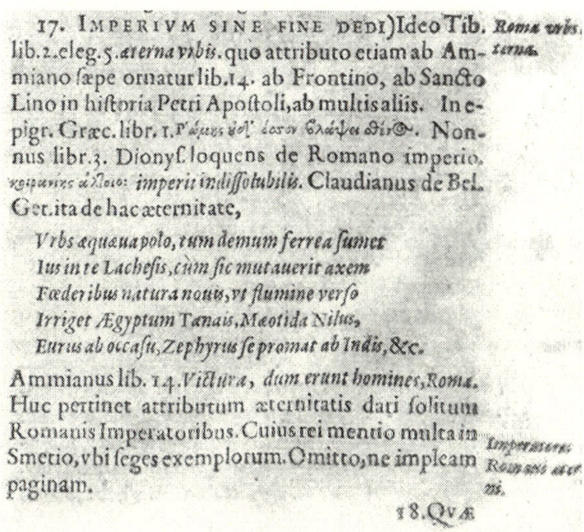
17. IMPERIVM SINE FINE DEDI)Ideo Tib. lib.2.eleg.5.*æterna vrbis*.quo attributo etiam ab Ammiano sæpe ornatur lib.14. ab Frontino, ab Sancto Lino in historia Petri Apostoli,ab multis aliis. In epigr. Græc. libr. 1. [illegible]. Nonnus libr.3. Dionys. loquens de Romano imperio, [illegible] *imperii indissolubilis*. Claudianus de Bel. Get. ita de hac æternitate,

Vrbs æquæua polo, tum demum ferrea sumet
Ius in te Lachesis, cùm sic mutauerit axem
Fœderibus natura nouis, vt flumine verso
Irriget Ægyptum Tanais, Mæotida Nilus,
Eurus ab occasu, Zephyrus se promat ab Indis, &c.

Ammianus lib. 14. *Victura, dum erunt homines, Roma*. Huc pertinet attributum æternitatis dari solitum Romanis Imperatoribus. Cuius rei mentio multa in Smetio, vbi seges exemplorum. Omitto, ne impleam paginam.

Roma vrbs æterna. *Imperatores Romani æterni.*

18. QVÆ

Towards the end of the 18th century, Christian Gottlob Heyne adopts la Cerda's views in his commentary (Fig. 2): "*rerum metas*, i. e. the boundaries of empire. *sine fine*, [i. e.] the eternal city, as on coins and monuments. This motif is variously treated and embellished by poets in countless passages".[26] Unlike la

(1965), 25-44. Cf. K. Balbuza, "The Idea of *aeternitas* of State, City and Emperor in Augustan Poetry", in *Klio* 96 (2014), 49-66.

26 | C. G. Heyne, *Publius Virgilius Maro, varietate lectionis et perpetua adnotatione illustratus. Vol. 2.* (Leipzig: Caspar Fritsch, ³1800), *ad Aen.* 1.278-9. The note is not changed by Wagner in his expanded 1832 edition of Heyne's commentary.

Cerda, Heyne lists none of these "countless" examples, emphasizing instead the diversity of media which advertise it: coins, monuments, poetry. Interestingly, two 19th century commentaries by Weidner and Conington (revised by Nettleship) silence the issue by not offering a note on *imperium sine fine* at all.[27]

Fig. 2: Heyne, Publius Virgilius Maro, 64 (partial photo), ad Aen. 1.278–9.

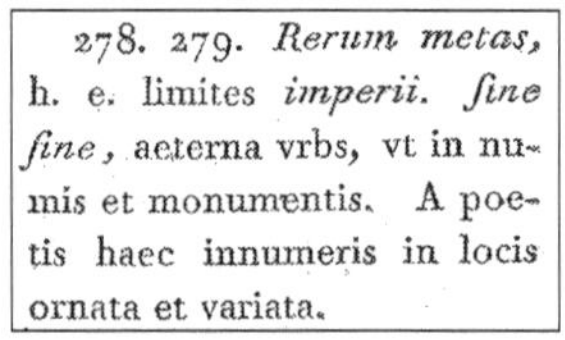

278. 279. *Rerum metas,* h. e. limites *imperii. fine fine,* aeterna vrbs, vt in numis et monumentis. A poetis haec innumeris in locis ornata et variata.

In the currently standard commentary on *Aeneid* 1, Austin continues where Heyne left off (Fig. 3).[28] He focuses again on *Roma aeterna:* "Jupiter sets no bounds of fortune or time to Roman power ... The splendor of eternal Rome is already settled. Here then is the concept of the Eternal City". Austin's eight-item list of parallels[29] (some of them quoted at unnecessary length) unravels, so to speak, Heyne's generic reference to "coins, monuments and poetry",

27 | A. Weidner, *Commentar zu Vergil's* Aeneis *Buch I und II* (Leipzig: Teubner, 1869); J. Conington and H. Nettleship, *The Works of Virgil, with a Commentary.* Vol. II. Fourth ed. revised with additional notes by H. N. (London: Whittaker & Co., 41884), *ad* 1.278-9 although not commenting on *imperium sine fine*, seem to favour the temporal interpretation themselves, noting that *meta* itself may be transferred from space to time, as it also happens in one other *Aeneid* passage (10.472, referring to the limits of an individual's life).

28 | R. G. Austin, *P. Vergili Maronis* Aeneidos *Liber Primus, with a commentary* (Oxford: Clarendon Press, 1971), *ad Aen.* 1.278f. On Austin's *Aeneid* commentaries in the wider context of 20th century classical scholarship, see Henderson, *Classic Commentaries on Latin Classics*, 37-69. I can only summarize here the main points of some other commentaries on the passage. R. D. Williams, *The* Aeneid *of Virgil, with introduction and notes.* 2 Vols. (London: MacMillan, 1972), *ad* 1.278-9 provides only a translation; G. Stégen, *Le livre I de l'*Énéide: *Texte latin avec un plan détaillé et un commentaire critique et explicatif* (Namur: A. Wesmael-Charlier, 1975), *ad* 1.278-9 also refers to the *urbs aeterna* motif, offering two parallels (Tib. 2.5.23, as in Austin, and a late antique passage, Claudian *Laud. Stil.* 3.159-60), but then discusses the ancient literary and philosophical tradition of the idea that "everything with a beginning must have an end", for which he offers no less than 11 parallels.

29 | I translate here only the most relevant sections of the parallels cited by Austin: "Romulus had not yet built the walls of the eternal city" (Tib. 2.5.23f.), "father of the eternal city" (Ov. *F.* 3.72), "a city founded for eternity" (Livy 4.4.4 and 28.28.11), "the

with the addition of non-poetic examples. The parallels Austin offers might, indeed, support an interpretation of *imperium sine fine* as the variant of the *urbs aeterna* idea, but in one case this is the result of incomplete quotation. In Livy 4.4.4 we read *in aeternum urbe condita, in immensum crescente* ("the city [of Rome] founded for eternity, growing to a measureless extent"). The distinction of temporal and spatial infinity here recalls Vergil's *nec metas ... nec tempora.* Austin's decision, however, to quote only the first half of the Livian passage hides this similarity and suggests that it specifically supports the temporal interpretation. The Livian passage, if quoted in full, rather shows that the idea of *Roma aeterna* can be easily coupled with that of unlimited expansion and that the Vergilian expression may, accordingly, might refer to the lack of limits for Roman power in both space and time.

Fig. 3: Austin, Aeneidos Liber Primus, 106–7 (montage), ad Aen. 1.278–9.

> **278 f.** Iuppiter sets no bounds of fortune or time to Roman power. The majestic pronouncement of 278 is confirmed, as it were, by the variation *imperium sine fine dedi* (a fine sweeping rhythm), where *dedi* is in strong contrast to the future tenses elsewhere: the splendour of eternal Rome is already settled.
>
> Here then is the concept of the Eternal City. The actual phrase appears first in Tibullus 2. 5. 23 f. 'Romulus aeternae nondum formauerat urbis / moenia' (so Ovid of Romulus, *F.* 3. 72 'aeternae . . . pater urbis'); cf. Livy 4. 4. 4 'in aeternum urbe condita', 28. 28. 11 'ne istuc Iuppiter optimus maximus sirit, urbem auspicato dis auctoribus in aeternum conditam huic fragili et mortali corpori aequalem esse'; and the noble peroration of Otho's speech in Tac. *H.* 1. 84 'quid? uos pulcherrimam hanc urbem domibus et tectis et congestu lapidum stare creditis? muta ista et inanima intercidere ac reparari promisca sunt: aeternitas rerum et pax gentium et mea cum uestra salus incolumitate senatus firmatur. hunc auspicato a parente et conditore urbis nostrae institutum et a regibus usque ad principes continuum et immortalem, sicut a maioribus accepimus, sic posteris tradamus'. Syme (*Tacitus*, p. 208 n. 1) notes an inscription of A.D. 32 (*ILS* 157) 'prouidentiae Ti. Caesaris Augusti nati ad aeternitatem Romani nominis', and observes that senatorial coins under Domitian are inscribed *aeternitas Augusti*: see his further references, and Ogilvie on Livy 4. 4. 4. Virgil's splendid lines show plainly the Augustan conception of Roman greatness. Marlowe has a fine rebuilding of Iuppiter's prophecy, in his *Tragedy of Dido*, Act 1.

As we have seen, the commentary tradition of the *Aeneid* passage is characterized by a focus on the temporal interpretation and especially on the *Roma aeterna* idea. This reading had never been explicitly challenged; implicitly, perhaps, by the lack of a note in two commentaries. Furthermore, we can also discover two further characteristics of this commentary tradition, both closely connected with the focus on *Roma aeterna.* First, by concentrating on this

eternity of our state" (Tac. *H.* 1.84), "the eternity of the Roman nation" (*ILS* 157), "Augustan eternity" (coins under Domitian).

related idea, commentators lose sight of the Vergilian expression itself and its linguistic form: they do not point out parallel passages where, for example, *imperium* and *finis* are combined in a similar (or contrasting) way. Second, the lists of parallels in both La Cerda and Austin focus on post-Vergilian examples (even Marlowe is included by the latter). Austin even emphasizes that the expression *urbs aeterna* is first found in Vergil's contemporaries (Tibullus and Livy). Thus, concentrating on the idea of 'eternal Rome', Austin (but, to a lesser extent, La Cerda as well) lets the Vergilian passage be seen as the forerunner of a literary and ideological tradition rather than as reflecting – or transforming – earlier Roman view(s) regarding the nature and limits of Roman power.[30]

Looking for Parallels with Digital Tools

Much scholarly attention has been paid to the development of Roman ideas of territorial expansion (based, to a great extent, on the tradition regarding Alexander the Great's conquests), to perceptions and representations of geographic space in ancient Rome, and to the transformations these perceptions seem to have underwent in the late republican and Augustan periods.[31] With the establishment of principate as a centralized political system, and in accordance with the *princeps*' political self-representation, Romans apparently began to see their possessions outside the city itself as parts making up a whole, a contiguous territorial empire, which can also be represented on a map rather than just as a list of all the distinct provinces and cities which happen to be under Roman rule. A related linguistic change can also be documented. Earlier, Romans had not referred to their 'empire' by the expression *imperium Romanum; imperium* had the meaning of 'command' or 'power' (of a magistrate or the Roman people). Such powers, however, were normally confined to certain areas, and

30 | Similar conclusions may be drawn by using *Cited Loci of the* Aeneid (aeneid.citedloci.org, accessed 06-27-2018) which indexes papers citing or quoting individual lines of Vergil's epic in the JSTOR database. Of the 42 individual papers listed for *Aeneid* 1.278 and 279, only around one third (13 papers) discuss the *Aeneid per se* and its earlier and contemporary intertextual context, while two thirds (29) focus on the antique or postantique reception of Vergil.

31 | See e. g. J. Vogt, "*Orbis Romanus*. Ein Beitrag zum Sprachgebrauch und zur Vorstellungswelt des römischen Imperialismus", in *Orbis. Ausgewählte Schriften zur Geschichte des Altertums*, 151-171. Freiburg/Basel/Wien: Herder, 1960; P. A. Brunt, *Roman Imperial Themes* (Oxford: Clarendon Press, 1990), 288-323, 433-80; Nicolet, *Space, Geography, and Politics in the Early Roman Empire* (with the review by N. Purcell, "Maps, Lists, Money, Order and Power", in *Journal of Roman Studies* 80 (1990), 178-82).

this implied spatial sense began to be emphasized in the late republican period until, eventually, the noun also acquired the now familiar meaning of 'empire'. Thus, part of the uncertainties about the spatial and/or temporal meaning of Vergil's phrase *imperium sine fine* might be due to the fact that the *Aeneid* had been composed in a transitional phase of the development of the word *imperium.*[32]

Had this study been conducted with the help of non-digital tools only, it would have commenced with a review of the literature on these topics, in hope that the relevant publications would also contain citations of passages which provide potential parallels for the Vergilian phrase (and especially for its spatial interpretation). Full text digital *corpora*, being more suited to detect verbal similarities than thematic and ideological parallels, facilitate the opposite approach: my digital case study starts with mapping the usage of expressions at least superficially similar to the Vergilian phrase, in hope that at least some of them will provide relevant parallels, and also reveal more of the cultural context of the *Aeneid* passage in question. This approach seems especially suited to my effort to compensate for the above discussed tendency of commentaries to focus on the idea of *Roma aeterna* instead of the expression *imperium sine fine.*

Commentators' predilection for the *Roma aeterna* motif may be explained, in part, also by the fact that Jupiter in lines 278-9 uses mostly ordinary, non-poetic words to construct a memorable utterance.[33] Not counting the pronouns, negatives and prepositions *(his, ego, nec, sine)*, most of the god's words belong to the basic vocabulary of Latin: *res* ('thing'), *tempus* ('time'), *pono* ('to put/state'),

32 | On the history of *imperium* in classical Latin, see in most detail J. S. Richardson, *The Language of Empire: Rome and the Idea of Empire from the Third Century BC to the Second Century AD* (Cambridge: Cambridge University Press, 2008). As he emphasizes (vii), his study could not have been carried out without digital *corpora;* on methodology see also J. S. Richardson, "Indexing Roman Imperialism", in *The Indexer* 24/3 (2005), 138-40. This monograph-length study of *imperium* can be compared to the author's earlier "pre-digital" paper on the same topic: J. S. Richardson, "Imperium Romanum: Empire and the Language of Power", in *Journal of Roman Studies* 81 (1991), 1-9. In Richardson's (sometimes too rigid) typology, *Aen.* 1.279 is an example for the traditional, not strictly territorial usage of *imperium:* Richardson, *The Language of Empire*, 132.

33 | Cf. the characterization "sonorous and unforgettable phrases" in Williams, *The* Aeneid *of Virgil, ad* 1.278-9; Y. Syed, *Vergil's* Aeneid *and the Roman Self: Subject and Nation in Literary Discourse* (Ann Arbor: University of Michigan Press, 2005), 44 treats *imperium sine fine dedi* as an example of the "sublime style" in the *Aeneid.* Williams, "The Opening Scenes of the *Aeneid*", 21 takes note of "the precise word order of Latin prose. There is no subtlety here, no embellishment, no verbal decoration, just the unadorned statement of a tremendous fact".

imperium ('power/empire'), *do* ('to give'). The only exception is *meta* ('cone/turning-post'), but even this word is not exceptionally rare or poetic. In other words, there is not much in the language used in these lines to trigger the reader's personal intertextual memory.

With the help of full-text digital databases it is possible to list occurrences of even such ordinary words, but choosing any one of them would no doubt generate hundreds or even thousands of results. Searching for bigrams, or co-occurrences of two words (even if common in themselves), on the other hand, will probably return a substantially reduced and thus much more manageable list of results to work with. In order to run such a query, given the high inflection rate and relatively free word order of Latin, we need a search engine able to find the two words in question 1) in any relative order, 2) in any inflected form, 3) even if separated from each other by intervening words. The latter two factors are most important when choosing which digital *corpus* and search engine to use for a particular query. Some words can be relatively easily queried by simple string searches. We can find all forms of *imperium* if we look for the string *imperi*, although this will return other words as well, some of them potentially relevant cognates like *imperito* ("to issue commands"), others unrelated words like *imperitus* ("inexperienced"). If we expect that the number of irrelevant results would be low, it is easier to filter them out during the review of the results rather than constructing a more complex search phrase. On the other hand, if we are looking for *res*, running a search for *re* (the stem common to all inflected forms) will also return, for example, countless occurrences of *rex* ("king") and any word having *re-* as a prefix. In these cases, the need is pressing for a search engine which is able to run "lemmatized" queries, i. e. to automatically look for all inflected forms of a given dictionary headword (and also account for some common suffixes as well as the connective *-que*).

In light of the above, it might seem that the latter kind of search engine is always the better but, in some cases, string queries offer more flexibility. It is always the research question (the particular words we are looking for and the types of parallels we hope to find) that decides which kind of search engine is more suitable to the task. This is also true with regard to the permitted gap between the two words of a bigram. Allowing for larger gaps and neglecting sentence boundaries leads to more results, but also allows us to find thematic co-occurrences more easily; accepting only smaller gaps and limiting bigrams to a single sentence will, in addition to reducing the number of results, foreground passages in which the two words have more chance of being syntactically related to each other. Again, the right tool can be selected only after clearly formulating our research question.

For this case study, I have decided to use Brepols' *Library of Latin Texts corpus* (henceforth *LTT*),[34] mainly for the flexibility of its search engine which can be used in both "string" and "lemmatized" mode – I have made use of both.[35] I have decided to look only for pre-Vergilian and contemporary parallels, for two reasons: first, because my primary aim was to reveal parallels from the period neglected by commentaries, and second, because discussion of even just the early reception of the Vergilian passage would require a separate paper. Consequently, my results will be valid only for Roman literature (both poetry and prose) up to Vergil's own times; had I concentrated on imperial literature, I might have arrived at different conclusions. In *LLT*, users can filter results by the dating of authors. In my case, I had to include authors ranging from the third century B. C. (the beginnings of Roman literature) to the early first century A. D. I had to include the latter period in order to see results from some contemporary authors who outlived Vergil; as a consequence, a number of evidently post-Vergilian authors also appeared in the lists of results. Some results thus had to be removed manually, and in the case of some roughly contemporary authors, I had to decide whether or not to include them. In the end, I decided to include as contemporaries the historian Livy, the architect Vitruvius and the poet Propertius, but exclude Ovid (clearly a poet of the next generation, showing the influence of Vergil in countless passages) and some other early imperial authors.

Among all the possible bigram queries based on a given passage, there will be probably some which do not return relevant results at all. Although my focus is on the expression *imperium sine fine* in this paper, I have also run queries (all of them lemmatized) for other combinations of the words making up lines 278-9: *meta* + *res*, *meta* + *pono*, *meta* + *tempus*, *meta* + *imperium*, and *tempus* + *pono*. None of them provide relevant pre-Vergilian or contemporary parallels. Even such negative results, however, might be interesting and it is thus useful to document them in publications: in my case, these negative results may be

34 | More exactly, the *LLT-A corpus* will be used (clt.brepolis.net/llta, accessed 06-27-2018); *LLT-B* contains texts which have not yet received the same editorial attention as those in the former.

35 | In string queries (called "regular search" in *LLT*), bigrams are found by default if both terms appear in the same sentence (irrespective of its length). It is also possible to look for bigrams spanning as many as three sentences, but I have decided not to use this setting. In addition to substantially inflating the list of results (no doubt with irrelevant results in many cases), this search option also has the odd effect of bigrams inside a single sentence or spanning two sentences appearing thrice and twice, respectively, among the results and thus distorting statistics. For lemmatized queries ("similarity search" in *LLT*), the user can select the maximum number of intervening words between 0 and 4; I used 4.

employed as an argument that (as far as we can tell) Vergil used ordinary words in our passage, but mostly in a novel combination, and this might also play some part (in addition to the lofty content: a promise of unlimited power) in making this passage memorable.

There were some further queries which returned potentially interesting results but will not be discussed here in detail to prevent this paper from becoming infinite itself. Such was my query for the expression *sine fine*, which returned 5 pre-Vergilian and contemporary instances, including Vergil himself; all of them, however, are also listed in the *Thesaurus Linguae Latinae*.[36] In this case, the use of a digital *corpus* did not provide more examples than the most exhaustive print dictionary of Latin– except for the information that the dictionary lists, indeed, all known occurrences of the phrase for the period concerned. The other (lemmatized) query not to be discussed was for *imperium + do*. My only summary remark here is that in 27 of the 30 the pre-Vergilian, Vergilian and contemporary passages containing any variant of the expression *imperium dare* ('to grant *imperium*'), the recipients are individuals elected for magistracies. There are only three passages where the recipient is a group or nation; moreover, all three are found in prophecies, two of them in the *Aeneid*.[37] Vergil thus seems to employ, twice in his epic, a widespread legal expression in a novel way.

My main query was for the two key nouns of line 279, *imperium* and *finis*. It seemed worthwhile, however, to include three further words (or word groups) as alternatives to *finis*. The first is *terminus/termino* ('boundary/to mark boundaries'), especially since the verbal form is present in line 286 (*imperium ... terminet*). The second is the adjective *infinitus* ('infinite', not found anywhere in Vergil) as the functional equivalent of *sine fine*. Finally, although I was primarily looking for parallels corroborating spatial interpretations, I also decided to include *aeternus/aeternitas* ('eternal/eternity'). This made it possible to check

36 | I searched for the phrase first as a single string, not allowing intervening words, then also as a bigram; the second query provided no additional results. *Sine fine* occurs once more in the *Aeneid*: Aeneas tells Dido that he had looked without end for his missing wife Creusa during the fall of Troy (2.771). The intratextual repetition, not mentioned by Austin, Aeneidos *Liber Primus, ad* 1.279 and R. G. Austin, *P. Vergili Maronis* Aeneidos *Liber Secundus, with a commentary* (Oxford: Clarendon Press, 1964), *ad* 2.771, is noted by N. Horsfall, *Virgil.* Aeneid *2: A Commentary* (Leiden/Boston: Brill, 2008), *ad Aen.* 2.771. Although Horsfall does acknowledge the use of digital *corpora* in his preface (ix), in this case he cites the *TLL* as authority.

37 | In addition to Jupiter's prophecy in 1.279, the Penates (protective gods of Troy) state that they "will grant power / an empire to the city [of Rome]" (*imperiumque urbi dabimus*, 3.159). The third passage is Livy 38.18.9.

if there are closer verbal parallels than *urbs* or *Roma aeterna* for a temporal interpretation of the Vergilian expression.[38]

Search engines all have their own syntax which users must become familiar with in order to formulate complex queries. After some experimentation, I have settled with the following as my search phrase in LLT, quoted here exactly (and then "translated" into English) to make my query reproduceable (Fig. 4):

(imperium, imperii, imperi, imperio) + (finis, finem, fini, fine, fines, finium, finibus, infinit*, termin*, aetern*)

In 'string mode' search, I am looking for bigrams found in a single sentence and constituted by any singular form of *imperium*[39] and either any form of *finis*, or words beginning with *infinit-*, *termin-* or *aetern-*.

Fig. 4: Advanced search options in LLT (clt.brepolis.net/llta)

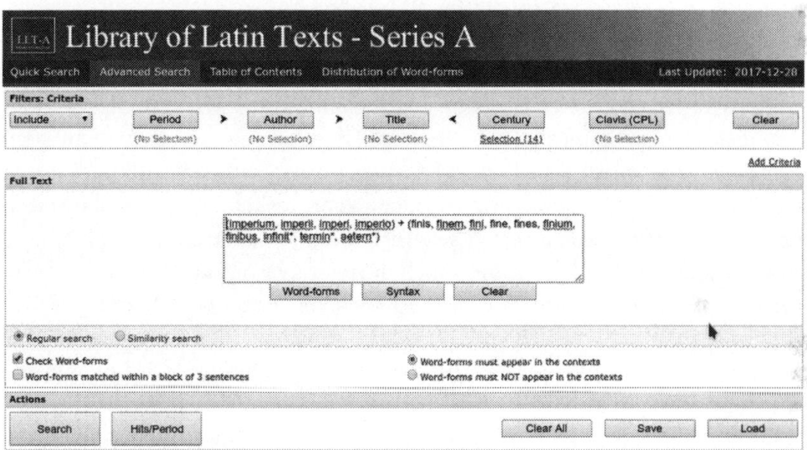

The query returned 109 passages in all. Given this high number of results, I had to go through multiple phases of selection and categorization, with each phase characterized by gradually "closer", more and more attentive readings.[40]

38 | Another reason for including this word is that the plural expression *aeternis imperiis*, in a different sense, is used by Venus in the *Aeneid* episode (at 1.230) with reference to the "everlasting commands" of Jupiter as governor of the world.

39 | Plural forms of *imperium* were excluded since they tend to have the meaning 'commands', as in Venus' words quoted above.

40 | Cf. A. Bilansky, "Search, Reading, and the Rise of Database", in *Digital Scholarship in the Humanities* 32 (2017), 511-27, esp. 518-9 on how full-text databases facilitate, through their search engines, the cooperative use of "distant" and "close" reading strategies, and N. K. Hayles, *How We Think: Digital Media and Contemporary*

The first phase, filtering[41] out the post-Vergilian passages, was the easiest and could be done by truly "distant" reading: I did not need to look at the texts themselves at all, only their authors and titles. The two Vergilian lines (*Aen.* 1.279 and 286) were themselves among the results, and 38 were post-Vergilian according to the definition outlined above. By the end of this phase, 69 pre-Vergilian and contemporary passages remained as possible parallels: still a quite high number.

The next phase was setting apart the "relevant" passages from the "irrelevant" ones. This was based on a still relatively distant kind of reading. It was my decision to put aside as irrelevant 1) passages containing false positives (e. g. homonyms of my search terms), and 2) passages in which the terms of my query seem not to be related to each other any more closely than by the simple fact that both happen to be present: for example, if they are found at a large distance from each other at the beginning and the end of a long periodic sentence, or closer to each other, but in separate clauses about different topics. In this second phase it was now necessary to "skim" the various texts themselves, but mostly without reading continuously, word for word. Digital search engines (be it Google or LLT) usually highlight the search terms in the resulting passages: they dynamically alter the texts (stored on the server without such alterations, of course) visually and typographically (Fig. 5). Such highlighting facilitates the initial processing of information by scanning and skimming without continuous and attentive reading. This evaluation strategy, we have to admit, raises the threshold above which the relevancy of a given passage can be detected. There is a greater chance of missing some details – especially if they are not highlighted – which could turn even an apparently irrelevant passage into a relevant one. We pay this price for quicker processing of a large number of results. It might also be argued, however, that attentive reading of all search results would make much more of them look interesting in some way or the other, and thus prevent us from seeing the forest for the trees: larger tendencies of discourse for individual texts.

Technogenesis (Chicago: Chicago University Press, 2012), 175-247 on the "symbiosis of narrative and database".

41 | On "filtering", "skimming" (see below) and other techniques of "hyper-reading", see J. J. Sosnoski, "Hyper-Readers and Their Reading-Engines", in *Passions, Politics, and 21st Century Technologies*, edited by G. E. Hawisher and C. L. Selfe, 161-177. Urbana: Utah State University Press, 1999 and Hayles, *How We Think*, 55-79; cf. N. K. Hayles, "Hyper and Deep Attention: The Generational Divide in Cognitive Modes," in *Profession* (2007), 187-99 on the generational aspects of favoring "attentive" and "hyper" reading strategies.

Fig. 5: Search results with highlighted search terms in LLT (clt.brepolis.net/llta).

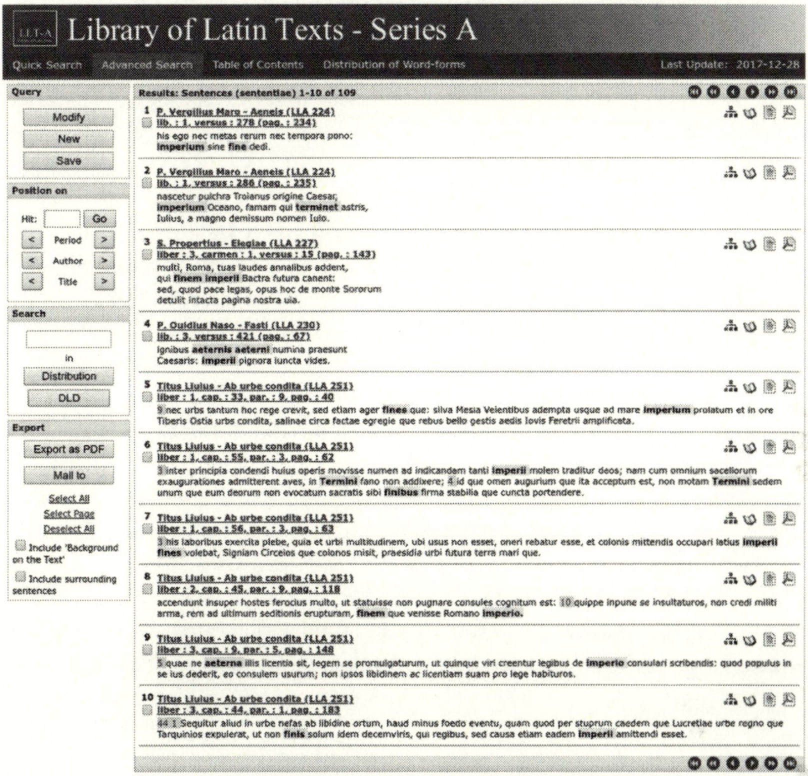

The second phase of selection ended with 32 (slightly less than fifty percent) of the 69 passages having been put aside as irrelevant for my study. The remaining 37 passages, mostly from Cicero and Livy (17 and 16 passages, respectively), were still too many and diverse to be treated and discussed as a single group. Some broad categorization was needed in order to reveal recurring topics and/or typical phrases. In this third phase of processing the results, I had to move one further step closer to the texts: the passages now had to be read word for word and, if needed, their broader contexts taken into consideration (by even more attentive reading). The seven categories I ended up with are thematic rather than lexical, and were gradually refined in the course of reading the individual passages:

1. extending the boundaries (of Roman rule) *(fines imperii propagare/proferre)* — 12 passages
2. frontiers *(fines imperii)* — 10
3. unlimited command *(imperium infinitum)* — 9

4. the temporal end of Roman rule *(finis Romani imperii)* 2
5. the cults of Terminus and Iuventas (Youth) on the Capitol 2
6. the conquests of Alexander the Great 1
7. eternity of Roman rule 1(+1)

The distribution of passages is in itself significant. The majority of them (categories 1, 2, 6; 23 passages in all) are concerned with space and geography; spatiality is also prominent in some of the 9 passages making up category 3. The two passages belonging to category 5 are concerned with the stability of Roman rule in both space and time.[42] By contrast, the topic of longevity is explicit in only four of the 37 passages (categories 4 and 7). It seems noteworthy, that the words *aeternitas* and *aeternus* are found only in two Ciceronian passages (category 7 and another passage which otherwise belongs to category 1).[43] All this suggests that the words *imperium* and *finis/terminus* etc. were used in pre-Vergilian and contemporary Roman literature, in similar collocations, in the context of the spatial infinity and expansion of Roman rule much more frequently than its temporally infinite nature; explicit references to the latter (as documented by the presence of *aeternus* etc.) are relatively rare.

All of the seven categories listed above have their own stories to tell, but I am going to discuss here, to represent the fourth phase of processing the results, only the topic and its expressions around which category 1 is built and which, in my view, is the most interesting result of my digital study on *Aen.* 1.278-9.

"Extending the Boundaries"

The 12 passages under category 1 are all concerned with (mostly Roman) territorial expansion. The idea is conveyed by a number of expressions.[44] Two passages – not noted by Austin –immediately stand out for their similarity with Jupiter's statement about Caesar "extending [Roman] rule to the Ocean, his fame to the stars" (*imperium Oceano, famam qui terminet astris, Aen.* 1.287), and bringing an era of peace. Pompey the Great is twice praised by Cicero for "ending all wars and bringing the frontiers of Roman rule to the end of

42 | The two passages of category 5 (Liv. 1.55.3, 5.54.7) are discussed in context of *Aen.* 1.278-9 by D. C. Feeney, *The Gods in Epic: Poets and Critics of the Classical Tradition* (Oxford: Clarendon Press, 1991), 141.

43 | Cic. *Rab.* 33, *Cat.* 3.26. Neither are cited by Austin, Aeneidos *Liber Primus*, *ad Aen.* 1.279.

44 | Prop. 3.1.15; Liv. 1.56.3; Sall. *Epist. Mithr.* 17; Cic. *Cat.* 3.26; *Balb.* 39; *Sest.* 67; and the passages listed in note 47.

the world" (*omnibus terris ... compressis imperium populi orbis terrarum terminis definisset, Sest.* 67; with the search terms underlined) and, even more hyperbolically, for "establishing the frontiers of [Roman] rule not in earthly, but in heavenly regions" (*finis vestri imperi non terrae, sed caeli regionibus terminaret, Cat.* 3.26). Vergil's Jupiter, ironically, praises Caesar/Augustus with the same rhetoric which was used by Cicero to praise both Julius Caesar himself (on other occasions) and Pompey (in the above two passages), Caesar's former ally, all-time political rival and eventual arch-enemy.[45]

Even more significant, however, seems to be the expression *fines imperii proferre/propagare,* "extending the boundaries of [Roman] rule". This is found, in different variants, in six of the twelve passages of the category.[46] If we run a second query, taking into account some elliptical variants as well (with either *imperium* or *finis* missing), the number goes up to 11.[47] In one case, this expression is combined with the motif of "reaching the end of the world", as in Jupiter's prophecy in the *Aeneid:* Lucius Scipio (brother of the famous Scipio Africanus) is praised for "having extended the boundaries of the Roman people's rule to the farthest regions of the world" (*imperium populi Romani propagaverit in ultimos terrarum fines,* Livy 38.60.4). Even more important, however, is a passage in Cicero's *Republic,* a dialogue written in the late fifties but with a dramatic date of 129 B. C. Cicero mentions "the honorary inscription carved on monuments of great generals: 'He extended the boundaries of [Roman] rule'" (*illa laus in summorum imperatorum incisa monumentis 'finis imperii propagavit', Rep.* 3.24). No such inscription from the republican or early imperial era has actually been found as of yet; nevertheless, Cicero's statement implies that the expression belongs to the formulaic language of cultural memory. This is also suggested by the relatively large number of examples among my results. The expression may be genuinely traditional or an example of late republican "invented tradition"; but by all means, it predates the Augustan era at least by

45 | These parallels are not noted by Austin, Aeneidos *Liber Primus, ad Aen.* 1.286ff. Cicero praising Caesar for reaching the end of the world: *Prov. cons.* 29–33, *Balb.* 64. Pompey praised himself in similar terms, as an inscription in Greek quoted by Diodorus Siculus (40.4) shows; cf. Brunt, *Roman Imperial Themes*, 292.

46 | Liv. 1.33.9 *nec urbs tantum hoc rege crevit, sed etiam ager finesque ... usque ad mare imperium prolatum;* 38.60.4 *imperium populi Romani propagaverit in ultimos terrarum fines;* Nep. *Ham.* 2.5 *finis imperii propagavit* (the only passage where the territory to be extended is not Roman); Cic. *Prov. cons.* 29 *finium imperii propagatio; Phil.* 13.14 *finis imperii propagabis; Rep.* 3.24 *finis imperii propagavit.*

47 | The search terms in this case were: "(finem, finis, fines, finium, finibus, imperi*) + (propag*, profer*, protul*, prolat*)". Additional results: Cic. *Mur.* 22 *in propagandis finibus;* Liv. 31.5.7 *prolationem finium;* 42.20.4 *prolationemque finium;* Sall. *Hist.* 4. fr. 70 *imperii prolatandi. Aeneid* 6.795, also among the results, is discussed below.

one generation. The repetition of this expression on various honorary inscriptions, as implied by Cicero's words, would suggest that these inscriptions commemorate military victories not just as individual successes, but also as stages in the process of conquering more and more territories for Rome. *Fines imperii propagare*, in that respect, conveys an idea similar to Vergil's *imperium sine fine*. It is the (potentially) never ending series of conquests that makes Roman rule "infinite": at any point in time, there are frontier zones (*fines*, in plural; cf. my category 2) which can *always* be pushed *farther* (*propagare, proferre*) until the end of the world is reached, and consequently there is no absolute limit (*finis*, in singular) for Roman rule either in space, other than the end of the world, or in time. Seen in this light, both expressions have spatial and temporal aspects at the same time, and they seem to be in a basically metonymic relation to each other. The Vergilian *imperium sine fine* focuses on the result, while *fines imperii propagare* reveals the historical process which leads to it; and Jupiter, obviously, highlights his own role and authority *(dedi)*, while the inscriptions focus on the contribution of the mortal generals *(proferre, propagare)*.

Jupiter's prophecy, although it is concerned with Rome's future conquests, does not include an account of the series of *fines ... propagare*. He singles out only two important events. One is the conquest of Greece as an act of revenge for the fall of Troy (*Aen*. 1.283-5); none of the generals are mentioned, however, who will make this conquest possible. In the second case, by contrast, the personal aspect is emphasized: Caesar/Augustus will reach the Ocean and initiate an era of peace – a kind of new Golden Age, as it will be heralded more explicitly later in *Aeneid* 6 by Anchises (*aurea condet condet saecula ... rursus*, "he will reestablish the Golden Age", 792-3). In the same passage it will be said that Augustus is going to "extend [Roman] rule over both the Garamantes and the Inds" (*super et Garamantas et Indos <u>proferet</u> <u>imperium</u>, Aen*. 6.794-5). The two people represent Africa and Asia, respectively: two continents to be conquered by Europe (Rome) in the process of establishing a world empire. The *Aeneid* 6 passage I quoted also belongs to my category 1 and is, indeed, among the results of my second query for elliptic variants of the "traditional" phrase (see above, n. 47). The two related *Aeneid* passages from books 1 and 6, when taken together, strongly suggest that both *imperium sine fine* and *proferet imperium* may be treated as elliptical variants of *fines imperii proferre*. Caesar/Augustus is presented by Jupiter and Anchises as the ultimate Roman conqueror: reaching the Ocean, the final frontier, he is the most important among the generals who have "extended the boundaries of Roman rule". Among all the statues and inscriptions referred to by Cicero, Augustus' would have to be placed in a prominent position.

Augustus is, in fact, granted a similarly prominent place by Anchises in his long speech to Aeneas in the Underworld. In the last section, he is showing his son some of the yet-to-be-born Roman heroes (6.789-846), and Augustus, although chronologically one of the last, is discussed among the first (791-805). This literary parade of heroes (the "Heldenschau") has also been compared to Augustus' "Hall of Fame", the statue gallery of great Romans *(summi viri)* in the porticoes of his new Forum inaugurated in 2 B. C. – some two decades after Virgil had written the *Aeneid*.[48] The statue of Augustus standing on a chariot was set up, to signal his prominence, in the center of the Forum and also the gallery. Suetonius (early 2nd c. A. D.), when discussing this monument in his biography of the *princeps,* also states that Augustus' principle was to select those generals "who made the empire of the Roman people grow from the smallest to the greatest" *(qui imperium populi Romani ex minimo maximum reddidissent),* to be treated as examples by himself and his successors (Suet. *Aug.* 31). Suetonius does not employ the phrase *fines imperii proferre* here,[49] but Augustus himself does use one of its variants in the *Res gestae,* his short political autobiography, where he proclaims that "I brought the Pannon tribes under the rule of the Roman people, and I extended the frontier of Illyricum to the banks of the Danube river" (*Pannoniorum gentes ... imperio populi Romani subieci, protulique fines Illyrici ad ripam fluminis Danuvi,* 30). Augustus refers to the expansion of a single province in this passage, but his statement can obviously be read *pars pro toto:* the expansion of Illyricum also meant the extension of the frontiers of Roman *imperium* in general. The formula "to bring under the rule of the Roman people" already appears in the title, stating (in the third person) that the *Res gestae* is about the deeds through which Augustus "brought the whole world under the rule of the Roman people" *(quibus orbem terrarum imperio populi Romani subiecit)* – or, in other words, by which he established the world empire described in the *Aeneid* by the words *imperium sine fine.* The expansion of a province, the extension of the frontiers of Roman rule and the establishing of the world empire are, as the expressions used in the above quotations suggest, tightly interconnected and represent three phases, or aspects, of the same process.

The texts and monuments discussed in the previous paragraph fall outside the chronological limits set earlier for my digital investigation. Still, they can provide a useful supplement to the digital queries which led to an interpretation of *imperium sine fine* different from (but reconcilable with) that "canonized" in the long commentary tradition by revealing some pre-Vergilian and contemporary literary parallels. The statue gallery in the Forum of Augustus, the

48 | On the statue gallery, see in most detail J. Geiger, *The First Hall of Fame: A Study of the Statues in the Forum Augustum* (Leiden/Boston: Brill, 2008) (with a bibliography on *Aeneid* 6 and the Augustan *summi viri* on p. 50 n. 89); cf. Brunt, *Roman Imperial Themes*, 443.

49 | See, however, Suet. *Aug.* 23.1 on Augustus prolonging the terms of provincial governors.

autobiographic *Res gestae* (datable, probably, to the last years of Augustus' life), and the biography by Suetonius belong to the first century of the reception of Vergil's epic. Obviously, we cannot treat them as documents of the early interpretation of the *Aeneid* in the same way as the commentaries of Servius and his colleagues; but they do seem to suggest that the parallel revealed between the Vergilian *imperium sine fine* and the formulaic *fines imperii proferre* could have seemed relevant also to readers living in the cultural and political climate of the early principate.

Updating the Commentary

It seems fitting to conclude my case study with producing my own version of a commentary note on *Aen.* 1.279. It is formulated to be a supplement to, rather than the replacement of, Austin's comments on *Aen.* 1.278–9. After Austin's list of examples for the *Roma aeterna* idea, my note would run on like this:

[...] The possibility of an end to Roman rule *(finis imperii Romani)* is, by contrast, brought up twice in Livy (2.45.10, 23.28.9).

Sine fine, just like *nec metas rerum* in 278, may also refer to the lack of spatial limits (except for the Ocean as end of the world: 1.286) for Roman rule (cf. 3.97, 6.781-2, 7.99-101). *Imperium* and *finis* (and synomyms) are collocated in pre-Vergilian and contemporary Latin only rarely in a temporal sense; the spatial sense is more frequent. See the expressions *fines imperii* and esp. *fines imperii proferre/propagare* (and its elliptic variants). The latter, according to Cicero, was a formulaic expression in inscriptions commemorating victorious generals (*Rep.* 3.24; see also e. g. *Prov. cons.* 29; Sall. *Hist.* 4. *fr.* 70, Liv. 38.60.4). The same language is to be reflected later in Anchises' speech (*Augustus ... proferet imperium,* 6.795): the *princeps* is the ultimate Roman conqueror, topping off the successes of earlier generals. *Imperium infinitum,* functional equivalent of *i. sine fine,* is found in Cicero only, always when he criticizes the virtually unlimited power of some magistrates (see e.g. *homini ... turpissimo ... quis imperium infinitum dedit?, Dom.* 23.8, and *Leg. agr.* 2.35.5 where *infinitum* is explicitly spatial).

There are only two further instances of *imperium dare* in contemporary and earlier literature where the recipient is a group or nation (rather than an individual), and both are found in prophecies: *Aen.* 3.159, Liv. 38.18.9. With regard to *sine fine* itself, cf. 2.771 with Horsfall 2008, *ad loc.*

Conclusion

Since my discussion of the *Aeneid* passage was part of a case study of how digital *corpora* can be used by classicists, I would like to close my paper with three points concerning methodology. First, I am not suggesting that my interpretation of this particular *Aeneid* passage is better than previous ones, or that the expression *fines imperii propagare* is a more relevant parallel than *Roma aeterna*. Nor am I of the view that digital tools are in general better than printed ones. It would have been hard, for example, to reveal *Roma aeterna* as a parallel for Vergil's *imperium sine fine* (had printed commentaries not discussed it) through digital queries because of the lack of common lexical elements in the two expressions. Rather, I would say that printed and digital tools (dictionaries, encyclopedias, papers, monographs, digital *corpora* etc.) complement each other: they help in answering different questions (or provide different answers to the same questions), and they promote different interpretative strategies.

Second, I have to confess that it would have been possible to reveal *fines imperii propagare* as a parallel for *imperium sine fine* also without the use of digital tools. Some instances of the former found through my digital queries are listed, for example, in relevant entries of the *Thesaurus Linguae Latinae* and the *Oxford Latin Dictionary*, the commentary notes by Norden and Horsfall on *proferet imperium* in *Aeneid* 6,[50] or some of the papers discussing the *topos* of world empire in ancient rhetoric which mention the prophecy of the Vergilian Jupiter as well, but without directly comparing *Aen.* 1.279 to the formulaic *fines imperii propagare*.[51] What could not have been revealed by all these printed tools added together is the total number of instances where variants of the formula are found; the number of relevant co-occurrences of *imperium* and *finis*, including the relative frequency of those focusing on the aspect of space and time, respectively. Digital *corpora* thus help in statistical evaluation of some linguistic and literary patterns and tendencies: in more systematic and in this

50 | *OLD* s. v. "finis" 1 (Liv. 38.60.5); *TLL* s. v. "profero" IA2b (Cic. *Rep.* 3.24, Liv. 1.33.9); E. Norden, Aeneis *Buch VI.* (Leipzig: Teubner, 1916), *ad Aen.* 6.794ff.; N. Horsfall, *Virgil,* Aeneid *6: A Commentary* (Leiden/Boston: Brill, 2013), *ad* 6.795. Both commentators mention as parallel the pseudo-Ovidian (thus post-Vergilian) verse *protulit in terras imperiumque novas* ("and he [Drusus] extended our rule over new territories", *Epicedion Drusi* 20); Horsfall also mentions Liv. 1.33.9 and Aug. *RG* 30. In the *Enciclopedia Virgiliana* entry on "imperium" (II. 927-8), Ilari discusses the plural *fines imperii* (cf. my category 2 above), but as a counter-argument against the spatial interpretation of *sine fine* (singular).

51 | See e. g. Brunt, *Roman Imperial Themes*, 293 and 297; Richardson, *The Language of Empire*, 75-6 and 132.

sense more representative mapping of the intertextual background of a given passage.

Finally, we cannot say that literary research done with the help of digital tools is more "objective". Of all the phases of work on my case study, only one was algorithmic and in this sense objective: if we run the exact same queries on the same version of the same database, the results will always be the same. Everything else was an interpretative decision: choosing the literary historical period and the individual texts to be studied, constructing the search queries, filtering out the results deemed irrelevant, categorizing and further interpreting the relevant ones. By changing just one of these parameters, I might have arrived at very different conclusions. Digital *corpora* (and other digital tools) may thus help in conducting "systematic" research and lead to "representative" results; but they do not exonerate the philologist of the burden and responsibility of interpretation.

Calendar View

Digitization and Big Data in the Historical Daily Press Research

Amália Kerekes

"[A] view where all the printings – authorized or not, skeptical or otherwise – configure a textual network of remarkable wit and complexity", thus Jerome McGann's proposal for the reconstruction of publication contexts of newspaper articles, which is directed against both the unilateral work- and author-centering and against the "stable hierarchy of relations" in conventional critical editions.[1] The endless centrifugal motions in the context of newspaper texts, which, in McGann's concept, parenthesize any perspectivization in favor of the former "multiple agents and relationships"[2] with a new historicist drive, put emphasis on problems of operationalization with the consequence that the groping, barely reflected broadening of historical press research, thanks to digitization, has been quickly maneuvered into a methodological cul-de-sac. However, this radical change in contemplation about new philological scopes in light of increasingly branched possibilities of contextualization as a consequence of the understanding of the quantitative concepts of Digital Humanities refers to the most tacitly accepted sore spot of historical press research, which is the problem of "insurmountable resistance" of journal articles, with registers only partially solved "against any categorization or systematization", as is the case with knowledge about magazines, as Nicolas Pethes points out. This insurmountable resistance, which cannot be banned with the help of digitization, will result in a new confusion. Pethes' diagnosis, however, resulted in

1 | Jerome McGann, "Philological Investigations I. The Example of Poe," in *A New Republic of Letters. Memory and Scholarship in the Age of Digital Reproduction* (Cambridge: Harvard University Press, 2014), 162, 165. I am grateful to Marcus Krause for referring on this text.

2 | McGann, "Philological Investigations," 167.

the utopian idea that "not only the journals themselves, but also their scientific analysis should be described as disparate, fragmentary and processual."[3]

These considerations, in many respects, mark a possible endpoint of the discussions enriched with numerous case studies by Almut Todorow and, among others, by Daniela Gretz and Susanne Düwell,[4] which, precisely because they are committed to the disclosure of the rhetoricity and interdiscursivity of the press, emphasize the importance of contextual knowledge. The operational or integrative strength of this idea of ensuring coherence within a number or a booklet or within serial formats, is particularly evident in those cases that end with a partial fiasco because things "march to a different drummer". However, this should not detract from the gained knowledge.[5] Todorow's concept of rhetorical media research based on the *Frankfurter Zeitung* was mainly tested on magazines.[6] Its further application to digitized corpora in typographically

---

3 | Nicolas Pethes, "Zeitschriftenwissen. Diskursive, printmediale und digitale Archive im 19. Jahrhundert - und heute," *Sprache und Literatur* 45, no. 2 (2014): 113, 116, own translation.

4 | Cf. Susanne Düwell, "'es soll das Mannigfaltigste [...] sammeln, und es für den Denker und Forscher aufbewahren'. Das Magazin zur Erfahrungsseelenkunde als dynamisches Fall-Archiv," Sprache und Literatur 45, no. 2 (2014): 57-73; Susanne Düwell, "Populäre Falldarstellungen in Zeitschriften der Spätaufklärung: Der spektakuläre Fall des 'Menschenfressers' Goldschmidt," in: Fall, Fallgeschichte, Fallstudie. Theorie und Geschichte einer Wissensform, ed. Susanne Düwell and Nicolas Pethes (Frankfurt/M.: Campus, 2014), 293-314; Daniela Gretz, "Kanonische Texte des Realismus im historischen Publikationskontext: Theodor Fontanes 'Frauenromane' Cécile und Effi Briest," in Zeitschriftenliteratur/Fortsetzungsliteratur, ed. Nicola Kaminski, Nora Ramtke, and Carsten Zelle (Hannover: Wehrhahn, 2013), 187-204; Daniela Gretz, "Ein literarischer 'Versuch' im Experimentierfeld Zeitschrift. Medieneffekte der 'Deutschen Rundschau' auf Gottfried Kellers 'Sinngedicht'," Zeitschrift für deutsche Philologie 134, no. 2 (2015): 191-215.

5 | To the dilemmas of creating interconnections cf. Madleen Podewski, Komplexe Medienordnungen. Zur Rolle der Literatur in der deutsch-jüdischen Zeitschrift "Ost und West" (1901-1923) (Bielefeld: transcript, 2013).

6 | Almut Todorow, *Das Feuilleton der Frankfurter Zeitung in der Weimarer Republik. Zur Grundlegung einer rhetorischen Medienforschung* (Tübingen: Niemeyer, 1996). To the actual state of the research with a short example for its application on the daily press cf. Barbara von Reibnitz: "Erstdrucke in Zeitungen. Zur editorischen Kontextdokumentation am Beispiel von Robert Walsers Feuilletons," in *Text - Material - Medium. Zur Relevanz editorischer Dokumentationen für die literaturwissenschaftliche Interpretation*, ed. Wolfgang Lukas, Rüdiger Nutt-Kofoth, and Madleen Podewski (Berlin: de Gruyter, 2014), 219-235.

compact avant-garde magazines[7] or in a combination that is interested in interdiscursivity with Moretti's "Distant Reading"[8] has not yet been able to provide a new profiling of the methodological issues. However, the results and insights (with or without digitization) can hardly be transferred to the daily press, especially because digitization itself is managed rather as a convenient service, an extension of analog research questions. Press historical questions, by contrast, which can only be generated thanks to digitization and which take into account the specifics of the daily press, are still scarce, which, due to the pioneering role of the digitization-savvy corpus linguistics that is mainly based on newspaper texts, never fails to astonish.

The consideration that daily press research is placed under intense methodological pressure as a result of digitization and that a methodological discussion should have to be made up, which partly raises questions other than the historical press research, concerns, however, only a tiny niche in philology, in which the extensive collection of examples rarely tends to pass into an intensive reading of texts. But perhaps this example can show to what extend the legitimacy of previous research techniques is challenged by digitization.

The fact that problems could benefit from new search procedures, especially in the field of historical semantics, should also provide a viable working hypothesis without any additional programming effort to exemplify continuities and changes between analog and digital research questions. The limitation of relevant corpora with regards to comparability, for example, of the profile or the prestige, would reset the interpretation of otherwise not detectable documents in the analog methodology, i.e. in a kind of manual topic modeling and would, by and large, activate the context knowledge. However, by opening such a corpus and to prove its singularity or its interdiscursive status in time, one enters the terrain of those asymmetries and released contingencies, which are interpreted as a productive reciprocal relationship between decentration and data-centering of knowledge in computer philology.[9] From this perspective it also becomes apparent how vulnerable the idea of comparability in the case of the press is after all, and how the corrections of the respective asymmetries can contribute to the increase of contingency. However, if one looks at the quantity

7 | Cf. the project: http://bluemountain.princeton.edu/exist/apps/bluemountain/index.html. <accessed February 8, 2018>

8 | Allen Beye Riddell, "How to Read 22,198 Journal Articles: Studying the History of German Studies with Topic Models," in *Distant Readings: Topologies of German Culture in the Long Nineteenth Century*, ed. Matt Erlin and Lynne Tatlock (Rochester: Camden House, 2014), 91-114.

9 | Cf. David M. Berry, "Die Computerwende – Gedanken zu den Digital Humanities," in *Big Data. Analysen zum digitalen Wandel von Wissen, Macht und Ökonomie*, ed. Ramón Reichert (Bielefeld: transcript, 2014), 47-64.

and width of evidence and give up the idea of representativeness in favor of penetrance, i.e. the research question is gradually detached from analogous patterns of interpretation, then the affinity of this access to Chris Anderson's frequently quoted Big Data idea about the task of finding causalities in favor of correlations is recognizable: "But faced with massive data, this approach to science – hypothesize, model, test – is becoming obsolete. [...] Petabytes allow us to say: 'Correlation is enough.' We can stop looking for models. We can analyze the data without hypotheses about what it might show."[10] The recording of these correlations may as well elucidate rhetorical techniques of serialization as the status of the constitutive "indeterminacy" of concepts[11], however, it only seems to leave behind the model-forming character of the classical approximations until the registration of contextual diversity, the "intended" and coincidental "contextual references" are contrasted with the "obstinacy" of individual documents[12] to escape the trap of a merely conclusive macro-analytical description, which was characterized by Dirk Baecker as follows: "Big Data, however, loses its relevance even more the higher this redundancy is. Big Data thrives on tracking down variance."[13] Research questions concerning profile development and editorial policy of the press, which strive for the proof of an idealistic coherence, or for the ritual of multiple utilizations, which usually undermine this idea, would be, against this backdrop, the cornerstones, in which the specifics of "newspaper knowledge" could be brought to light with the help of a quantitatively substantiated production of correlation and variance, such as the leveling effect of individual press formats or the relative independence of certain sectors. At the same time, this could be productively linked to the insight gained in the first studies, which concerned the handling of press digitized material, and according to which common practices, such as the "zoom-out" of article contexts with a kind of close reading or extensive browsing while reading the digitized material[14] is associated with the recognition of format and

---

10 | Chris Anderson, "The End of Theory: The Data Deluge Makes the Scientific Method Obsolete," *Wired*, June 27, 2018, https://www.wired.com/2008/06/pb-theory. <accessed February 8, 2018>

11 | Cf. Hans Ulrich Gumbrecht, "Pyramiden des Geistes. Über den schnellen Aufstieg, die unsichtbaren Dimensionen und das plötzliche Abebben der begriffsgeschichtlichen Bewegung," in *Dimensionen und Grenzen der Begriffsgeschichte* (München: Fink, 2006), 7-36.

12 | Reibnitz, "Erstdrucke in Zeitungen," 226.

13 | Dirk Baecker, "Metadaten. Eine Annäherung an Big Data," in *Big Data. Das neue Versprechen der Allwissenheit*, ed. Heinrich Geiselberger and Tobias Moorstedt (Berlin: Suhrkamp, 2013), 179.

14 | Cf. Gerben Zaagsma, "On Digital History," *BMGN – Low Countries Historical Review* 128, no. 4 (2013): 3-29, http://doi.org/10.18352/bmgn-lchr.9344; Paul Gooding,

pattern.[15] In this format, which correlates in many respects with the status of "assembling",[16] the sarcastic paraphrase of a basic insight by Clifford Geertz nevertheless largely remains valid: "[I]t is as if data analytics researchers seem to think that it is possible to understand phenomena without knowing them".[17]

This lack of knowledge as opposed to understanding also effects the scientification of the results outside the case studies in the field of Digital Humanities, to exemplify this with an example from these few examples that the press actually plows for a media historical question: The corpus on the subject of the production of volition, which was created with the aid of a historicist and which gained striking results, according to which the medial conveyance of the current crisis reverts to historical patterns,[18] left open the explanation for this result, as if a hermeneutic concept of understanding had replaced the positive concept of knowledge. This oscillation between understanding and knowledge, which is usually not reflected, could be identified as the crux of press history, which repeatedly presupposes an implicit consensus. This is the reason why, in terms of logistics, only a weak concept of representativeness as a modification of the idea of close reading can be used, and, therefore, we only have a concept of contextuality, which is based on consensus and previous knowledge. This concept, however, can only hint at the possible interconnectivity of the texts, at

"Exploring Usage of Digital Newspaper Archives through Web Long Analysis. A Case Study of Welsh Newspapers Online," Conference Paper, Digital Humanities 2014, Lausanne, http://dharchive.org/paper/DH2014/Paper-310.xml. <accessed February 8, 2018>

15 | Cf. the examples for dealing with Australian newspapers which include the illustrations and the functional entities of the print products, in: Clemens Neudecker, "Who cares about yesterday's news? Use cases and requirements for newspaper digitization," Conference Paper, IFLA 2016 News Media Conference, Hamburg, https://www.researchgate.net/publication/304012856_Who_cares_about_yesterday's_news_Use_cases_and_requirements_for_newspaper_digitization. <accessed February 8, 2018>

16 | Cf. the study by Pál Kelemen.

17 | Paolo Gerbaudo, "From Data Analytics to Data Hermeneutics. Online Political Discussions, Digital Methods and the Continuing Relevance of Interpretive Approaches," *Digital Culture & Society* 2, no. 2 (2016): 99, https://doi.org/10.14361/dcs-2016-0207.

18 | Tze-I Yang, Andrew J. Torget, and Rada Mihalcea, "Topic Modeling on Historical Newspapers," in *Proceedings of the 5th ACL-HLT Workshop on Language Technology for Cultural Heritage, Social Sciences, and Humanities* (2011), 96-104, https://www.aclweb.org/anthology/W/W11/W11-15.pdf. <accessed February 8, 2018>

the texts' "unruliness" without being able to prove the texts either in a qualitative or a quantitative way.[19]

However, the question arises – keeping the (analog) positivity in mind – to what extent the Big Data concept can principally be something fundamentally new in the already existing complexity. Among all definitions and in the case of daily-press digitized material, the most qualitative ones appear to be the most productive, which, as Christof Schöch, rely on diversity.[20] Or, to put it in the words of Boyd and Crawford, who state that networking is an ideal criterion: "Big Data is not sound because of its size, but because of its relationality to other data. [...] Big Data is fundamentally networked".[21] Taking into account both aspects – the diversity and interconnectedness of data – most of the case studies select "The New York Times Annotated Corpus", which currently provides a competitive range of search procedures in terms of journal projects: "Over 650,000 article summaries written by library scientists. Over 1,500,000 articles manually tagged by library scientists tagged with a normalized indexing vocabulary of people, organizations, locations and topic descriptors. Over 275,000 algorithmically-tagged articles that have been hand-verified by the online production staff at nytimes.com."[22] The fact that the efficiency of the work with this and similar databases is guaranteed in the automated and/or manually corrected article separation, which only insufficiently works in most press projects[23], or, together with key-wording, is not even taken into account, which not only negates the recognition of collocations, but also restricts the adaptation of possibilities of "topic modelling". However, there are already some approaches, the application of which to the historical daily press could be productive. An example would be the project idea of capturing "complex concepts of political theory formation", which tries to capture the collective identity using

19 | To the graduations of the connectivity of texts cf. the study by Hanjo Berressem.

20 | Christof Schöch, "Big? Smart? Clean? Messy? Data in the Humanities," *Journal of the Digital Humanities* 2, no. 3 (2013), 7, http://journalofdigitalhumanities.org/2-3/big-smart-clean-messy-data-in-the-humanities. <accessed February 8, 2018>: "In most cases, velocity does not play a key role in big humanities data right now. Also, the large 'volume' is less usefully defined in the humanities by a shift from databases to distributed computing. Variety of formats, complexity or lack of structure does come into play, however."

21 | danah boyd, and Kate Crawford, "Six Provocations for Big Data", Conference Paper, A Decade in Internet Time: Symposium on the Dynamics of the Internet and Society (2011), http://ssrn.com/abstract=1926431.

22 | https://catalog.ldc.upenn.edu/ldc2008t19. <accessed February 8, 2018>

23 | Cf. Günter Mühlberger, "Digitalisierung historischer Zeitungen aus dem Blickwinkel der automatisierten Text- und Strukturerkennung," *Zeitschrift für Bibliothekswesen und Bibliographie* 58, no. 1 (2011): 14, http://dx.doi.org/10.3196/186429501158135.

quantitative corpus linguistic methods,[24] or the visualization of geoscientific data in family sheets in connection with the question of the fine motor skills of colonialism.[25] Both questions, therefore, reach beyond the verification of existing knowledge and position the frequency analysis in the words of the two historians Gibbs and Owens, i.e. not only as a tool for testing hypotheses, but also as a means of detecting "abnormalities, trends, or unusual coincidences".[26] Against this background, the productivity of the search for the possibilities of systematic indexing seems to be rather doubtful because the development of natural language processing can enable the differentiated detection of variance and redundancy.[27] A similar procedure, also inspired by corpus linguistics, would be the testing of argument analysis in the daily press, which is usually rejected in newspaper articles because they do not operate with the sequence "premise, inference, conclusion".[28] However, what immediately caught the eye in the larger and colorfully composed text about the topos "Globe of Hungary", which stands for Hungary's incomprehensible (or too understandable) individualism, for self-dazzling, chauvinism, and megalomania, was the relatively stable and prominent placement of political metaphors at the beginning and/or at the end of the editorials.[29] The argumentative embedding of these metaphors or their absence could, of course, also be demonstrated manually on a smaller corpus; the change of magnitude of the test question of how far these metaphors separate, appear as ornaments or virtualize the entire execution, however, could possibly be justified by the penetrance of political metaphors, the scope and situational meaning of which is otherwise difficult to measure.

24 | André Blessing et al., "Computerlinguistische Werkzeuge zur Erschließung und Exploration großer Textsammlungen aus der Perspektive fachspezifischer Theorien," in *Grenzen und Möglichkeiten der Digital Humanities*. Special Volume of *Zeitschrift für digitale Geisteswissenschaften*, ed. Constanze Baum and Thomas Stäcker (2015), http://www.zfdg.de/sb001_013. <accessed February 8, 2018>

25 | Peter McIsaac et al., "Die Geowissenschaftliche Analyse von großen Mengen historischer Texte: Die Visualisierung geographischer Verhältnisse in deutschen Familienzeitschriften," in *Modellierung – Vernetzung – Visualisierung. Die Digital Humanities als fächerübergreifendes Forschungsparadigma*, Abstracts of the Conference (2016), 192-194, http://dhd2016.de/boa.pdf. <accessed February 8, 2018>

26 | Fred Gibbs, and Trevor Owens, "The Hermeneutics of Data and Historical Writing," in *Writing History in the Digital Age*, ed. Kristen Nawrotzki and Jack Dougherty (Ann Arbor, MI: University of Michigan Press, 2013), 168.

27 | Cf. the contributions by Charlotte Coch and Julia Nantke to this volume.

28 | Miriam Butt et al., "Argumentanalyse in digitalen Textkorpora," in *Modellierung – Vernetzung – Visualisierung*, 51.

29 | Amália Kerekes, "Kleine ungarische Globalgeschichte. Zur Karriere des Topos 'ungarischer Globus'" (under review).

This is something that is in line with a project that was established in Leipzig. This project aims at the diachronic investigation of Ernst Jünger's journalism and its contextualization in the press of the interwar period,[30] which is based on the already published samples and promises a possible extension of the techniques of the historical-critical editions.

Another field of research that reveals the specificities of the historical daily press relies on the radical delamination of the corpora, which are in any case difficult to segment, and, on the one hand, creates the possibility of exploring genre questions[31], or the presence of specific departments across the press landscape. On the other hand, one can assume, according to Ryan Cordell, that newspapers are rather functional "aggregates" and not original compositions. In Cordell's project of viral texts, the circulation of the articles is visualized to ultimately connect them with the question of the individuality of the particular press products.[32] In doing so, something is being put into practice that used to serve as a falsifying thesis in the research of Andreas Graf[33] and Arnulf Kutsch in connection with the hardly reconstructable functioning of the correspondence and feuilleton agencies "according to which the German newspapers very much cared for their own journalistic performance".[34] The fact that the decomposition of the newspaper numbers could run the risk of returning to the absolutization of the idea of authenticity in the last step rather than valorizing the stubbornness of hobbyists in smaller editorial offices as a research

30 | Dirk Goldhahn et al., "Operationalisation of Research Questions of the Humanities within the CLARIN Infrastructure – An Ernst Jünger Use Case," in Papers of the CLARIN Annual Conference 2015 in Wrocław (2015), http://asv.informatik.uni-leipzig.de/publication/file/336/CAC2015_Goldhahn_final_paper.pdf. <accessed February 8, 2018>

31 | Cf. Stefan Scherer and Gustav Frank, "Feuilleton und Essay in periodischen Printmedien des 19. Jahrhunderts. Zur funktionsgeschichtlichen Trennung um 1870," in *Vergessene Konstellationen literarischer Öffentlichkeit zwischen 1840 und 1885*, ed. Katja Mellmann and Jesko Reiling (Berlin, Boston: de Gruyter, 2016), 107-125.

32 | Cf. Ryan Cordell, "Reprinting, Circulation, and the Network Author in Antebellum Newspapers," *American Literary History* 27, no. 3 (2015): 417-445, https://doi.org/10.1093/alh/ajv028.

33 | Andreas Graf, "Literatur-Agenturen in Deutschland (1868 bis 1939)," *Buchhandelsgeschichte* 19, no. 4 (1998): B170-B188; Andreas Graf, "Feuilleton-Korrespondenzen (1871-1939). Publizistische Anfänge des literarischen Vermittlungswesens in Deutschland," *Buchhandelsgeschichte* 23, no. 2 (2002): B55-B64.

34 | Arnulf Kutsch, Friederike Sterling, and Robert Fröhlich, "Korrespondenzen im Deutschen Kaiserreich und in der Weimarer Republik. Rekonstruktion und sekundärstatistische Analyse eines medialen Sektors," *Jahrbuch für Kommunikationsgeschichte* 13 (2011): 169.

topic and capturing it as a form of serialization in the sense of franchising,[35] is ironically reflected as a gradual detachment of the macro-analysis of analog problem situations at the end of the study. How fluent the transition between analog and digital questions can be is also stressed by a quantitative study conducted with paper and microfilm by a larger research group, which, based on the mechanical separation of event report and analysis, anticipated much of what was used and offered in the Jünger project, namely the automatic markup of the names of persons and place names with CLARIN.[36]

This study is, as to the knowledge of the author, singular because the development of the emancipation of the press history from its existence as ancillary science is just as recognizable as the gradual extension of the close reading to research questions concerning social-scientific and media-economic issues. The phenomena of geographical precision, individualization or social contextualization of the figures appearing in the articles, or the number of events dealt with in an article, which could be more quickly identified with the aid of markups, provided clues to refute the popular explanation for the emergence of new long journalism because the development of this format had started much earlier than the appearance of the television, which is regarded as a tremendous competitor. Such a research would provide a relatively reliable basis for the question of which factors could be significant or could be formalized at all when talking about media competition in general, even if one eventually comes to conclude that all these factors are not even of secondary importance.

However, what Piersma and Ribbens recorded in a somewhat romantic sounding and only explicit comparison of microhistory of analog and digital about the necessity of "the early formalization of digital research questions",[37] does not only apply to many 19th century methods of evaluating the content of

35 | On franchise in combination with John Fiske's notion of "producerly" cf. the study by Hanjo Berressem.

36 | Kevin G. Barnhurst and Diana Mutz, "American Journalism and the Decline in Event-Centered Reporting," *Journal of Communication* 57, no. 4 (1997): 27-53, doi: 10.1111/j.1460-2466.1997.tb02724.x.

37 | Hinke Piersma and Kees Ribbens, "Digital Historical Research. Context, Concepts and the Need for Reflection," *BMGN – Low Countries Historical Review* 128, no. 4 (2013): 87, doi: 10.18352/bmgn-lchr.9352: "Historians are traditionally explorers of sources, digging around in archives for days to look for relevant material. During the research period, as they become familiar with the material and the historical process, the research question they formulate can be modified, adapted, or even changed completely, depending on where the material leads them. However, a digital approach of the research material requires the early formalisation of the research question."

the press in form of registers and repertories,[38] but also to the handling with press-digitized documents in the sense that the chaining of these formalized retrieval queries ultimately follows the classic analogous goal of press research, namely the proof of interdiscursivity.[39] But if it is not about the interpretation of anomalies, deviations, but simply about data poverty, inevitably the question of the status of originality and singularity, of "obstinacy", arises, which functions as a sticking point in a quantitative to be solidified press-trend research, which requires at least an addition-based "weak emergence".[40] To illustrate this question, or perhaps to rather illustrate the promise of demonstrating singularity in author- and work-centered traditional philological research questions with a special piece from reception history of Hungarian literature in Austria, the lack of the presence of Dezső Kosztolányi in the Viennese press between the World Wars seems to be a striking example, precisely because of the blatant differences. The fact that he was at loggerheads with the communist and social-democratic emigrants from Hungary, who were decidedly active in the press and provided further evidence for his authorship in an anti-Semitic rubric in the right-wing newspaper,[41] essentially explains the question. Only the finding, his story *Gray Glory* from 1916, appeared ten years later exactly in the social-democratic *Arbeiter-Zeitung*.[42] Translating a narrative about the disoriented language teacher could, in itself, be interpreted as a mocking or

38 | Cf. Michael Pilz, "Bibliographische Resonanzen. Presseschauen und Register am Beispiel der Zeitschrift *Das literarische Echo*," in *Zwischen Literatur und Journalistik. Generische Formen in Periodika des 18. bis 21. Jahrhunderts*, ed. Michal Pilz, Magdalena Bachmann, and Gunhild Berg (Heidelberg: Winter, 2016), 241-266.

39 | On the competency of the microhistory in caching the possibilities of interconnecting huge amounts of data cf. the study by Gábor Vaderna.

40 | Thomas Metten, "Medien/Ästhetik. Grundzüge einer kulturwissenschaftlichen Medienanalyse," in *Illustrierte Zeitschriften um 1900. Mediale Eigenlogik, Multimodalität und Metaisierung*, ed. Natalia Igl and Julia Menzel (Bielefeld: transcript, 2016), 123.

41 | Cf. András Lengyel, "Egy s más az Új Nemzedék Pardon rovatáról [This and that on the Column Pardon in the Newspaper Új Nemzedék]," *Kalligram* 18, no. 6 (2010): 89-99.

42 | Desider Kosztolányi, "Graue Glorie," *Arbeiter-Zeitung*, August 7, 1927, 4-5. Zur Interpretation cf. László Bengi, "Nyelv és közösség, irodalom és identitás. Kosztolányi Dezső identitásfelfogása kapcsán [Language and Community, Literature and Identity. Based on the Notion of Identity by Dezső Kosztolányi]," *Kortárs* 56, no. 3 (2012): 79-84; Amália Kerekes, "'Elegant möblierte Pester Wohnung': Zur Rezeption der ungarischen Belletristik in der Wiener Boulevardpresse 1923-1930," in *Verschränkte Kulturen: Polnisch-deutsche und ungarisch-deutsche Literatur- und Kunstbeziehungen*, ed. Zsuzsa Bognár and Zsuzsa Soproni (Berlin: Frank & Timme, 2018), 271-283.

admonishing gesture to the lost linguist Kosztolányi, which, however, should be rejected as an option because of the certainly clarified copyright issues with the author. Just as speculative would be the idea to interpret the publication as an indirect form of rehabilitation, even a self-revision of Kosztolányi.

This dilemma, the missing clues to contextualize press texts, can also be translated into the general question as to how far such methodological questions might develop a life of their own and position the press history as a special test field within the area of the Digital Humanities. This question should by no means be used as a joyful obituary for the field of research, especially because it requires a great deal of knowledge from analog practice concerning the search criteria, the economics of evaluation in the sense of blackboxing or the status of exemplary reading. What could prove to be an obsolete technique of interpreting in the long run is the form of curating of press analysis, which, whether in terms of representativeness or deconstruction, makes a short commentary on catchy quotes. This gesture can today be easily generated by machines because its interpretation and the experimental approaches of the digital humanities provide useful keywords and show exactly those sore spots that were tacitly accepted in the history of the press, especially for technical reasons. But since it was not just about the technology and the methodological self-oblivion of the research area was quickly exposed with Digital Humanities, the near future of daily press research as an auxiliary science of Digital Humanities does not seem rosy, but much more exciting than its recent past.

Micro and Macro, Close and Distant

History and Philology After the Digital Revolution

Gábor Vaderna

In memoriam Gergely Labádi (1975–2017)

When the digital revolution happened is an open question. Was it only a short period of time, or rather a longer transfiguration into a new type of culture? Has it ended, or is it still in progress? And anyway, is there a revolution, or do we only aspire to write down our cultural decline or ascension in a new and modern narrative form? Recently, Matthew L. Jockers asserted that we are already after the digital revolution. He wrote in his recent study *Macroanalysis: Digital Methods and Literary History* the following: "Though not 'everything' has been digitized, we have reached a tipping point, an event horizon where enough text and literature have been encoded to both allow and, indeed, force us to ask an entirely new set of questions about literature and the literary record."[1] He did not mention but definitely conceptualised this revolution in an English-based literary field. Fotis Jannidis and Gerhard Launer pointed to the year 2011 as a turning point when TextGrid Repository started operating; since then, they claimed, enough digitized texts have been available for macroanalytical research in proper quality.[2] On the one hand, this means that right after

1 | Matthew L. Jockers, *Macroanalysis: Digital Methods and Literary History* (Urbana/Chicago/Springfield: University of Illinois Press, 2013), 4.

2 | Cf. Fotis Jannidis and Gerhard Lauer, "Burrows's Delta and Its Use in German Literary History", in *Distant Readings: Topologies of German Culture In the Long Nineteenth Century*, eds. Matt Erlin and Lynne Tatlock (Rochester/New York: Camden House, 2014), 29-54, 30. The essay by Jannidis and Lauer is cited in Gergely Labádi's review on Jockers' book (Gergely Labádi, "Matthew L. Jockers: Macroanalysis", in *Irodalomtörténet* [Literary History] 97, no. 4 (2016), 496-500). Cf. Jean-Baptiste Michel, Yuan Kui Shen, Aviva Presser Aiden, Adrian Veres, Matthew K. Gray, The Google Books Team, Joseph P. Pickett, et al., "Quantitative Analysis of Culture Using Millions of Digitized Books", in *Science* 331, no. 6014 (January 2011), 176-182.

the Millennium, so many texts were encoded that we have to think it over – or think it again – what we talk about if we study arts and literature, what we discuss in our seminars and lectures at universities, and how we can deal with our subject. Of course, this shift from print culture to a digital one results in another shift: scholars who study the humanities have to try out new practices in research as well as in teaching. On the other hand, the revolution itself has achieved its goal, as the digital humanities already have institutions all over the world. Not only do grandiose enterprises like Google Books or Project Gutenberg come into consideration here; not only have professional and well-equipped research groups like the Stanford Literary Lab or the Cologne Centre for eHumanities emerged. In addition, not only do digital humanities research centres mushroom from Tokyo to Budapest and all over the world, but it is also a fact that every university curriculum offers courses for future digital philologists or historians, and that our BA-courses, maybe not only at the ELTE Budapest, had better avoid print literature if we hope for anyone to take a look at the set readings.

It is a cliché but true nonetheless that the digital revolution does not depend on the use of computers in science, rather on the approach. Using computers in literary studies is as old as computer science itself. *Index Thomisticus* by Father Roberto A. Busa was the first attempt in 1940.[3] But it does not mean that everyone was satisfied with the results. On the one hand, it seems that several issues can be resolved that were restricted by the human condition. One can follow the myth of machines in modernity: the machine never has fatigue; it does not lose interest in working; it does not make any human mistakes.[4] On the other hand, it is quite ambivalent how literary scholars deal with its functioning. It is a great tool for recording, modification, editing and searches, and it has no physical limits. Nevertheless, the computer is not only 'the maid of science', and 'humanities computing' turned into 'digital humanities' in an instant.[5] I argue that the digital humanities force a huge conceptual shift on

3 | About the consequences of this magisterial work, cf. Roberto Busa SJ, "Informatics and New Philology", in *Computers and the Humanities* 24, no. 5/6, Humanities Computing in Italy (December 1990), 339-343; Susan Hockey, "The History of Humanities Computing", in *A Companion to Digital Humanities*, edited by Susan Schreibman, Ray Siemens and John Unsworth, 3-19. Oxford: Blackwell, 2004, [http://digitalhumanities.org:3030/companion/view?docId=blackwell/9781405103213/9781405103213.xml&doc.view=content&chunk.id=ss1-2-1&toc.depth=1&brand=9781405103213_brand&anchor.id=0].

4 | Cf. Lewis Mumford, *The Myth of the Machine: The Pentagon of Power* (London: Secker & Warburg, 1971).

5 | About the conceptual shift cf. John Unsworth, "What is Humanities Computing and What is Not?", in *Jahrbuch für Computerphilologie* 4 (2002), 71-84, [http://comput-

how we think about history and provide not only a better tool, but call forth the problem of how the medial technique determines our perception (e.g. identifying a text as a text). And, it is only natural that our practices by the means of which we handle our materials have also changed, and fitting the technology to the content (and vice versa) is not a simple process of conversion.[6] Among the numerous heuristic and pessimistic forecasts for the future, I agree with Alan Liu's thought-through interpretation of the task: "the appropriate, unique contribution that the digital humanities can make to cultural criticism at the present time is to use the tools, paradigms, and concepts of digital technologies to help rethink the idea of instrumentality."[7] From this perspective, the question is which traditions and methods and practices can this redefinition rely on, and how to rethink the methodology of historical science during the reinterpretation of instrumentality.

In what follows, I would like to discuss how a special area of the humanities, i.e. microhistory, can be connected to the digital humanities. I do not view microhistory as a potential mode of history writing (one among many), but I assume that a certain philological approach was also associated with microhistory. After giving a brief overview of the history of microhistory (what it is and to what purpose it was called into being), I will attempt to rethink how the microhistorical approach fits the digital environment and the rapid everyday life of digital philology.

erphilologie.uni-muenchen.de/jg02/unsworth.html]; Patrik Svensson, "Humanities Computing as Digital Humanities", in *Digital Humanities Quarterly* 3, no. 3 (2009), [http://digitalhumanities.org/dhq/vol/3/3/000065/000065.html]. Cf. the article by Gábor Palko in this volume.

6 | The question can be asked from different aspects. Textology: David Greetham, "The Resistance to Digital Humanities", in *Debates in the Digital Humanities*, ed. Matthew K. Gold (Minneapolis/London: University of Minnesota Press, 2012), 438-451 [http://dhdebates.gc.cuny.edu/debates/text/47]; history: Sherman Dorn, "Is (Digital) History More than an Argument about the Past?", in *Writing History in the Digital Age*, ed. Jack Fougherty and Kristen Nawrotzki (Ann Arbor: The University of Michigan Press, 2016), 21-34.; in general: Willard McCarty, *Humanities Computing* (New York: Palgrave Macmillan, 2005).

7 | Alan Liu, "Where is Cultural Criticism in the Digital Humanities?", in *Debates in the Digital Humanities*, ed. Matthew K. Gold (Minneapolis/London: University of Minnesota Press, 2012), 490-509, 501, [http://dhdebates.gc.cuny.edu/debates/text/20].

Micro and Close

It is not clear whether microhistory is a school or a method, or a special viewpoint of historical research, and it is also very hard to decide which historical works belong to it.[8] Microhistory's state is also ambiguous because the main figures thereof are not fond of strict theoretical argumentations. Thus, microhistory can be characterized as a methodology for historical research that focuses on its subject on a small scale. Micro here simply means 'very small'. The historian does not look at history through a telescope as several historians of the *Annales* circle suggested, but rather through a microscope. The scope of the study changed as the matter of history is limited to small units: to locality (Emmanuel Le Roy Ladurie investigated a 14th century Occitan village, Montaillou through inquisition records[9]), to interesting cases (in the famous book of Natalie Zemon Davis, *The Return of Martin Guerre,*[10] a peasant disappeared, an impostor took his place and for a short period of time everybody – even Martin Guerre's former wife – accepted him as Martin Guerre, only other relatives started a legal process against the swindler, who seemed to win the process, as suddenly the original Martin manifested), to short and eventful periods (in Adam Zamoyski's book, *1812,*[11] the historian concentrates only on the catastrophic moment of the Napoleonic wars, when the French army tried to flee from Russia). These very different enterprises get on well with each other on many points.

Although some microhistorians disclaim the connection, I think microhistory was mostly inspired by historical anthropology. The first historically renowned work of the world which is regarded to be microhistorical was Carlo Ginzburg's *The Cheese and the Worms* (the original edition: Ginzburg, *Il formaggio e i vermi*). In this impressive work, Ginzburg presented the beliefs and worldview of Domenico Scandella, also known as Menocchio, who was an Italian miller from the village of Montereale. Menocchio was unable to stop talking; he told everybody his unfamiliar theories on how the world functioned. He had his own cosmology and spoke freely, because he felt he had done nothing wrong. Finally, he was arrested by the Inquisition. On his first

8 | On the question what microhistory is cf. Sigurður Gylfi Magnússon and István M. Szijártó, *What is Microhistory? Theory and Practice* (London/New York: Routledge, 2013), especially 1-7.

9 | Emmanuel Le Roy Ladurie, *Montaillou, village occitan de 1294 à 1324* (Paris: Gallimard, 1975).

10 | Natalie Zemon Davis, *The Return of Martin Guerre* (Cambridge: Harvard University Press, 1983).

11 | Adam Zamoyski, *1812: Napoleon's Fatal March on Moscow* (London: Harper Collins, 2004).

trial, on 7 February 1584, he confessed that he had said before that the Virgin Mary was certainly not a virgin and Jesus was born of man, but he added that he did so because he was tempted by evil. He tried to find an excuse for his sins and went further:

I have said that" – he argued –, "in my opinion, all was chaos, that is, earth, air, water, and fire were mixed together; and out of that bulk a mass formed – just as cheese is made out of milk – and worms appeared in it, and these were the angels. The most holy majesty decreed that these should be God and the angels, and among that number of angels there was also God, he too having been created out of that mass at the same time, and he was named lord with four captains, Lucifer, Michael, Gabriel, and Raphael. That Lucifer sought to make himself lord equal to the king, who was the majesty of God, and for this arrogance God ordered him driven out of heaven with all his host and his company; and this God later created Adam and Eve and people in great number to take the places of the angels who had been expelled. And as this multitude did not follow God's commandments, he sent his Son, whom the Jews seized, and he was crucified.[12]

These highly quoted arguments are considerably entertaining, although Menocchio was executed for them a few years later. Ginzburg claimed that Menocchio's heresy was not based on some kind of theological knowledge, rather it was an imprint of popular culture. Ginzburg collected the books that affected Mennochio's strange theses; there were popular versions of Biblical stories, Italian translations of picaresque novels, the *Decameron* and maybe a translation of the Quran. Ginzburg dug deeper and deeper into Menocchio's world, and asserted that one did not need to be educated to know vicious doctrines. Menocchio was not a typical member of his society, as he made his own vision from a bunch of ideas he got from popular culture and talked about it inordinately and sincerely. But from his blasphemous visions we understand something hidden in the history of Reformation and heresy.

The anthropological method, as it was disserted by Clifford Geertz is perceptible here. As microhistory tried to exceed history which explores the *longue durée* construction of great structures (e.g. Fernand Braudel's magisterial works such as *La Méditerranée et le Monde Méditerranéen à l'Epoque de Philippe II),*[13] Geertz's anthropology exceeded structuralism which sought the deep structures underneath the surface. "The danger that cultural analysis, in search of all-too-deep-lying turtles, will lose touch with the hard surfaces

12 | Carlo Ginzburg, *The Cheese and the Worms: The Cosmos of a Sixteenth-Century Miller*, translated by John Tedeschi and Anne C. Tedeschi (Baltimore: Johns Hopkins University Press, 1992), 5 f.

13 | Fernand Braudel, *La Méditerranée et le Monde Méditerranéen à l'Epoque de Philippe II.* (Paris: Armand Colin, 1949).

of life – with the political, economic, stratificatory realities within which men are everywhere contained – and with the biological and physical necessities on which those surfaces rest, is an ever-present one."[14] The only way to avoid this trap – claimed Geertz – is interpreting culture. There is no intact world outside culture from where social science would collect its bald facts – there are only well- or lesser-known cultural worlds. The social sciences should aim at describing these cultures and interpreting the interpretations of their own agents. Although Geertz himself was sceptical about historical anthropology, his interpretative method (the famous 'thick description') served as an example for the new wave of historians since the 1970s. Ginzburg's *The Cheese and the Worms* was undoubtedly under the effect of Geertz.

The novelty of microhistory is not only the fascinating application of the methods of Geertzism. Giovanni Levi, Ginzburg's Italian companion warned us in his essay, *I pericoli del geertzismo* that a thick description involved the oversimplification of cultural contexts as it arrayed every particular sign into a strict schema or system.[15] For Levi – I cite here another of his articles, *On Microhistory* – the essence of microhistorical research is the 'change of scope'. "Microhistory as a practice is essentially based on the reduction of the scale of observation, on a microscopic analysis and an intensive study of the documentary material."[16] According to Levi, it is obvious in anthropological research that a scholar has to take into account the problem of scaling. But for microhistory scaling is not only a problem among others, rather it is the essence of its approach. "For microhistory, the reduction of scale is an analytical procedure, which may be applied anywhere independently of the dimensions of the object analysed."[17] I suppose there is something important here that Levi observed when he criticised interpretative anthropology. Namely, as anthropology tried to avoid moving even further away from the very concrete cultural practices, it aimed only to find cultural contexts on a higher level – for Ginzburg it was popular culture. Levi suggested stepping back to the sources and reading them as closely as possible.

14 | Clifford Geertz, "Thick Description: Toward an Interpretive Theory of Culture", in *Interpretation of Cultures: Selected Essays* (New York: Basic, 1973), 3-30, 30.

15 | Cf. Giovanni Levi, "I pericoli del geertizsmo", in *Quaderni Storici* 58 (1985), 269-277, translation: Giovanni Levi, "Les dangers du geertzisme", traduction inédite de l'italien, par Pierre Savy, in *Labyrinthe* 8 (2001), 36-45.

16 | Giovanni Levi, "On Microhistory" in *New Perspectives on Historical Writing*, ed. Peter Burke (Cambridge: Polity Press, 1991), 93-113, 95.

17 | Ibd.

It's worth reminding ourselves of Robert Darnton's historical anthropology study, *Workers Revolt: The Great Cat Massacre,*[18] which is normally viewed as a master piece of microhistory. Darnton, on the basis of the memoirs of Nicolas Contat, 18th century French pressman, talks about how the apprentices suffering from bad conditions gave their master a lesson. One of them meowed under their master's bedroom window. After the second night of the 'cat music', the master and his wife ordered that the apprentices kill all cats in the area, except for the wife's favourite cat. The apprentices started the process of the 'great cat massacre', they pretended to have a court trial and then they ritually executed all of the cats, starting with the wife's favourite one. In Darnton's analysis, the case goes well beyond its own reach: the Capitalist logic of how the press operates is contrasted with the hundreds of years old legacy of popular culture (cat meowing, witch hunts). Darnton, inspired by cultural anthropology reconstructs the symbolic order of a culture. In any case, the debate which evolved thanks to the famous essay shows the limits of historical anthropology well. Roger Chartier wants Darnton to give an account of philological thoroughness: he thinks it is not worth interpreting the Contat text as a source of non-fiction, as it relies on literary traditions itself, and the symbolic layers reconstructed by Darnton so aptly could not be revealed in every social context at the same time. "This text [i.e. Contat's mémoire] exhibits the event, but it also constitutes the event as the result of the act of writing." [19] Perhaps it is not an overstatement to interpret such criticism as something that calls attention to the fact that the sources which provide the bases of the 'thick description' should also be subjected to philological criticism.[20]

Considering Levi and Chartier's standpoint, we can venture to state that this was quite an important methodological tool for microhistory: the *close reading* practices originated in literary studies (in the New Critique within that) combined with a careful philological attention to the sources. If one shifts their focus from the macro to the micro level, one steps closer to their objects – the historian steps closer to his sources – and applies the method of close reading to these. Besides, the shift between macro and micro focus can also lead to the general problem of the connection between the individual and the general.

18 | Robert Darnton, "Workers Revolt: The Great Cat Massacre of the Rue Saint-Severin", in *The Great Cat Massacre And Other Episodes in French Cultural History*, (New York: Basic Books, 1984), 75-106.

19 | Roger Chartier, "Text, Symbols, and Frenchness", in *The Journal of Modern History* 57, No. 4 (December 1985), 682-695, here 685.

20 | On the further debate cf. Robert Darnton, "History and Anthropology", in *The Kiss of Lamourette: Reflections in Cultural History* (New York: Norton, 1990), 329-354.; Dominick LaCapra, "Chartier, Darnton, and the Great Symbol Massacre", in *The Journal of Modern History* 60, No. 1 (March 1988), 95-112.

Despite their affinity or sympathy for historical anthropology, Davis, Darnton and Ginzburg's works were based on a strict analysis of one (and only one) documentary source. Davis worked after two contemporary books by Guillaume Le Sueur and Jean de Coras (he was one of the trial judges in Toulouse where the Martin Guerre case was heard), Darnton after Nicolas Contat's anecdotes (he was a member of the group that hanged the cats), Ginzburg after inquisition records. They all stayed as close to their only source as possible. It is not an accident that most of the criticism against these works tried to open up other contexts by listing other sources that might have been called in. Regarding this problem, the new microhistory frequently refers to the notion of 'exceptional typical' by Edoardo Grendi.[21] "The critics of microhistory" – said Matti Peltonen, a Finnish microhistorian, sarcastically – "seem to be convinced that the only possible links between micro and macro are exceptionality (famous persons or important events) and typicality (individuals or events that represent a larger group)."[22] "In new microhistory" – Peltonen goes on – "the link between micro and macro levels is not a simple reduction or aggregation. The movement from on level or sphere to another is qualitative and generates new information."[23] The paradox of the concept of 'exceptional typical' concerns the situation where the sources keep quiet obstinately and do not talk about the life of underclass people. In these cases, we can only gain information that is very far from typical (and due to this, they are rarely well-documented). Martin Guerre's doppelganger, Pansette, or Menocchio were not typical members of society, as hanging cats was also exceptional.

In 2003, Sigurður Gylfi Magnússon, an Icelandic microhistorian, outlined another concept of microhistory, in which he tried to find the answer to the problem of the shift between the two levels.[24] He asserted that microhistorical research should avoid great metanarratives. He criticised Ginzburg and others (among them his own former practice), as they all tried to fit the results of their study into a metanarrative. It is quite similar to Levi's criticism, but for Magnússon, the greater problem lays not in changing scales, but rather in losing the singularity of cases. Magnússon cited this place from Georg G. Iggers, who

21 | Cf. Magnússon/Szijártó, *What is Microhistory?,* 19 f.

22 | Matti Peltonen, "Clues, Margins, and Monads: The Micro-Macro Link in Historical Research", in *History and Theory* 40, No. 3 (October 2001), 347-359, here 356.

23 | Ibd., 357.

24 | Sigurður Gylfi Magnússon, "'The Singularization of History': Social History and Microhistory within the Postmodern State of Knowledge", in *Journal of Social History* 36, No. 3 (Spring 2003), 701-735; cf. Sigurður Gylfi Magnússon, "Social History as 'Sites of Memory'? The Insitutionalization of History: Microhistory and the Grand Narrative", in *Journal of Social History* 39, No. 3, [Special Issue on the Future of Social History], (Spring 2006), 891-913; Magnússon/Szijártó, *What is Microhistory?,* 119-133.

was critical of microanalysis: "While this book [*The Cheese and the Worms*] has argued for the legitimacy of microhistory, it has also shown how the latter has never been able to escape the framework of larger structures and transformations in which this history takes place. As we saw, almost all microhistorians have had to confront processes of modernization through their impact on the small social groupings to which they dedicated themselves."[25]

Although the microhistorians protested against such remarks one after another, and Iggers' approximation made them see red, Magnússon said that Iggers was, as a matter of fact, right. He suggested that historians should change their focus again. But our main task, he argued, is not only to go closer to the sources, but to avoid any kind of social history, to hold our matter in its own context. In this direction – he calls it 'the singularization of history' – he

> emphasize[s] that the linkage between units of research and metanarratives are not only undesirable but downright dangerous, since the latter tend to monopolize the scholar's attention. Macrohistorical research is particularly susceptible to such dangers, since it is precisely the linkings between different subjects that bring out its macrohistorical nature, i.e. the drawing of wide-ranging conclusions over long periods and variable areas of research. The subjects themselves, by whatever name they are known, are liable to disappear. Even microhistorians have their work cut out to remain faithful to their subject matter in the face of academic demands, and so put heavy emphasis on presenting links between their research and larger wholes. All this tends to produce a final form that is a distortion of general history.[26]

This concept, I think, tends to go even closer to the sources, and suggests excluding all the information we have beyond them.

> The singularization of history in this sense provides the researcher with a means of bringing out the oppositions that exist between the different 'discourses' of individual groups, and this is a precondition to our being able to approach ideas and points of view that in the general run do not come to the fore. In addition, this ideology brings into prominence the contradictions and inconsistencies in the mind of each and every individual and heightens the oppositions that move within each living person. To allow the contradictions and paradoxes freedom of expression, the emphasis must always be kept on squarely the subject matter itself and on nothing else. The key word here is singularization; the singularization of history is first and foremost a search for a way in which history can research its proper subjects in their proper logical and cultural

25 | Georg G. Iggers, *Historiography in the Twentieth Century: From Scientific Objectivity to the Postmodern Challenge* (London/Hanover, NH: Wesleyan University Press, 1997), 143. Cited: Magnússon, "'The Singularization of History'", 717.

26 | Magnússon, "'The Singularization of History'", 720.

context and thus disassociate itself from the 'manmade' ideological package of the metanarratives.[27]

Naturally, to think radically out of any context is a dream.[28] The more important thing for us is the mode of how Magnússon focuses on his subject: he divides and describes single units and then he interprets a brief passage of a single story. This method, like the method of close reading, emphasizes the single and the particular over the general, favours deep attention to individual language, inner controversy or parallelism, and prefers the order in which the texts unfold ideas when the historian works on the line of documentary source.

And finally, the last element by which I can characterize microhistory is the "carefully crafted narrative" – as Thomas Robisheaux recently called it.[29] The stories I have presented above are all very good and exciting stories. Based on the story of Martin Guerre, a French film was shot which starred Gérard Depardieu and was directed by Daniel Vigne (Natalie Zemon Davis was a consultant for the script). Later on, Hollywood also discovered the story; Jodie Foster and Richard Gere starred in the film, *Sommersby*, which put the story into the American context, as it was set right after the Civil War. Darnton's books are a kind of scientific bestseller; Ginzburg's book was translated into twenty-five languages. This is of course not just due to microhistorians' aspiration to gain easy fame, but because historical narratives are often preceded by closely and carefully read literary works.

Carlo Ginzburg once confessed that he was inspired by Leo Tolstoy's *War and Peace:*

But the impetus towards this type of narration (and more generally for occupying myself with history) came to me from further off: from *War and Peace*, from Tolstoy's conviction that a historical phenomenon can become comprehensible only by reconstructing the activities of all the persons who participated in it. This proposition, and the sentiments that had spawned it (populism, fierce disdain for the vacuous and conventional history of historians), left an indelible impression on me from the moment I first read it. *The*

27 | Ibd., 721.

28 | About this "dream" cf. de Man's commentary on the practical criticism: Paul de Man, "The Return to Philology", in *The Resistance to Theory*, foreword by Wlad Godzich (London/Minneapolis: University of Minnesota Press, 2002), 21-26, 23-25. Cf. the article by Marcus Krause in this volume.

29 | Cf. Thomas Robisheaux, "Microhistory and Story", presentation at the Workshop on Microhistory in Reykjavík, 27 June 2016. About this problem cf. Thomas V. Cohen's remark: "Microhistory Today", 14. (Robisheaux, Thomas, ed., "Microhistory Today: A Roundtable Discussion", in *Journal of Medieval and Early Modern Studies* 47, No. 1 (January 2017), 7-52).

Cheese and the Worms, the story of a miller whose death is decreed from afar, by a man (a pope) who one minute earlier had never heard his name, can be considered a small, distorted product of Tolstoy's grand and intrinsically unrealizable project: the reconstruction of the numerous relationships that linked Napoleon's head cold before the battle of Borodino, the disposition of the troops, and the lives of all the participants in the battle, including the most humble soldier. / In Tolstoy's novel the private world (peace) and the public world (war) first run along parallel lines, now they intersect; Prince André participates in the battle of Austerlitz, Pierre at Borodino.[30]

It is not only the approach to history that came from Tolstoy, but also the mode of narrativization. This is a crucial point of microhistorical research: how can one reach experiences of the historical agents? How can one constitute stories in which the train of thought sheds light on everyday events lived by everyday people? Maybe Tolstoy had a greater effect on writing history than we used to think. Beyond that, we can also say that microhistory provides a specific self-reflection on the problem of historical narratives.

Micro and Macro

Let us get back to the problem of the digital humanities, philology and microhistory. Their connection is far from being unproblematic.

On the one hand, the digital humanities try to deal with a large amount of data, and on the other, this is the very opposite of the microhistorical approach. When microhistory was born some forty years ago, its main enemy was the then current social history with its statistical method. At that time, social history was based on entering statistical models on computers and calculating with long-term data. Microhistory offered a new way of thinking; it ruined the great structures with single cases and short-term stories. After the digital revolution, historical thinking was given new tools and these new tools provoked new questions. We turned back to big data, but not to great structures. The main reason for this is the fact that the sources went online, and we have to cope with the great amount of data and new links between different types of them as well. Microhistory criticized social history because it positioned one main structure above others and missed the complexity of a culture. For instance, Braudel thought that economic structure gave stability to *longue durée* histor-

30 | Carlo Ginzburg, "Microhistory: Two or Three Things That I Know about It", translated by John Tedeschi and Anne C. Tedeschi, in *Critical Inquiry* 20, No. 1 (Autumn 1993), 10-35, here 24. As a side note: the above-mentioned book about Napoleon's fatal march to Moscow by Adam Zamoyski could not exist without the vision of history in *War and Peace*.

ical changes. Or, Le Roy Ladurie, before his microhistorical *Montaillou*, tried to prove that the economic and cultural decline of the Middle Ages was a direct consequence of climatic changes, i.e. the so-called Little Ice Age.[31] The new big data science rejects the concept of great structures.[32] And big data science also rejects the close reading of sources aspired to by microhistory.

The most famous and provocative attack against the pre-digital science was Franco Moretti's attempt at reading without reading texts. I mean the concept of 'distant reading' here, which is, at least at first glance, the very opposite of close reading. As it is well known by now, Moretti offered a new method for not reading and managing particular texts, but rather aggregating and analysing massive amounts of data. To get through this approach, let us take a look at Matthew L. Jockers' recent book, *Macroanalysis*. Jockers is a member of Stanford Literary Lab – a research group founded by Moretti in 2010 for analysing literature using software – and Jockers' complex method of research is called 'macroanalysis'. Macroanalysis intertwines the different methods of digital literary criticism, thus it is very useful here to take a look at the concept of distant reading in progress. In one of his case studies, Jockers presents a not-too-big database of American writers, containing 758 records. (In the age of big data, it is a kind of micro database.) Jockers created a differentiated database for a deeper analysis of historical change: "Each record in the database includes a full bibliographic citation, a short abstract, and additional metadata indicating the setting of the book: geographic coordinates and information such as state or region, as well as more subjectively derived information such as whether the setting of the text is primarily urban or rural. The records also include information about the books' authors: their genders and in many cases short biographical excerpts."[33] Jockers' former supervisor, Charles Fanning, in his Irish-American literary history came to the conclusion that a generation is missing between 1900 and 1930, as the number of titles dropped during that time. Fanning's analysis quotes dozens of novels, while he finely introduces that socio-cultural changes of the Irish community.[34] When Jockers searched for the data digitally, the new graph did not support Fanning's thesis.

31 | Emmanuel Le Roy Ladurie, *Histoire du climat depuis l'an mil, Nouvelle bibliothèque scientifique* (Paris: Flammarion, 1967), cf. András Vadas, *Weather Anomalies and Climatic Change in Late Medieval Hungary: Weather events in the 1310s in the Hungarian Kingdom* (Saarbrücken: VDM, 2010).

32 | About 'data scholarship' in the humanities cf. Christine L. Borgman, *Big Data, Little Data, No Data: Scholarship in the Networked World* (Cambridge/London: The MIT Press, 2016), 161-202.

33 | Jockers, *Macroanalysis*, 37.

34 | Charles Fanning, *The Irish Voice in America: 250 Years of Irish-American Fiction*. Second Edition (Lexington: The University Press of Kentucky, 2000).

What happened? – he asked. When Jockers did another, more differentiated calculation, he concluded that the publication practice of the Irish-American population is different on the east and west side of the Mississippi river, and that we should correct Fanning's thesis by adding that it was the number of Irish-American writers east of the Mississippi that dropped between 1900 and 1930, while the works published west of the river rose and reached its climax by around 1940. Further specification can lead to even newer conclusions: e.g. if we take gender distribution, the number of female writers dropped during the period in question in the East, while the number of male writers has been on the rise since 1860 in the West. Jockers' macroanalysis, for which he did not need to read the texts, points out that the researchers of Irish-American literature ignored the West and the changes of the weight of female literature. Macroanalysis then basically promised something very similar to what Magnússon set as his goal: to avoid the temptation of metanarratives by using them. The stylometric attempts of Jockers' book carry a similar promise, although they step closer to certain texts. He concluded that the epoch is the less important factor of the style (and this is an astonishing fact), and that it was preceded by genre, gender and nationality. He asserts that we have to revise our former great narratives about literary processes.

Just like the great structures and contextual metanarratives were the bogeyman of close reading fans, close reading is the bogeyman of distant reading fans. Of course, different scaling leads us to different results, and there are advantages and disadvantages of both approaches. Jockers compares literary scholarship to the workings of economics in one of his blog posts:

> Micro-oriented approaches to literature, highly interpretive readings of literature, remain fundamentally important. Just as microeconomics offers important perspectives on the economy. It is the exact interplay between the macro and micro scale that promises a new, enhanced, and perhaps even better understanding of the literary record. The two approaches work in tandem and inform each other. Human interpretation of the 'data,' whether it be mined at the macro or micro level, remains essential.[35]

Nevertheless, the situation is not so simple. One can be puzzled by the statement that there stood statistical analysis in the background at the birth of close reading. To consider a longer history, Yohei Igarashi stepped back to 19th-century statistics and pointed out that American New Criticism was based on those – although the followers of practical criticism rejected this connection. From this point of view, the digital humanities do not seem to be so radical or revolutionary. For Igarashi the most inspiring aspects are the new ways

35 | Matthew L. Jockers, "On Distant Reading and Macroanalysis", [http://www.matthewjockers.net/2011/07/01/on-distant-reading-and-macroanalysis/].

of education praxes by means of which one can be encouraged to cultivate "clarity of thought and expression". "Digital affordances", he writes, "allow for enlightening, valuable forms of statistical analyses of literary works and literary history, but this account suggests that there is also an opportunity for those in literary studies once again to learn from and contribute to reading research, which has studied interpretation and used statistics all along."[36]

Putting away Igarashi's visions about the humanities, it is relevant that close reading, albeit it officially denied any context outside the text, never stayed alone. The famous analysis by Roman Jakobson and Claude Levi-Strauss was written about one of Baudelaire's poems *(Les Chats)*, Cleanth Brooks's famous essay, the masterpiece of close reading was written about John Keats' verses *(Ode to a Grecian Urn)*. Paul de Man, the main critic and successor of New Criticism, presented his deconstructive interpretations on Nietzsche, Rousseau, Wordsworth, and Shelley. Each and every one of these interpreted authors is a member of the narrowest Western canon.[37] It is a well-known critique on these approaches that the interpreter had already known which texts were important, and after that he or she started to prove that any context outside the text did not matter.[38] Distant reading, we have seen this before, is very critical at this point. Moretti and Jockers stated that we missed our goal, because we used to read just a few texts, and we were not able to say why no other than those were outstanding, and in relation to what they were so important.

36 | Yohei Igarashi, "Statistical Analysis at the Birth of Close Reading", in *New Literary History* 46 (2015), 485-504, here 500. A few years earlier Alan Liu suggested something similar: "The Meaning of the Digital Humanities", in *PMLA* 128, no. 2 (2013), 409-423, here 415.

37 | Cf. Moretti's criticism at this point: "But the trouble with close reading (in all of its incarnations, from the new criticism to deconstruction) is that it necessarily depends on an extremely small canon. This may have become an unconscious and invisible premise by now, but it is an iron one nonetheless: you invest so much in individual texts only if you think that very few of them really matter. Otherwise, it doesn't make sense." (Franco Moretti, "Conjectures on World Literature", in *Distant Reading* [London/New York: Verso, 2013], 43-62, 48). Against this argues Michael Hancher, "Re: Search and Close Reading", in *Debates in the Digital Humanities*, ed. Matthew K. Gold and Lauren F. Klein (Minneapolis: University of Minnesota Press, 2016), 113-138. [http://dhdebates.gc.cuny.edu/debates/text/63].

38 | We can also add to this criticism those newer approaches which call attention to the definite ethical norm of the close reading ideology, such as Heather Love, "Close but not Deep: Literary Ethics and the Descriptive Turn", in *New Literary History* 41, No. 2 (Spring 2010), 371-391; or those which discuss the interpretative processes of new criticism as seen in a political context, such as Joseph North, *Literary Criticism: A Concise Political History* (Cambridge, MA/London: Harvard University Press, 2017), 24-25.

After all (and after the digital revolution), we have the chance to be critical of the microhistorical approach as well. Sigurður Gylfi Magnússon asked us to avoid great metanarratives, which he had good reason to do. If one tries to understand the specificity of Icelandic history, I am not sure that the best way of thinking is to follow the Western narratives of history. A very rich archive of written sources survived from 19th-century Iceland. But this literacy is not the same as the European one was. Our great narrative about the general alphabetization follows the story that in the 18th century, the number of printed books increased, and due to the educational reforms of enlightened absolutism, the state policy aimed at recording and archiving everything, and the whole society became part of a written culture. Book histories are full of this narrative. But in Iceland, most of the inhabitants were able to write, they continued long sagas from generation to generation, they kept diaries, although there was no modern educational system. What to do now with these sources? What to do with these 'barefoot historians'?[39]

However, the problem still looms before us: how can I avoid great narratives? Magnússon and his co-author, Davíð Ólafsson suggested to go as close to the sources as possible to reach a 'minor knowledge'. Naturally, we have to use narrative schemas for that, but even so, the great metanarratives are fraught with danger.[40] But how can one forget these framing stories? As Robert Darnton once pointed out, the Icelandic model of literacy (created by Ólafsson and Magnússon) was interesting because it differed from the model Darnton had created earlier, based on the circulation of French books.[41] We have to put inherited metanarratives in brackets in order to gain our own ones. And that is the junction where microhistory meets the digital humanities, as digital history also tries to avoid great metanarratives, and it also has a method for it, but sadly, as the digital humanities rather stay on the macro level, its aims are the very opposite of the ones Magnússon suggests.

Micro and Big Data

Is there any chance to combine the micro and macro levels? Maybe the question itself is misleading. Data is not the same as historical facts. However, there is something common to them. As facts cannot be applicable without interpreta-

39 | For the concept and problem of 'barefoot historians' see Sigurður Gylfi Magnússon and Davíð Ólafsson, *Minor Knowledge and Microhistory: Manuscript Culture in the Nineteenth Century* (New York/London: Routledge, 2017), 55-71.

40 | Cf. Magnússon/Ólafsson, *Minor Knowledge and Microhistory*, 1-8.

41 | Robert Darnton, "'What is the history of books?' Revisited", in *Modern Intellectual History* 4, No. 3 (2007), 495-508, here 505.

tion in historical research, the data of big data research is not innocent either. We can pick something out of a mass of raw material, but our data is prepared in advance. Databases put metadata beyond the material, and these metadata are already prepared for us. At the same time, we can handle so much metadata and search, link, and combine them so quickly that, although every data was brought into existence to answer a question, the data of structured databases can separate from their origin and in fact remain *raw* material. "So not only is evidence of value to our collaborative colleagues thick on the ground," said Willard McCarty a few years ago about the experience of the new science, "but it is also to be expected as a normal part of scholarship. But what about argument? By definition, evidence is information that backs up an argument. In other words, no argument, no evidence, only raw, uncommitted information."[42]

Remarkably, it is as if an old dilemma of microhistory was to recur. The main power of microhistory is not only the ability to avoid great narratives or build up popular historical stories, but the careful attention to the sources. For a microhistorian, the source itself is not a dead target, rather it is a knot of different discourses from which many of the links into other cultural worlds originate. It is very similar to the method of creating databases, anyway. But of course, the way in which digital databases are built and used is different. Borrowing Michael Frisch's idea about a digital humanities roundtable, there is great power in the web metaphor[43] – in the digital humanities, the spider makes a kind of multidimensional matrix with very complex links, but the spider does not think much about the paths; in microhistory the spider is interested in the linking of the different levels made by its thread. In the digital environment, microhistory can provide something special; it is a kind of metareflection in the ocean of metadata.

And, why should the digital humanities be useful for microhistory? Leaving aside what a huge amount of material can be reached via the internet and how the different search engines can assist microhistorical research – big data science can certainly support microhistory. A great problem of the micro–macro link is how one can imagine the possible activities of a historical agent. Menocchio told very strange things and Ginzburg's question was: how did he acquire these ideas? In the Occitan village, Montaillou, within what limits did the inhabitants act? The concept of historical agency is evidently important for

42 | Willard McCarty, "A Telescope for the Mind?", in *Debates in the Digital Humanities*, ed. Matthew K. Gold (Minneapolis/London: University of Minnesota Press, 2012), 113-123, 119, [http://dhdebates.gc.cuny.edu/debates/text/37].

43 | Cf. Daniel J. Cohen, Michael Frisch, Patrick Gallagher, Steven Mintz, Kirsten Sword, Amy Murrell Taylor, William G. Thomas, III and William J. Turkel, "Interchange: The Promise of Digital History", in *The Journal of American History* 95, No. 2 (September 2008), 452-491, here 469.

a microhistorian: understanding a particular case is impossible if we do not understand what a historical person can and cannot do; what he or she can conceptualize as a possibility of acting, and in what framework he or she made his/her decisions? Magnússon denied the importance of these questions, for him microhistory is against social history. But, if one is interested in another way of research and often tries to change the scope agency, this would eminently be a focal point of the study. Big data research in this regard can serve microhistory, as does social history. However, the skilful microhistorian can apply his research skills in previously unseen ways in the digital environment. The spider can discover a multitude of links, he can connect these and create new junctions which appear due to the logic of digital archiving.

Conclusion

Microhistory came into existence against the backdrop of *longue durée* great narratives. Instead of searching for the typical, it focused on idiosyncrasy and attempted to correct or at times reject the great historical narratives. Microhistorians learned a lot from cultural anthropology, and although they did not stress this, they were inspired by the practice of close reading of literary science. Although they did not reject contextual reading, they still attempted to focus and narrow down their view on a certain subject, source or area. According to one interpretation of close reading, the point was not so much the closeness but the changing pace of reading.[44] This change of scope in methodology is definitely a relative of the methodological suggestion of microhistory.

After the digital revolution, when we enter a new era of big data science, it is as if large scale is once again a more important point of measurement. At the same time, it is also as if the digital humanities were not going to return to the previous great narratives. Although they do not give up building historical narratives, they also refrain from stating that one ultimate narrative can be built out of big data, and historical sciences remain sceptical about judging what is typical and what is special. Distant reading and macroanalysis face methodological questions which were posed to the historical sciences by microhistory forty years ago. Rethinking the macro and micro levels and the close and distant reading techniques may happen by the help of microhistory. This way the spider may get a chance to also remember the thread whilst spinning its web.

44 | Jonathan Culler's essay refers to this idea ironically: "The crucial thing is to slow down, though 'slow reading' is doubtless a less useful slogan than either 'slow food' or 'close reading,' since slow reading may be inattentive, distracted, lethargic." (Jonathan Culler, "The Closeness of Close Reading", in *ADE Bulletin* 149 (2010), 20-25, here 23).

Securing the Literary Evidence

Some Perspectives on Digital Forensics

Melinda Vásári

Forensic practice is becoming a more and more prevalent motif in pop culture. The most obvious examples are the highly popular TV-series like *Sherlock, Dexter, CSI* and so on where forensics sometimes becomes the main driving factor of the criminalistic investigative narrative. In this sense, these modern kinds of popular detective series—which have a long-standing tradition of narrative pattern reaching back to enlightenment authors such as August Gottlieb Meißner—are different from their predecessors: here, one important factor of the narrative is that the viewer observes the technical, scientific procedure of securing and analysing the evidence and how its results evolve a meaningful interpretation in the course of the criminalistic investigation. And that is the key difference: while in the other kind of detective movies, the human detective has the only agency as an investigator who uses their interrogator skills (model: Columbo), here, they are at most skilled handlers of scientific tools and a reader of evidence. We, as audience, are observers, and the things, the traces, the tools have the *same agency* as the figures. And this points out that deduction can be based only on facts, only on evidence that is secured before the mental/interpretative process of deduction. So the first step of an investigation is securing material evidence, which constitutes the practice of forensics. This is what this paper is interested in: How would a forensic investigation of the digital traces of a literary writing process in a word processor look like, how does the forensic viewpoint on the philological record change our perspective on its literary features?

So, here, in the distinction between securing the evidence and deduction, we can see a difference between 'doing' and 'thinking', or 'working' and 'thinking',[1] between 'empirical' or 'rational' and 'speculative',[2] practice and theory, that is, between securing and interpreting traces, that is the evidence. In the second case, we are talking about a speculative, detective, hermeneutic activity, things that have had no meaning are assigned meanings, and in a material sense, nothing happens to them. In the practice of forensics, it is the material trace, the facts, that are dealt with (e.g. the traces of blood can be made visible with specific technology). Like the forensic expert in *CSI* says: "We don't speculate. The gun malfunctioned. That's it." We cannot say why—somebody tempered with it, the owner didn't clean it properly etc. –, it is open for interpretation, but it is not our task to solve the question. However, sometimes these roles cannot be separated from each other: the investigator becomes a forensic expert himself (like Horatio in *CSI: Miami*), the lab assistant and the investigator is one person. Here, the divided areas become intertwined, which leads to mental disturbance like in Sherlock's or Dexter's case, in the form of drug addiction, antisocial behaviour, even murder. At some point both of them use their trace reading ability to hide or disguise their actions. This points out that when the roles get mixed up, something is not right. I will return to this confusion later in regard to literary studies.

In the field of humanities, more closely, in the practice of philology, there has been always a tradition of reading traces. Just think of the practice of deciphering manuscripts—that is still not 'semiotic reading'. Besides, the philological practice regarded investigation as its model, which includes securing the traces as well. This precedes the act of deciphering and reading since at this point these traces are not signs but material things from which the practice of forensics secures and produces the evidence that only afterwards can be deciphered. In the digital age, leaving traces and then producing evidence from them becomes an automatic process of our everyday life. Archiving can be made visible only by programs that have been created in order to make the archiving processes traceable. These programs are the manifestation of the desire to see and understand these processes. In the digital age, there is a growing interest in this blind stage, to the "black box"[3] and to the automatic processes of the machine that an average person cannot access or observe, let alone comprehend.

The practice of writing has been the act of leaving traces, but today every act on the internet or on our computer leaves a trace. Since the software is con-

1 | As Stallybrass put it: Peter Stallybrass, "Against Thinking", *PMLA*, Vol. 122, No. 5, Special Topic: Remapping Genre (October 2007): 1580-1587.

2 | Carlo Ginzburg, "Clues: Roots of an Evidential Paradigm," in Ginzburg, *Clues, myths, and the historical method*, trans. Ann C. Tedeschi & John Tedeschi (Baltimore: Johns Hopkins University Press, 1992), 96-125.

3 | Cf. the articles by Gábor Palkó and Charlotte Jaekel in this volume.

stantly archiving, the act of production intertwines with the act of archiving. This is especially true concerning literature since many authors preserve their manuscripts for posterity, most leave them to a trusted person or an archiving institution.[4] We can say that this is one of the actual forms of the manifestation of 'legacy awareness' *(Nachlassbewusstsein)* that has developed in the first third of the 19th century.[5] In the digital age, this practice has become even more visible and accessible since the computer allows its users to archive and even to catalogue their own work by organizing the file system. The internet gives more and more possibilities to handle one's own private archive, it is, among other things, shareable by a click on the mouse. These digital techniques have transformed and improved the practice of self-preservation, and different forms of legacy awareness have been developed. I will discuss three types, or you could say, three degrees of this practice.

Hard Drive Philology: Digital Forensics

The first type, one can say, is the rawest, the most chaotic case: when the author gives his hard drives to a literary archive or to a trusted digital philologist. On the one hand, this way we have almost everything (his deleted files, temporary files, browser history etc.), on the other hand, we are faced with a vast amount of data that is unorganized and sometimes hardly accessible, and to access them one even needs special skills. This is the case when the practice of forensics—in the closest meaning—comes into the picture since when an author's HDD or floppy drive is given, the deleted files can be restored by the technology of digital forensics. However, one would need some previous knowledge and skills as well as the proper equipment (software emulators, forensics tools, floppy reader) in order to use computer forensics tools.

I, myself, encountered this technology in 2013, when I was editing a book in Open Office (on Ubuntu Linux) on a hot summer day in the university library where there was not (and still there is not) any air-conditioning. My computer was pretty old by then and shut down because of the heat, in a way that I lost the chapter I was working on the whole day. I had heard about data-recovery before and thought that there must have been a way to recover my work. So I went online and started to look for solutions. I found a program that was called 'foremost' and that was developed by Jesse Kornblum and Kris Kendall who served in the Air Force Office of Special Investigations at that time. It was

4 | Cf. the articles by Livia Kleinwächter and Julia Tóth-Czifra in this volume.

5 | Kai Sina, Carlos Spoerhase, "Nachlassbewusstsein Zur literaturqissenschaftlichen Erforschung seiner Entstehung und Entwicklung," *Zeitschrift für Germanistik* 23, no. 3 (2013), 607-623.

designed for Air Force investigators and then became open-source when it was released for the wider public in 2000. Later it became the basis of Scalpel, a more modern computer forensic tool that is still in use today. After studying it, I ran the program on my computer, and found every automatic save of my documents including the one I had lost and I was looking for. This was the moment when I started thinking about applying this technology to recovering digital manuscripts since, I thought, if we can recover automatic saves, we must be able to recover the whole writing process by comparing the different temporal variants of a given text with the already existing function of Word ('review'). Since then there are authors who give their digital heritage to archives and scholars who have started to 'carve' their hard drives to recover 'the born-digital dossier génétique', like Thomas Kling (poet) and Thorsten Ries (digital philologist).

In this case, the poet and the philologist is still clearly separated: Thomas Kling gave his archive, his hard drives, to the philologist, Thorsten Ries who then literally carves out fragments of poems from hidden places of the computer (the process is called 'file carving'). He reconstructs the writing process of Thomas Kling's "Herodot" in his paper "Philology and the Digital Writing Process" (2017). The fragments can be restored from different types of "places". Temporary files are automatically generated and can be 'undeleted' even those that were written on the hard drive before the author had clicked 'save' for the first time. Ries reconstructed the start of Kling's *Herodot* chapter in the automatically generated temporary and backup files.[6]

Fragments can be restored also from the 'slack' and the 'swap space' of what Kirschenbaum gives a clear definition:

> Most computers also use a portion of their hard disk as an extension of their RAM, a type of storage known as virtual memory or swap space. Forensic investigators recover all manner of otherwise-ephemeral matter, including passwords and encryption keys, from the swap space. So-called slack space—not to be confused with swap space—presents yet another opportunity for extracting remnants of supposedly long-discarded files: data on a magnetic hard drive are stored in clusters of a fixed length; 4096 bytes is typical. [...] But since files themselves are rarely the exact same size (and hence occupy variable numbers of clusters), it is also frequently possible to find the partial remains of earlier files at the end of a so-called cluster chain, a phenomenon known as "disk slack" (as opposed to file slack).[7]

6 | Thorsten Ries, "Philology and the Digital Writing Process," *Cahier voor Literatuurwetenschap* 9 (2017): 136.

7 | Matthew G. Kirschenbaum, *Mechanisms. New Media and the Forensic Imagination* (Cambridge/ London: The MIT Press, 2008), 51-52.

For recovering fragments from the drive slack, the forensic investigator has to have acquired the knowledge of how to use programs designed for data recovery, to emulate old software or an operating system in order to create a virtual working environment that is suitable for the digital material given by the author. And only then—after the hardest, most professionally skilled and most time consuming, one has to say, most enthusiastic and obsessed work—he is able to reconstruct the born-digital dossier génétique: "After extraction of the fragments, a minute philological reconstruction of the editing cycle is possible. For want of a digital, dynamic interface that would represent the reconstruction in a more accessible way, the following integral synopsis of the paragraph's editing process as recorded in [~WRS0003.tmp] encodes the identifiable genetic layers, including editing phases as well as revision of typing errors [...] [T]he genetic layering not only clearly shows the correction of typing errors, but the nonlinear development process of the whole text".[8] The result is a synoptic edition, it presents all the layers on one screen, in this, it does not defer from the analogue génétique edition, here, the philologist has to reconstruct as well. Of course, he applies technological tools as far as he can, and relies on the facts provided by the forensic tools.[9]

Excursion: Interdiscoursive Philology

Before I start to present the second type of legacy awareness, I have to stop for a moment and make an excursion and look at the practice of digital forensics and philology from a historical perspective. Like the name of the program, Scalpel, the file carver, the procedure described above, reminds us of autopsy or surgery or even of vivisection. All this refers back to analogue technology again, especially to investigation and to medicine. The series, *Crime Scene Investigation* has a spin-off that is called *CSI: Cyber*, and one can guess from the title that this one especially deals with cyber crimes and cyber investigations. In the first episode, the main character, the leader of the investigation, has to fight to take the cyber nature of the given crime seriously and securing the hardware as properly as the other evidence. Her key sentence is: "Treat every hardware like a dead body!" Here, in the metaphor of autopsy, investigation and medicine come together and its practice is applied to explain the practice of digital forensics. This appears in the choice of names for its tools: one of the basic tools of

8 | Ries, "Philology and the Digital Writing Process," 142.

9 | I am currently working on a hard drive provided by a poet, I will present the results of the analysis in another article.

forensics is called the 'Sleuth Kit', and its graphical interface wears the name 'Autopsy' (terms of investigation and medicine).[10]

Carlo Ginzburg also discusses philology together with medicine and investigation on the basis that they are all evidential or conjectural disciplines: "the group of disciplines which we have called evidential and conjectural (medicine included) are totally unrelated to the scientific criteria that can be claimed for the Galileian paradigm. In fact, they are highly qualitative disciplines, in which the object is the study of individual cases, situations, and documents, precisely because they are individual, and for this reason get results that have an unsuppressible speculative margin: just think of the importance of conjecture (the term itself originates in divination) in medicine or in philology, and in divining."[11] Since philology secures individual traces, and only then reads them as signs, that is, it makes conjectures, in this regard, its practice is similar to medicine and to criminal science. The individual traces correspond to evidence in forensics or to symptoms in medicine. For example, in the popular series *House MD* the assistants are the ones in the lab who first identify and analyse the symptoms (forensics), and only after can the doctor 'read' or interpret them (semiotics), and finally, treat the identified illness—it highly resembles the process of an investigation. Here, again, we can see the differentiation between forensics and semiotics. In this sense, medicine is another model for the practice of philology.

This is what manifests in the analogy between a dead body and the hardware as well. The 'autopsy' of the hardware appears in the practice of media archaeology, namely in the Medientheater of the Humboldt University. This reanimates the tradition of the anatomic theatre where the medical students could observe the autopsy of the human body: here, one can observe the autopsy of the hardware. Wolfgang Ernst describes the media theatre as it follows:

> The media theatre means more than a stage where the theatre is supplemented with new media; rather, it means the signal laboratory between them and the scene around us: the Grecian 'scene' as primarily a freely shapeable surface, thus a genuinely medial

10 | "The Sleuth Kit® (TSK) is a library and collection of command line tools that allow you to investigate disk images, and recover files from them. It is used behind the scenes in Autopsy and many other open source and commercial forensics tools." "The Sleuth Kit, Overview", accessed June 17, 2018, http://sleuthkit.org/sleuthkit/. "Autopsy® is a digital forensics platform and graphical interface to The Sleuth Kit® and other digital forensics tools. It is used by law enforcement, military, and corporate examiners to investigate what happened on a computer. Autopsy allows you to examine a hard drive or mobile device and recover evidence from it." "Autopsy user documentation", accessed June 17, 2018, http://sleuthkit.org/autopsy/docs/user-docs/4.3/.

11 | Ginzburg, "Clues", 106.

field combined with medial apparatus in the computing space. The modular levels of the theatre serve to give insight to medial operations, and conversely, to make you the objects of medial capture—and I am not speaking to you as a media theorist by coincidence since theory means theatre and insight at the same time. Therefore, the interests of two disciplines converge in the most fortunate way in the transformation of the studio theatre of the Department of Theater Studies/Cultural Communication to the media theatre of the Department of Media Studies. [...] The Media Theatre serves not only as the presentation of the medial action but also as a media laboratory where technological media can be explored as epistemological things both in their materiality and in their phenomenality. The workbench of the signal laboratory acquaints us in a practical way with the hardware and software of the media that is thematized in research and education—practised media archaeology.[12]

The best example for what Ernst describes here, is the 'anatomy' of the synthesizer built by Friedrich Kittler that was analysed by Sebastian Döring and Jan-Peter E. R. Sonntag. In their paper, they published photographs that were made during the process of dismantling Kittler's synthesizer. Here, we can see that the object is on a table surrounded by people observing it. However, they are in the dark, only the object is in the light, thus in the focus, just like in Rembrandt's painting, "The Anatomy Lesson of Dr. Nicolaes Tulp". They use philological techniques, for example, they date the components of the machine. They point out that the circuits are designed and drawn by Kittler himself, who even signed and dated them. There is the signature, 'AK 88'; as an autograph, AK most probably refers to Azzo Kittler; but at the same time it can also designate the famous Russian series of rifles.[13] The '88' can refer to more than one thing too, at first sight, it could be the year when he drew it, 1988, but the

12 | Wolfgang Ernst, "Vom performativen Theater zum operativen Medientheater." [Rede zur Eröffnung des "Medientheaters" am Semnar für Medienwissenschaft der Humboldt-Universität zu Berlin, im Rahmen der Langen Nacht der Wissenschaft am 12. Juli 2004].

13 | "With a special marker, Friedrich Kittler draw the lines himself to the Pertinax* motherboards from the 70s [...]—the circuit is a signed autograph—signed with AK as the AK-47 means Avtomat Kalasnyikov 47—probably the most frequently used rifle in the world –, and if we write it in full length then the AK simply means Azzo Kittler. According to Kittler the name Adolph, that he got after his father who got it after Gustav Adolf since he born after the battle of Lützow, after 1975 it disappears in favor of Friedrich. Despite, the AK remains as a sign for marking properties up until the 2000s on envelopes that contain building components and pictures." Sebastian Döring, Jan-Peter E. R. Sonntag, "apparatus operandi :: anatomie Der Synthesizer des Friedrich A. Kittler," *Tumult—Schriften zur Verkehrswissenschaft* 40, special topic: Friedrich Kittler—Technik oder Kunst (2012): 49.

number 88 is unfortunately also memorable because of its use by Neo-Nazis as an abbreviation for the Nazi salute *Heil Hitler*—the letter H is eighth in the alphabet, whereby 88 becomes HH. However, at the same time, it can refer to the number of keys on a typical piano—36 black and 52 white—for which a piano is sometimes called an 'eighty eight'. In this sense, it is a game with letters that fits very well with Kittler's theoretical thinking.

These signed autograph circuits raise the question whether we should treat these circuits like manuscripts—in this case, we can talk about machine philology. The 'anatomy or autopsy' of the machine is performed in a theatrical way, it is a unique event because it cannot be repeated since the seals have to be broken to open the machine and to look inside. They demonstrate Kittler's circuits on the body of the machine like in the tradition of the anatomic theatre: the doctors demonstrated on the body what was described in the anatomy books. The project is introduced on the webpage "Transmediale" as follows: "Following Kittler's circuits and codes, operating with and against him, encountering Nietzsche and going beyond Foucault, we are not just vivisecting the modular synthesizer the media philosopher constructed during the 1980s. By means of thinking and composing, we are conducting philology, exegesis and epistemology with its residue."[14] In this description, the terms of medicine and philology come together.

This way of thinking is what David C. Greetham (1996) in his text "Textual Forensics" investigates: how philology combines other discourses, and uses their vocabulary and methodology to define itself and its practice.

> Textual Scholarship is an antidiscipline because it does not occupy a permanent or consistent epistemological position and because it has no definable Fach, or subject matter. And textual scholarship is a postmodernist antidiscipline because it consists of co-opted and deformed quotations from other fields. Misappropriating concepts and vocabulary from law and jurisprudence, from ethics, philosophy, logic, theology, music, physics, mathematics, statistics, medicine, biology and genetics, sociology, and psychology, textual scholarship is a fragmented pastiche-in the words of Fredric Jameson, a 'blank without a central parody' governing figure or even a defined body of knowledge.[15]

14 | Jan-Peter E. R. Sonntag, Paul Feigelfeld, Sebastian Döring, Jussi Parikka, "Sources Synths Circuits. The Instrumentarium of Prof. Kittler", Transmediale, accessed June 17, 2018. https://transmediale.de/content/sources-synths-circuits-the-instrumentarium-of-prof-kittler.

15 | David C. Greetham, "Textual forensics," *PMLA* 111, no. 1, special topic: The Status of Evidence (January 1996): 32.

Stephen G. Nichols approaches this phenomenon from the other way around, from the perspective of practice and of the manuscript: he points out that we should regard the manuscript as a crossroad where various social and professional kinds of expertise meet. He considers it as a representational, multi-dimensional space of a given era.[16] He discusses the question concerning the Middle Ages but these observations can also be applied to the digital age. So while Nichols defines the manuscript as a multi-dimensional space, and the philological practice as a crossroad of different disciplines, Greetham examines the theoretical reflection of this practice that applies the terminology of several disciplines to define itself. Similarly, the digital manuscript that I am discussing here, manifests, on the one hand (e.g. Nichols), the cultural practices of today, and on the other, the problems that rise accordingly for the self-definition of philological practices (e.g. Greetham).

Saved Versions on the Hard Drive (The Case of "Product of Combustion" by László Potozky)

After this short excursion that we should keep in mind during the following discussion, let me introduce the second type of legacy awareness. In this case, the author saves the different phases of his work, thus creating its temporal variants on his computer. I use an example to examine the possibilities that this kind of digital manuscript gives to the philologist. I received the manuscript of a contemporary Hungarian novel, 'Product of Combustion' written by László Potozky. He shared a .zip file named 'versions.zip' via e-mail with me that contained 156 versions named "manuscript" and four versions named "edited", plus one called "final". By processing these versions, the philologist can create a digital, temporally layered manuscript by using the 'comparing documents' tool in Office which then shows the modifications in the 'review' mode.

16 | Stephen G. Nichols, "Why Material Philology? Some Thoughts," in eds. Tervooren, Helmut, Wenzel, Horst, *Philologie als Textwissenschaft. Alte und Neue Horizonte, Zeitschrift für deutsche Philologie* 116 (1997), 10-30.

Fig. 1: László Potozky: Product of Combustion, version 69 compared with version 113, Libre Office Compare Documents tool, screenshot by Melinda Vásári on her own computer, with the permission of the author.

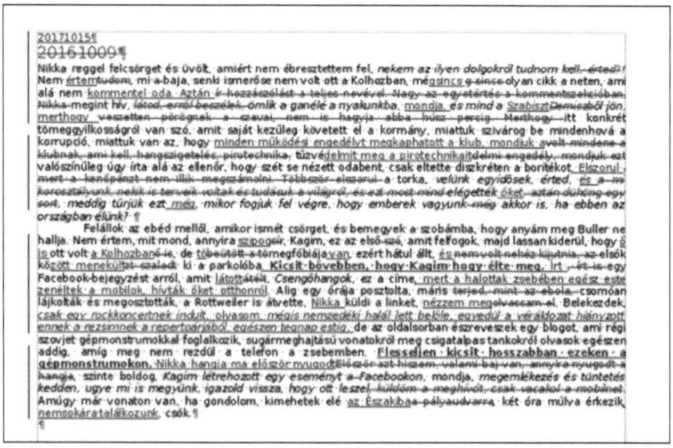

In Figure 1, you can see in blue the changes made by the author on 15 February 2017. The bold letters are instructions, for example, the first one sounds like this: "Pan out about how Kagim experienced it." These could be the notes of the author, or the suggestions of an editor or a friend who inserted it in the document. (Fortunately, here we can ask the author, and the first answer is the right one.) In this case, the philologist can create the version history of the novel. But it is, of course, not so easy. Here, you can see and follow the changes if you compare only two versions at a time, and we have 161! It would be theoretically possible to map the writing process, but, I think, anyone can agree that it would be a waste of time to go into so much detail. In the case of a novel, the tendencies can be interesting, and maybe we could make assumptions concerning the method of writing. Looking at the versions of this novel, we can see that, first, it is getting longer and longer, then, from a point, shorter and shorter. We can also observe that, when he started to write, the author went through the text he had already written before and corrected it, then started to continue the story. We can see when the author gives it to an editor, and we can even read the editor's notes, and investigate if the author accepted the suggestions, or not since we do not have an insight to the whole process.

Here, the writing process can be mapped similarly to the previous case but only in those phases that were saved and archived by the author. This way, archiving and production is deliberately separated after the act, the archiving did not happen at the moment of writing, just after one writing phase since the document was saved (and named and handled afterwards) as a version on the hard drive. However, the hard drive is not available for us, only the saved versions of the document which were regarded by the author as versions worth archiving. It is like making a hard copy, to print a document that we want to preserve. Now we save it to the hard drive, flash drive or in the cloud. This is exactly what Kirschenbaum calls archiving in the original sense in the digital age: "To archive in the realm of computation originally meant to take something offline, to relegate it to media which are not accessible or indexical via random access storage."[17] I would characterize this still as 'analogue thinking' since the archiving procedure follows the logic of the analogue archive, that is, making a hard copy in order to preserve the document. The philological agency is the same as in the case of paper: in the sense of legacy awareness the agency of the philologist and the author starts to be intertwined, but it is the author who makes the selection and the decisions.

Google Drive Philology (The Case of "Additions to a Colouring Book" by Mónika Ferencz)

The changes are more apparent on Google Drive where the writer—seemingly – works in one and the same document. And this would be the third, most developed and manageable technique that is provided by Google Drive where one can produce, edit or comment on, for example, a poem, and this way, the writing process becomes completely visible, traceable and most of all: shareable, even in the moment of production. Mónika Ferencz, a young Hungarian poet who is proficient in web technology, has shared the Google Drive versions of her poem with me.

As you can see in Figure 2, there is the "current version" of the poem, and on the right side, there are the different versions (seventeen to be exact) of the poem listed by the date when they were edited. It can be stated that the poem was written in four main phases then it was edited one last time for publication. For this reason, I chose (an act of selection) one version from each stage—I selected those versions where we can see the most changes.

17 | Matthew G. Kirschenbaum, "The .txtual Condition: Digital Humanities, Born-Digital Archives, and the Future Literary," *Digital Humanities Quarterly* 7 (2013). Accessed June 17, 2018. http://www.digitalhumanities.org/dhq/vol/7/1/000151/000151.html.

Fig. 2: Mónika Ferencz: Additions to a Colouring Book, Google Drive document of the author (version of 3 June 2016, 14:09), screenshot by Melinda Vásári on her own computer, with the permission of the author.

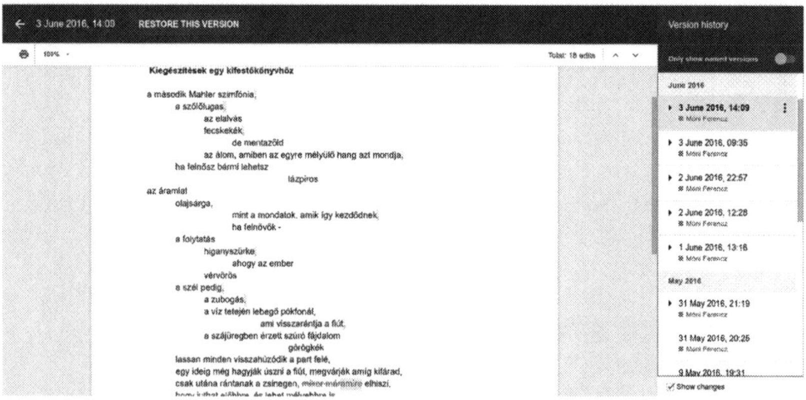

Fig. 3: Mónika Ferencz: Additions to a Colouring Book, Google Drive document of the author (version of 18 February 2016, 12:52), screenshot by Melinda Vásári on her own computer, with the permission of the author.

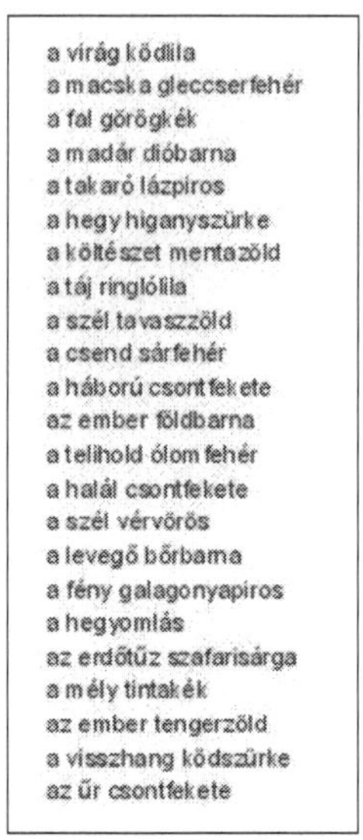

a virág ködlila
a macska gleccserfehér
a fal görögkék
a madár dióbarna
a takaró lázpiros
a hegy higanyszürke
a költészet mentazöld
a táj ringlólila
a szél tavaszzöld
a csend sárfehér
a háború csontfekete
az ember földbarna
a telihold ólomfehér
a halál csontfekete
a szél vérvörös
a levegő bőrbarna
a fény galagonyapiros
a hegyomlás
az erdőtűz szafarisárga
a mély tintakék
az ember tengerzöld
a visszhang ködszürke
az űr csontfekete

Fig. 4: Mónika Ferencz: Additions to a Colouring Book, Google Drive document of the author (version of 27 April 2016, 12:30), screenshot by Melinda Vásári on her own computer, with the permission of the author.

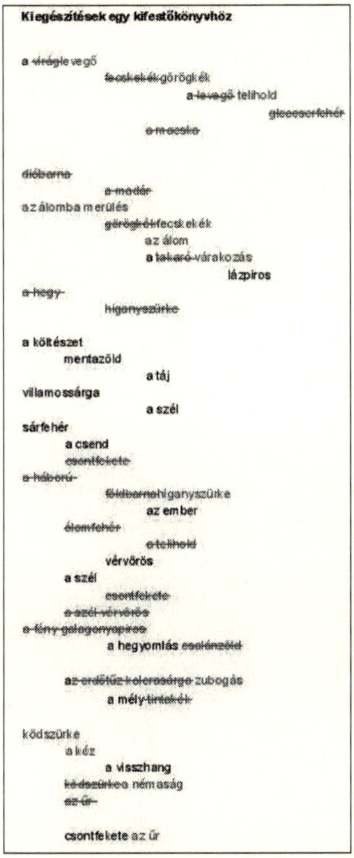

Kiegészítések egy kifestőkönyvhöz

a ~~virág~~levegő
~~fecskekék~~görögkék
a ~~levegő~~ telihold
~~gleccserfehér~~
~~a macska~~

~~dióbarna~~
~~a madár~~
az álomba merülés
~~görögkék~~fecskekék
az álom
a ~~takaró~~ várakozás
lázpiros
~~a hegy~~
~~higanyszürke~~

a költészet
mentazöld
a táj
villamossárga
a szél
sárfehér
a csend
~~csontfekete~~
~~a háború~~
~~földbarna~~higanyszürke
az ember
~~álomfehér~~
~~a telihold~~
vérvörös
a szél
~~csontfekete~~
~~a szél vérvörös~~
~~a fény galagonyapiros~~
a hegyomlás ~~csalánzöld~~

az ~~erdőtűz kolerasárga~~ zubogás
a mély ~~tintakék~~

ködszürke
a kéz
a visszhang
~~ködszürke~~a némaság
~~az űr~~

csontfekete az űr

Fig. 5: Mónika Ferencz: Additions to a Colouring Book, Google Drive document of the author (version of 31 May 2016, 21:19), screenshot by Melinda Vásári on her own computer, with the permission of the author.

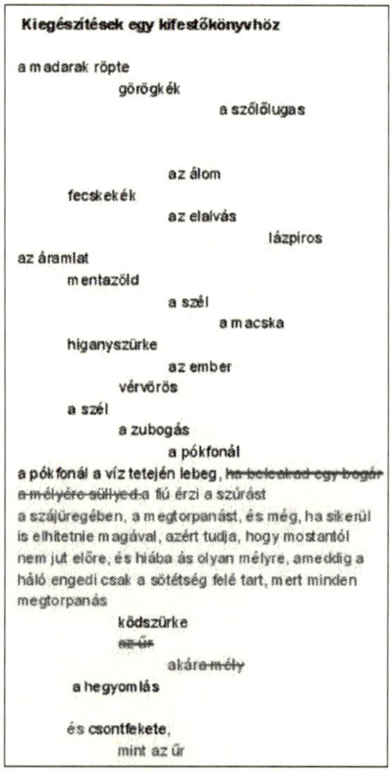

Kiegészítések egy kifestőkönyvhöz

a madarak röpte
görögkék
a szőlőlugas

az álom
fecskekék
az elalvás
lázpiros
az áramlat
mentazöld
a szél
a macska
higanyszürke
az ember
vérvörös
a szél
a zubogás
a pókfonál
a pókfonál a víz tetején lebeg, ~~ha beleakad egy bogár a mélyére süllyed~~ a fű érzi a szúrást
a szájüregében, a megtorpanást, és még, ha sikerül
is elhitetnie magával, azért tudja, hogy mostantól
nem jut előre, és hiába ás olyan mélyre, ameddig a
háló engedi csak a sötétség felé tart, mert minden
megtorpanás
ködszürke
~~az űr~~
akár a ~~mély~~
a hegyomlás

és csontfekete,
mint az űr

Fig. 6: Mónika Ferencz: Additions to a Colouring Book, Google Drive document of the author (version of 2 June 2016, 22:57), screenshot by Melinda Vásári on her own computer, with the permission of the author.

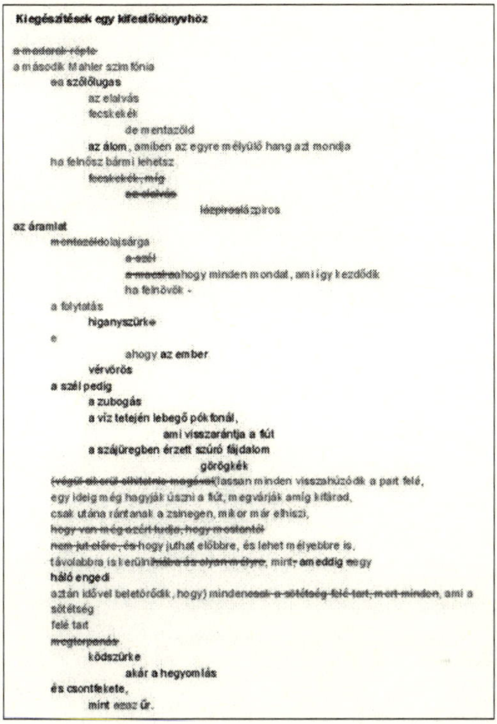

Kiegészítések egy kifestőkönyvhöz

a második Mahler szimfónia
ez szőlőlugas
az elalvás
fecskekék
de mentazöld
az álom, amiben az egyre mélyülő hang azt mondja
ha felnősz bármi lehetsz
lázpirosláz piros
az áramlat
mentazöldolajsárga
hogy minden mondat, ami így kezdődik
ha felnövök -
a folytatás
higanyszürke
e
ahogy **az ember**
vérvörös
a szél pedig
a zubogás
a víz tetején lebegő pókfonál,
ami visszarántja a fűt
a szájüregben érzett szúró fájdalom
görögkék
lassan minden visszahúzódik a part felé,
egy ideig még hagyják úszni a fűt, megvárják amíg kifárad,
csak utána rántanak a zsinegen, mikor már elhiszi,
hogy juthat előbbre, és lehet mélyebbre is,
távolabbra is kerülni, mint, **ameddig** egy
háló engedi
aztán idővel beletörődik, hogy) minden, ami a
sötétség
felé tart
ködszürke
akár a hegyomlás
és csontfekete,
mint ez az űr.

First you can see the very first stage of the poem (Figure 3), it is very simple, a list of things that are attributed a colour. Then there is one version from the second stage (the forth version, Figure 4), where we can see that the spatial arrangement of the poem has changed and several deletions and corrections were made. The third one (the tenth version, Figure 5) where a longer paragraph was added in which the enumeration is interrupted; after the nouns and adjectives (colours) come the verbs, and something happens, an action takes place which gives a frame to the whole poem. On the forth one (the 14th version, Figure 6), which dates from 2 June 2016 (22:57), one can see that the poet reworked the whole poem, added supplementary clauses, rearranged spatially some lines, and again deleted and corrected many parts of the text.

Following the stages of the production of the poem, without interpreting it in the usual way, it becomes obvious that Google Drive as the place of writing is not only used for archiving and sharing but for creation. It not only ensures a safe 'place' for the work in progress but a surface, a space for the production of the same work: the cloud (!), which is not even a real place since your work is not saved on your own hard drive but on a server, or more than one different servers somewhere in the world—so the writer and her writing is not even in the same place in the material sense. Which changes, again, a lot of circumstances: it makes possible the arrangement and rearrangement of the lines, corrections, additions and deletions without having to rewrite the whole poem, and still, the older version(s) can be revisited, nothing is lost and it can be easily read, not like in the case of the paper.

Finally, you can see the published variant of the poem in the author's book.[18]

Fig. 7: Mónika Ferencz, "Kiegészítések egy kifestőkönyvhöz [Additions to a Colouring Book]," in Mónika Ferencz: Hátam mögött dél [Behind my back South] (Budapest: Scholar, 2017), 30–31.

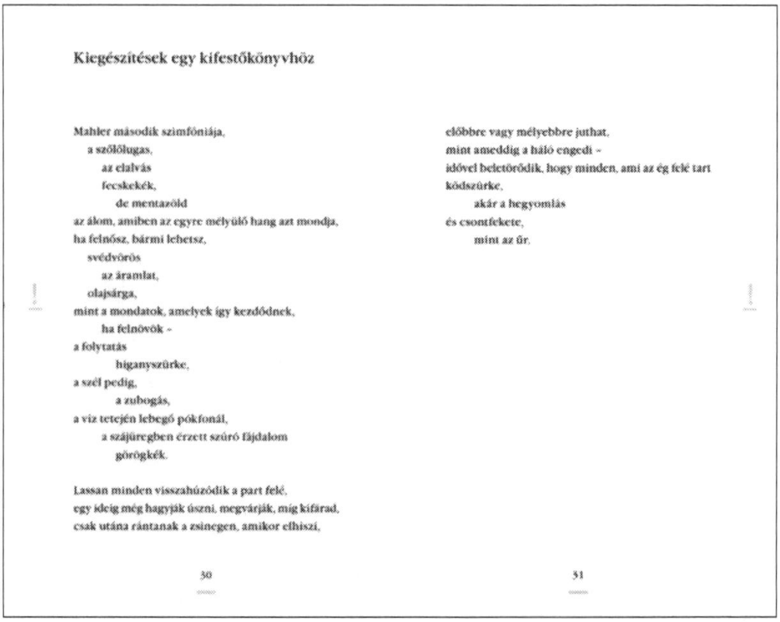

Kiegészítések egy kifestőkönyvhöz

Mahler második szimfóniája,
a szőlőlugas,
az elalvás
fecskekék,
de mentazöld
az álom, amiben az egyre mélyülő hang azt mondja,
ha felnősz, bármi lehetsz,
svédvörös
az áramlat,
olajsárga,
mint a mondatok, amelyek így kezdődnek,
ha felnövök -
a folytatás
higanyszürke,
a szél pedig,
a zubogás,
a víz tetején lebegő pókfonál,
a szájüregben érzett szúró fájdalom
görögkék.

Lassan minden visszahúzódik a part felé,
egy ideig még hagyják úszni, megvárják, míg kifárad,
csak utána rántanak a zsinegen, amikor elhiszi,

30

előbbre vagy mélyebbre juthat,
mint ameddig a háló engedi -
idővel beletörődik, hogy minden, ami az ég felé tart
ködszürke,
akár a hegyomlás
és csontfekete,
mint az űr.

31

18 | A raw translation of the poem *Additions to a Colouring Book*: "Mahler's second symphony, / the vine-arbour, / falling asleep / swallow-blue, / but mint-green / the dream where a deepening voice says, / if you grow up, you can be anything, / Sweden-red / the current, / oil-yellow, / like the sentences that start, / if I grow up–/ the sequel / mercury-grey, / and the wind, / the seethe, / the spider's thread floating on the top of the water, / the mordant pain felt in the mouth cavity / Greek-blue. // Slowly, everything recedes towards the shore, / for a while, they let her swim, they wait till she gets tired, / only then they pull the tie, when she believes, / she can get further or deeper, / than the web lets her–/ in time, she yields: everything that keeps towards the sky / fog-grey, / as the mountain-slide / and bone-black / like the void of space."

There were again some little modifications that were made even at the final stage, but maybe the most striking change is the spatial arrangement of the poem. The whole layout has changed, which is determined by the book format, now, we have two smaller pages thus, amongst other things, there is not enough space to play with the indents of the lines. But even after the publication, we can have access to the recorded version history of the poem if we are given permission by the author. If we are so lucky, every variant of the poem is accessible for us, with every modification (deletion, addition, rewriting or replacing of words), and even the exact dates of these modifications. In this way, the writing process is completely mapped, not afterwards, by a philologist, but in real time, in an automatic way, governed by the program. This is also true—just not so spectacular and obvious—when working on a hard drive since, as Kirschenbaum put it wonderfully,

> the preservation of digital objects is *logically inseparable* from the act of their creation – the lag between creation and preservation collapses completely, since a digital object may only ever be said to be preserved *if* it is accessible, and each individual access creates the object anew. One can, in a very literal sense, *never* access the 'same' electronic file twice, since each and every access constitutes a distinct instance of the file that will be addressed and stored in a unique location in computer memory. [...] [e]ach access engenders a new logical entity that is forensically individuated at the level of its physical representation on some storage medium. Access is thus duplication, duplication is *preservation*, and preservation is creation–and recreation. That is the catechism of the .txtual condition, condensed and consolidated in operational terms by the click of a mouse button or the touch of a key.[19]

Wolfgang Enrst created a term to name this attribute of the digital archive: "archaeography", that is, the archive writing itself: "The term *media archaeography* describes modes of writing that are not human textual products but rather expressions of the machines themselves, functions of their very mediatic logic".[20] He explains that technological media operates on the symbolic level (i.e., computing), this way, it is different from "traditional symbolic tools of cultural engineering (like writing in the alphabet)" because they register and process "not just semiotic signs but physically real signals. The focus shifts to digital signal processing (DSP) as cultural technology instead of cultural

19 | Kirschenbaum, "The .txtual Condition", 16.

20 | Wolfgang Ernst, "Media Archaeography: Method and Machine versus History and Narrative of Media," in *Media Archaeology Approaches, Applications, and Implications*, eds. Erkki Huhtamo, Jussi Parikka (Berkeley/Los Angeles/London: University of California Press, 2011), 242.

semiotics."[21] Ernst argues similarly that a shift is happening from the symbolic towards the technical. The same process that I discussed at the beginning: a shift from processing signs (semiotic reading) towards registering and securing traces (forensics). Finally, he states that technological media themselves became active archaeologists of physical realities that are often inaccessible to human senses.

Concerning Google Drive, this is even more sensible. Here, the production of literature and philology becomes intertwined: producing literature and its philological processing is happening at the same time, the author and the program—who takes over the place of the living philologist—work together. For this, the best illustration is the Google Chrome extension, 'Draftback' that records each and every revisions of the document, 2425 in this case, and plays the whole writing process if you ask for it at actual speed, while showing the date of every modification. It is stored in a way that it can be embedded and saved as an HTML file, archiving the archive (Figure 8).

Fig. 8: Playing the Draftback of the poem Additions to a Colouring Book, Google Drive document of the author, screenshot by Melinda Vásári on her own computer, with the permission of the author.

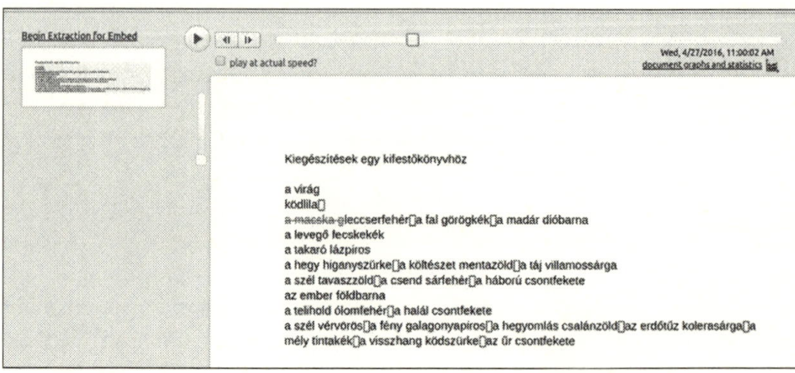

And there is more: the 'document data/stats summary' shows graphs and statistics of the creation of the document (Figure 9). It creates a graph of the timeline of activity showing how the length of the document changed and how many revisions happened at the given time. It also visualizes for the user where the document changed at the given times. Finally, it separates and displays the writing session: "This document was created over 19 distinct writing sessions (defined as periods where there wasn't more than a 10-minute gap between revisions)". It lists these sessions and define their time span, duration and that

21 | Ibid.

how many revisions were made in the given session. A complete inventory of the data of the writing process.

Fig. 9: The document data/stats summary of the writing process of the poem Additions to a Colouring Book, Google Drive document of the author, screenshot by Melinda Vásári on her own computer.

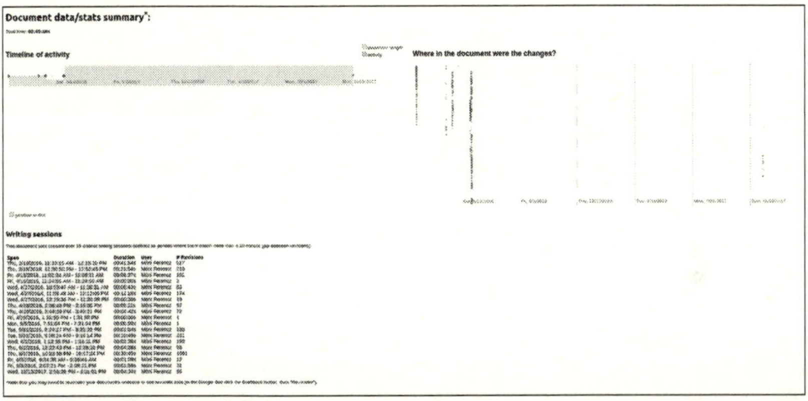

Therefore, the philological work does not happen posteriorly: there isn't authorial construction and philological reconstruction, but the two are intertwined in one single process in the software environment. Even the representation of the genetic process, that is, the design is defined by the program, this way, it is not elaborated by philologists but by software developers. This means that the principles that were accessible (and readable!) for everyone in the case of analogue philology become invisible since they are defined by algorithms which are not visible or accessible for everyone. Again, like in the Middle Ages, writing and reading, or now, designing software and understanding the way they work become the privilege of a few. Matthew G. Kirschenbaum also uses this metaphor concerning the digital age but in a slightly different relation: he talks about those who fear the coming of the "digital dark ages" when human records just vanish because of the obsolescent storage we cannot even access: "hard drives and floppy disks are actually easy in the sense that at least an archivist has hands-on access to the original storage media. The accelerating shift to Web 2.0-based services and so-called cloud computing means that much of our data now resides in undisclosed locations inside the enclaves of corporate server farms, on disk arrays we will never even see or know the whereabouts of."[22] Here, we are confronted with a contradiction: everyone can access the functions of Google Drive, everyone can be one's own 'philologist', but almost

22 | Kirschenbaum, "The .txtual Condition", 6.

no one can understand the principles and the mechanisms that determine the whole process.

Do we Need Analogue Philology?

The question rises again: in this changed technological environment, what is the function and importance of analogue philology—that is, the philological practice that is posterior to the process of creation? We examined three kinds of literary archives; in all three cases, the authors consciously devoted attention to not only archive their work but to make it shareable and accessible. This way, it becomes possible to create a highly detailed digital genetic edition and to present it in one single text on a screen which shows the different temporal layers of the manuscripts including deletions and modifications with the help of software. This is all very promising but what can we do with it? There is so much information displayed that the text itself becomes almost unreadable, one can only read it off, and interpretation gets into trouble. If we want to read in the sense of interpretation, then we have to choose one variant and work with that. And in this sense, at the end, we are back to the analogue. This raises the question what is worth to preserve. Greetham also asks the question of what can be significant in establishing the work of an author:

> 'everything'. what is everything? Where to stop? How to stop? How much information does an editor need to prove positions on such topics as intention, attribution, and style? The guidelines of the MLA Committee on Scholarly Editions, for example, have an even larger definition of everything than Foucault does, including 'second-party' materials such as letters sent to the author and revisions made by copyeditors, proofreaders, and others besides the author. In an attempt to discern two classes of everything, Japanese editing makes a distinction between bungaku collections, of literary works, and zenshu, 'everything written by the author,' although both terms imply completeness (Yamashita). In a prescription for variorum editing, Richard Knowles nicely catches the uncertainty about the evidence of everything when he cites R. P. Blackmur ('Use everything'), the Skeptic Pyrrho ('Trust nothing'), Richard Rorty ('Decide how well it works'), and Wittgenstein ('Only the exhaustive is interesting') (41).[23]

This, namely, the question what should be preserved and researched, is the question of curation. How can we know which files are relevant, and even if we know that, how can we find them amongst the millions of files? That is actually not the task of the digital philologist but the territory of the archives. It is the archive that collects the material evidence, the hard drives, processes them,

23 | Greetham, "Textual forensics", 34.

and then decides (discussing it with the author or with his/her successor due to privacy rights) what is to be accessed by the scholar. Of course, it is not this simple, rather a highly complicated, complex and differentiated process that demands a huge amount of time and resources, both human and technological.

A very exciting example to observe how the curation of such archive works, is the digital estate of Friedrich Kittler in the Marbach Literary Archive. The work of the DLA is well documented in the paper of Jürgen Enge and Heinz Werner Kramski, "Friedrich Kittler's Digital Legacy",[24] I will only summarize the main steps of the process. In case the author gives his digital heritage to the archive, first, the archivist has to create sector images of the hard drives—a sector image is a bit by bit representation of the drive—to work with them later on, so that the drive itself won't decay so fast physically. After the physical drives are secured (the preservation of these remains a great challenge due to the physical decay of digital objects), a disk image is created, and the archivist has to index each and every digital object. This means to assign an index to a file to define whether it is accessible to the public, can be researched by permission, is restricted or not yet been processed.

Concerning the Kittler Archive, the main problem for the DLA is to manage such huge amount of data: "the 756 replicated data storage devices (floppy disks, CD-ROMs, but also nine hard drives) already exceed the size of our entire digital archive of more than ten years; a simple selection of relevant files from around 1.7 million original files is not possible. Therefore, innovative software tools for the automatic analysis of large, unstructured packs of data are being developed. These tools will make the selection and indexing of relevant files possible."[25] It is not hard to understand that processing this vast amount of data is beyond human capability, thus humans need the help of the machine, software tools that do not exist yet but will be able to manage the problem after they have been developed for this particular task (in this case, the Indexer called 'Ironmaiden') not by but maybe with the help of philologists. As Enge and Kramski put it: "The first impression of 2012 seems to be confirmed. Kittler's digital estate is a testing ground, the complexity of which will not be seen again any time soon. The developed procedures, though, are principally applicable to other digital estates and more hard drives and media from other

24 | Jürgen Enge and Heinz Werner Kramski, "Friedrich Kittler's Digital Legacy—PART I—Challenges, Insights and Problem-Solving Approaches in the Editing of Complex Digital Data Collections," trans. Sandrina Khaled, David Hauptmann, *Digital Humanities Quoterly* 11, no. 2 (2017), accessed June 17, 2018. http://www.digitalhumanities.org/dhq/vol/11/2/000307/000307.html#d6931e836.

25 | "Digital Preservation of Holdings", Deutsches Literaturarchiv Marbach, accessed June 17, 2018. https://www.dla-marbach.de/en/preservation-of-holdings/digital-preservation-of-holdings/.

inheritances have arrived. The Indexer itself, which was developed without any funding, will be continued as a community project, perhaps in cooperation with the BitCurator consortium."[26] As we can see, here, the philologist works together with software developers, he does not work alone any more: to process born-digital materials, the philologist has to collaborate with the engineers. This could be his new role: the philologist as a forensic expert that results in a shared agency with the software/hardware environment.

I tried to show through these examples of philological practices of today, how digital technology has changed the process of writing, and the practice of archiving itself that manifests in the different degrees of the so-called 'legacy awareness' *(Nachlassbewusstsein)*. These three techniques of archiving technology that I introduced require different philological practices that demand proficiency in digital technology on different levels. The most extreme case is when the philologist reconstructs the digital manuscript by data recovery, thus by applying the techniques of digital forensics for philological purposes. Since the process of writing (corrections, rewritings, extractions, temporal layers etc.) can be reconstructed by the help of the software, the genetic presentation of a given text is possible. This digital manuscript can be analysed by applying previously existing philological methods and, at the same time, by developing a special methodology that considers the new medial environment. Furthermore, it is important to emphasize that the philological work is preceded by the preservation, curation and processing of digital heritage and making it available for research—namely, the curation of literary archives that has been also transformed by the appearance and then by the dominance of digital media. I presented some of the challenges that emerge as a consequence through the work of the Deutsches Literaturarchiv Marbach that curates Kittler's digital heritage.

My aim was also to introduce what kind of new possibilities, but, at the same time, new problems and questions arise once we are working in digital environment with born-digital documents. My main question is how literary studies, especially philology, can adjust to, apply and utilize this new, digital media environment. We can see that this is a still developing area of research, its methods, its legal frame, its skills are forming right now, mostly in the very act of practice. Each case is unique and becomes a case study that forms the principles and methods of digital philology. There are many challenges besides this fundamental level. At the philologist's side, one has to acquire special skills and knowledge, then decide what is relevant and irrelevant for the given research. At the author's side, she/he has to learn the best way to archive her/his work and learn these new archiving techniques. The archive and the curators need much more resources and time to be able to devote themselves to the curation of

26 | Enge-Kramski, "Friedrich Kittler's Digital Legacy," 35-36.

digital estates. It is the question of the future if the practice of philology can or want to adapt to these changes. The motivation of my research is to reinterpret, in the light of this, the already existing practices of literary studies, by which I mean both their application in practice and the theoretical reflection on these practices. From a broader perspective, in short: as Kittler investigated how our concept of writing had changed by the appearance of the typewriter, and what kind of consequences it had on our practice of writing in everyday life and in literature, I examine these questions in regard to digital writing.

On the authors

Hanjo Berressem (Dr. phil.) teaches American Literature and Culture at the University of Cologne. His interests include poststructuralist theory, environmental studies, science studies, media studies and 20th century literature, in particular the work of Thomas Pynchon.

Matthias Bickenbach (Dr. phil.), born in 1963, teaches Modern German Literature at the University of Cologne with a focus on the cultural techniques between literature and digital media.

Charlotte Coch (M.A.), born in 1989, teaches Modern German Literature at the University of Cologne. Her dissertation project is centered on literature around 1800 and the theory of literature, especially systems theory.

Charlotte Jaekel (Dr. phil.), born in 1980, teaches Modern German Literature at the University of Dortmund. Her research focuses on the literature of the eighteenth and nineteenth century and the materiality of literature.

Pál Kelemen (Dr. phil.), born in 1977, teaches Comparative Literature at ELTE Budapest. His research includes material cultures of nineteenth century literature, the history and theory of philology, and the culture of everyday life.

Amália Kerekes (Dr. phil.), born in 1976, teaches German and Austrian Literature at ELTE Budapest. Her research includes the history of the Austrian press and the popular culture in the 20th century.

Livia Kleinwächter (M.A.), born in 1987, graduated in theatre, media and literature studies in Bayreuth and Bochum. She works as a research assistant at the University of Cologne and pursues her dissertation project on "Note-taking – Epistemology, Mediality and Aesthetics of a Writing Scene". Her research interests focus on the theory of cultural technologies that emerge in the context of the production of literature as well as literary theory itself.

Dániel Kozák (Dr. phil.), born in 1980, is senior lecturer at the Department of Latin, ELTE Budapest. His main area of research is Roman poetry, focusing on epic and intertextuality.

Marcus Krause (Dr. phil.), born in 1974, is a member of the DFG research unit "Journalliteratur" (located at the universities of Bochum, Köln, and Marburg) and works in a subproject on "A Poetics of the Miscellaneous: On the Co-Evolution of the Periodical Press and the Modern Novel". His research interests include literary case studies, the history of psychological discourses, the archaeology of cinematography, and the mediality of modernity.

Gábor Mezei (Dr. phil.), born in 1982, his main fields of interest are 20th-21st century Hungarian poetry, media theory and the concepts of writing. He is the author of several articles on these topics, including a monography.

Julia Nantke (Dr. phil.), born in 1981, works as a researcher at the interdisciplinary graduate school "Document – Text – Editing" at the University of Wuppertal. Her research focusses on literary theory, digital literature and digital literary studies, materiality of literature and Avant-garde literature.

Gábor Palkó (Dr. phil.), born in 1973, senior researcher of HAS RCH Institute for Literary Studies, co-director of the Centre for Digital Humanities of ELTE Budapest. His research interests include digital philology, theory and practice of digital cultural heritage.

Nicolas Pethes (Dr. phil.), born in 1970, teaches Modern German Literature with a focus on Media and Science Studies at the University of Cologne. His research includes cultural memory studies, literature and science studies, the theory of the novel, and Actor-Network Theories.

Ádám Rung (M.A.), born in 1987, is an alumnus and temporary lecturer of the Latin Department at ELTE Budapest, where he is completing his PhD thesis on Roman myth in Augustan literature.

Björn Sonnenberg-Schrank (Dr. phil.), born in 1980, teaches at the University of Cologne's English department. His work focuses on American cinema, art, literature, objects, spaces, and popular and counter culture(s). In his book "Reassembling the Teen Film with Latour" he develops Actor-Network Theory as a model for a new film semiotics by engaging with American coming-of-age cinema; he currently works on books about the contemporary American author William T. Vollmann and on the cultural history of German humour since 1945.

Júlia Tóth-Czifra (M.A.), born in 1988, works as an editor at the publishing house Kalligram. Her research areas are 20th-century Hungarian literature, text editing, and the history and theory of textual scholarship.

Gábor Vaderna (Dr. phil), born in 1979, teaches literary history at ELTE Budapest. His main field of interest is the social history of Central European literature in the early nineteenth century.

Melinda Vásári (Dr. phil), born in 1986, teaches literary theory and contemporary prose at ELTE Budapest. She is an editor at "Műút", a journal of literature and culture. Her research concerns 20th and 21st century prose, media studies and digital philology.

Cultural Studies

Gundolf S. Freyermuth
Games | Game Design | Game Studies
An Introduction
(With Contributions by André Czauderna, Nathalie Pozzi and Eric Zimmerman)

2015, 296 p., pb.
19,99 € (DE), 978-3-8376-2983-5
E-Book: 17,99 € (DE), ISBN 978-3-8394-2983-9

Andréa Belliger, David J. Krieger
Network Publicy Governance
On Privacy and the Informational Self

February 2018, 170 p., pb.
29,99 € (DE), 978-3-8376-4213-1
E-Book: 26,99 € (DE), ISBN 978-3-8394-4213-5

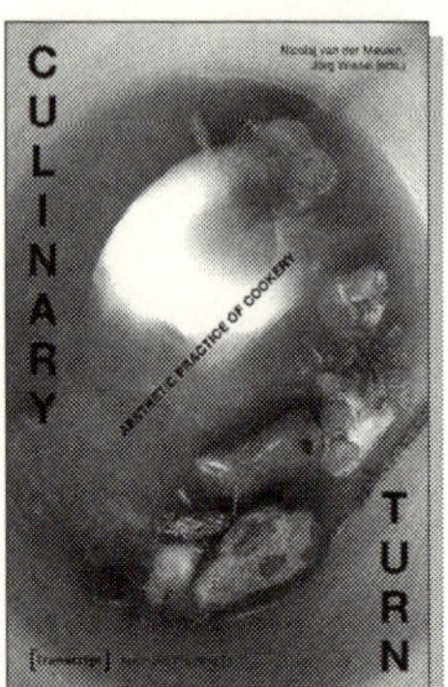

Nicolaj van der Meulen, Jörg Wiesel (eds.)
Culinary Turn
Aesthetic Practice of Cookery
(In collaboration with Anneli Käsmayr and in editorial cooperation with Raphaela Reinmann)

2017, 328 p., pb., col. ill.
29,99 € (DE), 978-3-8376-3031-2
E-Book available as free open access publication
ISBN 978-3-8394-3031-6

All print, e-book and open access versions of the titles in our list are available in our online shop www.transcript-verlag.de/en!

Cultural Studies

Martina Leeker, Imanuel Schipper, Timon Beyes (eds.)
Performing the Digital
Performativity and Performance Studies in Digital Cultures

2016, 304 p., pb.
29,99 € (DE), 978-3-8376-3355-9
E-Book available as free open access publication
ISBN 978-3-8394-3355-3

Suzi Mirgani
Target Markets –
International Terrorism
Meets Global Capitalism in the Mall

2016, 198 p., pb.
29,99 € (DE), 978-3-8376-3352-8
E-Book available as free open access publication
ISBN 978-3-8394-3352-2

Ramón Reichert, Annika Richterich,
Pablo Abend, Mathias Fuchs, Karin Wenz (eds.)
Digital Culture & Society (DCS)
Vol. 3, Issue 2/2017 – Mobile Digital Practices

January 2018, 272 p., pb.
29,99 € (DE), 978-3-8376-3821-9
E-Book: 29,99 € (DE), ISBN 978-3-8394-3821-3

All print, e-book and open access versions of the titles in our list are available in our online shop www.transcript-verlag.de/en!